P9-BIQ-820

The book of

INDIAN ANIMALS

The book of
INDIAN ANIMALS

S. H. PRATER, C.M.Z.S.

Former Curator, Bombay Natural History Society

With 28 coloured plates by
PAUL BARRUEL
and many other illustrations

BOMBAY NATURAL HISTORY SOCIETY
OXFORD UNIVERSITY PRESS
CALCUTTA CHENNAI DELHI MUMBAI

Oxford University Press, Walton Street, Oxford OX2 6DP

Oxford, New York,
Athens, Auckland, Bangkok,
Calcutta, Cape Town, Chennai, Dar-es-Salaam,
Delhi, Florence, Hong Kong, Istanbul, Karachi,
Kuala Lumpur, Madrid, Melbourne,
Mexico City, Mumbai, Nairobi, Paris,
Singapore,Taipei, Tokyo, Toronto,
and associated companies in
Berlin, Ibadan

© Bombay Natural History Society 1971

First published, 1948
Second edition, 1965
Third edition, 1971
Reprinted with correction, 1980
Tenth impression, 1997
Eleventh impression, 1998

ISBN 0 19 562169 7

All rights reserved. This book, or any parts thereof, or plates therein, may not
be reproduced in any form without the written permission of the publishers.

PRINTED BY BRO. LEO AT ST. FRANCIS INDUSTRIAL TRAINING INSTITUTE,
MOUNT POINSUR, BORIVLI (W), MUMBAI 400 103, PUBLISHED BY THE
BOMBAY NATURAL HISTORY SOCIETY AND CO-PUBLISHED BY MANZAR
KHAN, OXFORD UNIVERSITY PRESS, OXFORD HOUSE, APOLLO BUNDER,
MUMBAI 400 039.

Contents

Contents

Illustrations

COLOURED PLATES BY PAUL BARRUEL

MAP

MONOCHROME PLATES

Acknowledgements of copyright below plates

Preface to the First Edition

THE TITLE OF this book may appear confusing to those who quite correctly use the term ' animal ' to designate all living organisms which cannot be described as plants. But in popular usage the word ' animal ' has acquired a more restricted meaning. It is applied to Mammals, to that single class within the Animal Kingdom comprising animals which nourish their young by milk. Our title as such follows usage hallowed by custom. *The book of Indian Animals* describes the commoner or more conspicuous terrestrial mammals of India.

For many years, the Bombay Natural History Society, through the medium of its journal and other attractive publications, has endeavoured to create and stimulate in India an interest in the wild life of the country.

The necessity for this interest, particularly among our educated classes, is becoming more and more evident with the passing of time. During the past, extensive undisturbed areas of primeval forest, jungle, and desert gave safe harbourage to wild creatures, and provided guarantee of their survival. But changing conditions in the country, the gradual conquest of forests and waste lands, and, above all, the building of new roads and great improvements in methods and rapidity of transport have left few areas in the peninsula of India which are free from intrusion by Man. These factors have had and are continuing to have a disastrous effect on the wild life of the country. The danger to it has been accentuated in recent years by the enormous increase of firearms in use, and by the inability of many of the Provincial Governments to enforce such laws as exist for the protection of wild animals.

In the past similar conditions existed in most Western countries. Forests were cut down, streams polluted, and their livestock exterminated to meet the needs of the moment, with no thought of the morrow. Even in tropical lands, gradually permeated with the spirit of material progress, primitive Nature has had to give way little by little to invading towns and settlements. Ruthless destruction of wild life and a prodigal wastage of natural resources have invariably preceded the establishment of a material and prosperous civilization. Thus the magnificent animal life of many tropical and subtropical lands—and our country is no exception—is being driven to its ultimate retreat in fast diminishing forests, and is today threatened with extermination.

Even the great marine animals of the sea, the whales and fur-bearing seals, have not escaped this menace of extinction. The solitudes and vast spaces of the ocean have not been able to shelter them from the rapacity of man. Like terrestrial animals they have

been subjected to ceaseless persecution, made more easy by the perfection of means and methods employed in the destruction of life,
both human and animal.

But in recent years a gradual change has developed in man's
outlook upon the domain of Nature. This change has been brought
about partly by the spread of education and enlightenment. It is
engendering a growing opposition to this wanton destruction of life,
however much it may profit the destroyer. It is creating the more
humane conception that it is the duty of man to see that the wild
creatures of the world are not annihilated. But apart from humanity,
which in itself should impel man to grant to lesser creatures the right
of existence, there are other considerations which must influence
him.

The spirit of this age, with its urge for discovery and research,
with its marked tendency towards the popularization of science
among the masses and the dissemination of its truths and discoveries,
is fostering a widespread and intelligent recognition of the immense
value to man of the myriads of species, vegetable and animal,
which share this planet with him. Today there is no educated man
who does not realise that the realm of Nature provides science with
a vast and productive field for research. There is none who is not
impressed with the belief that such research has given, and will continue to give us, results of great practical and educational value.
There are numerous investigations, anatomical, physiological,
ecological, geographical, and evolutionary, which can only be made
by the study of animal life. While considerable data have been
accumulated by the study of dead specimens in museums, or of the
living creatures in the laboratory, the 'whence, how and where' of
his existence which man is seeking to discover cannot be discovered
by these means alone. The study of the living creature under the
natural conditions of its environment is equally important.

It is also true that there are material considerations apart from
the scientific. We have been accustomed to look upon beasts of prey
as creatures to be exterminated. But with a clearer understanding of
the role they play in maintaining the balance of life we know now
that even predatory animals have a distinct value. They are a controlling influence against overpopulation by species whose unchecked increase would adversely affect the interest of man. On the
other hand, there is the utilization for man's benefit of animal products such as furs, hides, and horns, which in themselves represent
a valuable economic asset. Furs collected from all parts of the world
and assembled in London for sale during a single year were assess-
ed at the value of £3,000,000. There is necessity for conserving the
sources of supply, which are not inexhaustible. Again, science has
revealed, and is continuing to reveal, hitherto undreamed of possi-
bilities in the uses of animal products and their employment in the
treatment of human debility and disease. Who can say what products still remain to be discovered which will one day be of price-

less value to man ? Finally the wild life of a country is a source of sport and enjoyment to its people. It gives healthy recreation to all classes, and is a constant attraction to visitors. It is also a definite source of income to the State because of the revenues realised from the sale of shooting licences and on imports of sporting arms and ammunition. But obviously it is also an asset which may vanish without reasonable efforts for its conservation. For these and other reasons, it is now admitted generally, both in Europe and America, that the natural beauties of a country, its varied fauna and flora, are an asset to its people, an asset to be protected and preserved to their own advantage and to the advantage of future generations. In its fauna and flora, Nature has endowed India with a magnificent asset, an asset which cannot fail to be generally appreciated by its people if they are led to know something of its worth and interest.

All those reasons which have made the people of Western countries strive for the protection of Nature within their borders apply with just as much if not more force to our country. Its wild life, in its interest, its beauty, and its marvellous variety, compares favourably with that of any country in the world.

There are more than 500 different species of mammals found within the Indian Region. They include the Elephant associated in India from time immemorial with the splendour of her princely pageantry, the Gaur or Indian Bison, the largest of existing bovines, the Great Indian Rhinoceros, the greatest of all the rhinos now inhabiting the world, the gigantic wild sheep of the Himalayas, probably the largest of their race, the Swamp Deer, the Thamin, the Spotted Deer, one of the most beautiful of all deer, and the Nilgai, the Fourhorned Antelope, and the Indian Antelope or Blackbuck, the only representatives of these genera. The beasts of prey include the Lion and the Tiger, the most magnificent of all the great cats, and such splendid creatures as the Clouded Leopard, the Ounce, and the Marbled Cat. Other species, like our Himalayan foxes, martens, gorgeous flying squirrels, and silky-haired langurs, are remarkable for the beauty and the value of their fur. The Musk Deer and the civets provide the musk of local commerce. Other species are remarkable for the beauty of their colouring. Our little Painted Bat (*Kerivoula picta*) with its brilliant vermilion and black wings is, without exception, the most vividly coloured mammal in the world. Peculiarity in form and structure is displayed by that strange creature, the flying lemur, which is neither lemur nor bat, but which bears the same relationship to the shrews as the flying squirrel does to the squirrels, or by the scaly anteater which, with its long scaly body, looks more like a reptile than any form of mammal. Apart from the interest in their symmetry of form, largeness of size, beauty of colouring, or strangeness of structure or habits, there is always that attraction and charm which the presence of wild life gives to our forests and plains, so dear to the many that live for the outdoor life.

A further interest attaches to our wild life from its association with the folklore and the legendary beliefs of the country. It is an interest not confined to India alone, but has spread among men of culture everywhere because of the esteem and admiration in which her sacred books and writings are held.

Some 30 different mammals are mentioned by name in the *samhitas* (i.e. the four principal Vedas).

Among them is the Elephant, the favourite of Indra, whose sanctity is enhanced by the belief that eight elephants guard the eight celestial points of the compass. The Langur or Hanuman monkey is held in veneration, as is commonly known, because of its association with other warrior monkeys who helped Rama in his campaign against Ravana. The Lion is one of the many incarnations of Vishnu. The Tiger finds mention in the later Vedic texts. The Mongoose figures in the *Mahabharata* as a teacher of wisdom to King Yudhistira. The Deer is always associated with Brahma the Creator, and is the constant companion of the god Mahadeva. The Wild Boar is referred to as the ' Boar of Heaven '. It is told how in the primordial floods Vishnu, taking the form of a boar, raised the submerged earth from the waters and supported it on his tusks. One could cite many more references from the sacred books concerning the animal life of the country. But apart from this, it is of much interest for us to know that the earliest known record of measures taken for the protection of animal life comes from India. The oldest record which we possess today is the Fifth Pillar Edict of Asoka by which game and fishery laws were introduced into northern India in the third century B.C. In this inscription the Emperor had carved on enduring stone a list of birds, beasts, fishes, and possibly even insects, which were to be strictly preserved. The mammals named are ' bats, monkeys, rhinoceros, porcupines, tree squirrels, *barasingha* stags, brahminy bulls, and all four-footed animals which were not utilised or eaten '. The edict further ordains ' that forests must not be burned, either for mischief or to destroy living creatures'. Centuries later, the Moghul Emperors, sportsmen, men of action, and born observers that they were, displayed a deep interest in the animal life of the country. Their writings are full of descriptions, some in great detail, of the animals, the plants, and the flowers of the country over which they ruled. While Babar, Humayun, the great Akbar, and Aurangzebe display in their writings their love of Nature, Jehangir was a born naturalist. It is said of him that, had he been the head of a great Natural History Museum instead of being the Emperor of India, he would have been a better and happier man. His profuse and engrossing memoirs are a real Natural History of the animal life of India.

We have endeavoured to show how great an asset to our country is its wild life and have given many reasons why we should do everything for its protection. But for the protection given to the Lion in Junagadh State and to the Great Indian Rhinoceros in Nepal and

Assam these two interesting animals would have been exterminated long ago. The Cheetah, or hunting leopard, once common in Central India, is now almost extinct in the wild state. The Lesser Onehorned Rhinoceros and the Asiatic Twohorned Rhinoceros, once said to be common in the grass jungles of Assam and the Sundarbans, have been practically exterminated in these areas. In many districts wild animals have been totally wiped out. In others, where they were once common, they are now hopelessly depleted. One does not wish to overdraw the picture. There are parts of India where the position of wild life is still satisfactory, though insecure. But equally, there are extensive areas where conditions are so appalling that, if left unchecked, they must lead to the complete destruction of all the larger wild creatures which live in them. There is yet another point which must be stressed. Any scheme for the protection of wild life would be incomplete without due provisions for the protection of our birds. Quite apart from a sentimental value, birds render incalculable service to man. While certain species may damage crops, such harm as is done by birds is overwhelmingly offset by the benefits we derive from them. Without their protection, our crops, our orchards, our food supplies would be devoured or destroyed by hordes of ravaging insects. Birds are the principal agency that controls the bewildering multiplication of insect life which, if unchecked, would overwhelm all life on this planet. Birds by reason of their predominating insect food are an indispensable balancing force in Nature. The abundant bird life of this country is one of its valuable possessions. Those who appreciate its value cannot but strive for its conservation. As far as our wild life is concerned, one cannot expect its preservation in urban land. Nevertheless, we believe that it is time that measures were taken for the protection of birds in urban areas. Areas actually under the control of Municipalities or Local Boards could with advantage be made bird sanctuaries, where the killing of birds is forbidden. There is need to put an end to the wanton destruction of familiar birds which takes place in the immediate vicinity of towns.

The second category, land under cultivation, provides at once the opportunity for a clash between the interests of man and animal. There are two main reasons for this. Firstly, the areas under cultivation in India are extending and will continue to extend to meet the needs of a rapidly increasing population. The need of increasing the available sources of food supply can be met only by the continued absorption of waste lands or forest, the natural domain of wild life. Secondly, there is the equally imperative need of protecting these cultivated areas from wild animals. The depredations of wild animals present one of the most serious handicaps the ryot has to face. In addition to loss of cattle, there is the damage done to crops and, not uncommonly, loss of human life. Therefore, whatever the views of the protectionist, this much is clear. Human progress must continue and in the clash of interests between man and animal human effort must not suffer. But this problem has been faced by other countries. Cannot a reasonable effort be made to face it in our own? That an intensive development of the agricultural resources of a country may accompany a sane and adequate policy for the conservation of its wild life is shown by the measures taken to this end by all progressive nations.

If our wild life is to find protection at all, it must find it somewhere in our forests. It is often claimed that the proximity of forests to agriculture makes them a constant source of harassment to the cultivator. If this argument is pushed to its logical conclusion, the only remedy would be to remove such protection as is now given to wild animals in our forests, for it would not be possible to remove this menace entirely until all the large wild animals in them are killed, or die of wounds, or are exterminated over large areas because of their inability to breed. Surely our goal is not the total extermination of our wild life, which is what must inevitably happen unless some form of protection is given to it within its natural domain.

While it is essential that the cultivator should have reasonable latitude to defend his property, it is equally essential that there should be certain areas or reserves where the shooting of animals is regulated and where the laws for their protection are rigidly enforced. Such reserves exist—roughly about one-third of British India and Burma consists of reserved forest—but, while we have extensive forests to shelter it and laws to protect it, our wild life is everywhere on the decrease. The time has surely come when it is necessary for us to review the position and to take such measures as are necessary to give real protection to the wild life of the country. It is the opinion of some that these great State-owned forests, where laws now operate for the protection of animals, are and must continue to remain the natural sanctuaries of wild life in this country, and that they will adequately fulfil the purpose of protection if they are effectively warded. The correctness of this view depends entirely on the actual conditions in a particular Province. The extent and nature of the forests, their accessibility, the density of the population, and the extent to which cultivation surrounds them are factors which must influence the issue. It may be found that in certain Provinces the establishment of a national park or reserve in specially selected areas will provide the only means of giving adequate protection to wild life without hampering agricultural development. It is certain that the creation of such a reserve or national park would give a special status to it, and thus facilitate the passing of special laws made applicable to such an area. Further, the actual selection and declaration of certain definite areas as a National Park would have the practical effect of forcing on the attention of successive generations of officials the importance of saving these areas from any danger of deforestation and the necessity for taking all practical measures to preserve the wild animals found within them.

The author hopes that this book will do something towards drawing the attention of people in India to the magnificent heritage which Nature has given them in this country, and that it will help them to realise the need for preserving this legacy to their own advantage and for the enjoyment of generations to come, who with the spread of education will be in a better position to appreciate its worth than we are today.

There is need for the creation of sane public opinion on the subject of wild life protection in India. At present such opinion hardly exists and, even if it does, in some quarters it may be antagonistic. This is mainly because people do not know, nor has any attempt been made to teach them, something of the beauty, the interest, and the value of the magnificent fauna of this country. In most Western countries there is a wealth of cheap and popular literature dealing with the natural history of those lands. In India such literature as exists is either unintelligible to the average reader or sold at a price beyond popular reach. Again, in most Western countries Nature Study is a serious part of the earlier stages of the school curriculum. While its main object is to develop the child's powers of observation, it creates a love of Nature and a sense of companionship with life out of doors. It is true that in India, Nature Study forms part of the curriculum in our primary and secondary schools. But often teachers are handicapped by the want of suitable books which they can consult. This book is therefore written with the purpose of providing a popular and well-illustrated account which will give people general information about the mammals of India.

The pages which follow contain illustrations and brief descriptions of the commoner mammals of India. They are based mainly on the observations of sportsmen and naturalists who have contributed to the pages of the journal of the Society during the past 50 years, and whose writings have added much to the sum of knowledge of the Natural History of India. Among the books consulted are :

Dunbar Brander, A. A.   Wild Animals in Central India.
Evans, G. P.   Big Game Shooting in Upper Burma.
Burrard, G.   Big Game Hunting in the Himalayas and Tibet.
Stewart, A. E.   Tiger and Other Game.
Stockley, C. H.   Big Game Shooting in the Indian Empire.
Champion, F. W.   With a Camera in Tiger-land.
Champion, F. W.   The Jungle in Sunlight and Shadow.
Lydekker, R.   The Great and Small Game of India.
Lydekker, R.   Catalogue of Ungulate Mammals (B.M.).
Blanford, W. T.   The Fauna of British India, Mammalia.
Pocock, R. I.   The Fauna of British India, Mammalia, Vols. I & II.
Jerdon, T. C.   The Mammals of India.
British Museum.   Game Animals of the Empire.

Our ability to undertake this expensive work was due to the generosity of the late Mr. F. V. Evans, a Vice-Patron of the Natural History Society and one of its most generous benefactors. Our thanks are also due to their Highnesses the Maharaja of Bikaner, the Maharaja of Morvi, the Maharaja of Bhavnagar, the Maharaja of Travancore, and the Maharaja of Mayurbhanj, the Sir Ratan Tata Charities, and Mr. F. E. Bharucha for their donations towards the cost of printing. The author wishes especially to thank Lt. Col. R. W. Burton and Mr. R. C. Morris who kindly read through the manuscript and offered valuable advice and suggestions.

Preface to the Second Edition

THIS SECOND EDITION, long overdue, has become possible because the cost is being shared by the Prince of Wales Museum of Western India. The text was fully revised by the author before his death in 1960. For the chapter on Marine Mammals, added later, the Bombay Natural History Society is indebted to its one-time Registrar Dr. E. G. Silas and its Curator Mr. J. C. Daniel. Some minor changes and additions have also been made in the text as revised by the author. The opportunity has been taken to revise the illustrations. A set of twenty-eight plates by the well-known artist M. Paul Barruel, depicting 141 species of animals, replaces the original coloured illustrations. Besides, there are several new monochrome plates, the originals of which were generously placed at our disposal by the owners of the copyright, to whom acknowledgement has been made in the appropriate place.

The nomenclature follows that of the CHECKLIST OF PALAEARCTIC AND INDIAN MAMMALS 1758 TO 1946 by Ellerman & Morrison-Scott.

In the preface to the first edition (1948) Mr. Prater noted that wild life was 'everywhere on the decrease' in India. A few years later, in 1952, the Central Government, impressed, perhaps, by representations made among others by the Society, established the Indian Board for Wild Life, whose functions include 'the devising ways and means of conservation and control of wild life through coordinated legislative and practical measures', the sponsoring and setting up of national parks, sanctuaries, and zoological gardens, and the promotion of public interest in wild life. The protection of wild life being a State subject under the Constitution of India, the Board works in an advisory capacity. Though several States have cooperated by enacting legislation implementing the Board's recommendations, the drain on wild life continues for want of effective machinery to enforce the law. As we have not the necessary statistical material we have not attempted in this handbook to indicate the extent of the deterioration. An assessment of the present position, so far as it is possible by a single individual, has been made by Mr. E. P. Gee (1964) in his book *The Wild Life of India*. The Society, through its representative on the Wild Life Board and in other ways, will persist in its efforts to secure effective action for the preservation of wild life in India.

Among our many helpers we thank particularly the Fauna Preservation Society, London, for the loan of the block of Plate 54 (*Rhinoceros sondaicus*), Mr. Humayun Abdulali who scrutinised the text of the new edition at all its stages and gave us freely of his knowledge, Mr. E. P. Gee to whom we turned again and again for assistance and information confident that we should not ask in vain, and Mr. D. E. Reuben who guided the publication from Mr. Prater's typescript to the final printing. Thanks are also due to the Society's Editorial Assistant Mr. J. S. Serrao for help given at all stages.

ZAFAR FUTEHALLY,
Honorary Secretary,
Bombay Natural History Society

Preface to the Third Edition

THIS EDITION is by photo-offset, a process which leaves very little latitude for change. The data now available on the primates, ungulates and other groups through the field studies of Jay, Southwick, Sugiyama, Poirer, Schaller, Spillett, Brosset, and the several articles and notes published in the Society's Journal have been consulted and the text revised where absolutely necessary.

Wild life in India is in danger, but there are certain encouraging developments. The reconstitution of the Indian Board for Wild Life under the Chairmanship of Dr. Karan Singh has injected new dynamism into the movement. The attention drawn to the critical situation by such scientific field studies as the book THE DEER AND THE TIGER by G. B. Schaller, have helped to create an awareness of the urgency for active measures for conservation. The Bombay Natural History Society is playing its part in the research currently in progress in the Gir Sanctuary in association with Yale University and the Smithsonian Institution. The studies involve an assessment of the habitat problems of the Gir Lions and the ecological requirements of the several herbivores which form part of the Gir environment. The International Union for the Conservation of Nature and the World Wildlife Fund have also shown a consistent and increasing interest in habitats and species studies in India, and many of these are likely to develop in the near future.

The revision of the text and the additional material on bats have been done by the Society's Curator, Mr. J. C. Daniel. We are very grateful to Mr. D. E. Reuben for his assistance.

ZAFAR FUTEHALLY
Honorary Secretary
Bombay Natural History Society

1. Mammals in General

WHAT IS A MAMMAL?

THIS BOOK describes and illustrates the commoner mammals of India and its adjoining countries. What is a mammal? Mammals are commonly described as quadrupeds or four-legged animals. Now most reptiles have four legs, while whales and dolphins, true mammals though they be, have legless fishlike bodies and might easily be mistaken for fishes. What then are the characters which distinguish a mammal from all other animals? The name 'mammal' in itself describes something which is distinctive of mammals. It refers to the possession of mammae or teats for suckling the young. Mammals are the only animals which have mammary or milk-producing glands. In all the world of Nature they are the only animals which nourish their young with milk.

It would be quite correct also to define a mammal as an 'animal with hair'. No other animal possesses hair. The hair-like growths on the body of a caterpillar or a crustacean are not hair. The so-called hairs of lower animals have neither the structure nor the mode of growth and development of true hair. Whereas every mammal, even the seemingly hairless whales, grows hair on some part of its body at some period of its life.

Other points of distinction are seen in the skeleton or bony framework of a mammal's body. The possession of a backbone classes mammals with the Vertebrates, that great subdivision of the Animal Kingdom which also includes birds, reptiles, fishes, and amphibians. But very distinctive in mammals is the mode of attachment of the lower jaw. It is directly hinged to the skull. All the other vertebrates have a loosely hung bone which links the lower jaw to the cranium. A mammal's lower jaw is again unique in its structure. It is made up of a single bone. In other vertebrates it is composed of several distinct bones joined together. This may seem a trivial point, yet it is sufficient to distinguish a mammal from all other animals. A lower jaw bone is all the evidence needed. Another important feature which distinguishes a mammal is that its heart and lungs are separated from its stomach and intestines by a muscular partition, the diaphragm. Except the crocodile, other animals have no diaphragm; heart, lungs, and bowels lie together in a single undivided body cavity.

Finally it may be said of mammals that the great majority of them bring forth their young alive and do not produce eggs as nearly all other animals do. Those curious mammals, the duck-bills and the spiny ant-eaters, lay eggs, but when the young hatch out they are suckled by the mother in the manner of true mammals.

These are some of the characters which distinguish mammals from other animals. Let us now try to get a picture of mammals as a class, the place they hold in the plan of Nature and how they are fitted to maintain life in the world in which they live. We can do this best by considering the main activities of mammals and then trying to discover how they are fitted and equipped by Nature to perform those tasks which make for successful living. It is rightly said that all animals have but two main occupations : (1) to care for themselves, and (2) to care for their young. Doing these two things successfully means successful living, in other words success in the struggle for existence. Now this struggle is nothing more or less than the struggle of an animal against the forces of its environment, against whatsoever is adverse to it in the surroundings in which it lives.

What is meant by ' environment '. Various factors together constitute or make up the environment of an animal and influence its life and well-being. We might analyse these factors into successive spheres of influence in accordance with the control they exert. First come such mechanical forces as pressure, gravity, currents, etc. They immediately exclude from an environment any animal which is not able to withstand them. No animal can, for example, lead an aerial existence unless it is equipped with wings or some device to overcome the force of gravity. Nor can it live in the greater depths of the sea unless its body is specially built to withstand the enormous pressure exerted by the weight of water flowing above and around it. Such forces make up what is known as the *mechanical environment*.

Then there are such factors as the nature of the food and drink available within the surroundings, the nature of the soil, or the salinity of the water. They make up the *chemical environment*. It is easy to see what an important bearing such factors must have in making an environment suitable or unsuitable to an animal.

An animal has also to cope with such factors as light, heat and cold, dryness and damp, summed up mainly in the term ' climate '. To live successfully an animal has to be able to withstand climatic and other physical conditions in its neighbourhood. These factors together make up its *physical environment*.

Finally there is the *animate environment* by which is meant other animals, including man, living in its neighbourhood. No animal lives or dies by itself alone. It has to live and compete with fellows of its own kind or with other species. It has to contend against enemies and parasites. In death it becomes the food of its neighbours. All these factors, mechanical, chemical, physical, and animate, make up the surroundings in which animals live, and by their action and interaction control the conditions of life within them.

An animal's ability to live within a particular environment depends then upon whether it is able to withstand whatsoever is adverse or inimical in the conditions of life which the environment presents. Its struggle against these adverse factors, animate or inanimate, is its struggle for existence. We must not conclude from this that all animals are prisoners in the grip of a tyrannous environment. While all animals depend for their existence on an appropriate environment, and while many are restricted by their structure and habits to a particular environment, most of the higher animals, mammals in particular, are to a large extent masters of their own fate. A higher type of brain has given mammals extensive powers of adaptation to varied modes of life under varied conditions. Many have spread from the countries of their origin over wide areas of the earth. In extending their territory they have chosen surroundings suited to their needs and have developed means to control or reduce in intensity factors in their environment which are adverse to their well-being.

In this business of caring for itself, the first and most important concern of an animal is to secure its food in sufficient quantity. Let us then first consider the food-getting activities of mammals. The better to appreciate their success and adaptability as food-getters let us turn for a while to their past history.

Mammals of the past. Though many species of mammals now inhabit the Earth, they form but a small proportion of those which flourished in the earlier periods of its history. The mammals of our time may be compared to the topmost branches and twigs of a giant forest tree whose trunk and larger limbs, represented by extinct species, lie buried and concealed under the ground. The earliest, the most primitive mammals, which we may liken to the roots of this tree, are believed to have had their origin in, or to be the descendants of, a group of primitive reptiles. The teeth of these reptiles, the development of their limbs, and yet other characters suggest such a kinship. Be this as it may, our concern is how did these primitive mammals live and secure their food? A study of their fossil remains, dug up from the earth, reveals that the earliest mammals, lineal ancestors of tigers, elephants, mice, whales, of all present-day species, great and small, were lowly obscure creatures. In build all conformed to a common type. Any one of them might be pictured as a small, hairy, long-tailed creature, with short limbs, and five-toed clawed and padded feet. From the form of the teeth we must conclude that they were omnivorous in diet. We find none with teeth especially designed to cut and tear flesh as are the teeth of modern beasts of prey, none with teeth especially made for the grinding of grass as are the teeth of modern grazing animals. Their bodily structure again suggests that they were mainly terrestrial in habit. None had limbs especially fitted for climbing and securing their food in trees, for flight through the air, or for a life in water. These primitive mammals obtained their food and earned their living mainly as ground dwellers. Compared with their present-day descendants, their mode and habits of life, their scope and opportunities for food-getting were very limited.

The mammal's greatest and most distinctive asset. But these primitive mammals, and their descendants to an increasing degree, developed one attribute which gave them an advantage over other animals in the struggle for existence. This attribute was a higher development of the brain, which distinguishes and places mammals above all other animals. Mammals, a class to which man himself belongs, are unquestionably the highest animals. The term 'highest' does not imply perfection of structure. A snake is as perfectly built as any mammal to follow successfully its particular mode of life. Unencumbered with limbs, it can glide through the grass, climb like a monkey, and swim like a fish, and can dart upon and secure its prey with speed and efficiency. The supremacy of the higher animals lies rather in a superior mental equipment which gave them that greater independence, that greater control, which they have attained over the forces of their environment. Man's superior brain has given him mastery over the impeding forces of Nature. He has conquered the earth, the sky, and the seas. He can go anywhere and live anywhere. All the resources of the earth lie open to him. In a lesser way, better minds and therefore a greater capacity for knowing, feeling, learning, and profiting by experience immensely widened the scope and the means by which mammals were able to earn their livelihood. In the competition for food, the essence of the struggle for existence, their intelligence and greater powers of discrimination enabled them to appreciate and seek out fresh sources for supply, to spread over the world, and to adopt and adapt themselves to every mode and condition of life in exploiting them.

Diversity of structure. The varying modes of life which mammals have adopted are associated with the great diversity in structure which they as a class display. For there is always an intimate relationship between the structure of an animal, its mode and habits of life, and the conditions under which it lives. Adaptation to the particular kind of life which various groups of mammals chose to follow led to the evolution of that bewildering diversity in form and structure seen among mammals today, a diversity which fits them for the most varied modes of existence. There are arboreal mammals, whose grasping limbs especially fit them to live and secure their food in trees. Others have acquired the means to progress through and to obtain their food in the air. With parachute-like folds of skin stretched between their extended limbs, flying squirrels can glide and sail from tree to tree. Adaptation to flight reaches perfection in the bats. With fingers enormously extended to provide struts for their leathery wings, bats fly with the ease and swiftness of birds. Among the ground dwellers there are some which have taken to living beneath the soil, and have acquired bodies which especially fit them for a subterranean existence. The thickset cylindrical body of a mole, its enormous forefeet modified for digging, fit it especially for a life underground. Many mammals have become fleet of foot, developing hoofed limbs especially designed to increase rapidity of movement. Others have agile bodies and limbs adapted for swift attack upon their defenceless neighbours. Many mammals sought their food and took to a life in rivers and lakes, and some of these aquatic forms invaded the sea ; among them are the whales, porpoises, and dolphins, whose fishlike bodies fit them for a marine existence almost as perfectly as fishes. Finally there are those mammals with that generalised type of structure which enables them to combine arboreal, terrestrial, and aquatic habits of life. There was also a progressive increase in size. The pedigree of the horse, the camel, or the rhinoceros commences with small insignificant animals which increase in size through successive generations and culminate in the large animals of our day. The early predominance mammals gained over other animals permitted of this increase in dimensions. (Plate facing p. 6)

The teeth of mammals. It will be seen that mammals more than any other class of animal display a diversity of form and structure which fits them to secure their food and earn a livelihood in a variety of ways. Subsisting as they do on many kinds of food, securing it and dealing with it in different ways, the teeth of mammals are distinctive in their great variety in design. Usually the teeth of animals are all of one type and built to deal with food in one particular way. There are mammals, porpoises and dolphins for example, with teeth of this uniform pattern, and others, like the whalebone whales and ant-eaters, which are quite toothless when adult. But the great majority of mammals have jaws well armed with different types of teeth. These teeth present differences of structure in different parts of the jaws. They are designed to perform different functions. In front of the mouth, there is usually a set of small cutting teeth, the *incisors*. Behind them rise sharp conical teeth meant for seizing and holding. These are the *canines*. Behind the canines lie the cheek teeth, *premolars* and *molars*, which are used for crushing, grinding, or tearing food. Incisors, canines, and molars display variations in pattern in accordance with the type of food the animal eats. The small pincer-like incisors of cats and beasts of prey are designed to scrape and tear away flesh and gristle from bones. The chisel-shaped incisors of squirrels, rats, and other rodents are especially built to gnaw hard-shelled nuts and seeds, the bark of trees, and tough vegetable substances. Canine teeth when present are usually set at the point of leverage of the great biting muscles which drive them in with great force. They are called canines because of their powerful development in dogs and beasts of prey. But of all teeth, the molars show best what kind of food an animal eats. The molars of purely carnivorous animals are mainly cutting instruments which ply against one another like scissor-blades. In mixed feeders the molars become broader and have tubercular crowns ; while insect-eaters have molars which bristle with sharp points. In purely herbivorous mammals the flat surface of the molars is complicated with folds and ridges of enamel to increase their efficiency as grinding organs. A very general feature of the teeth of mammals is the development of two sets of teeth—the milk teeth of infancy are replaced by the permanent dentition. In some mammals, milk teeth are shed before birth and in others not till a late period in life. The teeth of mammals in their form and structure are so closely associated with the food and feeding habits that they provide an important means of distinguishing between and classifying the various groups. (Plates facing pp. 7, 10)

Nails or claws are also useful guides to the classification of mammals. In some they are blunt and flat as in monkeys, in others sharp as in shrews. They are curved, powerful, sharp, and retractile in cats ; long, strong, and well adapted for digging in bears, badgers, and ratels. In herbivorous animals they are solid as in the horse which walks on a single toe encased in a hoof, or there may be two blunt, horny toes as in ruminants and some pachyderms.

Self-protection against other animals. Besides obtaining a sufficiency of food, self-preservation for the animal implies the ability to protect itself against other animals which live in its surroundings, against fellows of its own or other species, against enemies which seek to harm or destroy it. Here again a superior mental equipment gives mammals a considerable advantage in this phase of the struggle to exist. They display in a particular degree a superior development of the external organs associated with the higher senses of hearing, scent, and touch. The sense of touch is very delicate and usually concentrated in various organs, for example in the facial whiskers or vibrissae of cats and other carnivores, in the lips of the horses, or in the sensitive tip of the trunk of an elephant. The ears are usually well developed, sometimes extremely large and furnished with muscles to move them to take in sounds from many directions. The nose is always or nearly always conspicuous by its naked character, by the large, often moist, surface which surrounds the nostrils, and again by the muscles which enable it to be moved at will. The eyes are perhaps less marked in their predominance over the eyes of the lower vertebrates ; but they are provided as a rule with upper and lower eyelids and with a nictitating membrane. Quite apart from their general alertness and quickness of movement, characters in which they are equalled only by birds, mammals possess a varied armoury of weapons of offence and defence. The simplest device for the protection of the body is a tough leathery hide so common amongst hoofed animals, the usual victims of beasts of prey. A variation of this device is an armour-plating of heavy scales, which is the

PLATE 1

Diversity of structure in mammals

1. Climbing (monkey)
2. Preying (leopard)
3. Running (antelope)
4. Flying (bat)
5. Burrowing (mole)
6. Swimming (dolphin)

Plate 2

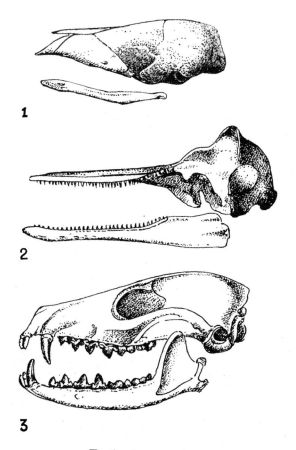

1

2

3

Teeth of mammals

1. The scaly ant-eater is toothless
2. The dolphin's teeth are all of one pattern
3. The fox displays teeth of varied pattern adapted to different uses

PLATE 3

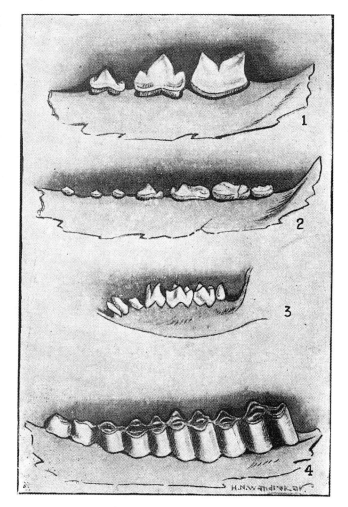

Molar teeth for various diets

1. Meat-eating (tiger)
2. Omnivorous (bear)
3. Insect-eating (hedgehog)
4. Vegetarian (deer)

PLATE 4

Himalayan scenery at the edge of the tree-line

Photo : Salim Ali

PLATE 5

Evergreen forest, Kerala

Photo : Salim Ali

PLATE 6

Tropical thorn forest

Photo : Harold Trapido

defence of armadillos and ant-eaters. The spines of hedgehogs and the bristling quills of porcupines are both offensive and defensive in purpose. These protective scales, spines, and quills are nothing more than modified hairs. An increasing thickening and stiffening of the hair produces the bristle, the spine, and the quill, while the scales of armadillos and ant-eaters are built up of masses of hair flattened and fused together.

The teeth, the essential purpose of which is to deal with food, may be turned into powerful weapons. In the case of the elephant the incisor teeth have been converted into huge defensive tusks, while boars and male musk deer and mouse-deer have great canine teeth which they use in defence and in combat. The horns and antlers of hoofed animals are countermeasures against the teeth and claws of beasts of prey. They are also weapons of offence and defence in combats with their own kind, so frequent during seasons of courtship. Quite apart from their keenness of hearing, scent, and sight, perhaps of greater value to these hoofed animals than any weapons is their speed. Their limbs are especially designed for rapid movement, for swift flight from pursuit. Concealment is also a very important factor in the relationship between predators and their prey. Both hunters and the hunted use it. Many of the weaker mammals conceal themselves under masses of rock or dig deep burrows. Many come out to feed only under cover of darkness. Such nocturnal habits have however produced in their turn a great cohort of night-hunting mammals.

The colours of mammals. Concealment may be effected by the colour and pattern of the coat. Speaking of colour, mammals do not generally display the bright colours of birds. Some apes have brightly-coloured tracts of skin ; the Indian Painted Bat with its vermilion and black wings is perhaps the most brilliantly coloured mammal in the world. These are exceptions to the usually sombre coloration of mammals. A colour which harmonises with the surroundings, such as the pale sandy tones of desert animals, or a pattern of stripes, spots, and bands which break up and mask the body form, are protective devices common to all creatures. The heavy stripes of a zebra or tiger, the spotted or dappled markings of a deer or leopard help to disrupt the body outline making its detection more difficult. Certain mammals display seasonal changes of colour. The extreme is seen in such animals as the Arctic fox and the Polar hare whose coloured summer coats give place to the white of the snowbound wintry landscape. Such a change must have its protective value. Lastly one must mention the use of nauseous fumes to repel an enemy ; such are the means by which the skunk, civets, and many small mammals seek to repel attack. Associated with this particular method of defence is a special type of colouring known as ' warning ' coloration.

Social life, living together in herds, flocks, or colonies, a habit developed by many groups of mammals, must also be counted among the means by which weaker mammals gain protection. Leadership of a herd of blackbuck is usually vested in an old and vigilant female, while the alertness of one among them may give timely alarm to a resting or feeding flock of wild sheep, or goats, or monkeys.

Protection against heat, cold, etc. Self-preservation to animals means yet more than the acquiring of food, successful competition with neighbours, or escape from enemies. To live an animal must be able to adapt itself to its surroundings. We have seen how mammals are adapted to seek their livelihood on the ground, in trees, in the air, or in the water ; but successful adaptation also implies the ability to withstand vicissitudes of climate and temperature, of heat and cold, drought and rain. How do mammals protect themselves against cold ? Hair to a mammal is what plumage is to a bird, a protection against cold. Hair takes many different forms. It may be converted into defensive quills, spines, or scales, or even form the substance from which horns are made. The solid horns of a rhinoceros or the horns of cattle and antelopes are but masses of hair welded together into solid structures. Hair is usually of two main types, the longer, usually coarser, hair which makes up the surface coat of a mammal, and that soft curly under-fur found commonly in aquatic mammals, seals and beavers, or in those which are liable to be exposed to intense cold. Every mammal living in the bare wind-swept plateaux of Tibet wears this warm woolly under-garment. Now hair is not only a protection against cold from without, it helps to retain the heat from within. It is an aid to the maintenance of a uniform body temperature. The temperature of mammals and birds does not vary with the temperature of their surroundings as is the case with the ' cold-blooded ' reptiles and fishes. It maintains a normal level. Now as this level is usually higher than the temperature of the surrounding medium we speak of mammals and birds as ' warm-blooded '. These highly organised animals have an intricate nervous mechanism which regulates the temperature of the blood, and the considerable heat given off by the body is retained by a ' blanket ' of hair in mammals or of feathers in birds. In cold regions an increase in the length and density of the hair during winter increases its effectiveness in preventing the loss of body heat. Hairless animals like whales usually have a dense layer of blubber beneath their skins which performs the same function as hair ; it acts as a heat retainer.

Of all animals, mammals possess the most effective device for protection against heat. This is a profusion of sweat glands which pour out on the surface of the skin a fluid which consists largely of water. Because of his ability to sweat, man can safely withstand heat much above his normal temperature. Wholly aquatic mammals like whales and dolphins have no use for sweat glands, and do not possess them. They are also lacking or poorly developed in moles and various rodents whose subterranean habits do not call for this method of temperature regulation.

Care of the young. After self-preservation, the second great concern of animals is the care of the young. Here again mammals have developed most effective means for the care and protection of their young, particularly in the earlier stages of growth and development. The eggs of creatures lowest in the scale of life are usually discharged into water. The delicate membranes in which they are encased offer scant protection against changes in external surroundings. The drying up of the water and exposure to the air frequently result in the drying up of the eggs and the death of the embryos. Such eggs are also the easy prey of numerous animals which devour them as food. Higher in the scale of life, we find the eggs better protected by a calcareous covering or a leathery shell. Reptiles and birds lay such eggs. They are laid on land without danger of drying up, and their development may be hastened with the warmth of the sun's rays. Some reptiles and almost all birds have advanced a stage further. They sit on or incubate their eggs, thus protecting the developing embryo from variations in temperature. Further, food for the developing embryo is provided within the eggs so that it is able to develop considerably before it hatches out and is exposed to the inclemencies of its surroundings. Finally we come to the stage when animals tend to become viviparous, to produce their young alive. The development of the embryo takes place within the body of the mother where the young are nourished, protected, and maintained under the most ideal conditions. Not all mammals have attained this perfect means of protecting their developing offspring. There are primitive mammals like the duck-bills and the spiny ant-eaters which lay eggs. Marsupials or pouched mammals like kangaroos have reached an intermediate stage. Their young, born in a very helpless and undeveloped condition, are transferred to a pouch on the belly of the mother where they remain glued to her teats until better able to fend for themselves. Except for these primitive forms, all mammals have reached the highest stage attained in Nature in the means employed for the nourishment and safety of their developing offspring. The developing embryo is encased in a membraneous structure called the *placenta.* This enveloping sac is so intimately in contact with the wall of the mother's womb that the blood-vessels of parent and young come into closest contact, and nourishment and the gases of respiration are diffused from one into the other. To the developing embryo the placenta acts as a lung, intestine, and kidney combined. The mother is thus able to house and nourish her offspring within her body until it is almost able to lead an active existence.

After birth, this protective association between the mother and her young is maintained and prolonged by her provision of milk for them. Parental care may continue long after the dependence of the

offspring on such nourishment has ceased. The young are guarded
and watched over, food is foraged for them, and such care may be
extended to training in methods of hunting, in avoidance of enemies,
and in other acquirements which make for successful living.

It has been shown that in the struggle for existence mammals have
gained supremacy over all other animals. Their superior brains have
enabled them immensely to widen means and opportunities of
securing their food, while a diversity of structure equalled by no
other class of animals fits them to obtain it in a variety of ways.
Their mental and physical equipment again gives them ascendancy
in ways and means of protecting themselves and their young against
whatever may be adverse in their surroundings. Life is expressed
on this earth in a myriad forms ; it attains its highest expression in
mammals and its most perfect in man, the highest of mammals
whose kingdom is all the Earth.

HOW MAMMALS ARE CLASSIFIED

Classification is the grouping together of things which bear the
same relationships or affinities. Mammals and other backboned
animals are grouped together in one great division of the Animal
Kingdom, the **Vertebrates**. The main characters by which any mammal can be distinguished from any other vertebrate have been indicated. These characters, common to all mammals, place them in
a distinct Class of the Vertebrates, the **Mammalia**. Differences in
the methods which they follow in caring for their young enable the
sub-classification of mammals into three groups : (1) the egg-laying
mammals or **Monotremes,** (2) pouched mammals or **Marsupials**,
and (3) the **placental mammals**. These groups are again divisible
on the basis of relationships and affinities into Orders, Families,
Genera, and Species. All rodents have chisel-shaped incisor teeth.
United in this character they form a natural Order, the Rodentia.
In the same way a distinctive dentition enables us to place all beasts
of prey in another natural Order, the Carnivora, and all insect-
eaters in yet another, the Insectivora. Of the seventeen such natural
Orders of placental mammals thirteen are represented in the Indian
Region. An Order may be divided into sub-Orders. The Order
Cetacea (whales) has, for example, two sub-Orders. One includes
Sperm Whales, Killer Whales, Porpoises, and Dolphins, which are
distinctive in having teeth ; the other includes Whalebone or Baleen
Whales which have baleen instead of teeth.   The Family is a subdivision of the Order or sub-Order. Squirrels have certain Family
resemblances which distinguish them from rats and mice, and these
again have common Family characters which distinguish them from
porcupines. The sub-Order containing all these animals is therefore
separable into distinct tribes or Families. Carrying the classification

further we pass from Family resemblances to particular distinctions between members of a Family. In the squirrel Family, flying squirrels, giant squirrels, and diminutive palm squirrels are quite distinctive. To specify these distinctions we place them in separate Genera. Finally the members of a Genus are distinguishable as different Species. We may go even further and reduce the classification to its smallest unit. Minor differences in size, colour, etc. may for example be seen in animals of the same species inhabiting different geographical areas. These variants are classed as sub-Species or geographical Races.

The classification of animals is based, as we have seen, on mutual relationships and affinities. It is work which requires knowledge not only of the external appearance and habits of animals, but also of their internal anatomy and structure. The imparting of such knowledge is outside the scope of this book. More detailed knowledge of the structure and classification of mammals may be had from text books of Zoology, and from the introductory chapters to Mr. Pocock's volumes on Mammals in the Fauna of British India series. These volumes, designed to replace Blanford's older work, provide the standard work on Indian mammals. The new edition is based largely on the results of a survey of mammals carried out for many years by the Bombay Natural History Society in India, Burma, and Ceylon. While it represents a great advance in our knowledge of Indian mammals, it also reveals how much remains to be learned, and how little is really known about even the commonest of Indian mammals. Take such a common animal as the Panther, we know little of its reactions to the changing conditions of its environment, its reactions to other animals among which it lives, its migrations and movements, its acquirement of territory. It is such knowledge as this which alone can give a truer picture than we now possess of the life and being of animals. Such knowledge cannot come from the study of dead specimens in museums, but from the study of the living animal in its natural surroundings. It is work which falls exactly within the province of field naturalists and students. It is to rouse and create the interest which may lead eventually to such work that this book has been written.

THE DISTRIBUTION OF MAMMALS

As this book was first published before the separation of Pakistan from India, the term ' India ' was used to include the area which is now Pakistan. Except where appearing otherwise from the context, it continues to be used in a zoogeographical sense to include present-day Pakistan. It also covers the Andaman and Nicobar Islands, and reference is made to Ceylon where Indian species extend to that island.

In the distribution of their wild life few regions of the earth

exceed India in interest. Covering an area of about 1,800,000
square miles (4,662,000 sq. km.), it displays in its physical characters and in its temperature and climate the most remarkable variation. Its widespread frontiers include the Himalayas, soaring for
thousands of feet above the level of perpetual snow, the deserts of
Sind and Rajputana, the luxuriant rain-swept forests of Assam and
the Malabar Coast, and the cold and arid plateaux of Ladak and
Tibet. Across our northern frontiers stands the chain of the loftiest
mountain range in the world, while our shores are washed by an
ocean which stretches south to the bleak Antarctic forming an in-
superable barrier to the dispersal of our wild life. Before describing
our mammals, I propose to give a picture of the varied conditions
under which they live, these conditions being the factors which influence their distribution.

Animals are dependent directly or indirectly upon plants for their
food. The vegetation of a country is therefore one of the main factors which influence the character of its animal life. But the type of
vegetation which will grow in any country depends much upon its
climate and the climate upon its physical features, the level of the
land, the presence or absence of mountain or hill ranges, the height
and aspect of these ranges. Hence the distribution of animal life
upon this earth, as we know it today, is based entirely upon the
changes which have taken place in its surface through the long ages
of its history. All through time the surface of the earth has been
changing. Mountain ranges stand in areas once submerged beneath
the sea. Expanses of land have broken up to become separate con-
tinents divided by oceans, and on the other hand dividing seas have
receded to form continuous stretches of dry land.

It is believed that during the early part of the Tertiary period the
peninsula of India, the triangular tableland which stretches from
the highlands of central India to Cape Comorin, was a large island.
This island during a still more remote period was perhaps united to
Africa. But during the Tertiary period it was separated from the
mainland of Asia by shallow seas which covered the plains of northern India and the whole of Kashmir. The Himalayan region and the
greater part of Tibet, formerly submerged beneath the sea, was then
a land of moderate elevation drained by great rivers, which flowing
east and west poured their alluvium and silt into the adjoining seas.
During the millions of years that elapsed, while no great changes
have been traced in the ancient island, the whole of those gigantic
forces which created the great Himalayan ranges exerted their influence. They raised the land and drained the seas covering Assam
and gave birth to the eastern Himalayas. Thus was formed the first
land connection between India and the continent of Asia. Thus was
provided a land bridge by which all the forms of life developing
in central Asia were able to enter and colonize the Indian peninsula.

It is believed that after a great interval of time, a second upheaval
took place. It produced the main Himalayan ranges and converted

what was left of the intervening sea into the plains of northern India. After an interval of quiescence, a third upheaval crumpled and ridged up a strip of this plain to form the outer ranges of the Himalayas, the group of hills known as the Siwaliks. So was formed in the course of ages the sub-continent of India.

Animals of the past. What animals inhabited the country during these distant ages? The remains of extinct creatures discovered in the upper layers of the Siwalik range and in other parts of the country give us a glimpse of a wonderful wealth of animal life during the Tertiary period. Mastodons and great herds of elephants of many species trumpeted and tramped through the swamps and reedy forests of this region. With them lived the hippopotamus, rhinoceroses of various kinds, and a colossal four-horned ruminant the *Sivatherium*. There were troops of giraffes, of large and pygmy horses, camels, herds of wild oxen, buffalo, bison, deer, many kinds of antelope, wild pig and pig-like creatures. Further the fossil beds reveal the existence in the Siwaliks of chimpanzees, orang-utans and baboons, of langurs and macaques. The beasts of prey included a type of cheetah or hunting-leopard, sabre-toothed tigers and various large and small felines, wolves, jackals, and foxes, civets, martens, ratels, and otters. The bears were represented by a species similar to our sloth bear, the rodents by various genera including bamboo rats, mole-rats, porcupines, and hares.

A striking fact, emerging from the comparison of the fauna of the past with that of the present, is the wonderful variety of forms which lived in those remote times and the relatively fewer forms of our day. It must be remembered that our records are incomplete. Yet we know that eleven different species of elephants and mastodons lived at various epochs in the Siwaliks as compared with the solitary living form we have now. There were six different species of rhinoceros and several representatives of the wild boar, some of gigantic dimensions. The beasts of prey were also more numerous than those now living in that region. This marked impoverishment of the fauna is not peculiar to India. The remains of extinct animals unearthed in various parts of Europe, Asia, and North America reveal a similar loss.

It is interesting also to note how many forms of life akin to those of that distant time still continue to flourish in India after millions of years. Langurs, macaques, various species of cats, hyenas, jackals, foxes, sloth bears, ratels, mole-rats, porcupines, hares, rhinoceroses, bison, and elephants, allied to those which lived in the Tertiary period, still live in this country. How many again still inhabit other regions of the earth though no longer found in India? Chimpanzees, baboons, hippopotami, and giraffes, eland, kudus, and other antelope survive in Africa, though not in India. A considerable affinity has been traced between the fauna of the Siwalik period and the wild animals now living in India and Africa. Rhinoceroses, elephants, antelopes, various species of felines, hyenas, jackals, foxes, ratels, mongooses, and several forms of rodents exist in both countries. It is believed that a very large proportion of the animals which formerly existed in the Siwaliks and the allied species now inhabiting Africa and India were derived wholly or partly from the same ancestors, which may have originally migrated southward from Europe and central Asia. The remains of extinct animals discovered in Europe and central Asia show that elephants, rhinoceroses, hippopotami, tapirs, antelopes, lions, and tigers once inhabited these regions. During that time, it is believed, the northern countries enjoyed an almost tropical climate, but owing to a change in climate and other causes all those forms of life which were unable to adapt themselves to changing conditions perished or migrated southwards.

It is known that during the latter part of the Tertiary period the climate of Europe was becoming gradually cooler, and that this refrigeration ended in a glacial epoch or Ice Age in which the northern countries were subjected to an Arctic climate. The Ice Age also produced glacial conditions in the Himalayan region, but whether these conditions extended into the peninsula of India is not known. It is assumed that all forms of life inhabiting the countries so affected were compelled to adapt themselves to the changing conditions, to migrate, or to perish. Some were able to react to the new conditions, many were exterminated, while others migrated southwards to colonize warmer tropical countries. Thus is explained the disappearance of numerous forms of life from the northern Hemisphere and the Himalayas, and the survival of their descendants both in India and Africa in our time.

Many forms of life, represented in the older fauna, disappeared from this country. Their place appears to have been taken by others, which subsequently migrated into India from the countries lying to the east of the Bay of Bengal. Many Indo-Chinese mammals, not represented in the older Siwalik fauna, are believed to have migrated into India from the hill ranges of Assam and the countries further east. The majority of them settled in the eastern Himalayas, while others spread through or colonized parts of the peninsula. About 70 per cent of the mammals living in the Himalayan forests between Kashmir and Bhutan are found equally in the hill forests of Assam, Burma, and south China, while some Malayan types, like the mouse-deer and the lorises, inhabit parts of the peninsula. A stream of migration has also come from the west. Such species as the Indian Lion, the Indian Gazelle, and the Urial of the Punjab and Kashmir, from their westerly range or their affinity with species inhabiting regions lying to the west, are believed to have extended into India through her western frontiers.

Thus we see that the wild life of India is derived not only from species which were indigenous to it, which are found in no other country in the world, but also from forms which are descendants of ancestors that migrated into India from the regions which adjoin its borders. It is composed of an admixture of Indian, Malayan, Ethiopian, and European elements. These foreign forms naturally predominate in parts of the country most suited to their habits. The Malayan forms abound in the damp, sheltered, forest-clad valleys of the eastern Himalayas and occur again with frequency in the rain-swept forests of the Malabar coast. The fauna of Kashmir and the higher Himalayas is marked by a predominance of European types. The main peninsula is described as the home of the true Indian fauna. The desert tracts of Sind and the Punjab shelter an animal life somewhat uniform with that of the great Palaearctic desert which extends westwards from Sind to the shores of northern Africa.

With this brief review of some of the factors which influenced the character and composition of the Indian fauna we may now consider its present general distribution.

India, with south-eastern Asia, forms part of the Oriental Region, one of the six great Zoological Realms into which the earth has been divided to study the distribution of its animal life. Each of these realms supports its characteristic animal life. That the animals and plants of one country or group of countries may differ from those of another must be apparent to most people. But India, while it forms part of the Oriental Region, presents in itself such contrasts in physical characters, such variation in climate and vegetation, that its animal life naturally varies with conditions in different parts of the country.

This vast sub-continent has been divided into various zones or sub-Regions each of which supports its characteristic assemblage of wild animals. There is no sharp line of demarcation between these zones. It would be difficult to plot them out exactly on a map. The animal life of one zone merges imperceptibly into that of another and there are widespread species which live in one or more zones. But on the whole it may be claimed that the animal life of a particular zone is sufficiently distinctive to be distinguishable from that of another. (Plates facing pp. 11, 16, 17)

The Himalayan Sub-Region

The Himalaya Mountains, between the Indus in the west and the Brahmaputra in the east, support an animal life more or less distinct from the rest of India. But the great range of altitude of these mountains has naturally resulted in marked peculiarities of distribution in its plants and animals.

Three distinct sub-zones, each with its characteristic assemblage of animals, are now recognised. The first, the Forest Zone, covers the whole of the forested slopes of the Himalayas from the eastern frontiers of Kashmir to Bhutan. The second includes the western

Himalayas from Kashmir and eastern Ladak to Chitral, the third the arid plateaux of eastern Ladak and Tibet. The bare towering peaks above the tree-line and a strip of upland grass country which lies between the main Himalayan range and the plateau of Tibet are regarded as a transition zone. Here the animal life of the Himalayan forests merges into one which is characteristic of Europe and central Asia.

The Forest Zone. The foothills and lower valleys or 'dhuns' of the Forest Zone are covered with dense tropical vegetation. These lower forests are inhabited mainly by animals which are found in the forests of the peninsula. Tiger, elephants, gaur, sambar, and munt-jac are common. In the swamps and forests of the Terai, the strip of low-lying country which adjoins the foothills, gaur are replaced by buffalo, and chital, hog-deer, and swamp deer are found.

When an altitude between 5000 to 6000 feet (1525 to 1830 m.) is reached the character of the vegetation changes. The forests become dark and gloomy. Oaks, magnolias, laurels, and birches covered with moss and ferns replace the sal, silk-cotton trees, and giant bamboos of the foothills. At an elevation of about 9000 to 12,000 ft. (2745 to 3660 m.) one enters forests of pine and fir trees, of yew and juniper, with an undergrowth of scrubby rhododendrons and dwarf bamboo. We enter a temperate zone with a temperate vegetation. But there is no sharp line of demarcation between the tropical and the temperate forests. The transition from one to the other is gradual, much depending on the height of the intermediate ranges and the depth of the inner valleys. In the eastern Himalayas, exposed to the full blast of the monsoon, tropical trees reach higher levels than in the colder and drier climate of the western Himalayas. The animal life of the temperate zone is distinguished by the absence of many species which inhabit the Indian peninsula, and by the presence of many Indo-Chinese forms, which do not occur in the peninsula but are common in the hill forests of Assam, Burma, and southern China. Pandas, hog-badgers, ferret-badgers, crestless porcupines, and those curious goat-antelopes the goral and the serow are some of the typical inhabitants of these temperate forests. They are not found elsewhere in India but range widely in similar forests through Assam and the countries further east. The Indo-Chinese element in the fauna is very marked in the eastern Himalayas but, as one travels westward, it gradually disappears until, in Kashmir and the countries further west, it ceases to be the principal constituent. The probable colonization of these forests by emigrants from the hill ranges of Assam has already been commented upon.

The Western Zone. The second great zone of the mountain system extends from Kashmir and western Ladak to Chitral. The Indo-Chinese mammals of the central and eastern Himalayas are here replaced largely by Indian species, and by an infusion of forms allied

to European and northern Asiatic types. Many animals living in the plains of India are or were found in this zone, among them the muntjac, the blackbuck, and the chinkara. The sambar is absent. The most distinctive deer is the Kashmir stag, a relative of the red deer of Europe. Again, typically northern animals such as the ibex and markhor range through these western mountains but, like the Kashmir stag, do not extend into the eastern Himalayas. The urial or shapu is also not found far beyond Kashmir but extends its territory westward through the Punjab, Baluchistan, and Afghanistan to the Persian hill ranges. Kashmir appears then to have received its fauna from the Indian peninsula and the countries lying to the north and west.

The Transition Zone. The bare peaks above the tree-line and the strip of luscious grass country lying between the mountains and arid plateaux of Tibet are described as a transition zone, a meeting ground between the animal life of the Oriental and the northern or Palaearctic regions. It is obvious that the huge mass of the Himalayas must be a great barrier to the free migration of animals. This obstacle combined with the great difference in climate north and south of the range has resulted in a fairly sharp line of demarcation at about 28° lat. between two distinct faunas, the Oriental in the south and the Palaearctic in the north. Evidence of this is particularly marked in the eastern Himalayas. Here north of this line live such typically northern animals as moles, water shrews, mouse-hares, marmots, musk deer, and the bharal, while south of it the forests are inhabited by typically Oriental animals like flying foxes, fruit bats, tree shrews, civets, mongooses, and Oriental squirrels.

The Tibetan Zone. The Tibetan plateau together with eastern Ladak is regarded as a distinct faunal area. The zone does not include the low-lying wooded portions of eastern Tibet, but covers the barren plateaux and uplands which lie beyond the Himalayas but within the northern frontiers of India from Kashmir to Bhutan. It is a windswept region of scanty rainfall, intense cold, and high elevation, and is described as the only region of the globe where both desert and arctic conditions prevail. The wild ass, which is found in various desert parts of Asia, lives in this zone, which also shelters the Woolly Hare. The great Tibetan sheep, the bharal, and the yak, are also typical inhabitants of these cold, desolate, and barren mountains. So much for the wild life of the Himalayan region. Its great range of altitude and variety of climate and temperature, its vegetation ranging from tropical to alpine, and its geological history make it one of the most interesting zoological regions in the world.

Assam and Burma. Assam and Burma are included in the same zoological province as the forest region of the Himalayas. There is the same gradation from tropical to temperate vegetation though the purely alpine flora of the higher Himalayas is largely absent. The distribution and character of the animal life is similar, except in Tenasserim where the fauna is distinctly Malayan in type. These Malayan types are traceable all through the province into the hill ranges of Assam, with an intermingling of peculiar forms. Of the wild animals of Burma some, like the gaur, are identical with those of India ; others, like the sambar or the thamin, are regarded as Burmese representatives of Indian forms.

The Indian Peninsular Sub-Region

India proper from the base of the Himalayas to Cape Comorin, with the exception of the Malabar coast, is regarded as a single sub-region, the cis-Gangetic or Indian Peninsular sub-region. The northern part of this sub-region comprises the alluvial plains of the Ganges, the Indus, and the Brahmaputra rivers, and their tributaries. It covers the greater part of the States of Assam, E. and W. Bengal, Bihar, U.P., E. and W. Punjab, and Sind. This immense tract of level land, from 90 to 300 miles (145 to 485 km.) wide and stretching for 1400 miles (2255 km.) from sea to sea, separates the main Indian peninsula from the Himalaya. South of the Gangetic Plain, the peninsula takes the form of a triangular tableland, varying in altitude from 1000 to 3000 ft. (305 to 915 m.), broken up at intervals by the valleys of its intersecting rivers. The northern side of the tableland rests on confused hill ranges known collectively as the Vindhya Mountains. Its two other sides are formed by the Eastern Ghats, stretching in fragmentary spurs down the Madras coast, and the Western Ghats, which form the almost continuous sea-wall of Mysore and Maharashtra. The face of the triangular plateau is scarred with scattered peaks and hill ranges, outliers of the Ghats. The most notable are the Nilgiris, the Anaimalais, and the Palni Hills of southern India.

The animal life of the Indian Peninsular region is characterised by the absence of many of those Indo-Chinese species which are so abundant in the hill forests of the Himalayas. It is the home of the true Indian fauna of which the spotted deer, the nilgai, the black-buck, the fourhorned antelope, and the sloth bear are typical representatives. They are found nowhere else. Other species like the gaur, the sambar, and the muntjac occur both in India and the Malay countries.

The Indian Desert Region. The trans-Indus districts of the Punjab, western Sind, and Baluchistan really form the eastern limits of a great desert region which extends through Persia, Mesopotamia and Arabia to the shores of north Africa. Naturally the character of the wild life of the Indian Desert region differs markedly from the rest of India. It consists mainly of species which have migrated into it from the desert lands lying beyond its borders, and of species from the peninsula which are able to live under the conditions prevailing in these arid and sandy wastes.

The Gangetic Plain. The general distribution of animals in this sub-region corresponds to a large extent to the character of the vegetation, which is again dependent on variations in climate and soil. In the great plain of the Ganges the rainfall is moderate and the winter temperature is correspondingly low. In the north-western portions of the plain, in E. and W. Punjab and western Rajputana, the vegetation gradually merges into that of the adjoining desert zone. In this area live many desert forms of animals such as the desert cat, the desert fox, the desert hare, and various species of desert gerbilles, colonists from the Desert zone. The desert forms disappear as one travels eastwards into the more humid part of the Gangetic Plain. A feature of the dry zone of the Gangetic Plain formerly used to be large herds of antelope and gazelle. In the humid plain of E. and W. Bengal, the semi-desert vegetation of the northern plain gives place to luxuriant groves of mangoes, figs, and palms, such as one finds in the moist coastal tracts of the peninsula. The wild life of this humid area differs little from that of the moister and more cultivated parts of the peninsula. Further east, at the mouths of the Ganges, the great plain is transformed into a wilderness of swamp and forest, the Sunderbans. It is a region of grassy savannahs and muddy islets covered with mangroves and dense evergreen forests. These forests shelter most of the larger animals found in the forests of the peninsula, with the addition of swamp deer and such other animals as have a preference for this amphibious terrain.

The Main Peninsula. While the drainage areas of its intersecting rivers are covered with green woods and cultivation, the greater part of the tableland which forms the main peninsula of India presents a scene of wide undulating plains separated by ranges of flat-topped hills. A portion of the plateau, comprising the eastern parts of central India, Gujarat, and the Deccan, is sheltered from the monsoon by the great wall of the Western Ghats. It is a dry region of moderate rainfall. This dry zone extends to the lowlands of the Carnatic and stretches south to the plains of southern India. These are again cut off from the monsoon by the southern hill ranges. The dry zone of the tableland has its characteristic vegetation due to climate and to soil. From the Bombay coast to the neighbourhood of Nagpur, from below Belgaum to Goona in central India, over some 200,000 sq. miles (518,000 sq. km.) of country, black cotton soil predominates. It is derived here from the underlying volcanic rocks known as Deccan Trap which form the unbroken substratum throughout this area. Black soil produces its characteristic wild and cultivated vegetation. The wide grass-covered plains and the bases of the flat-topped hills in the Trap country are scattered with clumps of thorny acacias, species of *Zizyphus*, small trees, and shrubs, which are either leafless or burnt-up in the hot weather. Forests, where they exist, are mainly deciduous and composed of stunted teak, bamboos, and sundry small trees. In the open grasslands and scrub jungle, herds of gazelle and antelope were once common. Other typical animals of the open country in the peninsula are the jungle cat, the common fox, the common mongoose, the Indian wolf, palm squirrels, hares, and a variety of field rats and mice. Gaur, sambar, spotted deer, sloth bear, and wild dogs are found in its open deciduous hill forests. As one leaves the Trap country and penetrates the humid region lying north and east of Nagpur, one enters a zone where the climate is somewhat similar to the plains of E. and W. Bengal, and the character of the soil and of the vegetation changes. Teak ceases to be the dominant tree of the forests. It gives place gradually to Sal, while the familar crops of the Trap country millet, pulses, and cotton yield to watery rice and sugarcane fields. The wild life of the forests of this humid zone is enriched by the presence of wild elephants, buffalo, and swamp deer, which occur in this area.

The Malabar Coast. The Western Ghats, in sharp contrast to the adjoining dry zone of the Deccan, present a region of great humidity and heavy rainfall. The forests covering the western slopes are at times very dense and composed of lofty trees, festooned with numerous perennial creepers. Bamboos form a luxuriant undergrowth. In parts of the range the forests are more open and the banks of clear streams running through them are covered with spice and betel groves.

The Nilgiris, an offshoot of the Western Ghats, rise precipitously to form extensive grassy downs and tablelands seamed with densely forested gorges or *sholas*. They are composed of tall evergreen trees with a dense undergrowth. Sholas, similar to those of the Nilgiris, occur in the Anaimalai, Palni Hills, and other south Indian ranges. They provide the main shelter to wild elephants, gaur, and other large animals of these hills. The most interesting feature of the higher level forests of the Nilgiris is their affinity to the higher forests of the Assam hill ranges. Many of the trees found in these high sholas, and some of the forms of animal life are common to both areas. The forests of the Western Ghats and the south Indian hill ranges have a richer fauna than the remaining areas of the Peninsular Region. Among the species limited to these forests are the Nilgiri langur, the liontailed macaque, the Nilgiri brown mongoose and the stripednecked mongoose, the Malabar civet, and the spiny mouse. In the higher levels of the Nilgiris and the Anaimalai are found such characteristically Himalayan animals as the tahr, the pine-marten, and the European otter.

CONCLUSIONS

From this general description of the composition and distribution of the mammals of India, and of the varied conditions under which they live, it will be seen that they share with all other living things the strong natural tendency to increase their sphere of action, to extend their territory. We find animals which have originated in countries beyond our frontiers or in our northern mountain ranges extending their range and colonizing the peninsula. When a species thus spreads into a new territory where the climate, the vegetation, and the enemies it has to face are different from its original home, it must adapt itself to these changed conditions or it will fail to establish itself. These different conditions may produce differences in its appearance and habits, in other words they may produce a variation from the typical parent form. If these colonists are subsequently isolated from the parent stock by impassable barriers, produced as a result of geological and other changes, they will tend in the course of centuries to differ more and more from the parent stock. Glacial conditions which obtained in the Himalayas during the Ice Age are believed to have driven the tahr with other animals to colonize the Indian peninsula, which is assumed to have enjoyed a more temperate climate during this epoch. The return of tropical conditions in India is believed to have resulted in the extermination of the tahr in the peninsular region. But those which were able to obtain a refuge in the temperate climate of the higher altitudes of the Nilgiris and Anaimalai hill ranges survived. Isolation from the parent Himalayan stock and different conditions of life produced in the course of centuries those differences in colouring and texture of coat, shape of horns, and other characters which now distinguish the Nilgiri from the Himalayan tahr. In other words, a new and distinct species was evolved. But if no impassable barriers are created, the new varieties evolved in different connected areas remain more or less alike. There is interbreeding and consequently an intergradation of characters between these varied geographical races linking them with the parent form. Thus, among many widespread species of animals we find more or less distinguishable geographical races, evolved as a result of the different conditions under which they live in different areas of their range. In the case of our Giant Squirrel, which extends through the forested tracts of the peninsula, there are well-marked differences in colouring which enable us to distinguish various races inhabiting different areas. (Map between pp. 24 and 25)

In the past naturalists were content to classify animals in accordance with the salient characters or marked differences between species. In recent years it has been recognised that it is not only necessary to classify species, but it is equally important to systematically record such geographical variations where they exist in a species. These data, when sufficiently multiplied, will in future furnish information for the investigation of problems connected with the variation and distribution of species. Therefore, in more recent publications dealing with Indian animal life, we find due attention paid to the description of geographical races wherever these occur.

It will also be seen that a knowledge of animal life gives us a better knowledge of ancient geography. It reveals changes which have taken place in the distribution of land and water, and shows how the present distribution of land animals has been brought about. We have seen also some of the factors which have influenced this distribution or produced changes in or the extermination of numerous forms. In our day, the agency which accelerates these changes is man. In India, irrigation by human agency in the desert tracts of E. and W. Punjab and Sind has resulted in the conversion of vast tracts of desert land into fertile country. This is bringing about a change in the character of the animal life of these areas. Desert species are retreating from them. They are being replaced by forms more adapted to the changed conditions. Again, man sweeps away forests, dams, rivers, and wipes out of existence races of animals which are the culmination of centuries of evolution. While man is a destructive agent, he can also become a preserver and protect wild creatures from the destructive effects of his own handiwork. The need for saving the wild creatures from annihilation is recognised in most countries of the world. Various factors, as a result of human activity, are threatening the wild creatures of India with extermination. There is, as we have shown, great need in this country for adequate measures to preserve wild life from the destruction which threatens it.

2. Apes, Monkeys, Lemurs

IN HIS CLASSIFICATION of animals man gives pride of place to himself and to the apes, monkeys, and lemurs. These animals have many of the same structural characters as man. Some of them resemble him more in one feature, some in another. They are grouped with man in a common Natural Order the **Primates**, the first, the highest of animals. Now there is nothing in the bodily structure of a primate which makes it superior to other animals. Creatures much lower in the scale of life are as well, some perhaps even better, fitted for their special ways of life. The ascendancy of the primate is purely mental. It is derived from a superior development of the brain and the higher intelligence which goes with it. But such predominance is not equally shared by all the members of the Order. In mental development some monkeys and lemurs are not much better than the lower mammals. At the other end of the scale is man, who in mental endowment stands alone and unapproachable among all creatures. The immeasurable superiority of the human intellect marks the line of cleavage between man and animal.

If we look for obviously distinctive characters in the animals which we class as primates, we find them in the structure of their hands and feet which are designed to serve the express purpose of grasping organs. As such they are admirably adapted to the particular habits and mode of life of the animals.

STRUCTURE IN RELATION TO HABITS

Hands and feet. The hands of apes, monkeys, and lemurs are constructed on the same plan as our own. The thumb is opposable to the other fingers. Such a hand can pick up and hold objects. But primarily their hands remain organs of locomotion. Many apes and monkeys have poorly developed thumbs ; some monkeys have no thumbs at all, or thumbs so small that they are almost useless. A gibbon's thumb is set far down the side of its slender hand, and parallel with the other fingers. It appears weak and ineffective. The thumb of a langur is rudimentary. Yet the long narrow palm of the gibbon and its long flexible fingers, when hooked over a branch, provide light and ideal suspension for its body. In rapid movement the hook can be fixed and released instantly, whereas a protruding thumb might catch against a branch or be otherwise injured in swift progress. The thumbless hand of some monkeys expresses a still more perfect adaptation to rapid movement through the trees ; an embarrassment in such movement, the thumb is either reduced in size or lost. Unlike apes and monkeys, all lemurs have well-developed thumbs, but curiously enough in some of them it is the index or first finger which is poorly developed.

To give the hand perfect freedom of movement the double bones of the forearm are quite free. Both bones are equally well developed and so articulated to the wrist that the palms can be turned upwards or downwards with ease. A similar provision gives the same facility of movement to the foot.

The feet of primates are built on much the same plan as the hands. The toes are long flexible fingers. The big toe is converted into a perfect thumb and like the thumb is easily opposable to the other digits. With such a foot objects can be seized and held. To fit these animals for climbing, the feet have become powerful grasping organs. The human foot has lost this prehensile power, though some of the primitive human types still retain it. But to live man has no need to climb, while apes, monkeys, and their lesser kin must. Their hands and feet and bodies are built for this special purpose. Such differences as we see in their hands and feet and in their limbs and bodies are but the result of differences in methods of climbing. Contrast the build of a langur with the build of a gibbon. A gibbon's excessively long arms, its powerful chest and shoulders, its weak hindquarters are all designed to aid its special method of progress through the trees. When moving rapidly a gibbon swings on his arms from branch to branch. It is a way of getting about quickly used by all the apes. The langur on the other hand displays no excessive lengthening of the arms. His legs are in fact longer than his arms, and his loins and thighs are powerfully developed. His particular build is associated with his particular method of swift progress. Like all monkeys, when moving fast a langur moves with leaps and bounds, springing from branch to branch, from tree to tree. In these flying leaps his tail helps to balance his body. (Plate facing p. 32)

Tails. The tail in primates is a variable feature. Apes have none. The tailless gibbon uses its outstretched arms to maintain its balance when walking erect on branches or on the ground. As for monkeys, there are monkeys with long tails, others with mere stumps, and yet others without a tail. When long, the tail helps to balance the body. Many American monkeys have prehensile tails and use them as a fifth hand. The end of the tail, hitched over a branch, gives additional support to the body in movement or in rest. None of the Old World apes or monkeys can use their tails in this way. For comfort when sitting the langur is provided with patches or callosities of hard tough skin on his buttocks. The provision is common to our gibbons and monkeys. It is absent in American species.

As with climbing, so with walking or running on the ground, the langur and the gibbon each has its characteristic way of movement. When it comes to earth, or walks along a branch, the gibbon walks

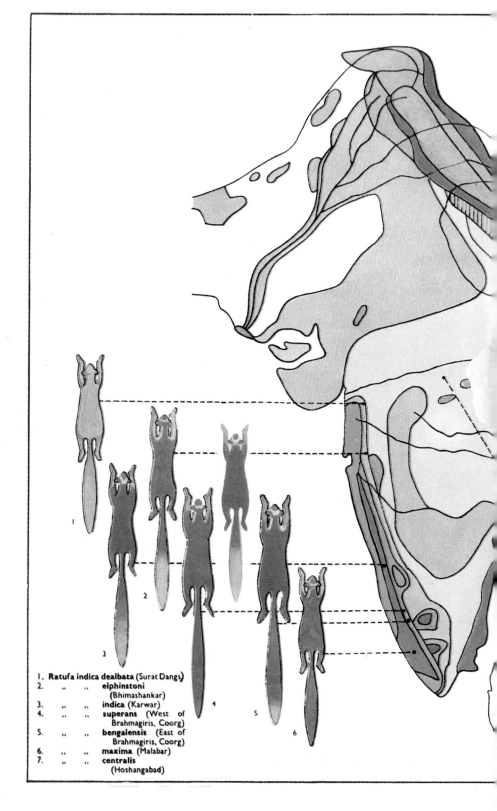

1. **Ratufa indica dealbata** (Surat Dangs)
2. " " **elphinstoni**
   (Bhimashankar)
3. " " **indica** (Karwar)
4. " " **superans** (West of
   Brahmagiris, Coorg)
5. " " **bengalensis** (East of
   Brahmagiris, Coorg)
6. " " **maxima** (Malabar)
7. " " **centralis**
   (Hoshangabad)

GEOGRAPHICAL RACES OF

THE INDIAN GIANT SQUIRREL

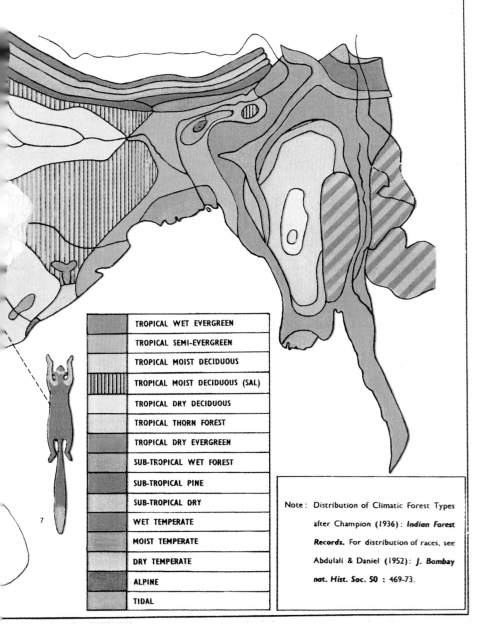

	TROPICAL WET EVERGREEN
	TROPICAL SEMI-EVERGREEN
	TROPICAL MOIST DECIDUOUS
	TROPICAL MOIST DECIDUOUS (SAL)
	TROPICAL DRY DECIDUOUS
	TROPICAL THORN FOREST
	TROPICAL DRY EVERGREEN
	SUB-TROPICAL WET FOREST
	SUB-TROPICAL PINE
	SUB-TROPICAL DRY
	WET TEMPERATE
	MOIST TEMPERATE
	DRY TEMPERATE
	ALPINE
	TIDAL

Note: Distribution of Climatic Forest Types after Champion (1936): *Indian Forest Records.* For distribution of races, see Abdulali & Daniel (1952): *J. Bombay nat. Hist. Soc.* 50 : 469-73.

7

erect on the soles of its feet, using its outstretched arms to maintain its balance. Except when very young the heavier apes cannot
do this. They maintain an erect posture with difficulty. They usually
walk or run on all fours. When doing this the body is supported
on the in-bent knuckles of the hand, and on the soles of the feet,
sometimes on the in-bent toes. Langurs and monkeys in general
walk and run as dogs and other four-footed animals do. The whole
of the palm is pressed to the ground, but not the entire sole ; the
heel is raised above the surface. As for progress in water, many
monkeys especially macaques are good swimmers. A troop of them
will drop from the trees into a stream and using the overarm or
breaststroke swim vigorously to the opposite bank. Having considered their fitness for climbing which is their special way of life,
let us now consider how apes, monkeys, and lemurs are fitted to
care for themselves and their young. In caring for itself the most
important business of an animal is to secure its food.

Teeth, and food. Apes, monkeys and lemurs eat leaves, flowers, and
fruit. This is their chief food. As vegetarians, most of them have
teeth suited to a vegetarian diet. Their molars or cheek teeth have
those broad crowns surmounted with cusps and ridges, which are
meant for grinding tough vegetable matter.

As to their ways of eating, most lemurs eat like other animals,
thrusting out for food with their long pointed snouts. Apes and
monkeys carry food to the mouth with their hands. They eat much
and eat fast. Eating, as wild animals do, under constant threat of
danger, many monkeys have special means of getting away with
large quantities of food in the shortest possible time. Some cram
food which they cannot eat at once into a large pouch in their cheeks.
Even when full, the pouch does not interfere with continued eating,
and this extra food hurriedly stowed away can be munched later in
some place of security. Macaques and baboons have these pouches.
Langurs have none. But for the langur the same purpose is achieved
in a different way. Its stomach does the work of a cheek pouch.
It is not the simple rounded sac usual in monkeys, but consists of
three separate pouches or compartments, somewhat like the stomach of a ruminating animal, of a cow, sheep, or goat. The ruminant's ' pouched ' stomach has a special chamber for receiving partly
chewed food. So has the langur's. With such a stomach food can
be hurriedly taken. Like ruminants, langurs are purely herbivorous ; their pouched stomachs are suited to their special food.
Baboons and macaques on the other hand are omnivorous. They
vary their vegetable diet with insects, grubs, and spiders. Some
even eat lizards and frogs, while one of the tribe has taken to eating
crabs. They have the type of stomach common to omnivorous
animals. Lemurs hunt for their food under cover of darkness.
Apes and monkeys feed only by day. Some monkeys, baboons and
macaques for instance, forage for food on the ground, some amongst

rocks and cliffs, but the great majority of apes and monkeys find their food in trees.

LIFE IN RELATION TO SURROUNDINGS

Animal neighbours. Apes and monkeys usually live on good terms with other wild animals. Deer and wild cattle will gather under trees where langurs or macaques are feeding, to eat the fruit and leaves which they wastefully drop. Their chief enemies are man and the larger beasts of prey. In India the arch enemy of the monkey is the panther, which waits in hiding for, or rushes up a tree to seize, its victim. The amazing speed at which a panther charges up a tree makes it a serious menace even to so nimble a creature as a monkey. Even the sudden rush or sudden roar of panther may send a monkey hurtling down from its perch. Highly strung creatures, they are obviously affected by loud and sudden sounds. There is an instance of a monkey in a zoo which dropped dead at a sudden clap of thunder. The larger reptiles are also their foes. A python will seize and strangle a monkey in its massive coils, and crocodiles kill and eat them when they come down to drink. Monkeys and apes recognise and have an instinctive dread of snakes, a recognition and fear not displayed by other wild animals.

Of their means of defence, it might be said that well-developed vision and hearing, extreme alertness and agility are their best means of escape. Concealment is a common device. To hide behind a heavy bough or foliage, or deliberately draw branches together to screen themselves from view is a thing which many monkeys do. But to flee from danger is the usual impulse. Very curious is the way some monkeys have of dropping down from the trees to sneak away silently through the undergrowth when frightened. Even such highly arboreal species as langurs do it. Why they leave the greater security of their treetops to face the more immediate risk of destruction below is behaviour difficult to explain. It must often bring death. Yet, it is behaviour which has been commonly noted. Apes and monkeys must derive protection or, to put it better, collective security from living together in communities. A threatened attack on one member of a troop draws aggressive demonstration from the rest. Mutual aid may be given to rescue the injured or threatened, and in defence of the young. Again, the vigilance of one becomes the defence of many. The alarm calls of langurs and macaques when fear or suspicion is aroused by the sight of a tiger, leopard, or other animal are well known, and are used by human hunters to locate a tiger. But there is no real evidence to show, as is often stated, that special sentinels are posted and that doing ' sentry-go ' is assigned to particular members of a troop. A warning cry from any langur will send the whole troop bolting, none stopping to discover the cause of the disturbance. Superior in mental development though they be, in their means of self defence apes and monkeys are as the lower animals. No monkey or ape has ever got the idea of using anything as a weapon. That is left to man. Being intelligent he has devised ways and means of killing the largest number of his fellow men in the shortest possible time! It is related that African baboons hurl stones at their attackers. It may be that stones and boulders are dislodged by these animals in their movements among rocks and rubble, but there is no authentic record of the deliberate picking up and hurling of stones. Their natural weapons of defence are their great canine teeth so formidably developed in many apes and monkeys. They are always larger in the males, which suggests that their special purpose is not for use against other animals, but for use in fights between rival males for dominance and lordship over females. Monkeys are not flesh-eaters and are therefore not prone to attack other animals. That they may attack in self-defence, or in defence of their young, is behaviour common to all creatures. Courage in these circumstances is largely an individual quality. One langur attacked by a dog covers his face with its hands and resigns itself to its fate, another sets upon and fatally mauls its tormentor.

Monkeys and man. As for man, the great apes have been unable to withstand civilised settlement in their domains, and have retreated before man into their utmost fastnesses. Protection alone can save them from extinction. The lesser monkeys, rated lower in intelligence, have been far more successful in adapting themselves to human company. Except where persecuted, they pay little attention to man. In most parts of India, where monkeys are not or are hardly ever molested, they have grown exceedingly bold. Troops of langurs and macaques settle down near or invade towns and villages, and loaf about railway stations ; they enter houses, pillage crops and gardens, and where too numerous make a complete nuisance of themselves.

Life in association with man must profoundly influence their ways and habits. One aspect of this influence is indicated later in considering the organisation of social life among these animals. While man serves as a provider of food, he also plays his usual role as an exterminator. Many species of monkey are persistently hunted for their furs. Because of the beauty of its rich black fur, the Nilgiri Langur (*P. johni*) is a victim to much persecution and is fast disappearing from areas where it was once common. The flesh of monkeys is commonly eaten by most of the forest tribes in India. The shyness or boldness of various species is usually dependent on protection or persecution by man.

The inanimate environment. Apes, monkeys, and lemurs are fitted by nature to live in a warm climate. Except for the Australian region, they inhabit all the tropical and sub-tropical countries of the

world. This does not mean that these animals cannot withstand
periods of intense cold. There are langurs which spend the winter
in the higher levels of the Himalayas, among the snow-laden pines
many thousand feet above the sea. The Assamese macaque has
extended its territory to the plateaux of eastern Tibet where it is
exposed seasonally to the intensest cold. Their protection is the
heavy coat of hair which they grow in winter time. It is particularly
long and fine in animals living in our northern upland regions, less
luxuriant for plain dwellers. With the onset of the hot weather this
heavy coat is shed and replaced by lighter summer pelage. The time
of shedding varies with the latitude and altitude of the habitat as
these factors control the early or late arrival of warmer weather.
Besides wearing light coats in summer, to escape the heat of the day
many of these animals seek the more sheltered levels of the forest.
Gibbons will sun themselves on the topmost branches of trees during
the chill hours of the morning, but they come down into the shade
of the lower levels at noontide. Langurs love to spend the hottest
hours of day dozing and resting in some sheltered grove or tree-
bordered watercourse. Rhesus monkeys frequently take to water,
swimming and bathing in the heat of the day.

The seasonal abundance or scarcity of food influence the local
migrations of monkeys. While many langurs winter in the pine forests
of the Himalayas, there appears to be some movement to the lower
valleys, associated probably with the quest for food which is more
readily available there than in the snowbound heights.

FAMILY LIFE AND CARE OF THE YOUNG

Means of communication. What are the means of communication
between the members of a monkey troop? It would be an exag-
geration to say that apes and monkeys talk to one another. At the
same time one may safely say that they excel all other animals in
the production of vocal sounds which have a particular meaning.
Many apes and monkeys have particular sounds to express different
emotions such as pleasure, anger, or fear. They have particular
calls to bring the members of a troop together, and distinctive cries
of caution and warning. Apart from vocal utterances the whole
range of emotions may be frequently read in the facial expression
of an ape or monkey. Another important means of intercommunion
is that almost universal habit of fur-picking. Such fur-picking is
not, as popular belief would have it, a hunt for lice or fleas. Apes
and monkeys are remarkably free from these vermin. What is got
out of this diligent search is usually nothing more than fragments
of skin, skin secretions, and other foreign matter. From the gentle
stimulus it provides fur-picking is a form of amative caress or courtship. Its repeated indulgence suggests that it is a powerful bond and
a means of social communion between members of a troop.

Family life. It was thought that the bond which keeps a troop of primates together is persistent sex attraction. However, recent studies show that this cannot be the basis for stable social grouping as many species show marked seasonal fluctuation in reproductive activities including, in some cases, complete cessation of copulation during a considerable part of the year. Broadly speaking, the evolution of social development in monkeys and apes is based on infant-mother relationship. Attachment to the mother creates suitable conditions for social learning within the intensely social group where the mother and her young are points of interest to the other members of the group.

The intricate social set-up among these animals gives them maximum advantage in their environment for protection from danger, living room, food, and species continuity. Social life considerably increases the chances of survival by making available several instead of one pair of eyes and ears to detect the approach of danger. There is shared knowledge of sources of food, and water, of areas free from danger, and safe sleeping places.

A system of pyramidal dominance knits the group together, and gives it order and a structure that provides predictable behaviour between the members within the group The main advantage is increased opportunity for learning. The group is a nucleus of knowledge and a pool of experience far exceeding that of any individual member. The protection provided by group living permits a learning period during which the juveniles acquire from the adults the knowledge necessary for their comfort and safety.

The mechanics of the social organisation follows a certain basic pattern in all species of apes and monkeys. Each troop or social unit does not range all over the habitat of the species but occupies its own particular territory. In a population of several troops living in one area, each has its home range containing all its requirements of food and shelter.

The territories of adjacent troops often overlap marginally, but disputes are unusual. Among langurs contact is avoided through vocalisation, and their loud whooping calls serve to orientate the troops with reference to each other.

Conflict is more frequent among troops of the Common Rhesus monkey living in urban areas in India, owing to the restricted availability of suitable habitat and the tension of living in a more than normally hostile environment. However, troops of these monkeys living in such circumscribed environments have an order of inter-troop dominance, and a fight is always avoided by the subordinate group if it can possibly do so.

Social organisation within a group is based on the principle of male dominance. The males in a troop are ranked in a linear hierarchy comparable with the pecking order seen among poultry. However, maximum dominance among the semi-terrestrial baboon of Africa and the Rhesus monkey of Asia does not depend on size and aggressiveness alone; the animal must have the ability to *enlist* support from other males within the troop. This is illustrated by an observation in a troop of African baboons. The leader male was actually subordinate to another male in the linear hierarchy, but his ability to enlist the support of the third and fourth-ranking males gave him maximum dominance. The three males formed a central hierarchy which determined group movement and faced threats from within the group and external dangers. The leader and his aides moved in the centre of the group surrounded by females with recently-born young.

In one troop of the common Rhesus Monkey of India whose social organisation was studied, the troops had smaller cohesive units within them. In this troop there was a central dominant group of two males of equal social status. The dominant male, according to the linear hierarchy, ranked higher than the central group males individually, but was jointly dominated by them. This male headed another sub-group. The females of the troop lived in these two sub-groups. A number of young but adult males of lower social status formed a third group. The females and young moved freely among these sub-groups and all united in defence of the territory and of members of the troop.

The arboreal Langur is, in all respects, a more peaceful and sober animal than the rhesus and ranking is not as easily visible as among the aggressive Rhesus. Dominance is established with a minimum of aggressive behaviour and exhibited more subtly. The indicators are complex. A pause while walking past another male, made at some distance from the stationary animal indicates that the moving animal is subordinate; if the sitting animal turns its head while another is passing, the sitting animal is subordinate. An indicator of status within the group is the personal space or area around a male when he is in a tense mood, into which area another male cannot enter without being threatened. The more dominant the male the larger the space.

These data were gathered from studies on langurs in north India. Conditions may vary with different populations, and the danger of generalisation is indicated by the work of a Japanese team at Dharwar. They found that several male leaders of groups studied by them were replaced by more aggressive outsiders who almost invariably killed all infants in the group of less than a year in age.

Care of the young. We know little about the birth and infancy of apes and monkeys in their native wilds. What we know is mostly learnt from the lives of captive animals. All primates usually produce their young singly. Occasionally twins are born. From the moment of its birth the baby monkey clings to its mother's body sucking her teats, clutching with its tiny hands and feet the fur of her breast and abdomen, maintaining its hold even during swiftest movement. When she sits down the mother may hold the baby to her with her arm, thigh, or foot, or even hobble along with it on three legs. A long-tailed lemur will bind her baby to her abdomen with a twist of her tail. When it is able to crawl she carries it on her back. Thus the young are never left alone, they are carried about in one way or another wherever the parents go. Such protection is not peculiar to primates. Bats, sloths, and armadillos carry their young about with them and the marsupials, the kangaroos and their kin, keep them in a snug pouch.

Apes and monkeys suckle their young for a long time. A baby gibbon was carried about by its mother until it was two years old and was never seen to take any food but its mother's milk. The change from milk to more solid food is slow and gradual. But as the mothers do not gather food for their young, they have to begin for themselves and probably start by nibbling at shoots and leaves and eating grubs and insects.

Youth and why it is prolonged. How long do apes and monkeys take to grow up? We know little about particular species but the question may be answered generally from the lives of captive animals. The answer is, generally, the better the brain an animal has the longer the period of its youth. If we take the group of Primates, animals with the best-developed brains, we find that man takes from 15 to 20 years to really grow up. He has the most highly developed brain. The man-like apes and bigger monkeys whose mental development is lower take 6 to 12 years, the smaller monkeys 3 to 5, while the little lemurs whose mental equipment is not much better than the lower mammals are full-grown in 2 or 3 years. Why should mental development regulate the duration of youth? The period of youth is a perilous time for animals and therefore a period to be got over as quickly as possible. And this is what is usual among the lower animals. They are creatures of lesser brain. What they do to live they do instinctively, and instinctive acts are done automatically without learning or practice. But the higher we go in the scale the better the brain, the longer the period of youth. As in man, so in the higher animals, the period of youth is a period of learning, a period of training for life. The baby monkey climbs instinctively but it cannot climb well at once, it has to learn and acquire skill in the acrobatics of climbing. A mother langur throwing its baby into the air and catching it up in her arms is unconsciously training it to use its limbs for grasping branches. To strip leaves and fruit from trees requires practised hands. How clumsy are the infant monkey's first attempts! Besides there is experience to be gained of what it may and what it may not eat. Experience to be gained in recognizing danger and avoiding it. Youth is the time when these experiences are gained, and the higher the type of brain the better the animal is able to store up such experiences which become an important influence in guiding the activities of the grown animal. Thus it is that man and his next-of-kin, the apes and monkeys who are at the top of the scale in mental development, take the longest time to grow up. Youth is prolonged so that fuller experience for the battle of life may be gathered. All through this defenceless period the baby ape or monkey lives under the fostering protection of its mother, who cares for it with a rough tenderness, controlling its too venturesome sallies, chastening it when necessary with a cuff, and cuddling it to her breast to calm its fractious shrieks and chattering. The first business of an animal is to look after itself, to provide for its wants, to satisfy its own appetites, but the care of its young begins a new life for it. So absorbing is the urge to protect its off-spring that life may be sacrificed in defence of the young, and laborious and selfless efforts given to its well-being. One must how-ever guard against ascribing the nobler human motives of devotion and self-sacrifice to the actions of animals. A monkey overlord risks his life to protect one of his followers, a troop rallies round a threat-ened or wounded companion, a nursing mother gives her life in pro-tecting her young. But monkeys behave exactly in the same way whether the object of their solicitude is alive or dead. A dead com-panion will as easily become the object of protection as a live one. A mother will continue to carry about the dead body of an infant long after the flow of her milk has ceased and the thing she carries is no more than a dried mummy. In brief, apes and monkeys like other animals are unable to recognise death, and as such their behaviour in the presence of danger cannot be interpreted as selfless devotion. It is not induced by conscious thought, but comes in response to a blind instinct, which in its operation is none the less beneficial for the preservation of the species and for the survival of the race.

CLASSIFICATION OF INDIAN PRIMATES

There are two main divisions or sub-orders of Primates. One in-cludes man and the apes and monkeys, the other the lemurs and their kin. None of the great man-like apes are found in India. The gorilla and the chimpanzee inhabit Africa, the orang-utan the forests of Borneo and Sumatra. The only tribe of apes inhabiting our country are the gibbons of which a single species, the Hoolock, is found in the forests of Assam and Chittagong. Like all apes they are distinctive in the great development of the arms, which are much longer than the legs ; further they are tailless.

The monkeys of the Old World are classed together in a group named **Cynomorpha** or dog-like, to distinguish them from the ape or man-like section. But why dog-like ? Not especially dog-like in form or feature, but dog-like in the way they walk. Monkeys walk as dogs and other animals walk, on all fours. This method of pro-gression is associated with peculiarities of structure which distinguish them from apes. They show no disproportion in the relative length

PLATE 8

Bonnet Monkey (*Macaca radiata*)

Photo : M. Krishnan

PLATE 9

Slender Loris
(*Loris tardigradus*)
Courtesy:
New York Zoological
Society

of their arms and legs such as is seen in apes. Their arms and legs are about equal in length. As for the tail, this might be quite long, short, or reduced to a mere stump. The longer the tail, the more arboreal in habit is the species, for the tail in these animals is essentially a balancing organ. The gibbon is tailless but he uses his long arms as a balance. But no other Indian monkey is tailless.

Indian monkeys belong to one family, namely the **Cercopithecidae** with two subfamilies, **Cercopithecinae** the macaques and **Colobinae** the langurs. A macaque can be told from a langur by its build which is sturdy, squat, and solid. A langur in contrast is tall and slim and stately. Besides macaques have cheek pouches. The langur has none. Such food as it cannot consume immediately goes separately into a special pouch in its stomach. So much for the general points of distinction between the two groups.

The lemurs entirely lack that human semblance marked even in the lowliest monkeys. A pointed snout gives the lemur a foxy animal expression. In brain and body it is on a much lower level than any ape or monkey. Yet brain and body reveal certain characters which entitle lemurs to inclusion among the Primates. Like all primates, lemurs have grasping hands and feet, the thumb and big toe, always well-developed, are prehensile and opposable to the other digits. But there is this about a lemur's foot which will at once distinguish it from any other primate, the second toe of the foot is always provided with a claw, quite distinct from the flat nails on the other digits. With this clawed toe the animal scratches itself and keeps its fur clean. Its comb-like incisor teeth are used for the same purpose. Lemurs are confined to the Old World and predominate in Madagascar where some thirty-five to forty different species live. A single family is found in India, the **Lorisidae** or Lorises, which inhabit Africa and south-western Asia.

THE HOOLOCK, or WHITEBROWED GIBBON

Hylobates hoolock (Harlan)

Plate facing p. 48

Local Names. Hindi *uluk* ; Arakanese *tooboung, myouk umaigyau.*

Size. Standing erect the Hoolock is a little less than 3 feet (90 cm.) high. Its grotesquely long arms are more than double the length of its legs measured from hip to heel. Weight, from 14 to 18 lb. (6 to 8 kg.).

Distinctive Characters. The only ape found in India. It has the distinctive build of an ape, arms much longer than the legs and a tailless body. Males and young females are black ; on reaching maturity, between the age of 5 or 6, the female's coat fades to a yellowish grey. A newly-born Hoolock is covered with yellow-tinted greyish-white hair.

Distribution. Forests of Assam; found in low-land forest also east of the Brahmaputra, Lohit and Dibang rivers to the Salween river in Burma. South to the Chittagong Hill tracts in Bangladesh. The range extends through upper Burma and the northern Shan States in western Yunnan.

Habits. Hoolocks live in hill forests. Normally, each family lives separately, parents and young forming a group seldom more than 6 in number. Abundance of food or other factors may cause a number of families to congregate together in a more or less limited area. A family of Hoolocks usually spends the night in a sheltered valley, and at dawn ascends the hill-sides to sun themselves and feed on the higher trees. Each family hunts within its own territory. Within this domain the family follows the same trail through the treetops day after day, much as chimpanzees do. The network of paths made by gibbons through the treetops can be traced by the worn condition of the branches, which each gibbon grasps as it makes its daily way through. They eat fruits, leaves, also insects, grubs, and spiders. Dew is sipped from the leaves or cupped in the hand. With the gathering light and warmth Hoolocks begin to howl. One starts, the rest of the family take it up, family calls to family, the forest rings with their calling. During the hottest hours of the day Hoolocks retire to the lower shadier tiers of the forest. It is a time for silence and rest. In the evening they are out again feeding and calling, but their chorus is less noisy. Swinging on their arms from branch to branch, running erect along the heavier boughs, dropping from one bending branch to seize another below, Hoolocks are more agile than any of the heavier apes. When walking they walk erect, using the outstretched arms as a balance. The male is content with a single mate. Whether he divorces her and takes another is not known. Nor do we know exactly how new families are founded. Probably males and females when grown-up desert, or are driven from the household, to find new mates. A young male is sometimes seen living on the edge of its family domain. It is too old or mature to live any longer with the family, yet loath to sever itself completely from all connection with it. Such a gibbon in time establishes its own territory, makes its own pathways to its own food trees and sleeping quarters, and finally taking a mate to itself establishes a family with its own domain. A mother gibbon is most assiduous in caring for her baby. When her journey through the trees includes some hazardous plunge she carries the baby on her back, or in one arm, making the leap with greater caution. Mating time is early in the rains and the young are generally born during the cold weather, December to March.

THE BONNET MACAQUE

Macaca radiata (Geoffroy)

Plate facing p. 48

[RACES IN INDIA : *radiata* (Geoffroy), *diluta* Pocock]

Local Names. Hindi *bandar* ; Marathi *makad, lal manga* ; Malayalam *vella manthi* : Tamil *korungoo* ; Kanarese *kapi.*

Size. Sitting on its haunches this monkey is just under 2 ft. (60 cm.) high. Its tail, longer than in most macaques, is longer than its head and body. The weight of a full-grown male is 13-19 lb. (6 to 9 kg.), of a female between 7 and 8 lb. (3 to 4 kg.).

Distinctive Characters. A medium-sized, long-tailed macaque. A bonnet of long dark hairs radiates in all directions from a whorl on its crown. The bonnet does not quite cover the forehead, where the hairs are short and neatly parted in the centre. A near relative, the **Toque Monkey** of Ceylon *M. sinica* (Linnaeus), wears the same headdress but is easily distinguishable by the pronounced whorls of hair on its cheeks. The coat of the Bonnet Macaque is variable both among individuals and with the season. In the cold weather it is usually lustrous olive-brown ; the underparts whitish. With the onset of the hot weather the coat loses its lustre, turns harsh and scraggy, and fades to a buffy grey.

Distribution. The Indian peninsula as far north as Bombay on the west and the Godavari River on the east. Bonnet Macaques from Travancore are considered a distinct race (*M. r. diluta*).

Habits. This is the little pale-faced monkey commonly seen with strolling showmen in southern India, where it is the counterpart of the northern rhesus described next. It is the common species in village and jungle, both in the foothills and in the plains. Troops of as many as 20 or 30 animals may be found feeding on the ground or in the trees. It is more arboreal in habit than most macaques, hence its longer tail. Bonnet Macaques eat anything eatable, fruits, berries, leaves and shoots, also insects, grubs, and spiders. Those living far from towns and in jungles are generally shy, but troops quartered near human settlements lose all fear of man, and will scarcely give place to him in a crowded street. Field studies show that Bonnet Macaques are very social and live in highly organized troops of both sexes of all ages in well defined territories which may be 2 sq. miles (5.20 sq. km.) or more in area. Social life is based on a well marked dominance hierarchy among the males, and social activation is controlled by a central core of highly dominant males who collaborate when necessary. Mating occurs throughout the year with a peak in October-November and births occur mainly from late January to late April, occasionally in June. Both sexes mature at about 2½ to 3½ years and males attain social maturity 2 to 3 years later. The average span of life in captivity is 12-15 years. One is reported to have lived 30 years.

THE RHESUS MACAQUE

Macaca mulatta (Zimmermann)

Plate facing p. 48

[RACES IN INDIA : *mulatta* (Zimmermann), *villosa* True, *mcmahoni* Pocock]

Local Names. Hindi *bandar* ; Bengali *markat* ; Kashmiri *punj, ponj* ; Burmese *meeauk*.

Size. Seated, a male rhesus is about 2 feet (60 cm.) high and scales about 15-23 lb. (7 to 10 kg.). Females are smaller and slighter in build. Head and body, 1½ feet (45 cm.) ; weight, 10-14 lb. (5 to 6 kg.). The largest and heaviest animals are found in the westerly ranges of the Himalayas.

Distinctive Characters. The Rhesus has the usual squat, thickset build of a macaque. The hairs on its crown radiate backwards from the forehead without the neat centre-parting, so distinctive in its relative the macaque of southern India. The orange-red fur on its loins and rump distinguishes it from any other Indian monkey.

Distribution. The Himalayas, Assam, and northern and central India as far south as the river Tapti in the west and the Godavari in the east, extending thence into Burma and adjoining countries. Three races are found in India.

Habits. Captive or wild, this is the common monkey of northern India. Large troops live near or in villages and towns and in groves round tanks and temples. In the jungle, they usually keep to the outskirts rarely penetrating into the depths, except where driven to seek denser cover. They have a decided preference for open country. Almost everywhere the Rhesus enjoys freedom from molestation. It is a common sight to see these monkeys mingling with the human element on the crowded platform of a railway station, accepting food from passengers, or stealing it when they can. To raid fields and gardens of a morning or evening is their common and established practice, to which popular and religious sentiment permits little check.   Capture and export on a large scale has now depopulated many areas.   Like most macaques, the Rhesus feeds mainly on the ground.   Some live habitually among rocks and cliffs. Ground plants, insects, and spiders are their usual fare.   In their feeding a troop of Rhesus will sometimes consort with a troop of langurs, each party going its own way at nightfall.   Protection against cold is supplied by a heavier winter coat, always more luxuriant in Himalayan animals, some of which winter in the pine forests quite 8000 ft. (2440 m.) above sea-level. They swim well both on the surface and underwater, using an overhand breast-stroke.   The social organisation of the Rhesus resembles that of other macaques being based on male dominance.

The Rhesus shows a definite breeding season, correlated with climatic conditions.   Mating was noted in all months of the year except March but the greatest frequency was from October to December. A major birth season (March to June) preceded the monsoon and a secondary brief postmonsoon birth season in September-October.   No new born young were seen from November to March.

THE ASSAMESE MACAQUE

Macaca assamensis McClelland

Plate facing p. 48

[RACES IN INDIA : *assamensis* McClelland, *pelops* Hodgson]

Size. Head and body a little over 2 ft. (60 cm.) ; tail, about 8 inches (20 cm.). A larger, heavier animal than the Rhesus. Weight of an old male, 26 lb. (12 kg.).

Distinctive Characters. The Assamese Macaque can be distinguished at once from the Rhesus by the absence of orange-red hue on its loins and rump. It cannot be confused with the **Stumptailed Macaque** (*M. speciosa* F. Cuvier. RACE IN INDIA : *speciosa* F. Cuvier), which inhabits the Assam hill forests, the tail of which animal is scarcely an inch long, or with the **Pigtailed Macaque** of the Naga Hills [*M. nemestrina* (Linnaeus). RACE IN INDIA : *blythi* Pocock] which carries its tail erect and arched.

Distribution. Himalayas from Mussoorie eastward to the hill ranges of Assam and the forests of the Sunderbans, extending into upper Burma and the adjoining countries. Two races are recognised. Animals from Assam, Burma, and beyond are distinctive in having shorter tails than the Himalayan form.

Habits. The Assamese Macaque has much the same habits, as its next of kin the Rhesus. It is perhaps less active but otherwise has the same general traits. In the Himalayas and Assam these monkeys inhabit forests ranging between 2000 and 6000 feet (610 and 1830 m.); about Sikkim and Darjeeling, they descend in the cold weather to between 2000 and 4000 ft. (610 and 1220 m.).

They usually haunt heavy forest, living in large or small troops. Their presence is recognised by a rather plaintive musical call, a low ' pio '. When threatened or alarmed these macaques display a habit, common to many monkeys. Leaving the comparative security of the treetops, they drop to the ground and seek to escape in the dense undergrowth. Their food is the usual food of macaques, a mixture of vegetable and insect diet. Like other macaques they are given to raiding cultivation when opportunity offers. About Sikkim and Darjeeling, they are hunted by the Lepchas for food and also because of the supposed medicinal value of their flesh. They are exceedingly shy and wary, but when unmolested display the customary indifference to man. Nothing is known of their breeding habits.

THE LIONTAILED MACAQUE

Macaca silenus (Linnaeus)

Plate facing p. 48

Local Names. Hindi *siah bandar* ; Mal. *nella manthi, chingala* ; Kan. *singalika* ; Tamil *karungkorungoo, arakkan*.

Size. Head and body, 20-24 inches (50-60 cm.) ; tail, 10-15 inches (25-38 cm.). Females slightly smaller.

Distinctive Characters. Distinguished from all other species of macaques firstly by a great mane of long dark-grey or brownish grey hairs growing from the temples and cheeks, and also by its glossy black coat.

Distribution. The Western Ghats from North Kanara southwards to Kerala and Kanyakumari District, Tamil Nadu.

Habits. The Liontailed Macaque inhabits the dense lonelier forests where it keeps to the evergreen tropical belt between 2000 and 3500 feet (610 and 1070 m.). With its dark colouring and shy and seclusive habits there is little wonder that it is seldom seen in these dimly lit forests. Like other macaques these monkeys are gregarious, living in herds of 12 to 20 animals or more. The call of the male is said to resemble the human voice. It is compared to the ' coyeh ' of a man trying to get in touch with his lost companions in the jungle, and again to the loud ' coo ' of a pigeon. Their movements through the treetops are usually slow and deliberate. A troop was seen climbing slowly down one tree and walking along the ground to the next, which they climbed, searched, and descended, going from tree to tree to repeat the process. Newborn young are seen regularly in September in south India. Destruction of habitat and poaching have made this animal an endangered species.

THE COMMON LANGUR, or HANUMAN MONKEY

Presbytis entellus (Dufresne)

Plates facing pp. 32, 49

[RACES IN INDIA: *entellus* (Dufresne), *schistaceus* (Hodgson), *hypoleucos* (Blyth), *dussumieri* (Geoffroy), *anchises* Blyth, *priam* (Blyth), *thersites* Blyth,? *achilles* (Pocock), *ajax* (Pocock), *achátes* (Pocock), *iulus* (Pocock), *aeneas* (Pocock), *elissa* (Pocock), *priamellus* (Pocock). CEYLON: *thersites* Blyth]

Local Names: Hindi *langur, hanuman*; Himalayas *pahari, dendoa*; Kumaon *gooni*; Lepcha *sahu kaboo*; Bhotia *propyaka*; Mar. *wana*; Gujarati *vandra*; Kan. *moosoo, moosoowa*; Coorg *kode*; Telugu *kumdamuchu*; Tamil *korungoo*; Bur. *meeauk*.

Size. Seated this langur is 2 to 2½ feet (60 to 75 cm.) high; tail, 3 to 3¼ ft. (90 to 100 cm.). Himalayan animals, particularly from the western ranges, are the largest and heaviest; weight 35-46 lb. (16-21 kg.). Peninsular animals scale from 20 to 35 lb. (9 to 16 kg.).

Distinctive Characters. This is the long-limbed, long-tailed, black-faced monkey, seen as much about towns and villages as in forests in India. Langurs from the Himalayas, peninsular and southern India, and Ceylon are not distinct species, but merely races of a single species, differing in size, heaviness of coat, and details of colour. Animals from the Himalayas are more heavily whiskered and coated, their pale almost white heads standing out in sharp contrast to the darker colour of the body. This contrast is much less apparent in peninsular animals, but among them there is variation in the colouring of the hands and feet. They are almost black in langurs from the plains of northern India, become paler as one travels southwards to the Deccan, and are almost white in the dry zone of south-east India. Langurs living in the rain-swept hill regions of the south-west are generally darker than those from the drier eastern zone.

Distribution: Practically the whole of India, from the Himalayas to Cape Comorin except the western deserts, and Ceylon. Within this area some 14 more or less distinguishable races are recognised.

Habits. Langurs are more arboreal in habit than macaques, but in parts of India some have taken to living on rocks and cliffs. In the Himalayas they inhabit forests from almost plains level to altitudes nearing 12,000 ft. (3660 m.). While many live in winter among the snow-covered pines and firs, in some parts of these mountains there is apparently a migration from higher to lower levels during this season, probably because of the scarcity of food in the snowbound higher reaches. In peninsular India, Langurs live in forests, haunt shady groves around tanks and temples, and establish themselves in towns and villages. They also exist in extremely dry areas where there is no other water in summer than that available in leaves and bark. Venerated by the Hindus and seldom molested, they have lost all fear of man. This is particularly marked among animals living in association with man. Forest dwellers are more shy and wary, particularly if hunted by forest tribes. Langurs are pure vegetarians, they eat wild fruits, flowers, buds, shoots, and leaves. They occasionally pillage gardens and cultivation, but are not such habitual thieves and raiders as macaques, displaying a sobriety of conduct in keeping with their staid and reverend appearance. Feeding commences at dawn. The hottest hours of the day are spent resting in some shady grove or nullah. In the evening they are out again. When feeding in troops, they display no objection to consorting with a party of macaques, but go their separate way at dusk. The inveterate enemy of the Langur is the panther. The sight of one, or of a tiger, or of any animal that rouses suspicion produces the guttural alarm note which sends the whole troop bolting. Quite distinct is the joyous 'whoop' emitted when bounding from tree to tree, or otherwise contentedly occupied. The agility of a Langur in the treetops, its stupendous leaps and bounds, and the precision with which it makes them are astonishing. On the ground progress is on all fours in the manner common to monkeys.

Langurs live in peaceful, relaxed, and fairly stable groups of all ages and both sexes. The average group size in north India is 18 to 25 but is slightly lesser in the south being around 15. All male groups have also been recorded. Each group forms a closed social system whose membership remains more or less constant. The range of a langur group varies from $\frac{1}{2}$ to 5 sq. miles (1.3 to 13 sq. km). The core area is usually located around the roosting tree, to which the animals retire at night to sleep squatting not on the thicker parts but towards the extremities of the branches, an instinctive precaution against heavy prowling beasts of prey. As in other primate societies, adult males are the leaders and the co-ordinators of group activity. The dominance interactions are milder than among the rhesus and there is seldom aggressive dominance display; the relations between individuals within a group being subtle and not easily distinguishable.

There is a marked breeding season with a peak birth period in north India in April-May though young are seen from February

onwards.   In south India most births are in January-February.
The gestation period is approximately six months.   A female becomes sexually receptive when 3½ years old and may have young
every two years.

THE CAPPED LANGUR, or LEAF MONKEY

Presbytis pileatus (Blyth)

Plate facing p. 49

[RACES IN INDIA: *pileatus* (Blyth), *brahma* Wroughton,
durga Wroughton, *tenebricus* (Hinton)]

Size. Males, head and body, 2 ft.-2ft. 4 in. (60-70 cm.); tail, 30-40
in. (75-100 cm.); average weight, 26 lb. (12 kg.).   Females: smaller
and lighter; head and body 1½-2 ft. (45-60 cm.); tail, 2½-3 ft.
(75-90 cm.); average weight, 22 lb. (10 kg.).

Distinctive Characters. A cap or crown of erect, long, coarse hairs
directed backwards from the forehead gives this monkey its name.
Its slender graceful build distinguishes it from the macaques, while
its colour distinguishes it from other langurs. The dark-grey
colouring of its back and limbs contrasts sharply with the
pale fulvous, orange, or golden red of the cheeks and underparts.
Newborn young have been described as golden, golden red, and
creamy white. Other langurs are black at birth.

Distribution. Assam to the adjoining districts of Chittagong and
upper Burma. Four races distinctive in details of colour inhabit the
hill ranges of Assam. A fifth occurs in Burma.

Habits. The Capped Langur or Leaf Monkey lives in the dense
forests which cover the hills of Assam and the Indo-Burma border.
The troops keep to the trees and, it is said, seldom come to ground
even to drink from the numerous streams which flow through their
habitat. They take their water from dew or rain-drenched leaves.
Like all langurs they are vegetarians, restricting their food to fruit,
flowers, and leaves. As forest dwellers, they are shy and wary,
quick to take flight or screen themselves behind foliage in the way
langurs do. The alarm note is a sharp guttural bark. The only
other vocal sounds noted are likened to squealing. Little is known of
the social life of these monkeys. During the cold weather troops
consisting of a male overlord, three or four wives, and their immature
young have been observed. Troops consisting exclusively of males,
probably those temporarily expelled from harems, have been seen.
All this suggests a social life similar to that of our Common Langur.
The time when breeding activity is especially marked is during the
cold weather. The period of gestation is not known, nor do we know
how long these monkeys take to become fully adult.

THE GOLDEN LANGUR

Presbytis geei (Khajuria)

Plate facing p. 49

Distinctive Characters. Coat, àn almost uniform deep cream colour in dull light, bright golden in sunlight, on flanks where the hairs are longer darker, almost red, lighter in summer, face, black; tail slightly tassellated. Young and the females appear silvery white to light golden yellow.

Distribution. Assam in the strip of country between the rivers Sankosh in the west and Manas in the east. Bhutan, forests up to 1600 m.

Habits. Inhabits evergreen forests in small troops of about 9 animals consisting of an adult male, one or more females and several subadults. Feeds on flowers, fruits and leaves. In captivity young have been born during July-August.

THE NILGIRI LANGUR

Presbytis johni (Fischer)

Plate facing p. 49

Local Names. Tamil *manthi* ; Mal. *karing korangu* ; Toda *turuni kodan, pershk* ; Badaga & Kurumba *kurri korunga.*

Size. Males : head and body, 2 ft. 7 in. (80 cm.) ; tail, 2 ft. 6 in.-3 ft. (75-90 cm.) ; weight, 24-30 lb. (11-14 kg.). Females : head and body, 2 ft. (60 cm.) ; tail, 2 ft. 6 in. (75 cm.) ; weight 25 lb. (11 kg.).

Distinctive Characters. A glossy black or blackish-brown langur with a yellowish-brown head. The rump and base of tail may be grizzled. Females distinguished by the presence of a white patch of hair seen on the inside of the thighs seen even in 10 day old infants. Young, reddish brown until 10 weeks of age, then jet black.

Distribution. The Western Ghats from Coorg to Cape Comorin, the Nilgiri, Anaimalai, Brahmagiri, Tinnevelly, and Palni Hills.

Habits. In the south Indian hill ranges the favourite haunts of these langurs are the *sholas* or stretches of dense evergreen forest which usually mark the nullahs and watercourses on their grass-covered slopes. They are not confined to forest and may invade gardens and belts of cultivated woodland. They live at levels ranging from 3000 up to 7000 feet (915 up to 2135 m.). Their food is the customary vegetarian food of langurs but shows considerable adaptiveness. Marked local food preferences exist and in areas planted with wattle (*Acacia melanoxylon* and *A. mollissima*) the flowers and buds have become a major source of food. Known to eat cardamom plant pith and other cultivated plants. They forage for food in the morning, rest at noontide, and come out to feed again in the cool of the evening. Their early morning whooping a deep ringing *hoo, hoo, hoo,* was once a familiar sound in their native forests. It is heard much less now, for constant persecution has sadly reduced these langurs. The beauty of their fur and the supposed medicinal value of their flesh, blood, and organs have caused them to be hunted more than any other species of Indian monkey, and have made them the most wary and unapproachable of all their tribe. Hunted with dogs and cornered they risk, to their own undoing, passage over the open ground from one patch of forest to another. Added to this the extensive destruction of its habitat makes this langur another endangered Indian mammal.

Nilgiri Langur troops vary in size from 3 to 25 averaging at 8 to 9 animals per troop. Troop organisation is on the basis of a single male leader, with an adult sex ratio of 1.2 female to 1 male. Males are occasionally to be seen by themselves, either alone or with other males. There is little antagonism among the social elements. The home range of troops varies in size from $\frac{1}{4}$ to 1 sq. mile (0.65 to 2.6 sq. km). There is apparently a distinct breeding season with a peak birth period in June and a subsidiary season in September.

THE SLOW LORIS

Nycticebus coucang (Boddaert)

Plate facing p. 49

[RACE IN INDIA: *bengalensis* (Fischer)]

Local Names. Hindi *sharmindi billi* ; Ben. *lajjar, lajjawoti, banar.*

Size. Head and body, 1 ft. to 1 ft. 4 in. (30 to 40 cm.) ; tail, a mere stump.

Distinctive Characters. A round-headed, round-eyed lemur, distinguishable as such in having its second toe clawed and the other toes furnished with flat nails. Stout in body and limb, with a coat of dense fur, variable in colouring. The head and shoulders may be silvery white, creamy, or grey ; the flanks and rump, rusty or buff or ash grey. Very distinctive is a brown stripe, marking the middle line of its back and terminating on the crown ; distinctive also are the brown circles round its lustrous, owl-like eyes.

Distribution. Three geographical races are known. The race found in India inhabits the forests of Assam, Tipperah, and Chittagong, extending thence into Burma and the countries eastward.

Habits. An inhabitant of dense forest, a creature of the night, the Slow Loris is seldom seen. What we know of its ways is known mostly from captive animals. Captivity may alter the ways of an animal, and individuals may acquire new habits, but in general it might be said that the Slow Loris spends the day in sleep, curled like a ball, preferably in some dark hole or crevice. Should the weather be hot it may come out of its hiding and stretch itself along a branch, sleeping on its belly with its legs a-dangle.

With the coming of dusk it wakes to hunt for its food, seeking fruits and leaves, hunting and eating insects of many kinds. Its movements are slow and deliberate. Its powerfully grasping feet never quit their hold of a branch till the hands have first secured a tenacious grip. For the size of the animal, the grip of a loris is unequalled by any primate. Stalking an insect and coming within reach, the quaint animal rises almost erect and, holding firmly with its feet, throws its body forward and grabs at its prey with both hands. The prey when caught is conveyed to the mouth and crunched. As an alternative to feeding upright, the animal hangs head downwards, clasping the branch with its feet and holding its food in its hands, the head held up to face backwards. It will also drink in this pendant position. In early captivity the loris is savage, growling and biting at any approach, but it tames easily and makes a docile and engaging pet. A single young is born after a gestation of 3 months. A young born in captivity had its eyes open at birth. Body was covered with dense fur having occasional long silver-grey hair which dropped off at 11 weeks. Up to 10 months of age young clung to the mother during the day. Took other food from about one month of age and was full grown in 10 months (1.6 kg.).

THE SLENDER LORIS

Loris tardigradus (Linnaeus)

Plate facing p. 33

[RACES IN INDIA : *lydekkerianus* Cabrera, *malabaricus* Wroughton. CEYLON : *tardigradus* (Linnaeus), *grandis* Hill & Phillips, *nordicus* Hill, *nycticeboides* Hill]

Local Names. Tel. *devanga pilli* ; Tamil *tevangu* ; Kan. *mala manushya, kadapapa, adavi manushya* ; Coorg *chinge kule*.

Size : Length of head and body, 8 to 10 in. (20 to 25 cm.) ; tail, absent or a mere suggestion; weight, males 10-12 oz. (280-340 gm.); females about 8 oz. (225 gm.).

Distinctive Characters. Much like the Slow Loris in form, but less pleasing because of its lean and lanky appearance. The limbs are longer and more slender, the ears larger, the snout more pointed, the eyes more close-set. The fur is less dense, yet soft and woolly. Its colour varies from dark grey to earthy brown with an embellishment of silvery hairs, the lower parts always much paler. The dark spinal stripe is never strongly pronounced and is sometimes absent. Eyes, circled with black or dark brown. Muzzle, white.

Distribution. South India and Ceylon. Two races occur in India. The typical race is described from Ceylon, in which island three other races are recognised.

Habits. The Slender Loris has the same secretive and nocturnal habits as the Slow Loris, but it is not confined to dense forest, and is found equally in open tree jungle. It does not keep exclusively to the trees, but comes down into bushes to feed, and must often cross open stretches of ground to enter isolated groves or to cross from one tree to another. It sleeps by day, hidden among foliage or in a hole or crevice, and starts its rambles at dusk. They have a fondness for the berries of lantana bushes which grow so profusely in scrub jungle, and also eat insects, lizards, small birds, and tree frogs, in fact anything that they can seize and overcome. They capture prey in the same way as the Slow Loris, there is the same stealthy approach, the same quick grab with both hands. Their movements are slow and circumspect, slower than their heavier and rotund relative. Moisture taken from the leaves is sucked up from the fingers. These animals will also eat and drink from a dish without using their hands. As to vocal sounds, besides screeching much in the way of our little spotted owl, they make slow chattering noises and utter a low growl when irritated.

From the way they fight when several are herded together in a cage it would appear that these animals are not gregarious. They are usually found solitary, sometimes in pairs. We know nothing of their mating in the wild state. The period of gestation is said to be over three months. Newly born young have been seen in various months of the year, May and June, October and March. Usually one, sometimes twins, are produced. The young are nursed for a long time and continue to suckle when half grown and no longer wholly dependent on maternal feeding. As with lemurs in all countries, a wealth of superstitious beliefs centre round these animals. The eyes are said to be a potent love charm, and are also used as a cure for certain eye diseases. Hence the capture and sale of these animals, which are cruelly hawked about exposed to the blinding glare of sunlight, to which by nature they are so ill-accustomed.

3. The Cats

THE HOUSE-CAT and the lion, the tiger, and the leopard, cats great or small, are members of one family, the **Felidae,** the foremost of all the Carnivores or beasts of prey. There are beasts of prey whose teeth are not expressly suited to a diet of meat. There are others whose blunted claws are useless as weapons of attack. Those characters which mark the perfect carnivore, claws especially adapted to strike and hold struggling prey, and teeth especially designed to bite into, cut up, and tear flesh, are most perfectly developed in the Cats. Among carnivores Cats stand supreme in equipment of tooth and claw, and supreme again in that combination of grace, strength, and agility which is the mark of the tribe. An excelling fitness for a predatory life is seen in the perfect adaptation of the whole being and structure of a Cat to the swift capture, killing, and eating of living prey.

STRUCTURE IN RELATION TO HABITS

Senses. The hunting of other animals as a means of livelihood requires high intelligence, and beasts of prey as a whole display an intelligence and brain development surpassed only by man and the higher apes. Hearing, vision, scent, all the higher senses, are highly developed in carnivores, particularly in those tribes which live habitually by hunting, such as the Cats. How long and prominent are the bristling whiskers of a Cat ! It has tufts of similar bristles on its forearms. They are sensory tactile organs. By means of connecting nerves they flash to the brain impressions gathered by feeling and touch. How acute is a Cat's hearing ! It is immediately conscious of any sound which betrays the presence of its prey. Its large upstanding ears are well adapted to pick up airborne sounds, and its sense of direction in respect to sounds heard is extraordinarily accurate. As for eyes, Cats have the largest eyes of all carnivores. A well-developed system of muscles within the eye contracts the pupil in bright light and protects the eye from glare. In the smaller Cats the pupil contracts to a narrow perpendicular slit, in lions, tigers, and leopards to a small circular opening. In the dark, the pupils dilate to allow as much light as possible to enter the eye. Attuned to work in the dark a Cat's eyes are quick to detect the movements of nocturnal prey. It is generally stated that, when hunting, the Cats as a tribe rely more on sight and hearing, the dogs on their sense of smell. But it is commonly said that a lion is guided more by scent when following its prey, a tiger or leopard by its eyes and ears. To what extent animals which hunt in the dark rely upon vision is a matter about which we have little real knowledge. It is difficult to believe that nocturnal animals do not make the fullest use of all their faculties, particularly in forests where the range of vision is so limited. It is probable that all senses play their part in the lives of these animals. Greater reliance on any one of them at a given moment depends upon what the animal is doing and what factors in its surroundings are influencing its action.

Feet. To take its prey by surprise is the essence of a Cat's hunting. The quarry is stalked by stealth or, lying hidden, the Cat waits for its prey to stray within reach and seizes it with a lightning rush or leap. In the tracks or ' spoor ' left by a tiger, or by your house-cat for that matter, one may read how well their feet are adapted to this method of hunting. A tiger's tracks show only the impress of the toes and of the great pad behind them. There is no trace of sole or heel. This is because Cats walk on their toes. Their walking is digitigrade. The raising of the sole and the heel above the ground alters the balance of its body, throws it forward, and increases the impetus of movement. Such digitigrade movement makes for greater speed and greater agility in running and leaping. A Cat's spoor shows the imprint of only four toes. No beast of prey has less than four toes. Cats have five toes on the forefoot and four in the hind, but the digit of the forelimb which corresponds to our thumb is set high up the foot and leaves no mark on the ground. The deep-cushioned pads under its feet muffle the Cat's tread and help its stealthy, noiseless progress. The movement of a tiger is aptly described as the ' flowing past of a phantom '. Such a gliding movement, so marked in the walking of the Cats, is due to the simultaneous advance of the limbs on each side of the body. In walking, the hindfoot of a house-cat is set exactly in the track of its forefoot. Its track recalls the track of a biped. This perfect register makes for silent movement. We see the action repeated in the spoor of a tiger. Ordinarily the tiger's feet leave a double track ; but in such highly controlled action as purposeful, silent approach to its prey the tiger's feet leave a single track. This muffled tread, this sinuous gliding movement combine to effect the Cat's stealthy approach to its prey. Apart from stealthy movement, the limbs and feet of Cats are marvellously fitted for striking down and holding prey.

Cats follow no rule in seizing and killing their prey. Even the great Cats pass from the awkward attempts of the young to the power and mastery of the adult. Equally must they adapt their strategy to the nature of their quarry and the conditions of its taking. There is the haphazard seizure of an animal in flight when desperate claws and teeth strive to retain and hold the moving body. There is the timely leap which takes the quarry in its stride and sends it hurtling to the ground. Different must be the killing of a standing animal. There are two ways in which a tiger does this. Coming with slow deliberate approach or bewildering rush it dips under and takes its prey by the throat, draws down and pins its head to the ground and, maintaining the pressure of the hold, strangles the animal. Or, rearing up on its hindlegs the tiger seizes the animal's neck in its jaws and, bringing one paw down upon the victim's head and shoulders, grasps the muzzle with the other and so takes it in violent hold and bears it to the ground. The ferocity of the hold and its ruthless violence may twist the neck of the animal or bend it back upon itself until it breaks. To break the neck of its prey is perhaps not the purpose of these great Cats. They take the animal by the neck or throat and attempt to strangle it. The neck may break from the manner of its seizure, from the force exerted, and most frequently from the stress of the hold and the opposing strain of the falling body. A tiger may seize a large animal by the hind legs, bite into it above the hock, and sever the tendons or break the bone. With one or both legs disabled heavy animals like a buffalo or a gaur fall easy victims to the tiger. Tigers in Burma appear almost invariably to ' hamstring ' large prey in this way. The method is less common in India. Let us now consider the weapons of Cats for striking and holding prey.

Claws. The claws of Cats are essentially weapons of attack. Let us consider their fitness for this purpose. The strong curving claws of a Cat reveal a perfection of development unequalled by other beasts of prey. A beautiful and peculiar device prevents them from being blunted by contact with the ground. In a Cat's foot the claw-bearing joint, in its normal position, lies folded back over the preceding joint. It is held in this reverted position by an elastic ligament. Thus folded back, the claw is raised off the ground. This is not all ; for its better protection the reverted claw is encased in a sheath of skin devised for its reception. When a Cat distends its paw to strike, a tendon connected to the great muscles of the limb pulls upon the reverted joint and draws it downward and forward. The claws instantly emerge from their sheaths, bared for action. These claw sheaths are by no means equally developed in all Cats. A cheetah or hunting leopard has the mechanism for retracting its claws. But the sheaths for their reception are so poorly developed that its claws are always bared. In tigers and leopards the lobes of the claw sheaths are large enough to completely cover the claws, and they are fully sheathed. Between these two extremes every stage in the development of claw sheaths may be seen in Cats.

Teeth. While claws are used to strike and hold, seizure of the prey is effected primarily by the jaws. In this action the canine teeth play a prominent part. Most animals have canine teeth, but in beasts of prey the canines tend to become large and strong. In the great Cats they develop into enormous fangs, much longer than, and well separated from, the other teeth. When the jaws close the canines interlock ; when the jaws open the canines stand clear and are driven full into the flesh of the victim. There are no contiguous

PLATE 10

Hoolock
(*Hylobates hoolock*)

Mature
♀   ♂ and
young ♀

Liontailed Maca que
(*Macaca silenus*)

Assamese Macaque
(*Macaca assamensis*)

Rhesus Macaque
(*Macaca mulatta*)

Bonnet Macaque
(*Macaca radiata*)

0   10   20   30 cm.

0   1 ft.

PLATE 11

Nilgiri Langur
(*Presbytis johni*)

Slow Loris
(*Nycticebus coucang*)

Golden Langur
(*Presbytis geei*)

Common Langur
(*Presbytis entellus*)

Capped Langur
(*Presbytis pileatus*)

teeth to obstruct their complete penetration. These great teeth are supported on short powerful jaws and controlled by great biting muscles for whose attachment special provision is made in the wide, sturdy cheek-arches and bony crest of the skull. Increased sturdiness and strength has been attained in the jaw bones of Cats by a reduction in their length. The comparative shortness of the jaws gives Cats that flatness of feature which contrasts so markedly with the pointed muzzles of civets, or the long snouts of dogs and bears. A Cat's jaws, its claws, and the great canine teeth are, as we have seen, perfectly adapted to the seizure, holding, and killing of prey.

Particularly well adapted to the eating of meat are the teeth of Cats. Canines and incisors provide the beast of prey with weapons for seizing, holding, and biting. The cutting up of the food is the work of the molar or cheek teeth. Among carnivores there is much variation in the form of teeth. Speaking generally, the more numerous the cheek teeth and the broader their crowns the more likely it is that the owner lives on a mixed diet; on the other hand a reduction in the number of cheek teeth and the compression of their crowns into sharp cutting blades indicate an exclusive diet of flesh. Carnivorous animals always have one molar tooth on each side, both in the upper and lower jaws, especially modified for cutting up meat. This is the ' carnassial ' or flesh-tooth. It is large and well-developed in pure meat eaters like the Cats. How do these teeth do their work ? Firstly they are set in that part of the jaws where the biting muscles exert the greatest pressure. Distinctive also in carnivores is the mode of articulation of the lower jaw. It moves on a small transverse hinge. The device gives strength to the joint, but deprives the animal of the power of moving its jaws from side to side, or backwards and forwards, as we do when chewing or masticating food. In beasts of prey movement of the jaws is limited to an up-and-down biting or snapping action. In such action the sharp-bladed cheek teeth, working against one another like scissor-blades, cut up and divide the flesh. The flesh teeth are ideal instruments for shearing the flesh from bones or crushing hard food. The incisor teeth have their special function. All carnivores usually have six incisor teeth. These small pincer-shaped teeth are used to gnaw the soft gristly ends of bones and scrape away the tendinous attachments of muscles. (**Plate facing p. 66**)

The tongue. But this is not all the Cat's equipment for dealing fully and completely with a meal. Remnants of flesh adhering to bones are licked clean by its rasp-like tongue. The tongue to us, and to most animals, is an organ of taste. But carnivorous animals which tear to pieces and swallow their food in great chunks, as Cats do, can scarcely derive much enjoyment from its taste. The taste glands of a Cat's tongue are small and set mainly on its margins. Most numerous and prominent are the conical papillae encased in horny, pointed sheaths which cover the tongue and stick into one's fingers

like so many pins. Their function is purely mechanical. These
numerous sharp and rigid points give the tongue the action of a
rasp, well-suited for licking bones clean. We have seen how the
Cats secure their food and how marvellously they are adapted to
the hunting, killing, and eating of other animals. No beasts of prey
are so highly specialised as they for their particular role in life.

Coloration. The colouring of Cats is varied. Spots and stripes,
longitudinal or vertical, upon a tawny ground is the prevailing hue
and pattern. The lion and puma are uniformly coloured when adult,
but spotted or striped when cubs. This is taken as an indication of
their descent from spotted or striped ancestors. How Cats got their
colours is another question, our concern here is colour as an aid in
hunting. It is believed that the tawny colours of the great Cats and
their spots and stripes make good camouflage. The colour harmonises with the surrounding tones of the jungle. Stripes and spots
by repeating broken lights and shadows deceive the eye. They break
up the body mass and confuse and obscure its contours. There is
little doubt that when sitting motionless in wait for prey the colouring of Cats helps in their concealment. It must also help them to
escape detection during stealthy approach. On the other hand, the
question arises how far does colour help the concealment of nocturnal animals. We do not know. We have little knowledge of the
extent to which beasts which seek their food at night rely upon
vision. We know however that the absence of spots and stripes on a
lion is no disadvantage to his hunting. Like the tiger, a lion hunts
in the broken light of forests. It hunts also in open bush or grassland, or in reed beds where a vertically striped coat would make
ideal camouflage. Again, both black and spotted panthers thrive
and hunt with success in the same jungles. All this suggests that the
pattern of the coat may play no essential part in the hunting. Cats,
great and small, owe their ascendancy to a perfect mastery in the
craft of hunting. Strong and active, of high intelligence, they display a perfection of senses and bodily organism which gives them
victory over creatures in whom a ceaseless struggle for existence has
tended to perfect the means of escape.

CATS AND THEIR SURROUNDINGS

The home of the great Cats. Though intimately associated with India,
the home of the tiger, the country of its origin, lies far north of our
frontiers. The earliest known fossil remains of the tiger were discovered in the New Siberian Islands, well within the Arctic Circle.
Time was when under a genial climate central and northern Asia
supported a rich vegetation and an abundant and varied animal life.
Reindeer, elk, bison, and many large antelopes roamed its vast
forests and grasslands, and they were the prey of tigers, leopards,

and other large carnivores. Most of these animals have disappeared from this now bleak and desolate region, but central and northern Asia is believed to be the home, the country of origin of the tiger, which still survives in Amurland. and Korea, in eastern Siberia, Mongolia, and Manchuria.

As for the lion, fossil remains discovered in England, France, and Germany show that in prehistoric times, lions ranged over the whole of central Europe. Even in historic times there were lions in Greece, and perhaps also in the Balkans and the valley of the Danube. Herodotus tells how the baggage camels of Xenophon were attacked by lions in the country of the Paeonians in Macedonia.

Coming now to the leopard or panther, all available evidence again points to the conclusion that this animal, like the lion and the tiger, came originally from the north.

Their migrations. From northern and central Asia the tiger extended its territory over the greater part of the continent. The westerly limits of its migrations appear to be the eastern slopes of the Caucasus and the Elburz mountains. Southwards and eastwards both the tiger and the panther, owing to climatic changes, gradually made their way through Amurland, Manchuria, and Korea down to Annam, Cochin-China, Siam, and the Malay peninsula whence some branched north through Assam into India and others south to Java and Sumatra. The tiger apparently entered India through the hill ranges of Assam. It first colonized the forested slopes of the Himalayas, and subsequently established itself over the greater part of the peninsula. How long ago the tiger came to India we do not know. Its absence from Ceylon suggests that it came south too late to take advantage of the land bridge which once connected the island with the mainland. It was prevented from colonizing the island by deep intervening seas. Other animals which failed to enter Ceylon are the Leopard-Cat, the Flying Lizard, and the Hamadryad.

From Europe, the lion spread into north-western Asia, and thence westwards into Africa where it established its dominion over practically the whole of the continent. During Biblical times lions were abundant in Asia Minor and Palestine. From these parts their territory extended across Iraq through Iran, to Baluchistan into India. The lion came to India by way of our north-western passes. It once inhabited practically the whole of northern and central India, from Sind to Bengal, from the Ganges and Indus to the banks of the Narmada. Its limited distribution suggests that the lion is a comparatively recent immigrant into India. Had our country been its original home, it would have spread over the whole of the sub-continent and perhaps into Burma. It is believed that it **did not have the time to extend its territory. It was virtually exterminated from India before it could do so.**

The panther has been the most successful of all in extending and maintaining its territory. It has established itself over the whole of

Asia except the more northerly parts, and over the whole of Africa
except the Sahara. By what route the panther entered India is uncertain. It may have come by way of our north-eastern or north-
western passes. That it was here before the tiger is suggested by its
crossing over to Ceylon. The subsequent disappearance of the land
bridge prevented the tiger from entering the island. It is not only
the great Cats that have thus extended their territory. There is also
evidence to show that the little Leopard-Cat of our forests, like the
tiger, came to us from the north. Spreading southwards it established itself over the Malay countries and India, but it came south
too late to get a footing in Ceylon. Originating in northern climes
these animals have, as we see, greatly extended their range and have
spread through new countries. Let us consider some of the factors
which limited or aided their migrations.

The choice of a habitat. In practice an animal is limited in its choice
of a habitat by its physical make-up, by its habits and inclinations.
It is able to sense what is dangerous to it in its surroundings, and it
chooses places to live in which are suitable to its needs. In spreading from the country of their origin, tigers have gone only where
there were forests or other adequate cover to shelter them. The tiger
did not colonize the Tibetan plateau where a combination of arctic
and desert conditions prevail, or the arid desert zone of north-
western India and the desert countries beyond. Southwards and
eastwards the existence of great belts of forests enabled the tiger to
spread from Arctic and semi-Arctic lands far into tropic and sub-
tropical regions. Climate was no obstacle to its spread provided it
could find shelter from the torrid heat. Forests gave the tiger the
shelter it needs and, where there are forests, there is always water to
quench its insistent thirst. Forests again make possible the assemblage of large herbivorous animals which the tiger must have for
food, and within forests it finds ample cover for its secretive methods
of hunting and its seclusive habits of life. Without forests or adequate shelter the tiger could not exist. Without forests or heavy
grass jungle there could be no tigers in India.

How different is the case of the lion ! Like the tiger, the lion
requires the propinquity of large animals for food, but it is much
less secretive, much less cunning than the tiger. It is not averse to
living in open country. It is better able to withstand exposure to
the sun. Absence of dense forests or heavy cover set no limit to the
extension of its range. Lions made their way into and established
themselves in the desert and semi-desert region of western Asia and
India, where no tigers could live, and where the tiger did not penetrate.

As for the panther, its physical make-up, its habits and inclinations gave it an even wider choice of territory. The panther thrives
in a parched and treeless terrain of rock and scrub, or in rain-swept
forests, under extremes of heat and cold, of dryness and humidity.
It can find shelter and concealment under the scantiest cover. Also

it can subsist on a variety of small creatures which would give no sustenance to a lion or a tiger. It has thus successfully established and maintained itself over an immense range of territory covering practically the whole of Asia and Africa. These are some of the factors which influenced its choice of a habitat. Let us now consider the effect of changed and changing conditions on these animals.

Geography and coloration. When we take into account the wide areas over which they range, the varying conditions under which they live, it is not surprising to find more or less constant differences in the external appearance of these great carnivores, differences which have enabled zoologists to recognise and distinguish various more or less distinct geographical races of these animals. These races are told from one another by various minor differences, distinctions in colour and markings. Such variations in colour appear to result from the different conditions under which these animals live in the several areas of their range. Temperature, dryness or humidity, an increase or decrease of light, all have their effect on the colours of animals. For example animals living in the Arctic regions show little tendency to bright colours. Whites, soft greys, and grey-browns are their prevailing livery. In more southerly latitudes, wherever there is a progressive increase in temperature and humidity, there is also a progressive darkening and enrichment of the colours of animals. This enrichment reaches its maximum in the forests of the Equator, where combined mean temperature and humidity is the highest. Probably, reduced light in these dense, dim-lit forests contributes to intensifying colour. We see this illustrated in the colour of tigers and panthers. While there is much individual variation in the colour and markings of these animals, and while dark and pale-coloured animals may be found in the same area, taken as a whole it might be said that tigers and panthers living in northern latitudes are paler in colouring than those inhabiting the hot and humid forests of India, and these again are less dark and rich in colour than tigers and panthers living in Malaya or the forests of Java and Sumatra, which are hotter and yet more humid being nearer the Equator.

Melanism and albinism. Black panthers are again more common in these rain-swept Equatorial forests. In fact, south of Malaya they appear to be the only type of panther found. They are less numerous, but still quite common, in the humid forests of Burma and Assam and in the rain forests of the lower Himalayas and the Western Ghats, but exceedingly rare in the dry open jungles of central India or in our desert zone. A black panther is not a distinct species. Both black and normal-coloured cubs may be produced in the same litter. Blackness, the general darkening of colour, is due to the excessive presence of a substance called melanin which intensifies pigmentation, and the production of melanin is increased where there is a combination of high temperature, great humidity, and reduced light ; hence the greater prevalence of black panthers in areas where these conditions obtain. The opposite conditions, dryness and intense light combined with high temperature, have the effect of reducing colour tones and of producing pale sandy yellows and reddish browns. Such are the climatic conditions prevailing in hot desert areas and such are the prevailing tones of desert animals. The panther of the Indian desert is sandy yellow and distinctly less rich in colour than the panthers living in our forest tracts. Again albinism, which is a condition opposite to melanism being the result of complete or partial absence of pigment, is more frequent in dry and desert areas than in moist tracts. White or partially white tigers are not uncommon in some of the dry open jungles of central India. Apart from physical conditions, there are other factors which influence the colouring of animals. Some of these are discussed in considering the coloration of the Rodents. While animals living in hot deserts have their special type of colouring, many living in cold deserts are distinctive in the loss of colour. In the cold dry wastes of Ladak and north-eastern Kashmir, where both desert and arctic conditions prevail, we have a repetition of Arctic colour tones, of whites, greys, and grey-browns. In the panther of these parts, the normal yellow coat is replaced by a coat of dull grey. These colour variations help to harmonize the colour of an animal with the colour tones prevailing in its surroundings. The soft grey of the Kashmir panther, the sandy hue of panthers in the Sind desert, or the dark rich colours of panthers which live in our moist forests, harmonizing with and adapted to the different surroundings in which they live, make for their better concealment. Geographical variation is also instanced in the length, texture, and density of the coat, variations which adapt animals to meet the rigours of climate. Tigers in northern Asia assume a dense and luxuriant winter coat which they shed with the coming of spring. Indian tigers go through a similar, though less marked change. They shed their heavier winter coats on the approach of the hot weather. The moult is at its height in March, and by April or May tigers in lower level forests are in their lighter hot weather coats. Panthers living in the deserts of Sind and Persia have longer, harsher coats than Indian animals. They too have to face extremes of cold which prevail in the desert during winter. This is one of the ways in which these animals, in common with others, control and modify adverse conditions in their surroundings. But not only is the external appearance of these animals influenced by their surroundings, but also their habits.

Habits and surroundings. An immigrant from cool northern climes, centuries of acclimatization have left the tiger still intolerant to tropical heat. To escape the heat he takes shelter in cave or covert and many tigers, particularly during the hot weather, take to water and lie in it during the sweltering hours of the day.

Changed conditions produced by the changing season profoundly influence the habits of beasts of prey. During the hot weather the Gir Forest, the last refuge of the lion in India, is bare and open, and the water supply over miles of country is limited to a few deep pools in the Hiran River and to some of the nullahs. Here game and herds of grazing cattle congregate, and where their food is there the lions also gather. But with the coming of the rains the whole nature of the environment changes. The days of torrid heat are over and the parched countryside is covered with luxuriant vegetation. There is water everywhere. This abundance of grazing and abundance of fresh water results in the wide dispersal of herbivorous animals. Lions following their prey stray out of forest limits into the neighbouring lands. Tigers again, in following their dispersing prey, become great wanderers during the monsoon and cold weather, roaming from place to place within a radius of 15-20 miles (24-32 km.). In the hot weather their movements are much more restricted. There is little cover or hunting, except where water is found. The onset of the monsoon also witnesses a general downward movement of larger animals from the higher levels of some of the hill ranges of the Peninsula, particularly those exposed to the full blast of the monsoon. Most mammals avoid the rain. They are less well-protected against it than birds. It permeates their heavy coats and exposes them to cold and chill. The coming of winter sees a similar downward movement of animals from the snowbound higher levels of the Himalayas to the lower valleys where food is more easily obtainable. The migrations of herbivorous animals are followed by the carnivores, for always their movements must be regulated by the movements of the animals on which they prey.

CATS AND THEIR NEIGHBOURS

The animal ' community '. An animal has to contend not only against inanimate factors in its surroundings, but also against its animate environment. It has to compete for its food with fellows of its own or other species. It has to contend against enemies and parasites. There is then an interdependence and interrelationship among animals living together in a particular area, however varied their species. The life of the Cats great and small, or of any animal for that matter, must be considered in terms of this interdependence. The animals living together in a forest, on a mountain top, or in a desert form so to speak a ' community '. They are bound together by common interests, they live together in a particular type of habitat because they find in such a habitat conditions which are best suited to their needs. They influence each other's lives, and by their separate activities contribute to the maintenance of the community as a whole. How they do so is best understood by a study of the organization of an animal community. The organization of an animal community, and the relationships maintained between its members, centre largely upon the question of food and its distribution. Plants form the basic food of animals. Therefore, in any animal community plant-eaters form the basic, the most numerous class. They are the foundation upon which the communal organization is built up. These plant-eaters provide food for and make possible the existence of carnivores or flesh-eating animals. A tiger's upkeep is dependent on the existence of plants, for without plants there would be no deer and other herbivores, and without these plant-eating animals to prey upon there could be no tigers. Both among plant-eaters and flesh-eaters there are animals which eat both flesh and vegetable food, which are omnivorous. But, essentially, the organization of the animal community is based on a primary or basic class of plant-eaters and a superposed assemblage of carnivorous animals which live upon them. Living within the community, as a class apart, there are animals who earn their livelihood as scavengers, feeding on the remains of other animals. Most carnivores, even the kings of the tribe like lions and tigers, sometimes feed on carrion; carrion-feeders like hyenas and jackals may prey on live animals, but essentially their profession is scavenging. Finally, within the community there is a class of weaker creatures which are unable to fend for themselves, which live as parasites upon their neighbours. This then is the organization of every animal community no matter where in the world it is established.

Within the community, each animal occupies a particular niche and plays a particular role. The plant-eaters act as a check on the too exuberant spread of plant life. The role of flesh-eaters is to control the over-increase of these herbivorous species.

To eat or to be eaten, this is the question in animal society. In practice it results in the control of numbers and makes for a more even distribution of food supply, which might be otherwise threatened by the superabundant increase of any one species. Now the rate of increase is highest among the smaller herbivores, the Rodents for example. To counteract this prolific increase rodents are preyed upon by a whole range of small carnivores, which themselves have a high rate of productivity. With an increase in the size of the animal there is a corresponding decrease in the number of young produced, and predators and prey diminish in numbers. Thus a certain balance of life is maintained within the community. The word ' balance ' is perhaps the wrong word to apply in Nature. There is not in fact that correctness and nicety of adjustment implied by the word balance. The numbers of animals living in a community fluctuate with time and season and change in surroundings. But the margin of increase and decrease established by the law of eating and being eaten and by other checks is kept within narrow limits, unless disturbed by external factors such as floods, prolonged periods of drought, epidemics, etc.

The role of carnivores. In fulfilment of its special function each carnivore plays its special part and becomes a check on a particular herbivore or range of herbivores. What herbivores it preys upon depends largely on its size, strength, and power. There are carnivores like wolves and wild dogs which hunt in packs and which are able to destroy large animals which they could not overcome by individual effort. But mainly, it is the size and strength of the predator which decides the nature of its prey. Commencing with the smallest herbivores and the smallest carnivores, predators and prey increase in size so that at the other end of this food chain we have the largest herbivores, which are preyed upon by the largest carnivores. In this check upon the over-increase of herbivorous species Cats, the most perfect of all beasts of prey, play an important role. The tiger is destined to be a check on the undue increase of the larger forms of deer and wild cattle. A panther may attack quite large animals, but usually its strength limits it to acting as a control on smaller species. It occupies a lower link in the food chain. There are Cats of intermediate size which prey upon yet smaller animals, and smaller Cats which kill hares, rats, and mice and become a check upon the superabundant increase of these all too prolific rodents. Checks such as these exist in every animal community no matter where established. The role of the tiger in India is taken by the lion in Africa, by the jaguar and the puma in the tropical forests of the New World. In India our Leopard-Cat functions as an exterminator of rodents in forest communities. The Jungle Cat plays the same role in scrub land and cultivation, and the Desert Cat in the community of desert animals. But what are the factors which control an over-increase of carnivorous animals, particularly those at the end of the food chain such as the tiger? There are many, but mainly it is a question of food and the supply available. Without its appropriate food no carnivore can exist. The extermination of game from large forest tracts in India has led equally to the disappearance of the tiger from these areas. The number of tigers that can exist in a particular area is controlled largely by conditions of shelter and food supply. This leads to a division of territory among tigers. A tiger settles in a favoured locality and establishes its rights over the territory. On its death its domain is taken over sooner or later by a successor.

Relationships with other carnivores. Carnivores are preyed upon and destroyed by fellows of their own and other species. Though supreme in his forests there is one enemy a tiger must fear and that is another tiger. He fears and avoids man, but competition with his own kind is the more intimate factor in his struggle for existence. Tigers living in the same forest are a danger of which the panther is acutely conscious. Panthers have been destroyed at their kills by tigers or by more powerful rivals of their own species. They have been killed, routed, and otherwise deprived of their right to a meal by wild dogs and hyenas. The rivalry and competition for food has had its marked influence on the habits of these great Cats, for their prey once secured and killed becomes an object of general and un-welcome attraction ; hence the common impulse of a tiger or pan-ther to drag its prey under cover, where it can be eaten in seclusion and without interference. In their anxiety to do this panthers and tigers have displayed remarkable ingenuity, even eating through the neck or leg of a tethered animal in order to carry it away. After feeding, what is left of the carcase is usually dragged and concealed under bushes, put away among the boulders of a nullah, and if there is no suitable hiding place an attempt may be made to cover up the food with leaves or with uprooted tufts of grass. Some pan-thers do not rest content until they have carried and placed the kill high up in a tree. These precautions are but devices to protect the food from rivals. All beasts of prey will feed on any carcase they discover. Besides professional hunters there are professional scaven-gers like hyenas, jackals, vultures, crows, and even eagles with plebeian tastes, all ready to appropriate a tiger's or a panther's food. Their efforts to conceal and otherwise to secure it arise from, and are an answer to, the thieving activities of their neighbours.

Relationship with man. Man is the centre of the animal community, its most disturbing influence. Man's activities have a profound in-fluence on the lives of animals. Man, who exterminated the lion in Europe and over the greater part of Asia—it is unlikely that it now survives outside India—has been equally responsible for its practical extinction in India, an extermination rapidly accelerated with the arrival of the European in India. Even in parts of Africa lions are steadily retreating before civilized settlement. The bolder, the more confiding habits of the lion, its herding instincts, the more open nature of the country in which it lives provided readier oppor-tunity for its direct destruction. The tiger, more cunning, more seclusive in habit, is better able to escape extermination. Its num-bers have been reduced mainly by making conditions of life impos-sible for it. The destruction of game and the destruction of forests has resulted in the disappearance of tigers from many parts of India where they were once common. This has been the case especially throughout a large area of Madhya Pradesh, parts of Bengal, and in several districts of Tamil Nadu and Maharashtra. Less im-pression appears to have been made upon the number of panthers living in this country. The panther's high rate of increase, its wider range of food, its adaptability to varied living conditions added to its marvellous powers of concealment have helped it to withstand efforts to reduce its numbers. Nevertheless rapidly changing con-ditions all over the sub-continent are now reducing the panther population in many parts of the country.

But this extermination of carnivores is not merely the killing of animals which are a possible threat to human life or human property. It does not end there. Ill-considered attempts to exterminate carnivorous animals have done more harm than good. Beasts of prey, as we have seen, have a definite role in the economy of Nature. In parts of England there was an organized killing of carnivorous animals, of weasels, stoats, badgers, etc. It was done to protect reared pheasants from their attacks, but it led to an overwhelming increase in the number of rabbits and consequently to serious damage both to crops and soil.

Apart from exterminating animals man, by providing them with opportunities for securing their food, or by reducing their food supply, profoundly influences their life and habits. There are many animals which take the whole or part of their food supply from man, feeding on his crops, his stores, and his domestic animals. Now it is usually the commonest and therefore the most numerous species which do this. The panther is an example. Pressure of numbers on food supply was one of the factors which compelled its spread and such pressure also compelled many panthers to take what food they could from man's domestic stocks. But the panther's ability to take full advantage of such opportunity was due to the readiness with which it has been able to adapt itself to the most varied conditions of life. This is a factor to which all those animals which are so common and so numerous owe their special success. It is due to their adaptability that they are able to live almost anywhere and have spread, increased, and multiplied accordingly. The growing population solves the pressure on its food by taking its surplus needs from man.

The tiger has been less successful than the panther. It is less adaptable. Its physical make-up, its habits and inclinations restrict it to living in forest or in places where there is sufficiently heavy cover. It is brought into less frequent contact with man and therefore has less opportunity to exploit human sources for food supply. Further, tigers have a slower rate of increase, they are less numerous, the need for adding to their food supply by taking what is available from man is less imperative. Left to themselves tigers would find a sufficiency of food in the wild animals which live in their forests, but human interference with their food supplies, the destruction and eradication by man of the larger animals upon which the tiger depends for its existence, compel it to prey upon domestic animals. Many become cattle-killers. Whether a tiger becomes a habitual cattle-killer, we do not know. It would appear that game animals are essential to the tiger's existence. How else could we explain its complete disappearance from large forested tracts in India where there are many cattle to prey upon, but where there are no large game animals left?

Association with man and the exploitation of his food supplies profoundly affect the ways and habits of these animals. Consider the life of a panther which lives habitually on wild animals. Its prey is varied in character and habit. It is not always concentrated within limited zones. Changes in environment brought about by season cause the concentration or the dispersal and wider ranging habits of both hunters and hunted. Panthers given largely to the killing of wild animals display in their method of hunting, seizing, and killing their prey many of the ways and habits of the tiger. In other words they display the truer habits of the species. How different is the life of the village panther which preys mainly on domestic animals. Its food is concentrated within a limited area, occasions for taking it are almost identical. Competition for food is frequently reduced by the elimination of rival beasts of prey for whom the environment is unsuitable, while the prey itself, its alertness enfeebled by domestication, is easily secured. Panthers living near human settlements probably maintain this mode of life through successive generations. The offspring of such panthers follow the example of their parents, for the life of the animal is not only the sum of its fixed instincts, a legacy born of the experience of countless ancestors, but of a parental tradition and experiences acquired in life. Thus the habit of cattle-killing may develop in a panther or tiger at an early age. So long as the supply of cattle is maintained an individual will establish a more or less permanent territory in the neighbourhood of a town or village. Failure or interruption in the supply will lead to migration to a similar environment where the accustomed food is available. But association with man not only brings about a change in habits of life, it has also brought about a change in the animals' attitude to man. Like other animals, panthers and tigers avoid man. Faced with a sudden apparition of man in regions rarely entered by him, the panther or tiger reveals the wild beast's usual curiosity or fear of the unknown. They stare at the intruder and then bound away. Experience gained by association may exaggerate this reaction in a panther, may develop great fear and suspicion in an individual, while familiarity with man and success in escaping harm may beget in another outrageous boldness, an indifference to human activity, to lights, sounds, or movements, and a complete disregard for human presence even in broad daylight. We have come to associate these attributes with the panther, because of their frequent and singular development in panthers living under the educative influence of human association. For domestic prey, the accustomed food of such animals, though easily taken, must be taken in competition with man, and such competition develops great boldness, cunning, and resource in these animals. Cattle-killing by tigers, lions, or panthers brings them in constant association with man, reduces fear of him, and leads often to man-eating.

Man-eating. The larger carnivores are not usually dangerous to man. A tigress or panther with cubs may make a demonstration of frightfulness and charge home. Again, taken unawares, these animals may attack in self-defence, or turn on their pursuers, as when wounded or harried in a beat, or the attack may be made in error a man being mistaken for more legitimate prey. This sometimes happens when people are sitting or moving in heavy cover. This chance killing of a man is suggested as one of the causes which lead panthers, tigers, or lions to man-eating. The reluctance to attack human beings, once overcome, may induce an individual to include human beings amongst its prey or convert it into a habitual man-eater. While many panthers occasionally take human prey, the number of habitual man-eaters is fortunately few. Insufficiency of food, or causes such as age or wounds or faulty dentition, which prevent the securing of it, may make one of these animals a man-eater. We have still to learn the causes which produce bad teeth in a particular tiger in a given area and induce it to man-eating. Such a man-eater is not necessarily an old or disabled animal. Man-eating is more frequent in females than in males. The difficulty of finding food for their young may initiate the habit and explain its greater frequency in the sex. One of the results of the great famine in Gujarat between 1901 and 1903 was marked increase in the number of man-eating panthers and tigers in that area. Man-eating may be acquired in age or in youth. The chance killing of man may initiate the habit in a young animal. Or a cub taking to the vice from its parents' example may retain the habit through life. Man-eating, like cattle-killing, may become a tradition passed on from parents to offspring. This is perhaps the explanation of the repeated occurrence of man-eating tigers or panthers in certain districts of India and their rarity in others. Brought into more frequent and intimate touch with man, the man-eating panther is more to be dreaded than the man-eating tiger. Familiarity with man and his ways makes it bolder, more difficult to circumvent, and gives it greater capacity for destruction.

How used by man. It is but natural that Cats, great or small, from their beauty and symmetry of form, from their habits and ways of life, have from time immemorial impressed the mind of man. A volume may be written on the domestic cat as an object of worship and veneration. The great carnivores have become the subject of legend, folk-lore, and romance ; and fear has made them objects of propitiation and worship. Sacred red-painted stones are placed to mark the spot where a tiger has slain a man. It is believed that worship at these shrines will avert a similar fate. It is a common belief that the spirit of a human being killed by a man-eater accompanies its destroyer to warn it of any approaching danger, while to certain forest tribes is given the power to protect tigers by turning aside the bullets of the hunter. Many products derived from the tiger are held for various reasons in high esteem. The fat is valued as an aphrodisiac and as a remedy for rheumatism. The clavicles or ' lucky bones ', which are the rudimentary collar bones found loose in the muscles of the lower neck near the shoulder joint, and the claws are prized as charms and ornaments. The whiskers may be used as a love-charm or be pounded into a mechanical poison to rid one of an enemy. The liver is eaten to impart courage, and the milk of a tigress is applied to soothe the ailments of the eyes. The beautiful furs of many of the Cats are naturally objects of value to man.

Conclusion. We have tried in this section to reveal something of the lives of the great carnivores considered in relation to their surroundings both animate and inanimate. A knowledge of the true life of these animals can only come to us by a greater knowledge of the many factors which influence their ways and habits. We have to study not only the animal but also the stage upon which it plays its role. We have still much to learn about the reaction of panthers and tigers to the varied conditions of their physical environment, to climate and to seasons, to new situations as also to the animal communities in which they live. We have still to learn about their migrations and their movements. Such knowledge can only come from continued field observation, more especially from controlled systematic investigations, surely worthwhile as to animals which play so definite a role in the economy of Nature in this country, and which are so surrounded with immemorial romance and interest.

THE FAMILY LIFE OF THE CATS

Vocal communication. One aspect which we discussed of the family life of apes and monkeys was means of communication. They have quite a vocabulary of special sounds by which they give vent to their feelings, and by which members of a family or a troop communicate with one another. The Cats are much more limited in their language. They have less need being unsocial in their habits. The lion is perhaps an exception. It is undoubtedly the most social of all the tribe and equally the most noisy and vocal. Its herding instincts and consequently its greater need for intercommunication may explain why lions are so noisy, much more noisy than tigers or panthers. Cats, in general, have a variety of sounds expressive of different emotions. There is the deep threatening growl of the angry tiger, the loud *whoof* by which it expresses surprise, and the harsh barking cough or terrifying roar which sometimes accompanies a charge. But usually among Cats vocal communication appears to be limited to mating calls and sounds by which mother and young communicate. In fact many carnivores never call except during mating time or when with young. At mating time tiger calls to tigress, repeating at short intervals a loud deep-throated roar. It is their mating call. They have a gentler puffing sound, which both tigers and tigresses give out during friendly approach. It is made by expelling air in panting jets through the nostrils. Then there is that curious call given out by both sexes, a call like the ' belling ' of a sambar. It would be fantastic to suggest that the tiger lures the sambar to its death by mimicking its call. No sambar would mistake it. A more plausible explanation is that this call, sometimes referred to as ' pooking' (' titting' in Burma), is an expression of suspicion or alarm ; or it may be merely another way of communicating with a mate, used in the season when tiger and tigress are a-courting. Lieut.-Col. R. W. Burton records that two tigers and one tigress dying of bullet wounds uttered a death-cry similar to a domestic cat being killed by dogs.

Courtship and breeding. Vociferous is the caterwauling courtship of domestic cats, but no less vociferous the courtship of their wild relatives, of lions, tigers, and panthers. There is little reticence in the courtship of a tiger or a panther. The procreative instinct appears to overcome all ingrained habits of concealment and secrecy. Their mating is accompanied by noisy demonstrations, by snarlings and spasmodic roarings, and by intervals of play, of gambolling and chasing, dictated by the receptive or resentive attitude of the female. Have the great Cats a particular time of the year for mating ? It would appear that in the forests of peninsular India there is no definite, well-demarcated breeding season. Cubs are born in any month of the year, though the birth-rate may increase markedly at a certain season. But we have a great deal to learn about the breeding of the larger felines. We have no definite knowledge about sexual periodicity in these animals. We do not know whether the males are sexually potent throughout the year, nor do we know the intervals of time which elapse between the periods when females are in condition to breed. The little we have learned of their mating, of the birth and care of the young, we have learned from captive animals.

Care of the young. A tigress gives birth to her young in some dense patch of cover in a cave or under a rough shelter of rocks. The panther does much the same, but being smaller it can use the hollow trunk of a tree or even a porcupine's burrow. The nursery is always well-concealed, its interior dark, and the site itself easily defendable. These are devices for the better protection of the young. Beasts of prey are usually born blind and helpless. Some baby lions can see at birth. The task of looking after the cubs falls chiefly on the mother. The tiger appears to desert its mate shortly before or after the cubs are born. The male panther and lion, on the other hand, remain with their families and, though they take little interest in their offspring, at least help in defending them and later, when they are somewhat grown, help them to secure food. But it is always the mother who keeps the nursery clean, who attends to the toilet of the cubs, licking them with her great rough tongue until they can lick themselves or each other clean. When they stray from their lair she brings them back, carrying them by gripping the loose skin of the neck with her teeth just as a house cat does. The young are insistent in their demands for attention, ever wailing and screaming. Newborn lion and tiger cubs have thin weak voices but in a few weeks they wail like house cats. They cry not only when hungry but also when cold, but wail the loudest when left alone. For the first few days the mother remains constantly with them ; later hunger compels her to go out and hunt. How long the great Cats nurse their young we do not know. We have scant knowledge about the period of lactation in these carnivores. Before they are weaned the cubs begin to scrape off fragments of flesh from prey the mother brings home. It is their introduction to meat-eating. Training in hunting and stalking begins in the nursery. The cubs crouch and leap at each other. What seems pointless play with the mother's tail is gaining of skill in approach and attack. They stalk its flicking tip, they leap at it as it is whisked away, they seize and worry it. They are unconsciously practising the elements of their craft. When strong enough to get about they are taken out by the mother or by both parents. Family parties of lions, tigers, and panthers have been frequently observed. An adult male present in a tiger family is probably a new mate acquired with the renewal of sexual activity in the female. During these family hunts the young gain experience. When a family of lions is hunting their hunt may be in the nature of a drive. Some of the troop, keeping in touch with each other by low grunts and growls, drive their quarry in the direction of others lying in wait to intercept and slay the victim. It is said that in these combined hunts it is the lion who drives and the lioness who kills, while the cubs waiting by her side rush in to tear at and feed on the prey. Family parties of tigers and panthers have been observed hunting in this way. A mother tigress hunting alone with her cubs will disable an animal so that it cannot escape the onslaught of her cubs, who come and take a share in the killing.

Col. Mosse describes the behaviour of a panther watching her cub making its kill. The cub was all concentration, while the mother affected complete indifference to the tethered bait and changed her position only to get a better view of the efforts of the cub. The conflict between the impatience of youth and the ingrained instinct for cautious approach was strikingly apparent in the efforts of the cub to stalk its quarry.

Beasts of prey have necessarily to be more intelligent than the herbivores which they hunt and kill, for their prey is intensely alert and wary. The young must exercise and develop their skill and craft if later they are to get enough food to keep themselves alive. They must gain experience in stalking, must learn how, when, and where to wait for their prey, and how to leap at the right time and strike effectively with tooth and claw. How clumsy are their early efforts ! The kills of the young show none of the mastery of the adult. They can be known by the clumsiness of the mauling. Much of this experience is gained during youth by following the example of their

PLATE 12

Tiger
(*Panthera tigris*)

♀

Lion
(*Panthera leo*)

♂

Snow Leopard
(*Panthera uncia*)

Leopard
(*Panthera pardus*)

0	30	60	90 cm.
0	1	2	3 ft.

PLATE 13

Clouded Leopard
(*Neofelis nebulosa*)

Golden Cat
(*Felis temmincki*)

Fishing Cat
(*Felis viverrina*)

Leopard Cat
(*Felis bengalensis*)

Marbled Cat
(*Felis marmorata*)

0   10   20   30 cm.

0   1 ft.

Jungle Cat
(*Felis chaus*)

parents. It is then that vices like man- or cattle-killing may also be acquired.

We have gained a fair amount of knowledge about the youth and growth of beasts of prey from captive animals. But it must be remembered that captivity may make a difference. It probably hastens growth. Lions and tigers take from three to five years to become fully adult. But males and females are capable of breeding soon after, or even before, they are three years old. Leopards, lynxes, and caracals are generally full-grown in one and a half to three years. The smaller Cats are almost adult when a year old. The period of youth in man and in apes and monkeys, it is seen, varies with the degree of intelligence attained by the adult. Civilized man the most intelligent takes the longest to grow up. The smaller monkeys, the least intelligent, complete their youth very quickly. But it is impossible to arrange the carnivores in an ascending scale of intelligence. They all show considerable intelligence, wild species no less than the domesticated forms. But it might be said that among them youth is never so long as in the Primates. Lions and tigers, much larger and more powerful animals than any ape or monkey, reach maturity quicker.

THE TIGER

Panthera tigris (Linnaeus)

Plates facing p. 64

[RACE IN INDIA : *tigris* (Linnaeus)]

Local Names. Hindi *bagh, sher* ; Central India *nahar, sela vagh* ; Mar. *wagh* ; Tamil & Tel. *poolee*; Mal. *kaduwa* ; Kan. *hoolee* ; Bur. *char.*

Size. Measured in a straight line between pegs few Indian tigers exceed 10 ft. (300 cm.) in length. The average is 9 ft.-9 ft. 6 in. (275-290 cm.) ; females, 8 ft. 6 in. (260 cm.). Average weight, male 400-500 lb. (180-230 kg.) ; females about 100 lb. (45 kg.) less. Tigers from the Himalayas generally show a slight superiority in size over tigers from Madhya Pradesh and southern India.

Distinguishing Characters. The Indian Tiger is a rich-coloured well-striped animal with a short coat. We have still to learn whether the Indian Tiger varies in the different States, and what differences in its coloration are produced by season and age. Individual variation is great.

Distribution. Over the wide area of its range, 6 races of the Tiger have been distinguished. The Indian race, designated as the typical Tiger, is found practically throughout India from the Himalayas to Cape Comorin, except in the deserts of Rajasthan, the Punjab, Cutch, and Sind. Its range extends into Burma.

Habits : In India the Tiger has left its tracks in the winter snows of the Himalayas at an altitude of 10,000 ft. (3050 m.). It lives in humid evergreen forests, in dry open jungle, and in the grassy swamps of the terai, while in the Sunderbans it leads an almost amphibious life in a terrain of trees, mud, and water. Three things are essential to the Tiger, the neighbourhood of large animals upon which it can prey, ample shade to sleep in, and water to quench its thirst. Ordinarily the Tiger hunts between sunset and dawn, but should the day be cold or clouded with rain it will be up and about. The Tiger's method of hunting and killing its prey have been considered in a previous chapter. It hunts game of all kinds including elephants (usually females or young), gaur, and buffalo. It preys on deer, nilgai, wild pig, bears, and porcupines, and will kill and eat panthers and other tigers. Driven by hunger it will eat almost anything, fowl, fish, reptiles, or carrion. Many, in the absence of game animals or from opportunity, take to cattle-killing. The habit may be acquired in age or by following parental example when quite young. The same applies to man-eating, a vice acquired in circumstances which have been discussed. In spite of its heavy build the Tiger is endowed with astonishing suppleness of movement. It takes to water readily and swims with ease. Though not given to climbing it will climb trees should need arise. In India many Tigers seem to mate after the rains and the majority of young are born between February and May. Whether the Tiger is always monogamous is not known. Tigers with more than one female in train have been seen. Association between the male and female appears to end when the cubs are born, but there may be some companionship for a varying period after that. The period of gestation is said to be fifteen to sixteen weeks. Usually 2-3, but as many as 6, may be produced in a litter. The cubs wander about their lair, and when about 6 months old accompany the mother in her hunting and may stay with her until quite two years old, and even after she has acquired a new mate.

Sexual maturity is attained at 3 years of age by the tigress and at 4 by the tiger. The life span of the Tiger is estimated to be about 20 years.

The rapid decline of the tiger population in the country, resulted in a complete ban on their shooting in 1970. With international co-operation a project for their preservation was organized by naming 9 sanctuaries with different habitats as Tiger preserves for rehabilitation of the species. At the commencement of the project there was believed to be less than 2000 tigers in India.

PLATE 14

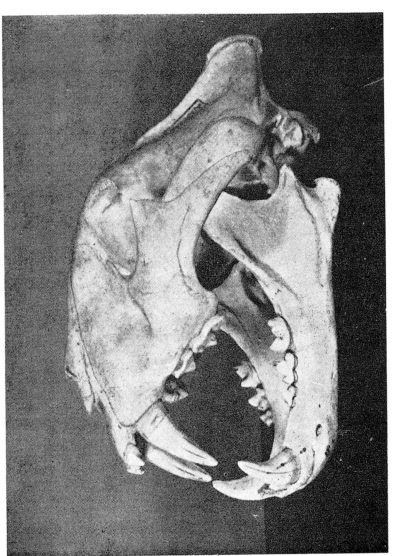

Skull of Tiger (*Panthera tigris*)

Note the widely separated canines, the few blade-like cheek teeth, the powerful jaw bones, and the sturdy cheek arches which support the great biting muscles.

PLATE 15

Lion (*Panthera leo*) in Gir Forest

Photo : E.P. Gee

Panthera leo (Linnaeus)

Plates facing pp. 64, 67

[RACE IN INDIA : *persica* (Meyer)]

Local Names. Hindi *sher, sher babar, singh;* Guj. *untia bagh;* Kathiawari *sawach;* Mar. *sinha;* Mal. *Simham;* Tam. *Singham.*

Size. The average length of Asiatic and African lions is the same, a few inches over 9 ft. (275 cm.). The largest recorded measurement of an Indian Lion is 9 ft. 7 in. (292 cm.), of an African Lion 10 ft. 7 in. (323 cm.).

Distinguishing Characters. On the average the Asiatic Lion has a scantier mane than the African, but curiously enough in combination with this character a fuller coat, a longer tassel of hair at the end of its tail, a more pronounced tuft of hair on the elbow joints, and a fuller fringe of hairs on its belly. The mane is light or dark, rarely quite black. It may be full-developed or scraggy. This is true also of African lions. Cubs, spotted or striped.

Distribution. The Asiatic Lion is probably no longer to be found in Iraq and Iran. It was once found over the whole of northern and central India as far south as Narmada. It is now restricted to the Gir Forest in Kathiawar, Gujarat.

Habits. The Gir Forest lying within Junagadh District, covering some 500 sq. miles (1280 sq. km.) of rugged country, is composed mainly of stunted teak trees, palas, jambul, and *ber* and patches of small bamboo, with an undergrowth of thorny shrubs and bushes. This is the nature of the only forest where the Lion is now found in India. The habits of the Indian Lion do not differ from those of the African. By day they rest under the shade of trees and at dusk go in quest for food. Their roars are heard throughout the night, more noticeably at dusk and again just before daybreak. In the Gir Forest they prey mainly on game and cattle. At dusk the cattle-killer makes straight for the nearest village to wait for cattle coming home, or it takes its victims when they are driven out to pasture long before dawn.

There appears to be no particular breeding season. In the Gir many Lions mate between October and November and the young are produced between January and February. The period of gestation is about 116 days. The male stays with the family and helps to defend the young and later to get food for them. Young are produced at intervals of at least 18 months to 2 years. The female Lion is said to have her first litter when she is between 2½ to 3 years old. The ordinary litter numbers two, sometimes three; it may contain as many as five. A Lion is in his prime when five years old. The number of Lions living in the Gir in 1978 was less than 200.

THE LEOPARD, or PANTHER

Panthera pardus (Linnaeus)

Plates facing pp. 64, 78

[RACES IN INDIA : *fusca* (Meyer), *?pernigra* (Gray), *?saxicolor* Pocock, *sindica* Pocock, *millardi* Pocock. CEYLON : *fusca* (Meyer)]

Local Names. Hindi *tendwa, chita, sona chita, chita bagh* ; Mar. *karda, asnea, singhal, bibalya wagh* ; Kan. *chirchu, chirate, siwangi, keeraba* ; Tamil *chiruthai* ; Tel. *chinna puli* ; Bur. *thit* ; Mal. *pulli poolee*.

Size. The average total length is 7 ft. (215 cm.), females about 1 ft. (30 cm.) less. An exceptionally large male may reach 8 ft. (245 cm.). Weight 150 lb. (68 kg.), female about 110 (50 kg.). These are maximum weights. Ordinary weights are 115 lb. (52 kg.) and 85 lb. (39 kg.). There is much variation in size in various parts of India.

Distinguishing Characters. A typical Panther from the Indian peninsula is a sleek short-haired animal with a fulvous or bright fulvous coat marked with small close-set black rosettes. There is however considerable colour variation. Animals from the desert zone are paler. Panthers from Kashmir have soft deep-furred grey buff coats with small, thick-rimmed rosettes.

Distribution. The Indian Panther ranges over the whole country and extends into Burma and Ceylon. Panthers from Sind, Kashmir, and Baluchistan are regarded as distinct races. So is the Panther of Sikkim and Nepal. Pocock has named and described eleven races of panther as found in Asia (*Journal of the Bombay Natural History Society* 34 : 64, 307). According to him three of these races occur in India. It is likely that research will reveal a small dark race in the Nelliampatti Hills in Cochin. Attention was first drawn to it by Mr. R. C. Morris.

Habits. Panthers are able to live and thrive almost anywhere. They are not restricted to forests or heavy cover like tigers, and thrive as well in open country as among rocks and scrub. Being more tolerant of the sun they frequently hunt by day, particularly if they have failed to secure food at night. The Panther will kill and eat anything it can overpower with safety, cattle, deer, and monkeys, the smaller beasts of prey, and larger rodents, like porcupines. The bill of fare is extended to include birds, reptiles, and crabs. A big sambar or *barasinga* stag, or a bull nilgai are perhaps more than a match for the Panther, and these he usually leaves alone. The Panther's chief enemy is the tiger. Wild dogs and hyenas frequently come off best in encounters with Panthers. The Panther's habits bring it into far more frequent contact with man than the tiger, and as such it has become a greater potential scourge on human life and property.

Panthers living near human settlement, particularly outside forest areas, prey mainly on domestic animals, calves, sheep, and goats, on ponies and donkeys, and quite commonly on dogs. Very different must be the life of the game-killing Panther which lives by the killing of wild prey. It displays many of the habits and ways of tigers. Like the tiger the forest Panther follows roads or paths or the beaten tracks of animals through the forest, or waits for its prey in hiding. It seizes its quarry from the ground or leaps on it from a height such as an overhanging branch. The strength of the Panther is amazing. To find security for its kill a Panther has scrambled up a tree carrying a full-grown chital stag in its mouth. Familiarity with man and his ways makes the man-eating Panther more to be dreaded than the tiger.

Panthers breed all the year round. In captivity the female produces the first litter when $2\frac{1}{2}$ to 4 years of age. Gestation period varies from 87 to 94 days. Normally 2 cubs per litter are born, occasionally 3 or 4. Eyes open between the 4th and 8th day after birth. Weaned at about 4 months.

THE SNOW LEOPARD, or OUNCE

Panthera uncia (Schreber)

Plate facing p. 64

Local Names. Tibetan Bhotia *ikar, zig, sachak* ; Hills north of Simla *barhal he* ; Kunawar *thurwagh* ; East of Kumaon *burhel haye* (*burhel* killer).

Size. Somewhat smaller than a panther with relatively longer tail. Head and body, 3 ft. 3 in.-3 ft. 8 in. (100-110 cm.); tail, 3 ft. (90 cm.).

Distinctive Characters. The Snow Leopard is distinctive in the shortness of its muzzle, its high forehead, and vertical chin. The ground colour of its coat is soft grey paling to pure white on the underside. The grey is sometimes tinged with buff. The spots are unbroken and distinct on the head, nape, and lower parts of the limbs. On the body they break up into larger, paler rosettes. These rosettes are less pronounced in the luxuriant winter coat. Except for a few black blotches the fur of the undersides is pure white. Newly born cubs are darker than the adults.

Distribution. In India Snow Leopards range along the whole Himalayan chain from Kashmir to Bhutan. Northwards their territory extends into Tibet, central Asia, and the Altais.

Habits. Little is known about the habits of this animal. The inaccessibility of its haunts makes observation difficult. Its home is the higher altitudes of the Himalayas, in that region of stupendous rock and cliff above the tree-line, some 12,000-13,000 ft. (3660-3965 m.) above sea-level. Lying up by day, Snow Leopards hunt at night, preying on wild sheep and goats, on musk deer, hares, marmots, and other rodents, perhaps also on the larger birds. In summer when the upland pastures are open to grazing, they follow their prey to these higher reaches and find opportunity to take domestic goats, sheep, or ponies from the herdsmen. As with panthers and tigers, individuals establish territory near human settlements and take more or less habitually to preying on domestic stock. At the onset of winter, Snow Leopards follow the general downward migration of animals, coming down with them to altitudes as low as 6000 ft. (1830 m.). Like other beasts of prey their movements are wholly regulated by the movements of their accustomed prey.

The gestation period is about 3 months; young number 2 to 4. In common with all other creatures whom Nature has given a special endowment of beauty, Snow Leopards are persistently sought after and hunted for their valuable fur. Its soft colouring and luxuriant beauty is scarcely rivalled.

THE CLOUDED LEOPARD

Neofelis nebulosa (Griffith)

Plate facing p. 65

[RACE IN INDIA : *macrosceloides* (Hodgson)]

Local Names. Lepcha *pungmar, satchuk*; Bhotia *kung*; Nepali *amchita*; Bur. *thit kyoung.*

Size. A large male measured, head and body with tail, about 6 ft. 5 in. (195 cm.). Weight, 40-45 lb. (18-20 kg.).

Distinctive Characters. The animal has a long body and tail and short limbs, rounded black ears relieved by a greyish patch in the centre. The structure of its feet is much like that of the panther and its near relatives, the tiger and the lion. It differs from the great Cats mainly in the structure of the skull and the set of the teeth. Very striking in the Clouded Leopard is the enormous relative development of the upper canine teeth, which present the nearest approach among living Cats to the great tusks of the extinct sabre toothed tiger.

The markings of the Clouded Leopard give it a beauty and distinction equalled by few of its tribe. The general colour of the body varies from grey or earthy brown to pale or rich yellowish brown fading to white or pale tawny on the underparts. Indian animals are generally darker and greyer with less yellow. The face is marked with the usual cheek stripes so common in the smaller Cats, and the head is spotted. Two broad bands, with narrower bands or elongate spots between them, run from between the ears to the shoulders and extend more or less regularly in the form of large oval or elongate marks on the back. The clouded pattern of the flanks is formed by dark blotches more or less lined with black and divided by paler interspaces. The limbs and underparts are marked with large spots, and the tail ornamented with rings frequently imperfect on the sides.

Distribution. In India the Clouded Leopard is found in the forests of Nepal, Bhutan, and Sikkim, whence its range extends eastwards into Assam, Burma, S. China, and the Malay countries.

Habits. The Clouded Leopard is largely arboreal. It inhabits dense evergreen forests where it hunts its prey by night. Its powerful jaws and great canine teeth and sturdy build adapt it to the killing of deer and equally large animals. It sometimes visits Bhotia and Lepcha villages to prey upon goats and pigs. There is a record of one cattle-killer which was slain while advancing to attack a herd-boy who split its skull with his *dah*.

It brings forth its young in the hollow of a tree. The litter size is two. It has been bred in captivity.

THE MARBLED CAT

Felis marmorata Martin

Plate facing p. 65

[RACE IN INDIA : *charltoni* Gray]

Size. Rather larger than a domestic cat ; 3 ft. (90 cm.) in total length, half of which consists of tail.

Distinctive Characters. As a sub-genus (*Pardofelis*), the Marbled Cat is distinguished from the leopard-cat and other Oriental relatives by structural peculiarities of the skull which, among other points of distinction, is short and broad and more rounded, and has wider cheek arches. The teeth, especially the canines, are relatively more robust, and the chin more vertical. The Indian race is said to be quite distinctive in its thicker, longer, rich ochreous-brown coat, whose luxuriance tends to obscure the marbled pattern, more apparent in typical examples from Java and Sumatra.

The general pattern on the coat of these Cats consists of stripes on the crown, neck, and back, of large and small blotches making the so-called marbling on the flanks, and of spots on the underside of the limbs and on the tail. The marbled pattern on the flanks is variable even in individuals inhabiting the same region. In the Himalayas it is limited to a few wavy greyish buff stripes which break up the ground colour of the flanks into large ochreous-brown patches. The heavily spotted legs are of the same rich hue as the body. The tail is darker in tone and its pattern is obscurely defined. Though much smaller in size, the Marbled Cat resembles the clouded leopard in colour and pattern, so that young clouded leopards are easily confused with this species.

Distribution. Nepal, Sikkim, and Assam, extending into Burma and the Malay countries. A single race occurs in India.

Habits. Nothing is known about the habits of this Cat. It is conjectured that it is a purely forest Cat of arboreal habits, feeding on small mammals like rats and squirrels and birds. The supposition is supported by the structure of its feet which show no adaptation to ground-dwelling habits. Its tree-climbing and nocturnal habits are suggested as a reason for its rarity in most collections.

THE GOLDEN CAT

Felis temmincki Vigors & Horsfield

Plate facing p. 65

[RACE IN INDIA : *temmincki* Vigors & Horsfield]

Size. Little over 4 ft. (120 cm.) in total length ; tail, about 1½ ft. (45 cm.) long.

Distinctive Characters. With the exception of the clouded leopard the Golden Cat is the largest of the group of smaller Oriental felines. It is included in a separate sub-genus, *Profelis*. It is a fine sturdily-built Cat. Its coat is golden brown to dark brown, bright red, or grey. Black examples are also known. There is usually little or no trace of pattern on the body. When the coat is short and smooth, as in summer, there may be a more or less distinct pattern of greyish lines on the flanks and shoulders. Kittens have longer and thicker coats than the adults, but show no pattern. But whether the body pattern in the adult is retained or lost, it is always conspicuous on the face of this cat, and gives the animal a very striking aspect. Most conspicuous is a horizontal white or buff cheek stripe, sometimes edged with black, running from below the eye to behind the gape. On the inner side of the eye there is always a whitish stripe which bifurcates above and is continuous with a more or less distinct greyish stripe passing on to the crown. Occasionally there are curved lines running back from above the eye to between the ears.

Distribution. Nepal, Sikkim, Assam, extending into Burma, S. China, and south-eastern Asia, generally as far south as Sumatra. Three races are recognised ; the Indian is the nominate form.

Habits. Nothing definite is known about the habits of this Cat. The Mishmis say that it breeds in hollow trees and has two young. The Lushai hunters state that it lives among rocks and does not climb trees. There is however a record of one which took refuge in a tree from a dog. This individual did not display the fierceness usually ascribed to this species, which in Burma is known as *kya min*, signifying that it dominates other Cats, even tigers. The Golden Cat preys on poultry, sheep and goats, and small deer. One was shot near Maymyo on a calf that it had killed ; another was speared at Victoria Point, Mergui, after killing a buffalo calf. The young born in captivity in April was black in colour, weighed 110 gm. and was 29 cm. in total length.

THE LEOPARD-CAT

Felis bengalensis Kerr

Plate facing p. 65

[RACES IN INDIA : *bengalensis* Kerr, *horsfieldi* (Gray), *trevelyani* (Pocock)]

Local Names. Hindi *chita billi* ; Ben. *ban bilar* ; Mar. *wagati*.

Size. Head and body, just under 2 ft. (60 cm.). Tail exceeds half length of head and body. Weight about 6-8 lb. (3-4 kg.).

Distinctive Characters. The Leopard-Cat (sub-genus *Prionailurus*) is about the size of a domestic cat but rather longer in the leg. Its colour and markings give it the aspect of a miniature panther. The prevailing colour of the body is yellowish above, white below, ornamented throughout with black or brownish spots. Both colour and pattern are very variable in the species. The ground colour may show a tendency to grey, as in animals from N. Kashmir, or rufous, and the spots, usually arranged to form regular lines along the body, may coalesce into uninterrupted longitudinal bands. Among other markings are four more or less distinct bands running from the crown over the neck, which break up into short bars and elongate spots on the shoulders. There is a pair of horizontal cheek stripes, the lower joining a black bar across the throat, and the usual two black bars on the inside of the forearm. The spots on the tail form cross bars towards its end.

Distribution. Forest regions of India from Kashmir and the Himalayas to Cape Comorin ; south-eastern Asia generally northwards to Manchuria and Korea. Three races occur in India.

Habits. This beautiful forest Cat preys upon small birds and animals. It is nocturnal in habit and seldom seen. Hollows in trees are a favourite shelter. It is common about villages in Coorg, where it is said to be very destructive to poultry. Young have been obtained in March and May. 3-4 may be born in a litter. A kitten a few months old was taken in August in the Nilgiris. It became quite tame and though driven off by domestic cats returned more than once to its owners after a sojourn in the forest. Instances of its interbreeding with domestic cats have been observed.

In southern India and in the W. Ghats up to the Dangs and in some parts of Kashmir, there is an allied species, the **Rustyspotted Cat,** *F. rubiginosa* Geoffroy. It is about half or three-quarters of the size of a domestic cat. A slightly built active creature, with a soft, smooth fawn grey coat, patterned with brown bars and spots arranged in more or less regular lines. The markings on its head and shoulders are dark brown; they change to rusty on the flanks and are reduced to smaller round spots on the hind quarters. The underparts are nearly white with black spots. It frequents grassland, scrub, and jungle, and is to some extent arboreal in habits. The litter consists of two to three kittens. The typical race *F. r. rubiginosa* Geoffroy occurs in India. One race, *F. r. phillipsi* (Pocock), is found in Ceylon.

THE FISHING CAT

Felis viverrina Bennett

Plate facing p. 65

Size. The body of a large Fishing Cat measures about 3 ft. 3 in. (100 cm.) and its tail is about a foot (30 cm.) in length. It scales 25 to 32 lb. (11 to 15 kg.).

Distinctive Characters. Sub-genus *Prionailurus*. The Fishing Cat is distinguished from the leopard-cat by its much larger size and shorter tail, which is much less than half the length of its head and body. This Cat is short in limb and rather stout in build. Its body is covered with short, coarse, earthy-grey fur, infused with brown. The body markings consist of a series of elongate spots arranged in more or less longitudinal rows. They vary in size and sharpness of definition in individuals. From 6 to 8 dark lines run from the forehead over the crown on to the neck, breaking up into shorter bars and spots on the shoulders. The cheeks are greyish white with two usually well-defined horizontal black or brown stripes. Markings on the limbs are indistinct or wanting. The two usual dark bars appear on the inside of the forearm. The lower parts of the body are spotted, and the tail is more or less distinctly ringed with black. The forefeet of this Cat have moderately well-developed webs between the toes, the claw sheaths are not large enough to completely envelop the retracted claws, the ends of which project considerably beyond the sheaths.

Distribution. Inhabits forests up to 5000 ft. (1525 m.) in the Himalayas and the swamps at the base of these mountains and in parts of West Bengal, Uttar Pradesh. Unknown in the peninsula except in Keonjhar district and the vicinity of Chilka Lake in Orissa and on the West Coast from Mangalore to Kanyakumari. Sind (Pakistan), Bangladesh, Sri Lanka, Indo-Chinese countries and Java (Indonesia).

Habits. This Cat lives in or near heavy jungle, or in scrub, frequently in grass swamps, or in reed beds, about rivers and tidal creeks. It preys on any animal and bird that it can secure, and has been known to kill calves and sheep, to carry off dogs, and even children ! There is the record of a newly-caught male which killed a leopardess twice its size after breaking through the partition which separated their cages. It is given to feeding on fish and freshwater molluscs. Its method of fishing is to crouch on a rock or overhanging bank and to scoop up the fish with a blow of its paw. It does not enter the water in pursuit of its prey.

Nothing is known about the breeding habits of this Cat. A single kitten was taken in Cannanore in June from a lair in a beaten down patch among reeds with tunnelled approaches from either side. A female with two kittens was seen in Champaran (Bihar State) in April.

THE JUNGLE CAT

Felis chaus Güldenstaedt

Plate facing p. 65

[RACES IN INDIA : *affinis* Gray, *kutas* Pearson, *prateri* Pocock, *kelaarti* Pocock. CEYLON : *kelaarti* Pocock]

Local Names. Hindi *khatas, jangli billi* ; Ben. *ban bilar* ; Mar. *baul, baoga* ; Tel. *junka pilli*; Tamil *kartu poonay*; Mal. *kartu poocha* ; Kan. *kada bekku* ; Bur. *tor chaung.*

Size. Head and body, little over 2 ft. (60 cm.) ; tail, about a foot (30 cm.) long ; weight, 10-12 lb. (5-6 kg.).

Distinctive Characters. With its long legs and comparatively short tail the Jungle Cat has a very distinctive appearance. Its pale green eyes give it a coldly cruel expression. The colour of its fur varies from sandy grey to yellowish grey. The tail is ringed with black towards the end and has a black tip. The paws are pale yellowish, black or sooty brown underneath. The ears are reddish, ending in a small pencil of black hairs. The underside of the body is paler, with vestiges of stripes on the underside and flanks.

Distribution. The Jungle Cat has established itself over a wide territory ranging from north Africa through south-western Asia to India, Ceylon, Burma, and Indo-China. This is the common wild cat of India and is found practically all over the Peninsula from the Himalayas to Cape Comorin. The Himalayan form is distinguished by its heavier winter coat. The north-Indian plains form is smaller, shorter in tail, and lighter in weight. There is a sandy-coloured desert r. ce ; and a south Indian race with a short coat much suffused on the back with grey, and showing a speckling of black and white.

Habits. Jungle Cats inhabit the drier and more open parts of the country, keeping more to grassland, scrub jungle, the reedy banks of rivers and marshes. In Kashmir, where they are common in the neighbourhood of towns, many live among rocks or find shelter in old buildings. The Jungle Cat is frequently about by day, more usually in the mornings and evenings. Its movements in the open are much like those of a small panther. It preys on small mammals, birds, and when near villages on poultry. There is record of one making bold to seize its prey even in the presence of the owners. Very swift and exceedingly strong for its size, it is quite capable of bringing down larger game. Crump, writing of these Cats in Kumaon, says that it was not at all uncommon to find the quills of porcupines, which they had killed or attempted to kill, embedded in their paws.

Births have been recorded between January-April and in August and November. Litter size usually 3 but occasionally up to 5 kittens. The eyes open 11 to 15 days after birth. The kittens are easily tamed and purr like a domestic cat when content.

THE DESERT CAT

Felis libyca Forster

Plate facing p. 96

[RACE IN INDIA : *ornata* Gray]

Local Names. Cutch *jhang meno.*

Size. Head and body, two feet (60 cm.) ; tail, about 1 ft. (30 cm.) ; weight 6-8 lb. (3-4 kg.).

Distinctive Characters. In the Indian desert region and in the dry zone of central India, where both jungle cats and Desert Cats are found, the Desert Cat is easily distinguished by its spots. Not much larger than a domestic cat, the Indian Desert Cat has pale yellowish fur, more or less infused with grey and marked with numerous black spots. The terminal half of its tail is ringed with black. It has two horizontal stripes on its cheeks, numerous dark cross lines on the outside of the limbs, and the usual two distinct black bars on the inner side of each forearm. The chin, throat, and breast are white and unspotted. The ears are coloured like the back, with a few black hairs at the tips.

Distribution. The deserts of north-western India extending into the drier parts of central India and to near Poona in the Deccan. Westward the range extends through desert lands from Sind to northern Africa. Northwards into the steppes of central Asia.

Habits. Very little is known about the habits of this Cat, except that it lives in deserts and scrub jungle, where its prey must consist mainly of desert gerbilles and other small rodents and birds. One was shot while feeding on the carcase of a sheep. Breeding habits, unknown.

THE CARACAL

Felis caracal Schreber

Plate facing p. 96

[RACE IN INDIA : *schmitzi* Matschie]

Local Names. Hindi & Persian *siyeh gush.*

Size. Head and body, a little over 2 ft. (60 cm.) long ; tail, about 9 in. (23 cm.).

Distinctive Characters. Sub-genus, *Caracal*. The Caracal has the broad head and tufted ears of the lynx. Like the lynx it stands higher on its hind limbs than on the fore, but it is smaller and lighter in build, has a longer tail, and no ruff of hairs around its face. Its skull bears a general resemblance to that of the lynx, but is narrower in the cranial and facial portions, and recalls in some of its structural characters the skull of the typical Cats (*Felis*). Its coat, though not as dense as that of the lynx, is yet thick and soft. The colouring is a uniform reddish grey above fading into buff or white below. Faint indications of spots are present on the undersurface and sometimes on the back.

Distribution. Baluchistan, Sind, and Cutch. Said to be common in the north and north-west hills of Cutch. Also found in the drier parts of the Punjab, Rajasthan, Uttar Pradesh, and central India. Outside our limits its range extends westwards into Iran, Iraq, and Arabia, and over the greater part of Africa.

Habits. An uncommon and elusive animal, fast approaching extinction in India, little is known about the Caracal in the wild state. It is a creature of desert and scrub jungle, where it preys on birds, which it is said to take in flight by springing up at them, and on rodents, antelope, and small deer. There is a record of a Caracal attacking a man in the Mirzapur District, U.P., but it is believed that the individual was driven to the act by hunger. It was in a very emaciated condition, so perhaps it made the attack in desperation. A captive Caracal in the Mysore Zoo killed and partly ate a large cobra which had entered its cage.

Like the cheetah, it is easily tamed and trained to show its prowess in hunting small deer, gazelle, hares, and foxes, and also birds such as peafowl, crane, and pigeon. It relies for success upon its extraordinary agility. So perfect is the accord of eye and foot, that champion performers in this sport once popular in Persia may kill 9 or 10 of a flock of feeding pigeons before they can leave the ground. It is interesting to note that of all the species of Cats the Caracal comes nearest to the cheetah in the structure of its hindfeet, though it cannot compare with it in speed or staying power. It is trained to hunt in much the same way as the cheetah.

Nothing definite is known about the breeding habits of the animal in India. It is said to rear its young in porcupine burrows, in hollow trees, or crevices among rocks, the average litter being 2 to 4. Two cubs were obtained in October in Rajasthan.

THE LYNX

Felis lynx Linnaeus

Plate facing p. 96

[RACE IN INDIA : *isabellina* Blyth]

Local Names. Kash. *patsalam* ; Lahul *phiauku.*

Size. Head and body, 33 to 35 in. (85 to 90 cm.) ; tail, 7 to 9 in. (18 to 23 cm.) ; weight, 60 lb. (27 kg.).

Distinctive Characters. The long erect tufts of hair on the tips of its ears distinguish the Lynx from other Cats ; from the caracal the Lynx is distinguished by its short tail reaching only half way to the hocks, and by the distinct ruff or fringe of pendant hairs framing its face. In summer its coat shows a sprinkling of spots which may persist, but which usually disappear in the heavier winter coat.

Distribution. The Lynx, which occurs within our limits in the upper Indus valley, in Gilgit, Ladak, and Tibet, is a race of the Lynx of northern Europe and Asia. It is distinctive in its pale sandy-grey or isabelline colouring, hence its racial name *isabellina.*

PLATE 16

Leopard (*Panthera pardus*) on the prowl

Photo : F.W. Champion

PLATE 17

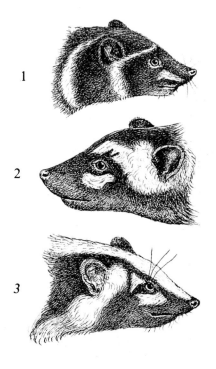

H. N. Wandhekar

Warning Colours: Facial Masks

1. Polecat (*Vormela peregusna*)
2. Toddy Cat (*Paradoxurus hermaphroditus*)
3. Chinese Plam Civet (*Paguma larvata intrudens*)

Habits. The Lynx shelters in the dense cover provided by willow scrub, patches of reeds, and tall grass. It hunts such animals and birds as it can overcome, hares, marmots, partridges, pheasants, and takes its toll from flocks of sheep and goats. In summer it covers a wide range of altitude having been seen at levels between 9000 (2745 m.) and 11,000 feet (3355 m.). Its keen eyesight and hearing are proverbial. Little is known of the breeding habits of this animal. It is said to have 2-3 young, the mother usually hiding her litter in a cave or a hole among rocks. Half-grown cubs have been seen in August.

PALLAS'S CAT

Felis manul Pallas

Plate facing p. 96

[RACES IN INDIA : *manul* Pallas, *nigripecta* Hodgson, *ferruginea* (Ognev)]

Size. That of a small domestic cat.

Distinctive Characters. Pallas's Cat (sub-genus, *Octolobus*) is a small, long-tailed Cat, distinctive in its broad head, low forehead, and short widely separated ears, which appear to be set very low behind the cheeks, giving the cat a strange and peculiar aspect.

Observation of the behaviour of a specimen in captivity suggested an explanation of its low forehead and the peculiar set of its ears. When behind some rock or point of vantage watching its prey, this species need not lower its ears in the accustomed manner of Cats. It is able to reveal a relatively small part of its head without depressing or partially folding its ears, a habit which must to a certain extent interfere with quick hearing in other species.

The prevailing colour of the face is grey, that of the neck, back, and body silvery or iron grey. The hairs on the back are sooty black at the base, then white, and again black at the tip. Traces of dark transverse stripes appear on the loins and sometimes on the limbs. The distal portion of the tail is ringed and ends in a black tip. The fur of the throat, chest, belly, and thighs is considerably longer than on the flanks. It is perhaps an adaptation, which gives protection to the Cat when lying or sleeping on snow-covered or frozen ground. A parallel lengthening of the hairs on the thigh and underparts of the body is seen in the yak which, like Pallas's Cat, is a denizen of the bleak uplands of Ladak and Tibet.

Distribution. A central Asian species, occurring within our limits in Ladak and Tibet.

Habits. Nothing is known about the habits of this Cat in the wild state. It is said to live among rocks and to prey on small animals and birds. In captivity, its behaviour was distinctive from that usual in most other small felines. It showed no fear of spectators nor a desire to avoid them and was very silent, never uttering the familiar snarling growl or hiss. Its mew is described as recalling a ' combination of the bark of a small dog and the hoot of an owl.'

THE CHEETAH, or HUNTING LEOPARD

Acinonyx jubatus (Schreber)

Plate facing p. 96

[RACE IN INDIA : *venaticus* (Griffith)]

Size. Head and body, a little over 3 ft. (90 cm.); tail, about a foot (30 cm.) less.

Distinctive Characters. The Cheetah looks like a long-legged, slim-built leopard. Distinctive, however, is its small round head, relatively smaller than that of any of the other Cats. Distinctive also in profile is the steep outline of the forehead and dome-like cranium. It is sometimes said incorrectly that the Cheetah has non-retractile claws. Its claws are almost, if not quite, as retractile as the claws of some Cats. Their peculiarity lies in the total absence of claw sheaths ; these sheaths are present in varying degrees of development in all Cats. Hence the Cheetah's claws are always bared. Its coat varies from tawny to pale buff and is heavily patterned with solid close-set black spots.

Distribution. The Cheetah's range extends over the greater part of Africa and through the desert countries of south-western Asia into India. like the Lion, the Cheetah came to India by way of our north-western passes. It established itself in the plains and lower hills of northern and central India straggling southwards as far as the Deccan and Mysore. Whether the Cheetah still survives in the wild state in India or other parts of Asia is not known, but it was not infrequently met with up to fifty years ago.

Habits. When the Cheetah lived in India, it lived most commonly in low rugged hills, and came down from its lair amidst rocks and boulders to hunt in the neighbouring plains. It hunted gazelle and antelope, and probably smaller animals and birds. Sometimes it attacked goats and sheep. Its way of hunting is suggestive both of the hunting of cats and the hunting of dogs. Crouching belly-to-earth the Cheetah takes advantage of every inch of cover or inequality of ground, stalking its prey in the manner of a cat. But the prey is not taken with a cat's sudden unexpected leap. It is pursued as dogs pursue their prey, in open chase. The Cheetah's initial burst of speed is amazing. It can attain a speed of 66 miles (110 km.) an hour, faster than the fastest greyhound, and can keep it up for about 400 yards (366 m.). This exceptional speed was developed to one purpose, the capture of fleet-footed prey ; and all those characters which distinguish the Cheetah from other Cats, the small head, the narrow deep chest and body, the long sinewy limbs, and the bared claws which secure firmer hold on the ground, arose from its accustomed way of hunting antelope, gazelle, and other swift-running prey. For centuries the Cheetah, tamed and trained, has been kept by man and used in hunting. In India, the Cheetah is taken blindfolded to the scene of the hunt. It is unhooded and released in the proximity of a herd of antelope. A short crouching stalk, a few bounds of great length and rapidity, and the hunt is over. Either the quarry escapes, or the Cheetah fells it by means of the powerful dew-claw hooked into a hindquarter or by knocking its feet from under it, and grips it in a stranglehold by the throat; the victim's throat is cut and the captor rewarded with a drink of warm blood collected in its accustomed feeding bowl.

Nothing is known or recorded of the breeding habits of the Cheetah in India.

The last authentic record of the Cheetah in India is of the three males wantonly shot together in Korea, Bastar Dt., M. P. in 1948.

4. Civets

CIVETS, PALM CIVETS, Linsangs, and Bear-Cats, a diverse assemblage of animals, are grouped in a single family, the **Viverridae**. The nearest relatives of the family are the Cats (Felidae).

While Cats and Civets show certain resemblances in structure, they differ in many ways. No one could mistake a Civet for a Cat. A Civet is long in body and short in limb. It has an elongate head and pointed muzzle, quite distinct from the long limbs, rounded head, and flattened muzzle of a Cat. Different habits of life account for these differences in structure. Cats live wholly by hunting. Civets do not ; many live partly or even mainly on vegetable food. As such the whole build of a Civet shows a lesser degree of fitness for a predatory life. Contrasted with the short, sturdy jaws of a Cat which are specially designed for gripping struggling prey, the jaws of Civets are long and slender, their canine teeth are comparatively feeble, and their shorter claws less powerful. Yet, though less well equipped as beasts of prey, these animals are well fitted for their particular ways of earning a livelihood.

STRUCTURE IN RELATION TO HABITS

To secure their food, Civets have keen eyes, a sharp sense of smell, and acute hearing. The facial vibrissae or whiskers, prominent in these animals, are very mobile and can be switched backwards and forwards. A captive Himalayan Palm Civet was seen always to touch its food with its whiskers before eating. It seemed to use them to sense the nature of its meal.

Feet. When they hunt, Civets hunt in the manner of Cats, taking prey by surprise, stalking it stealthily or pouncing on it from hiding. Some of the family live more by hunting than the others. The Linsangs (*Prionodon*), for example, live almost entirely on animals which they kill. They are the most Cat-like of all Civets. Among other things, their feet are built much like those of Cats, the claws well protected with sheaths and fully retractile. The feline characters of these Civets are in keeping with their highly predatory habits. In other members of the tribe, true civets (Viverrinae) and tree civets (Paradoxurinae), the feet are less highly specialised for the capture of prey. The claws vary in retractability. They are bare in some species and more or less protected with sheaths in others. These animals depend less on hunting for a livelihood and live partly on animal and partly on vegetable food. But different ways of living and food-getting have produced marked differences among them. The true civets, though they can climb well, rarely climb trees for their food. They seek it on the ground. Their feet are built for terrestrial progress. They walk on their toes. Their paws are small and compact. The first digit on the fore-and the hindfoot, set well above the other toes, is functionless. The pads under the feet are well cushioned and the soles well covered with hair. These characters adapt the feet better to movement on the ground. Quite different are the feet of tree civets. These animals live and find much of their food on trees. Their feet are built for climbing. Their gait is almost plantigrade ; in walking, practically the entire sole is pressed to the ground. The foot is short and broad, all the toes are set a-level, and all of them function. The sole-pads are broad and the soles hairless. All these characters are designed to adapt the feet for climbing and securing a better hold on branches. Different and distinctive also is the build of tree-climbing civets. They have longer and more sinuous bodies and longer tails. Each group, as we see, is fitted for its particular way of earning its livelihood, the Cat-like Linsangs to take their prey by hunting, the true civets to secure their food on the ground, and the tree civets to take it in trees. Let us now consider the teeth of these animals in relation to their feeding habits.

Teeth. The meat-eating Linsangs have molar teeth with sharp blade-like crowns, much like the molars of Cats. The molars of omnivorous Civets are different in design. They are built for both cutting up meat and grinding vegetable substances. How far they serve this double purpose depends on the extent to which the owner is omnivorous. The true civets live on meat and vegetable matter. They have broad-crowned many-cusped molars designed both for cutting and grinding. The palm civets are more herbivorous than carnivorous. Their molar teeth have yet broader crowns and are even less specialised for meat-eating than the true civets. These animals show the intimate connection between teeth and diet. Here within a single family we see a marked variation in the form and character of teeth, based entirely on the different types of food the different species eat. One more point in relation to food. Civets have smooth tongues. The sharp conical papillae which convert a Cat's tongue into a rasp are absent. Civets have no need for such a rasp to lick bones clean. They eat as dogs eat, crushing and swallowing the bones of the small animals they kill. So much for general structure ; though their equipment as beasts of prey is inferior to the Cats, Civets, as we see, are well fitted for their humbler role in life. Let us now consider the life of these animals in relation to their surroundings, in relation to their inanimate and animate environment.

CIVETS AND THEIR SURROUNDINGS

The home of the Civets. Civets are found all over the Oriental Region
and in Africa, whence they have passed into southern Europe ;
but the headquarters of the family appears to be India and the
Malay countries, where the largest number of species live. There
were true civets (*Viverra*) living in India in prehistoric times. Their
fossil remains have been discovered in a cavern in Madras and in the
rocks of the Siwalik Hills. They are obviously ancient inhabitants
of the tropical forests of the Old World. In the Indo-Malayan
region, the great majority of the family keep to humid tracts where
there is a heavy or a good rainfall. Rain forests, rich wood and
grasslands are their chosen habitat. In this terrain they live from
plains level to an altitude of about 7000 ft. (2135 m.). This is about
the limit of their upward range in the Himalayas and the south
Indian hills. Two species only, the Small Indian Civet and the Common Palm Civet, have succeeded in establishing themselves in arid
and open country. Their territory extends into the dry scrub lands
of central India and Rajputana, though not into the actual true desert
zone beyond. Compared with the Cats it may be said that Civets,
as a group, show a lesser degree of adaptability to varying conditions of environment. Adaptations to conditions of climate are
seen mainly in the growth of a long and luxuriant winter coat, which
may be supplemented by a soft warm vesture of woolly under-fur.
The luxuriance of the winter coat appears to depend but little on
altitude. Civets living near the Himalayan foothills have as fine
coats in winter as those inhabiting the mountains. Latitude makes
a difference. Civets in southern India, where the difference between
summer and winter temperatures is less marked, show but little
difference in their summer and winter pelage. The finest winter
coats are developed by animals living in the cold dry climate of the
western Himalayas, or in the arid lands of central India and Rajputana, where there is little humidity and where extremes of heat
and cold obtain. The shedding of the winter coat and its replace-
ment by the short sleek summer pelage varies with the time of onset
of the hot weather in different latitudes. While there is much variation in colour and markings, even among individuals of a species
living in the same area, there is little difference in colour and pattern
between Civets inhabiting different geographical areas. There is
however this about colour and markings in relation to geography.
Diffused and faint in the heavy winter coat, markings become more
evident in the short summer pelage. The temporary obliteration of
the pattern is more pronounced in northerly forms; the pattern is
obscured by a luxuriant winter coat. It is less evident in Civets inhabiting southerly latitudes, where the difference between the summer
and winter coat is less marked.

Of the more intimate life of these animals in relation to the surroundings, we know little. Does the monsoon bring about any

change in the habits of life ? What are their movements in relation to food, in relation to changes of climate ? In the south Indian hill ranges the ripening of the coffee berries brings about a large concentration of palm civets around the coffee estates ; they disperse when the fruiting season is over. But there is much more to be learnt, and such knowledge can only come from continued observation in the field. Let us now turn to the life of Civets in relation to their animate environment, in relation to man and other animals living in the neighbourhood.

CIVETS AND THEIR NEIGHBOURS

As beasts of prey, Civets as we have seen play a lesser role. As hunters they are a check on a host of lesser creatures, small animals, birds, reptiles, etc.

Nocturnal and diurnal animals. The majority of Civets seek their food by night. Now there is this to be said about nocturnal and diurnal animals ; though living together in the same area they may never meet, simply because they become active at different times. Thus the carnivores and the herbivores which they eat make up more or less distinct nocturnal and diurnal food chains. Night-roaming carnivores are linked up with and live upon night-roaming herbivores, while daylight produces a different set of hunters and hunted. There are of course predators and prey which feed both by day and by night, and others which feed only at dusk or at dawn, while many nocturnal animals come out to feed on dark and cloudy days. But, taken as a whole, an animal community has its set of day- and night-workers which, working at different times, collectively help to maintain an optimum density of population. This influence of day and night on the character of animal communities is more marked in tropical and sub-tropical countries where the majority of animals are nocturnal ; but as one travels into temperate lands, nocturnal animals tend to become fewer, till in the Polar regions there are no nocturnal animals at all. Here in India we have still much to learn about the influence of night and day on the life of our varied animal communities. We know little that is exact about when the different species come out to feed, or about their food relationships, or to what extent their nocturnal movements are influenced by temperature and other factors. All this remains a subject for study and investigation.

Stink-glands and warning colours. While Civets feed on smaller animals they themselves become the prey of the larger carnivores. What are their means of defence ? Apart from their equipment of tooth and claw, Civets are armed with yet another defensive device, i.e. stink-glands. When in imminent danger, some Civets discharge a vile stream of yellow fluid at the attacker, the product of the anal glands. It is the animal's extreme defence, used when there is no other means of escape. So unexpected, so acrid is this discharge, so repellent and nauseating its odour, that it temporarily blinds, discomfits, or otherwise frustrates the attacker, and gives the Civet a chance to escape. Most Civets are equipped with this means of defence. Nauseous fumes or fluids discharged in self-protection are common weapons in the armoury of Nature. They are used by diverse animals, including man, who in adopting this weapon increased its deadliness a thousandfold. Man is intelligent ! With poison gas, he is able to kill his fellowmen with devastating effect ! But to come back to less intelligent animals, there is an interesting point about this means of defence in animals. It is usually associated with a particular type of coloration. Animals which discharge nauseous fumes or fluids generally wear a special livery. Contrary to what is usual in Nature, their colour and markings advertise rather than conceal their presence. This particular livery is described as warning coloration. It is explained that after experiencing the malodorous and repellent character of its victim an enemy learns more easily to recognise a fellow of its species because of its bold and conspicuous display of colour. It associates repellent qualities with such colour and pattern and avoids animals which wear it. Warning colours are displayed by nauseous insects, such as stink bugs and blister beetles. Many wear red and yellow boldly banded with black. Mammals with defensive stink-glands have their special warning display which becomes prominent in time of danger. Skunks and polecats, notorious for the nauseous fluids discharged from their anal glands, have their faces masked with bold black and white patches. Under stress of excitement the long black hairs of a polecat's body stand erect displaying its contrasting white or yellow under-fur. A sombre, otherwise protective livery, is converted in time of danger into one that is bold and conspicuous. Civets have the same type of coloration. They wear ' masks ' marked with dark and light bands. In excitement there is the same bristling up of the longer dark hairs of coat and crest, and the same vivid display of light-coloured under-fur. As with skunks and polecats, the colouring is associated with their special and repellent means of defence. It is warning coloration which enemies remember and avoid. And it would seem, the more likelihood there is of attack the more conspicuous the warning colour and pattern. It is pointed out that Chinese palm civets, living in the northern areas of their range in China and Burma where they have many enemies, are boldly masked in black and white ; whilst civets of this species living in the Andamans where there are scarcely any enemy carnivores to warn off wear much less conspicuous facial masks. **(Plate facing p. 79)**

The influence of man. Man and his works have influenced the life and habits of these animals. Like other mammals many civets have become partly parasitic on man. The various species, particularly where common and numerous, supplement their food supply by invading human domains to prey on poultry, and on rats and other vermin which flourish in such numbers in and around human settlements. Besides, to these omnivorous animals there is the added inducement of fruit plantations where so much food is to be had for the taking. So much so, that some individuals depend more or less on human effort for food and shelter. Many Small Indian Civets (*Viverricula indica*) and Common Palm Civets (*Paradoxurus hermaphroditus*) have forsaken the forests to live permanently in villages, or even in crowded cities, finding shelter in drains or in the roofs of houses, where they have ample opportunities for stealing food.

Civets and plants. Then there is also a relationship between civets and plants. As many of them are fruit eaters they must play some part in the dispersal of seeds, which they pass out in their droppings. Accumulations of seeds of the coffee berry passed by palm civets are sought after by estate coolies who add the recovered beans to their store for the market. Seeds of the common peepul tree are swallowed and dispersed in the same way by these animals.

FAMILY LIFE AND CARE OF THE YOUNG

Means of communication. Civets, as far as we know, are silent animals. Except for the Binturong or Bear-Cat, which is said to howl loudly in its forests and to utter low growls and hissing sounds when on the prowl, none of the family appear to give out calls or communicate vocally with one another. These animals apparently have other means of communication. This is effected by scent glands, which leave their powerful odour over the trail where a civet has passed.

Scent glands. Except for the Linsangs, which are more Cat-like than other members of the tribe, all civets possess scent glands. In fact the name 'civet' is derived from the Arabic term *zabat*, a term given to the scent derived from these glands. The structure of these scent glands differs in different civets. It may differ to some extent even among males and females of the same species. In the true civets (*Viverra* and *Viverricula*) the scent gland, situated in the perineal area, can be seen externally as a fairly large pouch with hairy swollen lips which close and open it. The scent glands of palm civets and their kin (Paradoxurinae) are quite different and less elaborate in structure. The secretion of the gland is discharged into a fold of skin, not into a pouch. The secretion contains free ammonia, resin, fat, and a volatile oil to which its odoriferous properties are due.

Care of the young. There is little known about the family life of civets. How long the sexes remain together is not known. These animals are usually found solitary, and the period of association between parents is apparently brief. Nor do we know whether civets have a definite breeding season. The young of the Small Indian Civet appear at any time of the year. As with other animals, there may be a period when breeding activity is more marked. Baby Palm Civets (*P. hermaphroditus*) are seen more commonly between October and December. For a nursery, civets usually use a hole in a tree, or a shelter under overhanging rocks. Species which have taken to living near man may bring up a family under the rafters of a house, or in a drain, or in some such place of concealment. How long the young remain with the mother is not recorded, nor do we know the age at which these animals become fully adult. It is reported of the Himalayan Palm Civet (*Paguma larvata*) that the growth of the young was much more rapid than with kittens or puppies; when only three months old they almost equalled their parents in size. The colouring of the young usually differs from the adult in this, that the bold face markings which make up part of the warning livery are less evident in baby civets. The warning colours are apparently fully attained only when the animals leave the protection of the mother and fend for themselves. From records of animals kept in captivity the average span of life appears to be from twelve to fifteen years.

Uses of Civets. The Genet, a species of civet found in southern Europe and Africa, appears to have functioned as a domestic cat among the ancient Greeks ; and so recently as the times of Belon, we are told by him that genets were common and tame at Constantinople. Civets are good ratters and great destroyers of these vermin. Those living in or near human dwellings do man a real service by helping to reduce the swarms of rats which infest our fields and houses. The Threebanded Palm Civet of Tenasserim (*Hemigalus*), which feeds largely on squirrels, is described as a factor in keeping down the numbers of those rodents, which are so destructive in coco-nut plantations. Apart from their service to man as exterminators of pests, the secretion of their scent glands is used both for perfumery and medicinal purposes. In India it is held to have valuable medicinal and aphrodisiac properties. In this country the secretion is collected from the scent glands of the Large Indian Civet (*V. zibetha*) and to a greater extent from the Small Indian Civet (*V. indica*). It is much sought after by the Brahmins of Malabar, and as much as Rs 10 per tola (12 gm.) is paid for the pure essence. The civet essence obtained from the bazaars is much adulterated with butter and oil to increase its weight. The so-called civet perfume of commerce which is imported into India comes from America. It is not obtained from civets but is taken from the beaver. In India the best prices are paid for the entire pouch cut from a freshly killed animal. The more usual method of collection is to scrape the secretion from the pouch with a wooden spoon. Small Indian Civets are kept at Kolar and in other places in east Mysore for the collection of ' civet '. ' Civet ' is also used for flavouring tobacco particularly by the Javanese.

THE SPOTTED LINSANG, or TIGER-CIVET

Prionodon pardicolor Hodgson

Plate facing p. 112

[RACE IN INDIA : *pardicolor* Hodgson]

Local Names. Bhotia *zik chum* ; Lepcha *suilyu, silu.*

Size. Head and body, about 15 inches (37 cm.); tail, an inch (2.5 cm.) or so less ; weight, 1¼ lb. (570 gm.).

Distinctive Characters. While typically civet-like in build, with pointed muzzle, elongate body, and short limbs, its golden colouring and bold pattern of large black spots distinguish it at once from other civets. The absence of scent glands in both sexes is also distinctive.

Distribution. Nepal, Sikkim, Assam, extending into upper Burma, and southern China.

Habits. This beautiful civet is nowhere common. It lives in mountain and hill forests and has been taken at levels varying from 500 ft. (150 m.) to 6000 ft. (1850 m.). Hodgson wrote about these animals in Nepal wellnigh a hundred years ago, and to this day but little has been added to our knowledge of their habits. Linsangs, as we have seen, show a remarkable combination of feline characters in their structure ; they are equally Cat-like in their ways. They spring and climb with great power and live mainly by hunting. Their prey is small mammals, and more commonly birds, which they capture both on trees and on the ground. While the feet of the Linsang appear to be better adapted to terrestrial progress, it is perfectly at home on trees, which are its accustomed shelter. A specimen kept in confinement was fierce and impatient, but by degrees became gentle and playful and, when allowed to leave its cage in search of sparrows and other small birds, it caught them with great skill, leaping on them from its hiding place in the tall grass. Hodgson, writing of another captive taken in Darjeeling, says that it was very gentle and fond of being petted and very sensitive to cold. It refused fish, eggs, and fruit, and lived only on raw meat. It never uttered a sound and was perfectly free from all odour.

These animals are said to breed in hollows in trees. Breeding time is in February and again in August, there being two litters a year. The number of young produced is two.

THE LARGE INDIAN CIVET

Viverra zibetha Linnaeus

Plate facing p. 97

[RACES IN INDIA : *zibetha* Linnaeus, *picta* Wroughton]

Local Names. Hindi *kattas* (used for several other animals also) ; Ben. *mach bhondar, bagdos, pudo gaula* ; Nepal Terai *bhran* ; Bhotia *kung*.

Size. Head and body, about 2 ft. 8 in. (80 cm.) ; tail, 1 ft. 6 in. (45 cm.). Males and females do not differ much in size.

Distinctive Characters. A sturdily built animal with a long head, long compressed body, and short stumpy legs, a build typical of true civets. An erectile crest of long deep-black hair runs down the centre of the back. This crest is distinctive and differentiates the large civet (*Viverra*) from the small civets (*Viverricula*). General coloration dark hoary grey, usually washed with yellowish or brown. Dark bands may ornament chest and shoulders and form loops and rosettes on the hindquarters. The markings are not always discernible and are usually obscured in the more luxuriant winter coat.

Distribution. Nepal, Sikkim, Bhutan, upper Bengal, and Assam, extending eastwards into Burma, southern China, Siam, and the Malay peninsula.

Habits. The Large Indian Civet is a solitary creature sheltering in woods, under bushes, or in heavy scrub jungle, sleeping by day and coming out to hunt by night. It is one of the commonest carnivores in Sikkim and around Darjeeling. It preys on small animals and birds, and is destructive to poultry. Like most carnivores it feeds on anything worth killing ; as such, its food may include snakes, frogs, crabs, and even insects. Equally addicted to a vegetable diet, berries, fruits, and roots provide a seasonal supplement to its animal food. It is recorded as breeding between May and June and is said to have three to four young. The scent glands are large in this animal, measuring about 2.5 in. × 1.5 in. (6 cm. × 4 cm.). Dogs are greatly excited by the scent and are said to leave that of any other animal for it.

A second species of large civet, the **Malabar Civet** (*V. megaspila* Blyth. RACE IN INDIA : *civettina* Blyth) was once very common in the coastal districts of Malabar and Travancore. It lived in the wooded plains and in the adjoining hill slopes. But at the present time it is scarcely ever seen and appears to be nearing extinction.

THE SMALL INDIAN CIVET

Viverricula indica (Desmarest)

Plate facing p. 97

[RACES IN INDIA : *indica* (Desmarest), *bengalensis* Gray & Hardwicke, *deserti* Bonhote, *wellsi* Pocock, *baptistae* Pocock. CEYLON : *mayori* Pocock]

Local Names. Hindi *kasturi* ; Ben. *gando gaula, gandhagokul* ; Deccan *mushak billi* ; Mar. *jowadi manjur* ; Kan. *poonagubekku, poonugu kotthi* ; Tel. *punagu pilli* ; Tamil *punagu poonay* ; Mal. *meru* ; Bur. *chaung kado*.

Size. A well-grown adult male is slightly over 3 ft. (90 cm.) in entire length,. the tail being a little over a foot (30 cm.) long. Weight 6-8 lb. (3-4 kg.).

Distinctive Characters. A tawny grey or greyish brown animal, lined and streaked on back and croup ; spotted more or less in rows along the flanks. There are usually some cross bars on the neck. Typically civet-like in build, the absence of the dorsal crest distinguishes it from the Large Indian Civet.

Distribution. The peninsula of India from Sind, the Punjab, and the Himalayan foothills southwards to Cape Comorin and Ceylon. Eastwards its range extends to Burma, southern China, and the Malay countries. Five different races are recognised in India, the distinctions between them being based on colour, size, and cranial and other characters.

Habits. Dry or moist conditions make no difference to the choice of habitat of this civet, but it keeps out of heavy forest and prefers long grass or scrub to live in. It shelters in holes or under rocks or lies up in grass or under bushes. Many live near villages and some straggle into crowded towns finding refuge in drains and outhouses. Like other civets its usual habit is to hunt by night. Though it climbs well and can scale a vertical trunk with ease, it seeks its food on the ground, preying on rats, squirrels, small birds, lizards, insects and their grubs, on anything which it can catch and kill. Given opportunity it preys on poultry. This food is varied with fruits, roots, and other vegetable matter. It has a fondness for the berries of the *ber* tree. The young are seen at all times of the year. There does not appear to be any marked period of breeding activity. The nursery selected is usually a small chamber excavated at the end of a short burrow, usually dug under a rock or at the base of a tree, or in a field drain. The care of the young is left entirely to the mother as pairs are seldom seen together. Four to five young may be produced at birth. The young produce a piercingly loud cat-like *meow*. The adult civet when contented and happy makes a *tick-tick* like clicking noise. This civet is easily tamed. Some are kept under domestication for the regular extraction of 'civet' from the scent glands.

THE COMMON PALM CIVET, OR TODDY CAT

Paradoxurus hermaphroditus (Pallas)

Plates facing pp. 79, 97

[RACES IN INDIA : *hermaphroditus* (Pallas), *bondar* (Desmarest), *pallasi* Gray, *laneus* Pocock, *vellerosus* Pocock, *scindiae* Pocock, *nictitatans* Taylor. CEYLON: *hermaphroditus* (Pallas)]

Local Names. Hindi *lakati, khatas* ; in the South *menuri* ; Ben. *bhondar* ; Mar. *ud manjar* ; Kan. *mara bekku, mantta* ; Tel. *manu pilli* ; Tamil & Mal. *marra nai, marra meru*.

Size. Head and body, about 2 ft. (60 cm.) ; tail, of equal length ; weight, 6-10 lb. (2.7-4.5 kg.).

Distinctive Characters. A black or blackish-brown civet with long coarse hair. Underwool, when present, whitish, buff, or a rich yellow ; usually hidden in the heavier winter coat. When this is shed the new coat, before it is fully grown, generally shows a pattern of longitudinal stripes on the back and spots on the flanks, shoulders, and thighs. The limbs are always black or dark brown. Facial markings variable, the most usual pattern is a white patch or spot below the eye, sometimes one above it, and one on each side of the nose.

Distribution. Kashmir, the Himalayas, and Assam southwards through the whole of the Peninsula, except in the desert zones of Sind, the Punjab, and the old N.W.F.P. Eastwards, Burma and the Indo-Chinese and Malay countries.

Habits. This civet is more common and abundant in well-wooded regions. It lives much on trees, lying curled up by day among the branches or in a hole in the trunk. Near towns and villages large mango trees or palm trees are a favourite shelter. But many have forsaken an arboreal existence and have adapted themselves to a life in human settlements, even in the heart of crowded cities, selecting a roof, an outhouse, or drain as a place of hiding. They seek their food at night, in trees or on the ground, killing birds and small mammals and feeding also on fruit. Those which have become partly parasitic on man prey on rats and mice which swarm round his dwellings, become poultry thieves, and raid plantations. Pineapple and coffee plantations are a favourite resort in the fruiting season ; and where palms are tapped for toddy these civets are known to climb the trees to steal the sweet juice which collects overnight in the pots. They are easily tamed, becoming quite domestic and even affectionate.

The young are born at all seasons and are usually produced in holes in trees or under a shelter of rocks. The usual litter is from three to four.

A second species, the **Brown Palm Civet** (*P. jerdoni* Blanford) is found in North Kanara and the hill ranges of south India. A shy forest animal, rarely entering houses, it is distinctive in its rich deep brown colouring. Its general habits are similar to those of the *jerdoni* Blanford and *caniscus* Pocock. They attain sexual maturity at about 11 months.

THE HIMALAYAN PALM CIVET

Paguma larvata (Hamilton-Smith)

Plates facing pp. 79, 97

[RACES IN INDIA : *grayi* (Bennett), *wroughtoni* Schwarz, *neglecta* Pocock. ANDAMANS : *tytleri* (Tytler)]

Size. Average length of head and body, 2 ft. (60 cm.) ; tail, about the same ; weight, 8-11 lb. (3.6-5.0 kg.).

Distinctive Characters. The Himalayan Palm Civet is distinguished from other Indian civets by its white whiskers and by the absence of any trace of spots or stripes on its body. Its coat ranges from uniform grey to tawny ; the underparts white. Underwool brownish, grey, or sooty. Facial markings, variable ; usually a white band on the forehead and nose, another beneath the ears passing over the cheeks, and a blotch below each eye.

Distribution. Kashmir, western, central, and eastern Himalayas, and the Assam hill ranges. Beyond our limits its range extends eastwards into Burma, and the Indo-Chinese and Malay countries, the Andaman Islands. Three Indian races are recognised. One race occurs in the Andaman Islands.

Habits. The habits of the Himalayan Palm Civet are very similar to those of the Common Palm Civet. It lives in mountain and hill forests sheltering in holes in trees, and hunting its food in the treetops or on the ground. In diet, it is perhaps more of a vegetable feeder than the Common Palm Civet. It lives mainly on fruit ; but like all civets it preys on such small animals and birds as it can capture and kill. Hodgson, writing of a caged animal, says that it thrived on boiled rice and fruits, which it preferred to animal food. When set at liberty, it would lie in waiting for sparrows and mynahs, springing on them from cover like a cat. It would also pounce unerringly on sparrows which entered its cage to pick up grains of boiled rice. Of another captive pair it is written that the female, when given an apple, usually took it in her forepaws, and squatting up on her haunches ate it in the manner of a squirrel eating a nut. Hodgson describes his caged specimen as ' very cleanly, its body ordinarily emitted no unpleasant smell but, when it was irritated, it exhaled a most unpleasant stench, caused by a discharge of a thin yellow fluid from four pores, two of which are placed on either side of the anal opening '. This was obviously a discharge from the anal glands, described when discussing the methods of defence of these animals.

In Nepal this civet breeds in holes in trees. A litter of four young was found on one occasion. A female in the Zoological Gardens, London, produced a litter of three during the summer.

THE BINTURONG, or BEAR-CAT

Arctictis binturong (Raffles)

Plate facing p. 97

[RACE IN INDIA : *albifrons* (F. Cuvier)]

Local Names. Assamese *young* ; Bur. *myouk kya.*

Size. Head and body, 2 ft. 6 in. (75 cm.) to 3 ft. (90 cm.) ; tail, 2 ft. 4 in. (70 cm.).

Distinctive Characters. The Binturong is easily distinguished from other civets. Its tufted ears, its long shaggy coat suggestive of a bear, its tail markedly thick at the base and covered with large bristling hairs, longer than those of the coat, are distinctive. Colour, very variable : mostly black but an intermingling of partly white and buff hairs may give the coat a grizzled appearance. In some animals the white and buff is so pronounced that the coat takes a straw-coloured or grey tinge.

Distribution. In India, the range covers Nepal, Sikkim, Bhutan, Assam, extending into Burma and the Malay countries. Two races are recognised. The Indian form is said to be distinctive in its fuller and more luxuriant winter coat and a more marked tendency to a grizzled coloration.

Habits. The Binturong is a creature of dense forests. It is mainly arboreal and spends the day curled up in a hole in a tree, its head tucked well under its bushy tail. These animals come out at dusk to seek their food. Their movements through the trees are slow and deliberate, but they climb with ease and use their tails to aid their climbing. The tail, very muscular at the base, is prehensile at the tip and is hitched round a branch as an anchorage, particularly when descending. Baby Binturongs are able to support themselves by the extremity of the tail alone. Like other civets, Binturongs are omnivorous, living on small animals, birds, insects, and fruits. When on the prowl they are said to grunt and to make a hissing sound by expelling air through partly opened lips. From the build of the animal it would seem that most of its food is obtained in trees. The species, though particularly fierce, when taken young is easily tamed, becoming very gentle and playful. Because of its secretive nocturnal mode of life, the animal is rarely seen and nothing is known of its breeding habits.

5. Mongooses

OUR COMMON MONGOOSE, so frequently exhibited by wandering snake charmers, is familiar to most people in India. In appearance it is typical of its family, somewhat like a ferret in build and movement, long-bodied, short-limbed, with bright beady eyes, a sharp snout, and a trailing bushy tail. Naturalists first classified these animals in one of the primary subdivisions of the Civet family ; but as they possess a number of structural characters which distinguish them clearly from civets, mongooses are now grouped in a family by themselves, the **Herpestidae.** One can, for example, immediately distinguish a mongoose from a civet by the size and shape of its ears. Civets have comparatively large ears. The ears of a mongoose are more or less semi-circular in shape, and so small that they never project above its head or nape. The structure of its ear is also different. It is made up of a series of complicated folds which can shut down over one another so as to completely close the ear-opening. Then, civets have short-clawed compact feet. The feet of a mongoose splay out more, the digits are freer, and the claws are long, sometimes very long. Again our mongooses have no perfume glands. Except for the linsangs, all civets have them. Like civets, all mongooses have anal glands ; but the anus in these animals is enclosed in a naked glandular sac, a thing not seen in civets. Lastly there is a difference in habits. Mongooses as a family are more predatory than civets. They live mainly by hunting, while most civets have taken largely to a vegetable diet.

STRUCTURE IN RELATION TO HABITS

Mongooses take vegetable food, but have a preference for meat. This is shown in the structure of their teeth which are compressed, sharp-bladed, meat-cutting teeth. Their manner of hunting is distinctive. Cats and civets hunt by stealth, they take their prey by crafty approach or by pouncing upon it from ambush. The method of the mongoose is direct, open, and headlong attack. Seeing its prey, a mongoose goes for it, but if the distance is too far for a rush or pounce, it will stalk for a sufficiently near approach. Or following its quarry by scent, a mongoose may trail it to its burrow and, entering, dig its victim out. Its pointed head, small ears, lissom body, and short legs are well fitted to give the mongoose easy entry. The habit explains its ferret-like build. Ferrets and weasels hunt in the same way.

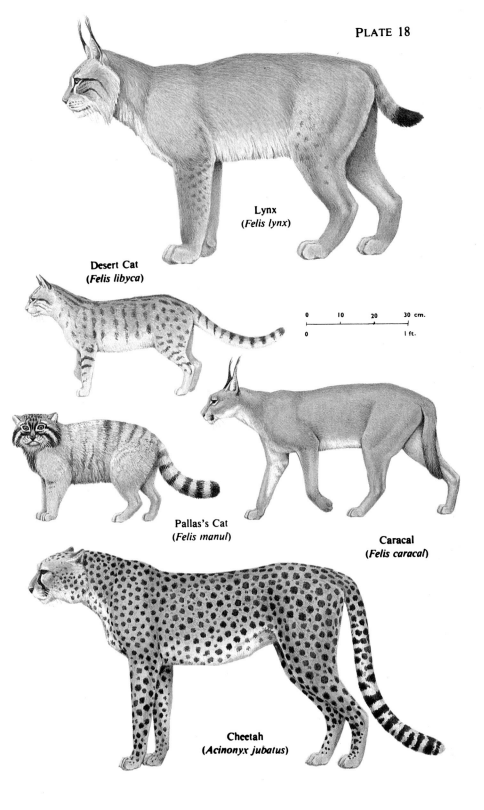

PLATE 18

Lynx
(*Felis lynx*)

Desert Cat
(*Felis libyca*)

0   10   20   30 cm.

0   1 ft.

Pallas's Cat
(*Felis manul*)

Caracal
(*Felis caracal*)

Cheetah
(*Acinonyx jubatus*)

PLATE 19

Large Indian Civet
(*Viverra zibetha*)

Small Indian Civet
(*Viverricula indica*)

Toddy Cat
(*Paradoxurus hermaphroditus*)

Himalayan Palm Civet
(*Paguma larvata*)

Binturong
(*Arctictis binturong*)

0   10   20   30 cm.

0   1 ft.

The claws, especially long and well-developed in the forefeet, are digging claws; while the contrivance for closing the ear, which we have noted, is designed, apparently, to keep out dust and dirt when burrowing. When hunting, a mongoose often sits up on its haunches, or stands on its hindlegs, to take a look around, a habit which must increase the range of vision of these low-bodied animals. The prey when caught is bitten and crunched to death and eaten, or the mongoose is content with drinking its blood. This is what usually happens when there is wholesale slaughter in a poultry-yard. Birds' eggs, a favoured food, are held in the forepaws, a hole is bitten into the egg, and its contents sucked out. More usually, lifting the egg in its paw, the mongoose rears up on its hindlegs and bangs one end of the egg on the floor. The Ruddy Mongoose (*H. smithi*) smashes the shells of large snails by beating them against stones; this is also the Crabeating Mongoose's way of dealing with crabs and hard-shelled molluscs.

LIFE IN RELATION TO SURROUNDINGS

Tropical Africa is believed to be the original home of mongooses. This is where most genera of mongooses live. A single genus, *Herpestes*, has spread from Africa to Spain and the southern parts of the Asiatic continent. Six species of this genus inhabit southern Asia. All of them are found in India. Of these, two, the Common Mongoose (*H. edwardsi*) and the Small Indian Mongoose (*H. auropunctatus*) have adapted themselves to every condition of climate and surroundings. They live in cultivated lands, jungle, or arid desert, in the plains or in mountain forests 7000 ft. (2135 m.) up in the Himalayas. In India all the other species keep to hill forests.

Colour and geography. As with other animals, different conditions of life in different habitats influence the coloration of mongooses. The coat of the Common Mongoose (*H. edwardsi*) has a grizzled, ' pepper and salt ' appearance. This is because each hair is alternately ringed with black and white. In mongooses from northern India the white rings to the hairs are more prominent and give the whole coat a paler hue. In the southern part of the Peninsula the black ringing is more dominant and the tone of the coat becomes darker. In the desert zones of Sind, Baluchistan, and north-west India, the rings on the hairs are often red and the coat takes on a bright ferruginous tint. But the pale-coloured animals found in this region appear to be the true desert form—the red form is a desert variant. This tendency to erythrism is seen in many desert animals. The Small Indian Mongooses (*H. auropunctatus*) which inhabit our north-western deserts are also paler in colour than those living in the humid lands further east. The various geographical races based on colour distinctions are difficult to determine. Animals living in one geographical area tend to intergrade in colour with those inhabiting adjoining areas, and again mongooses identical in colour may be found in the middle of different racial zones.

Size and geography. Different conditions of environment influence the size attained by the Small Indian Mongoose (*H. auropunctatus*). Those living in the deserts are the smallest in build. As one travels eastward these mongooses increase in size, the largest being found in Burma in the eastern extremes of their range. Again, with the Common Mongoose (*H. edwardsi*) the largest animals are found in southern India.

Seasonal changes. Change in season brings about the accustomed change of coat. In the north, the Common Mongoose gets its full winter coat about October or November. It is not only fuller but brighter, the black and white speckling of the hair is very pronounced. The summer coat seen in June and July is scantier and drab; the black ringing of the hair fades to brown and the white loses its brilliance. As a protection against cold these animals assume a heavy vesture of soft underwool.

During the monsoon there is a large assemblage of snakes and frogs in the flooded fields which must provide a ready food supply for mongooses living in these areas. During the dry season with the cutting of the crops, rats and mice find less ample shelter and are more easily hunted. Factors like these must influence the lives of mongooses, their feeding habits, and their relationships with other animals.

MONGOOSES AND THEIR NEIGHBOURS

With beasts of prey, the size of the prey usually depends on the size and strength of the predator. But there are some whose smallness in size is made up for by boldness and ferocity in attack. Such are the mongooses. They may attack and kill animals much larger than themselves. But their usual prey is rats, such birds as they can catch, reptiles, frogs, insects, crabs, scorpions, and other invertebrates. Keeping these prolific animals in check is their special role in the economy of nature. Within the animal community, they belong more to the group of day-workers. Mongooses commonly hunt by day, usually early in the mornings and in the evenings. As to enemies, they are chiefly man and the beasts of prey.

Mongooses and snakes. Mongooses prey upon snakes, often on highly venomous species like cobras. How does the mongoose protect itself against so deadly a foe? Its strategy may be a headlong frontal attack, or a more circumspect waiting for opportunity such as the seizure of the lowered head after the snake strikes. What protects the mongoose is its extreme agility in evading a bite. Other factors which prevent a fatal issue is the mongoose's way of bristling the hairs of its body. Under stress of excitement the hairs stand erect making the mongoose appear twice as large as it really is. This might easily cause the snake to strike short. There is a prevalent belief throughout Oriental countries that a mongoose, when bitten, eats a root or herb (known in India as *mangus wail*) which counteracts the poison. Burmans also point to a thorny patch on the mongoose's tongue which is said to contain the antidote to snake poison ! The patch really consists of thorny papillae used for rasping flesh from bones. It is true that the mongoose is less sensitive to the venom of snakes and is able to withstand doses of poison potent enough to kill other animals of equal size. But the immunity is by no means absolute. A mongoose well and truly bitten and injected with venom in sufficient quantity dies from the poison like other animals. Such partial immunity is not especial to the mongoose. Certain animals like pigs and hedgehogs display similar powers of resistance to snake venom. Cats for instance are less affected by it than dogs, and pigs to a lesser extent than cats.

Stink-glands. Though bold and courageous in attack, mongooses are alert and wary animals, ready to scamper into cover at the slightest alarm. Among their means of protection one must refer to a defensive device used by certain animals. It is a type of defence already mentioned when speaking of the civets. We have seen how, as a last resort, civets defend themselves by discharging a foetid fluid at the attacker, the acrid, vile-smelling secretion from their anal glands. All mongooses have these stink-glands but only the two largest species, the Stripednecked Mongoose (*H. vitticollis*) and the Crabeating Mongoose (*H. urva*) have been observed to use them in self-defence. As with skunks and civets, this protective device is associated with warning coloration. Both species have broad distinctive neck stripes. These markings, combined with the bright red colouring of *H. vitticollis* and the badger-like grey and white of the Crabeating Mongoose, are warning liveries designed for advertisement and ready recognition.

The influence of man. Like other animals, mongooses avail themselves of opportunities for food-getting provided by man. This is particularly the case with species like the Common Mongoose and the Little Indian Mongoose, which can adapt themselves to any conditions and are widespread and numerous. They enter or take up residence in houses, they hunt in fields and cultivation, seeking prey among the large and varied assemblage of creatures which always live in and around human settlements. Rats and snakes are the attraction, but given opportunity a mongoose, always predatory in habit, attacks poultry, and given the chance creates havoc in a hen-house, killing for the lust of killing more than it can consume.

While mongooses do a certain amount of damage to poultry and smaller livestock, they more than compensate for such damage by the amount of vermin, rats and mice in particular, which they destroy. A mongoose rapidly rids a house of rats, mice, snakes, scorpions, and various insects, and will do it far more effectively than a cat. Its utility to man in this respect has been recognised from ancient times. The bones of a small mongoose were found in the basement of a house in Ur, suggesting that the ancient Chaldeans kept these animals in their homes to keep down vermin.

The Small Indian Mongoose (*H. auropunctatus*) was introduced from India into Jamaica for the express purpose of destroying rats and snakes which infested the plantations. They did their work exceedingly well and received honourable mention in Parliament. The species has now established itself in the West Indies firmly and, as an omnivorous feeder that kills ground-nesting birds and attacks the sugar-cane, has itself become somewhat of a pest.

FAMILY LIFE AND CARE OF THE YOUNG

Communication. Little is known about means of communication among these animals. The Common Mongoose gives out a hoarse mew, and calls to its young when they stray by yelping querulously. The strongly odorous anal glands probably play a part in communication and recognition between fellows of the same species. Mongooses have the habit of rubbing these sacs over surfaces where they rest or pass, and must leave behind a trail of their own perfume.

Breeding and care of the young. The Common Mongoose and the Small Indian Mongoose, our commonest species, do not appear to have a particular breeding season. Their young are seen in any month of the year. As with most carnivores the male takes no part in the care and upbringing of the young. This is left to the mother. The place she selects for a nursery may be a burrow dug by herself. Sometimes she enlarges and excavates a chamber within the galleries of a termite mound, or chooses a hole under rocks or at the foot of a tree. In human settlements the family may be reared in the roof of a house, in a drain, in any suitable place of concealment. The period of gestation varies with different species. The litter is small, usually two to three, but the small number of young is compensated for by frequency of breeding. A Common Mongoose produced five litters within a year, which helps to explain why the species is so common and numerous. The mother guards and protects her cubs assiduously, instantly attacking animals much larger than herself in their defence. Under conditions of captivity or semi-captivity an individual, otherwise quite tame, may become fierce and intolerant when with young ; another may permit without concern the handling of her babies. Should need arise she carries them in her mouth gripping her whelp by the loose skin of its neck. How long it is before the young are weaned is not known. But growth is rapid, and in a few months the young are able to go out hunting with the parent. They run close to her side, stopping when she stops, following her every movement. It is their period of training in what and how to hunt. We have still to ascertain how long mongooses take to reach maturity. A young male Common Mongoose was seen to mate with its parent seven months after it was born. As to length of life what we know is known from captive animals. From the available records it would seem that the smaller species, like the Common Mongoose and the Small Indian Mongoose live from seven to eight years, whilst the larger forms, e.g. the big Striped-neckea Mongoose (*H. vitticollis*), may have a life-span of 13 years and more.

THE COMMON MONGOOSE

Herpestes edwardsi (Geoffroy)

Plate facing p. 112

[RACES IN INDIA : *edwardsi* (Geoffroy), *nyula* (Hodgson), *ferrugineus* Blanford. CEYLON : *lanka* (Wroughton)]

Local Names. Hindi *mangus, newal, newara* (north and central India) ; Mar. *mungoos* ; Guj. *nurulia* ; Tamil, Mal., & Kan. *keeree* ; Tel. *yentawa mangisa* ; Bur. *mweyba*.

Size. Total length, nearly 3 ft. (90 cm.) of which 18 in. (45 cm.) is tail ; average weight, about 3 lb. (1.4 kg.). Males considerably heavier and larger than females.

Distinctive Characters. A tawny yellowish-grey mongoose with no stripe on the side of its neck. The alternate light and dark rings on its hairs gives its coat a grizzled ' pepper and salt ' tinge. The tail, which is as long as its body, is tipped with white or yellowish-red, never black. Three Indian races are recognised : a north and central Indian race (*nyula*) with a fuller, somewhat darker winter coat, a desert form (*ferrugineus*) with reddish fur, and the typical south Indian form (*edwardsi*) with a shorter, finely speckled winter coat.

Distribution. The whole of India from the Himalayan foothills to Cape Comorin, extending westwards to Persia and Mesopotamia and southwards to Ceylon.

Habits. This is not a creature of forest, but of open lands, of scrub jungle, and cultivation. It lives in hedgerows and thickets, among groves of trees and cultivated fields, taking shelter under rocks or bushes, lying up in a hollow in the base of a tree trunk, or digging a hole for itself in the ground. Those living in the deserts usually shelter in deep burrows to escape the heat. Termite mounds are sometimes occupied. Mongooses which have taken to living in towns or villages find shelter in the roofs and rafters, or in drains. They hunt their food by day or by night. They hunt singly, or a male and female hunt together, and sometimes one sees a family party, a mother with her train of young. They prey on rats and mice, on snakes, lizards and frogs, insects, scorpions, and centipedes, in fact on anything that can be overcome. Birds' eggs are eaten, and to some extent fruits and roots provide a variation to the customary diet of flesh. Like most carnivores, mongooses eat carrion and are frequently seen taking a share of the kills of large animals. About towns and villages many mongooses become habitual poultry thieves. In a hen-house or pigeon-coop a mongoose may achieve wholesale slaughter. Its prowess at killing snakes has already been discussed. The Common Mongoose breeds all the year round and three litters may be produced in a year. The period of gestation is about 60 days. They make charming and useful pets, speedily ridding a house of rats and vermin.

A second species, the **Ruddy Mongoose** (*H. smithi* Gray) as large as the Common Mongoose, lives in the forested areas of central and southern India. The species is readily distinguished from the Common Mongoose by the black tip to its tail. Its food and habits are much the same. Being a creature of forests it is less commonly seen. The typical race *H. s. smithi* Gray is found in India. One race *H. s. zeylanius* Thomas occurs in Ceylon.

THE SMALL INDIAN MONGOOSE

Herpestes auropunctatus (Hodgson)

Plate facing p. 112

[RACES IN INDIA : *auropunctatus* (Hodgson), *pallipes* (Blyth)]

Size. 18 to 20 in. (45 to 50 cm.) in total length.

Distinctive Characters. Its smaller size, shorter tail (shorter than the body), its olive-brown, gold-flecked, soft silky fur are distinctive. Two races are recognised in India. The desert form (*pallipes*) is distinctive in its pale general colouring. The animals in the more fertile parts of N. India (*auropunctatus*) are a darker brown minutely speckled with gold.

PLATE 20

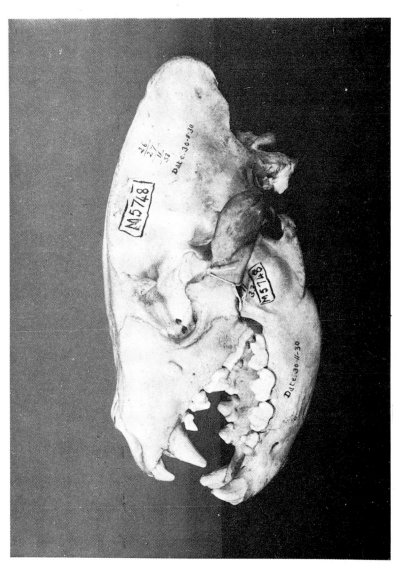

Skull of Hyena (*Hyaena hyaena*)

Few carnivores have jaws and teeth comparable in strength and bone-crushing power with those of the hyena.

PLATE 21

Striped Hyena (*Hyaena hyaena*)

Photo : F. W. Champion

Distribution. Northern India from Kashmir to Bengal, Orissa, and Assam extending eastwards into Burma and the Malay countries and westwards into Afghanistan, Baluchistan, Persia, and Mesopotamia.

Habits. The Small Indian Mongoose lives in holes burrowed by itself. It is diurnal in habit and is seen hunting its food about bushes, hedges, and in cultivated fields. It is a cautious creature generally keeping to cover. Its presence can usually be detected by the worn tracks it leaves along the hedges. It uses the same path day after day. It feeds on anything it can kill, on rats, mice, snakes, scorpions, centipedes, wasps and insects of all kinds. Like its larger relative, it is useful in ridding a house of vermin.

What we know of the breeding habits of this mongoose is gathered mainly from notes on a female kept in a semi-wild state in Ghazipur. She paired with a wild male in July and after seven weeks produced a litter of three young, one male and two females. A second litter, both females, was produced in the following April, and a third three months later in July. The newborn young are described as being remarkably ugly, practically hairless, and of a dark mouse colour. Their eyes opened on the 16-17th day after birth. When suckling they purred like cats. The mother also gave vent to a purring sound whenever she was given a drink of milk. She was restless, and for the first two or three weeks constantly moved her offspring from place to place, carrying them about as a cat carries her kittens. While the young were helpless, she was savage in their defence. This mongoose has lived in captivity for 8½ years.

THE STRIPEDNECKED MONGOOSE

Herpestes vitticollis Bennett

Plate facing p. 112

[RACES IN INDIA: *vitticollis* Bennett, *inornatus* Pocock. CEYLON: *vitticollis* Bennett]

Local Names : Tamil *sare keeree;* Mal. *chen keeree;* Kan. *kemp kerree.*

Size. This is the largest of all Asiatic mongooses, attaining a total length of nearly 3 ft. (90 cm.) and weighing about 7 lb. (3.2 kg.).

Distinctive Characters. The black neck-stripe reaching backwards from the ear to the shoulder is distinctive in this mongoose. Its coat is grizzled grey, tipped with chestnut-red, the red increasing in intensity on the hindquarters. Two races are recognised. The typical form (*vitticollis*, Coorg and Kerala) is characterised by the dominance of chestnut-red on its coat. The second race (*inornatus*, N. Kanara) has the red tinge confined to the rump and absent in the fore-body.

Distribution. The Western Ghats from North Kanara, southwards to some of the adjoining S. Indian hill ranges and Ceylon.

Habits. This mongoose is typically a forest animal and is less commonly seen around human habitation, though it enters cultivation and is frequently seen hunting its food in rice-fields. Unlike other mongooses it is little attracted by rats, poultry, and other food to be had in and around human dwellings. Large and powerfully built, the Stripednecked Mongoose can be very destructive to game. In Ceylon it is recorded as preying on mouse-deer, hares, bandicoots, field rats, and birds and reptiles. Its habit of hunting by the banks of rivers and frequenting swamps and flooded rice-fields suggests that frogs, fishes, and land crabs may be part of its diet. Fruit and roots also enter into its bill of fare. Little is known of its breeding habits. In Ceylon a female was discovered with three young just able to move. She was suckling them on a dry patch of earth under an overhanging mass of rocks.

A second species of mongoose, the **Brown Mongoose** (*H. fuscus* Waterhouse) is found in the forests of the south Indian hill ranges at 3000-6000 ft. (900-1850 m.). It is a large, heavily built, blackish brown mongoose, more or less speckled with yellow or tawny. Paws almost black. Head and body 19 in. (50 cm.) ; tail 1 ft. (30 cm.) ; weight about 6 lb. (2.7 kg.). The species is fairly common around coffee plantations. Only the typical race *H. f. fuscus* Waterhouse is found in India. Four races occur in Ceylon where it is described as a great pest to poultry keepers, though somewhat beneficial in ridding estates of vermin. They are *flavidens* Kelaart, *maccarthiae* (Gray), *siccatus* Thomas, and *rubidior* Pocock. It is said to breed in burrows beneath rocks and tree roots, and to have 3-4 young.

THE CRABEATING MONGOOSE

Herpestes urva (Hodgson)

Plate facing p. 112

Size. A large, powerfully built mongoose. Head and body, 18-21 in. (45-50 cm.) ; tail without hair at the end, 10-12 in. (25-30 cm.); weight, 4-5 lb. (1.8-2.3 kg.).

Distinctive Characters. The white stripe running from the angle of the mouth along each side of the neck to the shoulders is distinctive in this mongoose. Its long coarse fur and somewhat ragged coat is a dusky iron grey, long light tips to the hairs paling the general tone. The woolly under-fur is dark brown at the base and pale brownish yellow at the tips.

Distribution. Nepal to Assam, eastwards to Burma, south China and the northern part of Malaya.

Habits. This mongoose is more aquatic in habit than other species. It is an expert swimmer and diver, fearlessly entering water to take the frogs and fishes and crabs which abound in Himalayan and Burmese hill streams. These appear to be its chief food. In Kurseong one of these mongooses is reported to have come repeatedly to a tank stocked with live gold fish. It took many of them and must have dived from the side of the tank to take its prey. The Crabeating Mongoose hunts along the banks of streams feeling under stones and in rock crevices with its paws for lurking crabs and snails. It has been confirmed in the case of snails (JBNHS 69: 411-12). It is recorded of an animal kept in captivity that it would take hold of any hard object, such as a stone or golf ball, and holding it in its forepaws stand up and crash it to the ground, hurling it with great violence between its hindlegs, and jumping clear to avoid the rebound. The habit is probably an indication of the way in which this mongoose kills and breaks up hard-shelled crabs and molluscs on which it feeds. Like other species it lives in holes in the ground. Its habit of squirting out a foetid fluid as means of defence has been commented on. The fluid is shot backwards with great force from the large anal glands. Breeding habits not known. It has lived in captivity for 10 years.

6. Hyenas

THE BUILD AND general appearance of a hyena suggest its relationship with the Dog family. Its legs and feet are typically those of a dog ; but the structure of the skull, the teeth, and other points in the anatomy of the animal definitely place it in the Felid or Cat section of the Carnivora. Heavy and ungainly in build, a hyena carries a broad head with large, pointed, upstanding ears. While its forelimbs are sturdy and long, its deep and massive body ends in weak drooping hindquarters supported on short knock-kneed hindlegs. The animal walks on its toes. There are four on each foot. The claws are short and blunt. They have no protective sheaths and are non-retractile. Hyenas have no scent glands, but are provided with anal glands contained in a large sac hung above the anus. All in all the animal is built neither for attack nor for swift pursuit of prey. Its structure fits it for its particular mode of life, which is to feed on prey killed by other animals.

STRUCTURE IN RELATION TO HABITS

A scavenger by profession the hyena seeks its food by scent. Sight plays little part in its search ; hearing none at all. Those sensitive organs, the facial vibrissae or whiskers, so large and conspicuous in cats and civets, used by them when hunting and to discern the nature of food, are poorly developed in hyenas. They are not hunters, nor is there variety in their food. They live chiefly on the carcasses of animals, more truly on what is left of a carcass after a tiger or panther has done with it and the vultures and jackals have eaten their fill. The hyena's share is then mostly bones and coarse remains. The powerful jaws of the hyena and its large teeth are admirably adapted to bone crushing. The whole shape of the skull has been changed to provide good attachment for the powerful muscles which work the jaws and teeth. The canine teeth, weapons of attack in typical beasts of prey, are comparatively small. The distinctiveness of the hyena's teeth lies in the great size and strength of the molars as compared with the canines, more especially in the massive conical crowns of the second and third premolars in both jaws. These teeth have a large basal ridge which acts as a guard to protect the gums when bones are being crushed. Few carnivores have jaws and teeth which can compare in strength or bone-crushing power with those of hyenas. **(Plates facing pp. 102, 103)**

PLATE 22

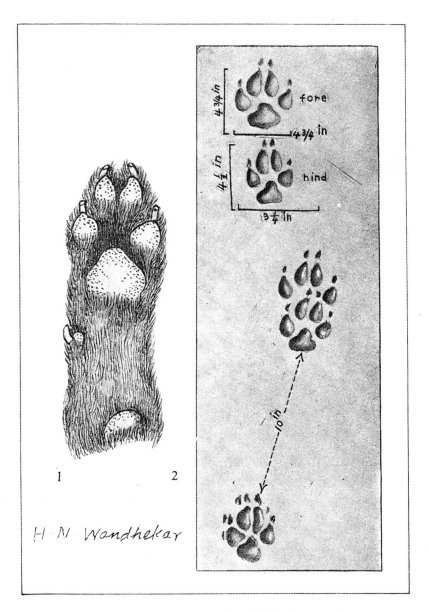

Foot (1) and spoor (2) of Wolf (*Canis lupus*)

The foot is small and compact, the toes rest on deep cushioned pads, the claws are short and blunt.

PLATE 23

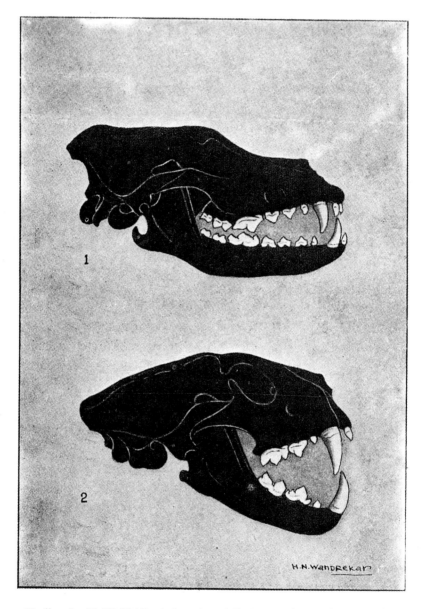

Skulls of : (1) Wolf (*Canis lupus*) and (2) Leopard (*Panthera pardus*)

Note difference in length of jaw-bones and number of teeth.

LIFE IN RELATION TO SURROUNDINGS

The hyena family contains but two genera, the Striped and the Brown Hyenas (genus *Hyaena*) and the Spotted Hyena (genus *Crocuta*). The Spotted and the Brown Hyenas are found only in Africa. The Striped Hyena is an inhabitant of peninsular India whence its range extends westward through Iran and Iraq into north Africa. Probably Africa was·the original home of the tribe.

The type of surroundings hyenas like best are bare open plains, desert, rocky scrub-covered hills and nullahs, grass or open jungles. They usually avoid the interior of heavy forests and live more commonly in the drier parts of India. A hyena finds shelter from the heat of the day in caves, among boulders, in a hole dug by itself, or in one dug out by a porcupine. Against the cold it grows a heavy winter coat, full and soft and thickened with underwool, quite different from the short and scanty summer wear.

HYENAS AND THEIR NEIGHBOURS

We have seen that hyenas live on dead animals. Within the animal community their role is the role of the scavenger. They do their work by night. As to competition for food, while most carnivores will eat carrion, the hyena's more habitual rivals are vultures and jackals. Vultures a hyena seldom meets, as they usually feed by day. Further, jackals and vultures eat the flesh and lighter pickings. The hyena gets the heavier bones and coarser remains, which it is especially fitted to eat. But feeding on the kills of tigers and panthers is dangerous work and disputes arise when a tiger or panther comes on the scene. Against the tiger the hyena has little chance. It is sometimes more than a match for a panther ; in such encounters it is the hyena which is not infrequently the victor. Food is the most serious business of animals. And in defence of its food, the hyena, a creature which usually avoids a quarrel with any animal which can injure it, stands its ground even against so formidable a rival as a panther, displaying great courage and determination. But in other circumstances a hyena shows little or no fight at all. Cornered and harried by dogs, with no means of escape, the beast may lie prone and motionless submitting to its tormentors. They, finding no interest in an apparently lifeless body, desist from attack. Similar tactics have been developed to a fine art by the American opossum. This most unusual behaviour is aptly described as ' shamming dead '. But no animal actually ' shams dead ', simply because no animal except man knows what death means. The behaviour is not reasoned but instinctive. It is an instinctive reaction displayed by certain animals and insects under stress of attack.

Hyenas and man. The hyena is brought into contact with man chiefly during its prowls round the outskirts of towns and villages. Though scavengers by habit, they sometimes attack such animals as can be easily overcome, both wild or domestic. Sheep, goats, and calves, and dogs in particular become their victims. In Africa the Striped Hyena is apparently more aggressive. It has been known to run among a herd of sheep, killing half a dozen or more from sheer lust for slaughter. As for man, hyenas fear and avoid him. But there is one authentic instance of a hyena carrying off a child, which was rescued from the beast's jaws by its mother, and another case of a woman attacked at a well who beat off her attacker. Lt.-Col. R. W. Burton reports having shot a hyena near Nowgong, Madhya Pradesh, which had killed and eaten one woman and mauled another.

Uses. As a scavenger the hyena is a useful animal, helping to keep the neighbourhood of human settlements clean. In some parts of India the tongue and the fat of these animals are prized as medicine, the former to reduce tumours and swellings, and the latter as a remedy for rheumatism. In Egypt peasants in the Nile Valley eat the heart of a hyena to obtain its courage. They use the whiskers as charms and the poorer among them eat the flesh.

FAMILY LIFE AND CARE OF THE YOUNG

Hyenas give vent to various weird noises and cries, among them a loud, unearthly, laughing chatter. In captivity a hyena can be induced to chatter in this way at the sight of food. But the significance of the various calls and the part they play in communication between the sexes remain to be interpreted.

We know very little about the hyena's family life. We do not know whether they breed in any month of the year or whether there is a restricted breeding season. Nor do we know how long the male and female live together. These animals are often seen in pairs. But in the few recorded instances where hyenas were found with cubs the mother appeared as their sole protector. The nursery selected is the accustomed cave or hole. The young, three to four in number, are born, like most carnivores, with their eyes and ears closed. They are covered with short silky white hair and have the usual stripes, but have no mane which is the adornment of the adult. How long it is before the cubs are weaned and how long they take to grow up is not known. The life span of the Striped Hyena, as known from captive animals, is from 12 to 24 years, the average being 16.

THE STRIPED HYENA

Hyaena hyaena (Linnaeus)

Plates facing pp. 103, 130

[RACE IN INDIA : *hyaena* (Linnaeus)]

Local Names. Hindi *hundar, lakkar baghar* (north India), *teras* (south India) ; Mar. *taras;* Tel. *dumul gundu, korna gundu* ; Tamil *kalada koratu, kaluthai puli* ; Kan. *kathe keeruba, kathe kuruba, nai hooli.*

Size. Total length of male, 5 ft. (150 cm.) ; height, about 3 ft. (90 cm.) ; weight 85 lb. (38.5 kg.). Females, about 10 lb. (4.5 kg.) less.

Distinctive Characters. A dog-like build, massive head and fore-body, weak hindquarters, and a heavy dorsal crest of long hairs, sharply defined from the rest of the coat, distinguish the hyena. Its colour varies from cream, buff, or tawny to the grey or dirty white of the harsh scanty summer coat. Transverse stripes on body and limbs usually well defined, less so in the full winter coat.

Distribution. India, south-western Asia, northern Africa.

Habits. The hyena is rare in forested districts, abundant in open country, especially where low hills and ravines offer convenient holes and caves for shelter. Many lie concealed by day in high grass, under bushes, or in cane fields, but the den usually preferred is a cave amongst rocks, or a hole dug in the side of a hill or ravine. Quite often a hyena enlarges a porcupine's burrow to suit its needs. They come out in quest of food by night, retiring before sunrise. Pairs usually go about together, sometimes a group of 5 or 6 is seen but this is probably a family party. In search of food the hyena tramps many miles. Few tracks of wild animals are more common in India than those of the hyena. Its ' spoor ' is much like a dog's except that the imprint of the forefoot is much larger than that of the hind, and that of the main pad is uneven and oval. Animals that have died of disease or those killed by the larger beasts of prey are the usual food of the hyena. Its share is the coarser remains, the heavier bones which the others reject. These it breaks and crushes with its powerful jaws and teeth, swallowing and digesting great fragments. Portions of the meal may be carried to the den to be eaten in greater security. Its place of retreat is usually marked by a litter of bones and its peculiar dung, which dries into hard white balls and seems to be composed chiefly of crushed bone. A large male hyena killed in jungles of Hyderabad (Deccan) had a greatly distended stomach which contained only sun-dried, dessicated bones, all uncrushed, and apparently swallowed whole. Though scavengers by profession, performing useful services as such, hyenas do not feed wholly on carrion; occasionally sheep and goats and quite often stray dogs are carried off by them. Some individuals, developing the cattle-killing habit, become perfect pests on livestock. Larger cattle are seldom attacked. Despite its bulk and power our hyena does not attack big animals, though an individual may be quite prepared, if need be, to appropriate the kills of panthers or even tigers. There are many instances of hyenas depriving panthers of their food and of routing them in such disputes. The weird laughing chatter of the hyena has already been referred to. Little is known of the mating habits of this quite common animal. Mating time is said to be in the cold weather. The young are born during the hot season. Hyenas are easily tamed and even when full grown remain docile and trustworthy.

7. The Dog Family

AS MAN'S COMPANION and friend, the dog has made us familiar with many of the characters and ways of its family. Wolves, jackals and foxes, dogs domestic and wild, together compose this family, the **Canidae**. All these animals have a strong family likeness. They are built on the same general plan, a well-shaped head, long pointed muzzle, large erect ears, deep-chested muscular body, bushy tail, and slender, sinewy limbs. Their perfectly digitigrade feet have blunt, nearly straight, and non-retractile claws. Except for the Cape Hunting Dog, all dogs have five toes (including dew-claws) on the forefeet, and four on the hind. As to colour, again with the marked exception of the Cape Hunting Dog, all the family have sombre-coloured coats, usually of some shade of grey, or yellowish or reddish brown, without any stripes or markings. Such are the main external characters. The whole build of these animals is designed to fit them for their special way of getting their food. Though all of them occasionally eat vegetable food and some, like the jackal, live mainly on carrion, the family, as a whole, are professional hunters living on animals large or small which they kill. But their way of hunting is not the way of the Cats and other beasts of prey. The custom of most of the family is to secure prey by swift and open chase. How perfectly Dogs are fitted to do this becomes clearer, when we consider just how these animals find, pursue, kill, and eat their prey.

STRUCTURE AND HABITS

Senses. To see quite clearly this relationship between structure and food-getting habits let us follow a pack of wolves in their quest for food. Our wolves trail their prey, nose to the ground. Dogs hunt by scent. The sense of smell is exceedingly keen in all canines. How easily wild dogs follow the scent of an animal even on dry sun-baked ground ! Sight and hearing are acute and must be of help when hunting. Our wolves approach their quarry with that alertness and cunning which is so markedly displayed in the family. Coming within range they attack at once or they lie around hidden, waiting for an opportunity. They lie belly to earth, nose resting between forepaws, ears bent forward, bright eyes watching. Sight and hearing come into full play, while the prone position helps the animal the better to pick up sound vibrations conveyed through the ground. An antelope strays near. There follows the swift rush on

the unwary victim, the headlong flight, and the relentless and untiring pursuit.

Feet. In their pursuit there is no undue hurry, no violent outburst
of speed. Dogs move with a lobbing tireless canter which in the
end brings them to their exhausted prey. Once determined on the
chase, the quarry is doomed. Food, as we see, is secured by open
chase. To do this these animals must have not only sufficient speed
to keep up with swift-footed prey, but also the endurance and staying power to outrun it. Those who have hunted wolves, jackals, or
foxes on horseback know something of the speed and amazing
endurance of these animals. A wolf pursued by a hunter on horseback kept up its tireless canter for well nigh two hours and covered
some 18 miles before it was ' done '. Endurance and lung power is
indicated in the deep-chested muscular body, so general in the
physique of the Canidae, speed in the long sinewy limbs and their
digitigrade (on the toes) action. The foot is small and compact.
The toes are held close together by elastic-rimmed webs and rest on
deep, well-cushioned pads. The claws are short and blunt. The foot
as such is designed neither for striking nor for seizing prey. It is
not built for climbing—none of the family climb for their food.
Nor is it especially designed for swimming, though all Dogs swim.
The feet are adapted to one purpose, the pursuit of prey over hard
ground. **(Plate facing p. 106)**

On coming up with the quarry the method of attack will depend
upon circumstances, among other things upon the kind of animal
which is being attacked, upon the number of attackers, upon
whether the victim is standing at bay or in flight. Wolves attack a
running sheep or an antelope by leaping at its throat. Seizing its
neck, the wolf jerks the victim's head downwards so that it crashes
nose to earth, and is stunned by the violence of a fall during rapid
movement. Or like wild dogs, they spring at the flanks of a running
animal and, snapping at the soft under-belly, they usually succeed in
disembowelling it. If an animal has been brought to bay, wild dogs
ordinarily launch themselves in a frontal attack, seizing the eyes,
ears, nose, and lips of the victim, or whatever part they can get hold
of. If the pack is a large one, some attack from the rear. Large or
dangerous game is only attacked when the Dogs are numerous.
Then a simultaneous attack from front and rear becomes effective
strategy. Those in front attract the victim's attention ; those behind
snap at its hindquarters. During the attack, the prey may be emas-
culated. This is the result of chance, and not of deliberate effort
as is commonly believed in India. Equally prevalent is the belief
that wild dogs sprinkle bushes with urine, and drive their quarry
through the bushes to blind them with the acrid fluid ! There is a
somewhat similar belief about wolves in Europe, that they dip
their tails in water and shake or whisk it into the eyes of an animal

PLATE 24

Spotted Linsang
(*Prionodon pardicolor*)

Common Mongoose
(*Herpestes edwardsi*)

Small Indian Mongoose
(*Herpestes auropunctatus*)

Stripednecked Mongoose
(*Herpestes vitticollis*)

Crabeating Mongoose
(Herpestes urva)

PLATE 25

Wolf
(*Canis lupus*)

Jackal
(*Canis aureus*)

Red fox
(*Vulpes vulpes*)

Indian fox
(*Vulpes bengalensis*)

Dhole
(*Cuon alpinus*)

0   10   20   30 cm.

0   1 ft.

to blind it ! These are myths. But observe how well the whole build of the Dog, its deep-chested muscular body, sinewy limbs, and sturdy feet fit it for its method of hunting by pursuit. In pursuit and attack, these animals work in marvellous union. Their mutual helpfulness in bringing down their quarry bespeaks their high intelligence.

Jaws and teeth. So much for methods of attack. Let us now consider how the prey is seized and the equipment for its seizure. Wolves or wild dogs hold their prey with their jaws and teeth, and once having held never let go. This tenacity of hold is their mainstay in attack. It has been attained in the Canidae by a lengthening of the jaw bones. The long jaws provide space for a great array of teeth, whose vice-like grip is controlled by powerful cheek muscles. In no other genus of quadrupeds are the jaws so well, or so variously, armed with teeth. With but a few exceptions, the total number of teeth in Dogs is 42, compared with an average of 30 in Cats and 40 in civets. Notwithstanding the crowded array of teeth, sufficient space is left between the canines and the neighbouring incisors and cheek teeth to allow of their interlocking. These interlocking canines are efficient and formidable weapons for seizing or lacerating living prey. The incisors are well adapted by their shape and forward position for biting, gnawing, or stripping the skin from flesh. This is a thing these animals often do to make an entry to the meat. A portion of skin is neatly stripped away. To cut and divide the meat the dog uses its cheek teeth, cutting sideways with its jaws. Some of the cheek teeth have compressed triangular crowns, while the ' flesh teeth ', the largest of all, have two great cusps and are well suited for such work. Large chunks of meat are cut away by their scissor-like action, tossed upwards, and bolted whole. The tuberculated crowns of the cheek teeth are also adapted for the cracking of bones and the crunching of food both animal and vegetable. In number and general form the teeth of Dogs are not very different from the teeth of civets, which as we have seen are omnivorous. Though meat is their customary diet, most of the Canidae also eat grass, herbs, and fruit. Their cheek teeth fit them equally for such a diet. **(Plate facing p. 107)**

THE DOG FAMILY AND ITS SURROUNDINGS

The home of the family. The Canidae are among the most widely distributed of all the beasts of prey. Most species inhabit the northern Hemisphere, suggesting that their original home lay in northern latitudes. In course of time the family has spread practically over the whole of Europe, Asia, Africa, and America. No member of the family inhabits Madagascar or the Australian Region. The dingo or wild dog of Australia is believed to be derived from domestic dogs originally brought by the aborigines from south-west Asia.

With a distribution extending over arctic, temperate, and equatorial lands, it is clear that conditions of climate, however rigid and adverse, have done little to prevent the family from invading and settling in new countries. The wolf, the red fox, the jackal, and the wild dog are immigrants into India from the north. They probably entered the country by way of our north-western passes. Here as elsewhere they have adapted themselves to life under con-trasting conditions of heat and cold, of dryness and humidity. In this, the jackal has been perhaps the most successful. It has spread over the whole of India. It has colonized both desert and forested regions, plains and high mountainous country. Not so the wolf and the fox. In the Indian plains, wolves and foxes have selected for settlement the more open parts of the country. In contrast, wild dogs have kept exclusively to forests. In forests, wild dogs find food and a ready water supply on which they are so depen-dent. In this the wild dog resembles the tiger. Like the tiger, the wild dog must have entered India by way of our north-eastern frontiers. Like the tiger it extended its range to our most southerly limits avoiding treeless and desert portions. Both species were unable to enter and colonize Ceylon, suggesting their arrival at the southerly limits of their range after the submergence of the land bridge between the Peninsula and the Island.

Geography and variation. Yet wherever they live, no matter how wide their range, and how different the conditions of life, Dogs and their kin show no essential changes in structure. The wolf in India, the red fox of the Himalayas and our north-western deserts, our jackal, and our wild dog do not differ in any essential character from those of their kind living in other lands. The Indian repre-sentatives are merely geographical races of their widely distributed species. Such differences as these animals show in different areas of their range are but minor distinctions arising from adaptations to local conditions of climate and other physical factors. The most marked difference in the various races is the length and luxuriance of the winter coat. It is naturally at its fullest and finest in the Arctic regions or in the uplands of central Asia, and in the Tibetan zone where both arctic and desert conditions prevail. There is also a difference in size. The wolf in Europe, living as it does under conditions more favourable to its species, is a larger animal with bigger skull and teeth than the wolf of the Indian plains, a lean and leggy creature. The same may be said of the jackal, the red fox, or the wild dog. Animals from northern latitudes are bigger in build than those living in the southern extremes of their range. As to colour, in all these animals the colour of the coat varies among individuals living in the same area, and varies also with the season ; but it might be said that there are colour distinctions

PLATE 26

H.N.Wandrekar

Relative sizes of Wild Dog (*Cuon alpinus*) and Sambar (*Cervus unicolor*)

PLATE 27

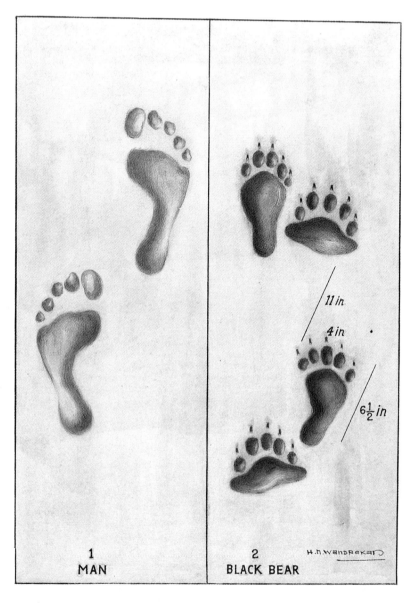

1
MAN

2
BLACK BEAR

11 in

4 in

6½ in

H.N.WANDREKAR

Tracks of man and bear

more or less associated with geographical areas. The wolf in Europe is generally a drab grey, in the Himalayas and central Asia it is more tawny, and in the plains of India a sandy fawn. Jackals from the desert are paler in colouring than those living in the Himalayas or southern India. The wild dog's coat, which is pale or tawny in northern latitudes, grows redder in India and redder still in the jungles of Nepal, Burma, and Malaya. But these distinctions in the length and luxuriance of the winter coat, in size, and in colour, while they are marked in animals living in the northern and southern extremes of their range, so completely integrade in the intervening areas that it is difficult to say exactly where one geographical race ends and the other begins. An interesting form of variation is exhibited by the Red Fox (*Vulpes vulpes*). In America ' red ', ' hoary ', and ' black ' or ' silver tip ' phases of these animals occur in the same locality or even in the same litter. In the Himalayas we have a similar production of colour phases. There are foxes with ' bright red ', ' fulvous ', and ' black ' or ' silver-tipped ' coats. As far as is known, the black and red phases are commoner in the western Himalayas, and the yellow in the eastern part of the range.

Habits and surroundings. While wolves, jackals, and foxes are generally tolerant of the sun's heat, their habits are nevertheless influenced by conditions of temperature. They seek their food by day or by night, the jackals being perhaps more nocturnal than the wolf or the fox ; yet, in the cold weather or on a cloudy day, jackals frequently come out to hunt by day. Again, in very hot weather jackals take to water and lie in it to keep cool, a thing which wild dogs also do. But, in the plains, living as they do in open country, wolves, jackals, and foxes ordinarily spend the hottest part of the day under shelter. Our wolves lie up in tall grass, under trees, or in scrub. Jackals and foxes retire to their dens. In the desert where there is little shade wolves get into deep holes in the sand dunes. Smoked out of its den in the midday heat, a desert wolf cannot evade its pursuers for long. Contact with the burning sands soon blisters its feet and disables its running.

Food and feeding habits also vary with surroundings. Wolves in temperate lands hunt both in forest and open country. They have a larger variety of animals to prey upon than Indian wolves, which confine themselves to open country and must prey only on animals which live in this open terrain. It is the same with the Red Fox. In temperate lands it has a wide choice of food, while its brother in the Indian desert is compelled to live mainly on gerbilles and other desert rodents. Change of season also brings about changes in feeding habits. In summer time in the uplands of Ladak and Tibet wolves live sumptuously on marmots, hares, and other small animals and birds. But in winter these small animals are more difficult to get, and wolves then take more to the hunting of bigger game, such as wild sheep and antelope. But large prey is more easily secured when there are more wolves to help, which explains the great assemblies of wolves seen during winter in Russia and other northern lands. Such large and numerous packs are never seen in India simply because here food getting is not more difficult in winter than it is at other seasons. Again, a rigid winter may bring about a change in the feeding habits of our Himalayan foxes. Driven by hunger they become partial scavengers and come to human dwellings to pick up offal and scraps of waste food. But besides meat, foxes and jackals eat a great deal of vegetable food, consequently their diet changes markedly with the season. During summer in the Himalayas, Red Foxes feed abundantly on acorns, nuts, and berries, and our jackals, during the cold weather, are able to vary their diet of carrion with the fallen fruit of *ber* trees or with coffee berries which litter the ground in plantations. Even wild dogs get an opportunity seasonally to supplement their meat with fruit. In the south Indian hill ranges they are said to feed greedily on the fallen fruits of *bael* and blackwood trees.

Apart from food, there are other changes in habits made in response to surroundings. It is a subject about which much remains to be learnt. There is one such change recorded of the Common Indian Fox. This little animal usually digs its burrows in flat open plains. In alluvial country subject to inundation they have taken to digging their burrows in high mounds and bunds to avoid being flooded out during the rains.

THE CANIDAE AND THEIR NEIGHBOURS

Let us now consider dogs and their kin in relation to their animate environment, to their neighbours animal or human. While some species have become scavengers, the majority of the tribe are professional hunters, living on animals which they kill. As such their relationships with neighbours is largely the relationship between predator and predator, and predator and prey. Now we have seen that what an animal kills, what food rivals it is associated with depends much on its size. The largest herbivores become the prey of only the largest carnivores, because they are big and strong enough to kill them. The smaller beasts of prey do not enter into this competition. Size is then one of the chief factors which regulates the relationship between carnivore and carnivore and a carnivore and its prey. But with dogs and their kin we come upon an exception to this common rule. The family contains no animal as big as a lion, a tiger, or a leopard ; yet, though much smaller in build, wild dogs and wolves kill the same large prey as the great Cats. They increase their effective size and therefore their power to kill by the strategy of numbers. They hunt in packs. It is true that

a lone wolf or wild dog may pull down and kill a large deer without
the aid of its fellows. But it is when assembled in a pack that these
animals grow bolder, and more prone to attack large prey. Those
members of the family, species like the maned wolf of South
America, or foxes, which do not hunt in packs, kill only small
animals. They become food rivals of the small carnivores ; while
wolves, wild dogs, and other pack-hunters compete for food with
the larger beasts of prey. (Plate facing p. 114)

Interrelationships with other carnivores. This relationship is governed, as we have said, mainly by the question of food and competition for it. Now apart from size, what other animals a carnivore competes with depends also on the type of habitat in which
it chooses to live. Each type of habitat has its characteristic animal
community. In peninsular India wolves do not compete for food
with tigers. They live in separate animal communities, the wolf
with animals of open country or desert, the tiger with forest communities. In its own territory the wolf's chief competitor for large
prey is the panther. In open lands there is usually more human
settlement, and here both species live largely on food made available by man, on cattle, sheep, and goats. The supply is normally
sufficient and constant, and competition is somewhat reduced. The
case of the wild dog is different. It lives in forests where tigers,
panthers, and other carnivores compete with it for large prey.
A pack of hungry wild dogs, if sufficiently numerous, will not hesitate to attack a panther, a bear, or even a tiger. There is sufficient
evidence to show that occasionally tigers are killed by wild dogs.
But ordinarily, conflicts arise not because the dogs seek the large
carnivora as prey, but from chance meetings or, as often happens,
when the dogs appropriate the kill of one of these great Cats. In
forests the food problem is usually more acute. There is less opportunity for supplementing supplies from human sources and animals
have to depend on what Nature provides. Such provision is less
stable and certain, among other reasons because the number of
animals, both of hunters and hunted, is constantly changing.
Marked changes in the density of the animal population profoundly
influence food supply and therefore the relationship between the
members of the community.

The influence of numbers. While the various species which compose
an animal community remain more or less constant, their numbers
vary. Many observers have noted how the number of wild dogs
living in a particular area periodically increases, attains some
unknown peak, and then declines. Fluctuations like this are not
peculiar to wild dogs. Many species of mammals both carnivores
and herbivores are subject to changes in density of population.
Now food relationships within the community being what they are,
so complex, so interlocked, any undue increase or decline in the

number of one species affects the lives, habits, and economy of many others. How profound must this influence be in the case of animals like wolves and wild dogs ! Ordinarily, even when there is some balance between their number and the available food supply, they make great demands upon the stock. They are very destructive to life, more destructive than the biggest carnivores. They kill more than they can eat, they make no attempt to save the remains of a meal, they do not return to feed on it, but having killed go out to kill again. The effect of an over-increase in their number becomes rapidly evident. Most of the game animals living in the area are either killed or driven out. The bigger beasts of prey, deprived of their natural food, are also forced to leave the infested area. They follow their prey or change their feeding habits, take to cattle-killing for example. This is what happens to tigers and panthers in forests overrun with wild dogs. There must be other repercussions on the life of the forest community. It is an interesting subject for study. Of equal interest would be the discovery of the causes which bring about periodic fluctuations in the number of wild dogs. In Canada records maintained by the fur-trading companies show that the periodic fluctuations in the number of foxes coincide exactly with the periodic rise and fall in the number of lemmings, their basic food. What factors influence the periodic increase in the number of wild dogs, we have still to discover. On attaining a peak number a rapid decline is brought about by disease, the shortage of food lowering the resistance to it. Faced with food shortage in one area animals, as we have seen, go elsewhere to seek it, or change their feeding habits. Wild dogs may follow their prey over wide areas, or a shortage of their customary prey may cause them to take to cattle-killing. When faced with a serious and widespread shortage of food, wolves in Canada were found to develop mange and other diseases. In India, Mr. R. C. Morris records how wild dogs, when unduly increased in number in the Billigirirangan Hills, also developed mange. The disease was observed during the same period 70-80 miles (115-130 km.) further south in the Nilgiris, where the dogs had also attained a peak number. Many were found dead. Epidemics of one kind or the other are undoubtedly the factor which ultimately controls an over-increase in the number of these animals, and restores the population to its appropriate density.

Messmates. While much has been written about wild dogs and wolves and their association with other carnivores we have little data from our country about other member of the tribe. There is of course the interesting food relationship which jackals sometimes establish with other carnivores. From early times the jackal was given the name of ' lion provider '. Legend has it that the jackal led the lion to its prey and was rewarded with the remains of the meal. In India it is commonly believed that jackals perform the

same service for the tiger. Actually a jackal may accompany a
tiger in its hunting, not as a guide but as a follower seeking an
opportunity to feed on the tiger's kill. Jackals also become messmates of hyenas, and they have been found hunting with a pack
of wild dogs. Many animals form relationships such as this. One
species becomes the commensal or messmate of another, taking a
share of the food it obtains. Better opportunity for food-getting is
the object of such relationships. But what are the interrelationships
between different members of the Canidae ?

Inter-family relationships. In India there is little opportunity for
food rivalry between the different species of the family. Wild dogs
hunt in forests, wolves in open country. Some of our foxes live
in the same animal communities as the wolf, but seek smaller prey.
As for jackals, their main trade is scavenging. They eat what is
left by their neighbours. But what of rivalries between animals of
the same species, between different packs of wild dogs or different
packs of wolves ? There is an old Chinese proverb which says
' two tigers cannot share the same hill ', meaning that each hunts
in its own preserve. This makes for a better division of food and
reduces competition. Is there such territorial adjustment between
packs of wild dogs hunting in the same forest ? Does one pack
ordinarily establish hunting rights over its territory and resent the
intrusion of another. It is a point which still requires investigation.
Then again, do the various members of the tribe prey on each
other ? Wolves have been seen coursing foxes, and both wild dogs
and jackals in certain circumstances may attack domestic dogs, or
domestic species attack the wild. Yet there seems to be a common
bond of recognition between various members of the family. Jackals
and wolves consort with domestic dogs, they have been known to
hunt with them, and interbreeding between the wild and tame
species certainly takes place. Of the wild dog, it is said that it
attacks neither a jackal nor a hyena, ' respecting them as blood
brothers '. As for its relationship with domestic dogs, Mr. Dunbar
Brander says that, when attacked by dogs of sufficient size and
determination, wild dogs will show fight but, if the dogs set against
them are small and it is no longer a question of self-protection,
there may be no fighting but rather an attempt at making friends.
He tells of wild dogs fawning on and gambolling with his terriers,
following them in play to within a few yards of where he stood.
So much for relationships between the family and its fellows, or
between the family and other carnivores. Let us turn to relationships between the family and its prey.

Relationships with prey. The range of food of the Canidae, as we
have seen, is extensive. Large mammals to rodents, birds big and
small, and even such insignificant creatures as insects, crabs, and
molluscs enter into the dietary of one or the other of its species.

The family thus functions as an effective check on the over-increase of their victims. Yet though a constant menace to other animals, wild dogs attract little attention in a forest. Their movements are not heralded by that chorus of alarm calls and cries which ring out when a tiger is seen on the prowl. Curious indeed is this scant attention which other animals pay to wild dogs or wolves when they are not actually hunting. In the American prairies, wolves have been seen moving among grazing bison which continued their feeding unconcerned. Here in India, wild dogs have been seen intermingling with a herd of grazing sambar, the one paying no attention to the other. Animals seem to know when their enemies mean business and when they do not. Cattle and deer were found quietly grazing near a panther absorbed in feeding on its kill, and it is said that zebra and other animals commonly hunted by lions in Africa take little notice of their roars by day. They seem to know exactly when the roars threaten danger.

Means of defence. Apart from their powerful equipment of teeth and jaws, the collective strategy of wild dogs and wolves and of other species which assemble in packs must be a powerful means of self-protection. There is no animal, man excluded, bold enough to deliberately attack such an assemblage. Speed and untiring endurance, for which the family is noted, are other potent factors in defence. In fact, for species which do not combine in packs this is perhaps the main means of escape. How remarkable is the speed of our little Indian Fox ! How dextrously it twists and turns and doubles on its course to gain ground on its pursuers. ' Shamming dead ', lying prone and inert under overwhelming attack, a habit noticed in the hyena, is also adopted by some of the family. Wolves are known to ' sham dead ', and jackals frequently resort to this ultimate means of escape. The holes, caves, and cavities in which many of the tribe shelter are a means of protection both from climate and enemies. A fox's burrow is specially designed for ready escape. There is always more than one tunnel leading to the central sleeping chamber ; should an enemy enter by one, the fox makes its exit by another. Then there is that alertness, intelligence, and cunning which dogs and their kin pit against an enemy. Finally, the fecundity of the species, the large number of young they usually produce, makes for preservation and the maintenance of their numbers. In fact there are no wild animals which are a serious menace to the family. Ultimately, undue increase in its species is controlled by disease-producing parasites. These are the real enemies of the family, and of course man, who has made himself the centre, the dominant influence in the animate environment of animals.

The tribe in relation to man. The influence of man is seen firstly in his role as exterminator. Man has brought about the extermination and disappearance of the wolf from large areas where it was once common. This has happened in Europe and America and is now happening in India. Everywhere the wolf is retreating before human settlement. Its chance of survival in this country lies in the existence of extensive waste lands and deserts where human interference is still negligible. This is also true of our foxes, though everywhere foxes have been more successful in escaping extermination than wolves. The hand of man has been against the fox from time immemorial, but foxes still persist in lands from where the wolf has been long driven. As for the wild dog, its domain is the forest, where man is yet no serious threat to its numbers. Yet in India the cutting down of forests and the extermination of game upon which wild dogs are dependent for food has driven them from many areas where they were once common. Man, by taking from animals their means of living, drives many to live by taking such food as they can from him. They have no other resource. In India many wolves living near human settlement live habitually on cattle, sheep, and goats. Larger wild animals in such areas are scarce or non-existent. Wild dogs avoid the haunts of man and seldom prey on cattle except in time of dire food shortage. Jackals reverting to the predatory instincts of their family sometimes attack poultry, young lambs, and goats. Red Foxes in the Himalayas have the same habits as their cousins in Europe and, given opportunity, raid poultry yards. The Indian Fox on the other hand is seldom a pest to the poultry keeper.

As for man-eating, the chief culprit in the tribe is the wolf. Stories of attack by wolves when driven by hunger, particularly on travellers in Russia in winter, are well known ; and here in India, sporadic outbreaks of man-eating occur. Wolves hunting in pairs or in small packs terrorize a neighbourhood, pulling down women and children, and sometimes men. Wild dogs scarcely if ever attack man. But dogs and their kin may bring death to man in other ways, e.g. by the transmission of disease. Rabies is a disease which appears in many animals, but especially in the Canidae. Wild dogs and jackals develop it, though there is reason to believe that it was originally a disease of the domestic dog communicated by dog to man and other animals. Domestic house-dogs are known to be the cause of a parasitic disease of the liver in human beings. This is rare in India but not uncommon in Australia.

Domestication of the dog. We have spoken of man in his role as an exterminator ; there is another aspect of his association with the family, his role as a preserver. It is said that the Age of Mammals is passing, and that ultimately only such species will survive as are useful to man, and which man seeks to preserve. High among these is the domestic dog. How man came by his dog is a question about which naturalists are not agreed. But the modern view is that the wolf is the principal if not the sole ancestor of the domestic dog. How wolf-like are some breeds of domestic dog, Alsatians and Eskimo dogs for example ! In structure the wolf and the dog are identical, except that wolves have bigger teeth. From wolves our dogs have inherited some of their special habits, that curious habit of rolling on evil-smelling substances, or of turning round before sitting or lying down. But jackals also display some of the habits of domestic dogs. They do not turn round before sitting, but they smile as some dogs do and wag their tails when pleased. A jackal will hide a bone, pushing it into the earth with its snout exactly as some dogs do. There are competent naturalists who hold that the jackal also contributed to our domestic strains. That wolves and jackals interbreed with domestic dogs in India there is little doubt, and both species appear to have left their stamp on some of the Indian domestic breeds.

Uses to man. The usefulness of the domestic dog to man is sufficiently recognised ; we are here concerned with the wild species. Wild dogs and wolves serve man indirectly by keeping down the numbers of animals which would otherwise become a still greater threat to his crops. In India wild dogs prey consistently upon wild pigs which are so destructive to cultivation. Foxes again are useful as destroyers of rodents and smaller vermin, and more than repay such damage as they may do to poultry. Besides, the beautiful furs derived from these animals are a source of immense profit to man. Fox farms have been established in many parts of the world as a readier means of securing their valuable pelts.

FAMILY LIFE AND CARE OF THE YOUNG

Means of communication. Vocal communication is well developed in the tribe, particularly among species which live in packs. There are sounds, like whines, growls, and snarls, by which an individual gives expression to fear, anger, and other emotions. The weird cry sometimes given out by a jackal is commonly associated with one in attendance on a tiger. And such an animal is called a *pheal, phiou,* or *phnew,* the name being an inept imitation of this blood-curdling cry. The cry is an expression of fear or alarm, but not necessarily associated with the presence of a tiger. Jackals have been heard giving vent to it in places where there were no tigers. Nor is this agonising cry peculiar to jackals. A domestic dog was heard to emit a similar cry when stirred by fear. Wild dogs may give vent to a hyena-like chattering, when startled or alarmed. A pack was once heard giving out a bewildering cry, a shrill chorus, uncanny and all-pervading. This was when a hunter rushed towards them to protect his dogs.

But apart from these emotional expressions, there are definite calls and cries which the various species employ to communicate with their fellows. There are calls which assemble a pack of wolves or wild dogs, there are directive sounds given to the hunt by leaders when pursuing prey, and yet other sounds by which individuals of a pack keep in touch when not hunting. The wailing howls of jackals at dusk or before dawn are familiar enough to most people in India. Just as African tribesmen signal by drum beat across vast distances, so the howling of jackals is heard and repeated by other jackals and by others, more distant, and so carried across the countryside. The meaning of this howl remains to be interpreted. Is it a signal to assemble ? Jackals often collect in packs, especially after dark, and this may be one means by which they get together. But in many parts of India the chattering cry of the small Indian Fox is heard almost every evening, and these animals do not gather in packs. Besides these calls, there are calls associated with sex, special cries by which males and females communicate. Wolves and wild dogs have such mate calls. Finally, there are the sounds by which parents and young keep in touch. A wild dog deprived of her young was heard calling to her offspring through the night. She gave vent to a particular wailing, quite unlike other cries uttered by her species. The calls and cries of animals may be inborn and develop naturally, or they may be picked up and learned from parents or from other individuals. Wolves do not bark, dogs do, but in certain conditions dogs give up barking altogether and captive wolves may learn to bark like dogs. Jackal cubs reared in captivity never gave vent to the accustomed howling of their wild neighbours, from which it is concluded that these particular sounds are not innate in these animals but are learned or perfected during life. Apart from vocal communication there are other means by which the species communicate. A dog marks the path by which it has travelled by repeated urination, and wild dogs are said to leave their droppings in regular spots. This is one way by which many species of animals find their fellows. All canines have a scent gland typically marked by a black spot on the upper basal half of the tail. Perineal or anal scent glands seen in civets and mongooses are absent. Scent is a powerful means of communication in the tribe. The Red Fox leaves a trail of scent on the ground from skin glands between the pads of its feet. Wild dogs may leave a strong scent behind them. Scent plays a vital part in communication between the sexes. Females in condition to breed are recognised by their scent.

Breeding. In peninsular India, wolf, jackal, or wild dog cubs have been taken in almost every month of the year. They appear to have no fixed breeding season, though breeding activity may be more pronounced and more young produced at particular seasons. The nursery selected is a natural hole, cave, or cavity among rocks, or a burrow dug by the parent. A number of females may select a favoured site and form a breeding colony. Wild dogs sometimes do this. The period of gestation is about 60-63 days in wolves, jackals, and domestic dogs, 70 days in the wild dog, and about 51-53 days

in the fox. Fecundity is very high and the large litters produced by
most species are a factor which makes for survival. As with most
carnivores the young are born blind and helpless, the mother caring
for them with utmost solicitude. With most species the male remains in faithful attendance. The male wolf kills and brings food
for the young and stands guard in their neighbourhood. The mother
is equally watchful. We read of a mother wolf standing for hours in
the broiling sun keeping a wary eye on a party of travellers camping
near her nursery. It is also recorded how, when two cubs from a
litter were taken, the parents came by night and removed the others
to safety. In fact wolves are said to mate for life, and it is believed
that Red Foxes and coyotes also form permanent partnerships.
The wild dog is believed to select and live with its mate long before
union. How long the partnership continues is not known. Males
sometimes found hunting alone are probably in attendance on a
family. The period of partnership in jackals and our little Indian
Fox is not known. The domestic dog is promiscuous in its mating.
But this is probably the result of domestication. A house dog has
no need to bring food to a mate and to defend its young. The
period of lactation is not known. It is probably brief. Wild dogs
and foxes grow rapidly. They are full-grown and capable of breeding when about one year old. Wolves take longer. They mature in
the third year. The young display their hunting instincts from the
earliest stage. Captive wolf cubs when only three weeks old attacked
a baby gazelle, flying at its throat. Wild dog cubs are equally savage
and pugnacious. Whelps reared in captivity fought with each other
continuously till they were seven or eight months old. Thereafter
all wrangling ceased. There emerged the ' top dog ', the largest and
strongest among them. To him the others now paid marked de-
ference. He became their leader. Thus probably in puppyhood are
future leaders of packs made. When weaned the cubs are first fed
on food regurgitated by their mother, this is their gradual introduction to a diet of meat. As soon as they are strong enough, they are
taken out on hunting expeditions. The common belief that there are
two breeds of wild dogs in India, a small breed which hunts sheep
and goats and other small animals and a larger breed which seeks
bigger game, probably originated in these family hunting parties.
The packs of small dogs are really parents taking their cubs out to
hunt, and naturally they commence with animals which are easier
to kill.

How packs are formed. Social life in the tribe originated in the
prolonged association of parents and young. The family
continues to live and hunt together. It forms a pack. In time such a
pack or family may unite with another family, or two or several
families may join forces to form quite a large assemblage. Wolves
in Europe do this in winter, and in India families or packs of wild
dogs get together in large assemblies, especially during the hot

weather and the rains. With collective effort bigger prey can be secured ; besides, these assemblages give the younger generation a better opportunity to find mates. But with the coming of the main breeding season the big assemblies dissolve and pairs settle down to family cares.

THE WOLF

Canis lupus Linnaeus

Plate facing p. 113

[RACE IN INDIA : *pallipes* Sykes]

Local Names. Hindi *bheriya, nekra, bighana, hundar, hurar* (northern and central India) ; Mar. *landga* ; Kan. *thola, vraka* ; Tel. *toralu* ; Tamil *onai* ; Tibetan *changu*.

Size. Height, 2 ft. 2 in.-2 ft. 6 in. (65-75 cm.) ; body length, 3 ft.-3 ft. 6 in. (90-105 cm.) ; tail, 14-16 in. (35-40 cm.) ; weight, 40-60 lb. (18-27 kg.). On the average, Himalayan animals are larger and heavier in build.

Distinctive Characters. Its size, large skull, and teeth distinguish the Wolf from the rest of the family. Colour variable. In general, animals from the plains of India have sandy fawn coats stippled with black. The fawn may bleach to grey and the black become less evident in the scantier summer wear. Wolves from Tibet, Ladak, and the northern slopes of the Himalayas sometimes have black or blackish coats. Their winter coats are variegated with long, black and white or black and buff, hairs and dense, grey or bright buff, underwool.

Distribution. Europe, North America, northern, central, and southwestern Asia. Within Indian limits, Tibet, Ladak, and parts of Kashmir, extending into the desert zone and dry open plains of peninsular India.

Habits. Wolves may live in forests, but in India they are more common in bare and open regions. In the barren uplands of Kashmir, Ladak, and Tibet they live as nomads coming down to the valleys in winter, migrating with game and grazing flocks to the snow-line in summer. In these parts, holes, caves, and cavities in rocks provide them with shelter in winter, and thickets of reeds and scrub with a refuge in summer. In the Indian desert Wolves shelter from the heat in burrows dug in the sand dunes. Elsewhere, there is more shade and they remain above ground, lying up in fields, or patches of scrub and thorn forest. They hunt by day or by night. What they hunt depends on the nature of the habitat. Near human settlements where there is little else to eat, Wolves prey mainly on cattle, occasionally carry off children and, when driven by hunger, become a serious menace to human life. In areas more remote from human influence they hunt blackbuck and gazelle, course after hares and foxes, in fact eat any animal or bird they can capture. Contrasting winter and summer conditions bring a more marked change in the diet of Himalayan wolves ; rodents, and smaller animals are their main food in summer, wild sheep and gazelle their prey in winter.

In India, the main breeding season is at the end of the rains and the majority of cubs are born in December. In the Himalayas they breed later and cubs are produced in the spring or early summer. Three to nine whelps are born in a litter. The duration of life is 12-15 years. Young Wolves are easily tamed.

THE JACKAL

Canis aureus Linnaeus

Plate facing p. 113

[RACES IN INDIA : *aureus* Linnaeus, *indicus* Hodgson, *naria* Wroughton.   CEYLON : *lanka* Wroughton]

Local Names. Hindi *gidhar* (north India), *kola* (Deccan & South) ; Mar. *kolha* ; Ben. *shial* ; Tamil *nuree* ; Kan. *nuree, kunni nuree* ; Tel. *nakka* ; Mal. *koorukan* ; Bur. *kway at.*

Size. Height, about 15-17 in. (38-43 cm.) ; length, head and body, 2 ft.-2 ft. 6 in. (60-75 cm.) ; tail, 8-11 in. (20-27 cm.) ; weight, 17-25 lb. (8-11 kg.). Animals from north India are on the average bigger and heavier in build.

Distinctive Characters. The Jackal's long-drawn, eerie howling at dusk or just before dawn is perhaps more familiar to most people than the animal itself. Its nearest wild relative is the wolf, but the Jackal is smaller in build and meaner in aspect. It lacks the arching brows and elevated forehead which give the wolf its nobler profile. Coat, variable with season and locality. Typically, a mixture of black and white washed with buff about the shoulders, ears, and legs. Himalayan animals have more buff on their coats and a deeper tan on ears and legs. Black variants are not uncommon in north India.

Distribution. South-eastern Europe, south-western Asia, throughout India and Ceylon, extending some way into Burma and south-eastern Siam. Three Indian races are recognised.

PLATE 28

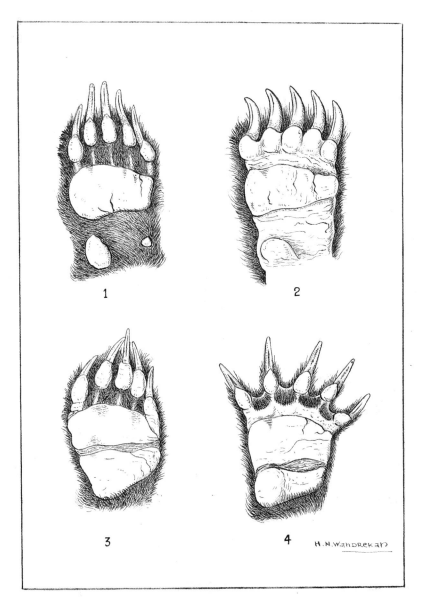

H.N.WAhDREKAr

Feet of bears

1. Brown Bear   3. Himalayan Black Bear
2. Sloth Bear   4. Malayan Bear

Note the hairy soles of the Brown Bear and the naked soles of the tree-climbing species.

PLATE 29

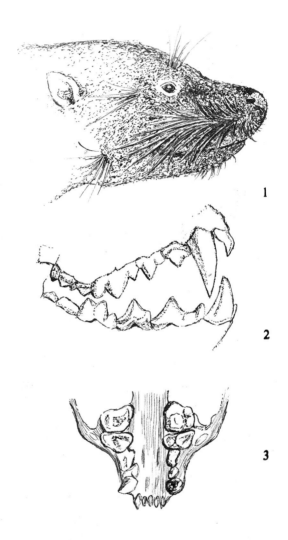

Head (1) and teeth (2 and 3) of Common Otter (*Lutra lutra*)

Habits. Jackals live in almost any environment, in humid forest country, or in dry open plains, or desert. They have been found at a height of 12,000 ft. (3660 m.) in the Himalayas and are well-established round hill-stations 4000-7000 ft. (1220-2135 m.) above sea-level. The greater number live in the lowlands, about towns and villages and cultivation, sheltering in holes in the ground, among ruins, or in dense grass and scrub. Jackals usually come out at dusk and retire at dawn ; but in cool or cloudy weather they may be up and about by day ; also on a very hot day Jackals often come out in quest of water to drink or lie in. Sometimes they form packs, but usually go about alone, or two or more may hunt together. They do good work in the clearance of carcasses and offal, providing, with vultures, the only sanitary service known to many of our towns and villages. The hunting instinct is not wholly dormant in the Jackal, some become poultry thieves, or take to killing lambs, kids, and sickly goats and sheep. Any small or wounded animal may be attacked. They have been known even to collect in a pack to hunt small deer or antelope much as wild dogs do. In season, Jackals raid melon patches and sugarcane fields and gather during the cold weather in coffee plantations. Where *ber* trees grow, they collect to feed on fallen fruit. Little is known about the Jackal's family life—it is so secretive in habits. How long the male remains with its mate or family, what part, if any, it plays in caring for the young, their upbringing, growth, and dispersal, all remain to be discovered. Cubs are born at any time in the year, usually in a hole in the ground, in a drain, or any natural shelter. The duration of life is about 12 years. A jackal can run at a speed of 40 km. per hr. when pressed.

THE RED FOX

Vulpes vulpes (Linnaeus)

Plate facing p. 113

[RACES IN INDIA : *montana* (Pearson), *pusilla* Blyth, *griffithi* Blyth]

Local Names. Hindi *lomri*, Kash. *loh*, Nepal *wamu*, English *Hill Fox* (Himalayas), *Desert Fox* (Desert Zone).

Size. Length of head and body 2 ft.-2 ft. 4 in. (60-70 cm.) ; tail inclusive of hairs, 18-20 in. (45-50 cm.) ; weight, 10-12 lb. (4.5-5.5 kg.).

Distinctive Characters. A richly coloured fox with long silky fur and a superb brush. The black backs to the upper half of its ears and the white tip to its tail distinguish it from other Indian foxes. Red is the dominant colour of its lovely coat, but this is very variable ; bright yellowish, grey, silvery, and black individuals occur. In spring, when the luxuriant winter coat is shed, the Red Fox is scarcely recognizable ; the dark under-fur showing through the moulting coat gives it a grey-brown tinge.

Distribution. Within Indian limits, Tibet, Ladak, Kashmir, and the Himalayas as far east as Sikkim, extending into the desert zone of north-western India. Beyond our frontiers the range extends mainly north and west over the greater part of the northern Hemisphere as far as the shores of Arctic lands. Three races of the Red Fox are recognised from India : a mountain form, the **Hill Fox** (*montana*) of the Himalayas, a northern desert form (*griffithi*), and a western desert form, the **Whitefooted Fox** (*pusilla*) ranging from Rajputana, Cutch, and Sind westwards into south Baluchistan, Persia, and Mesopotamia.

Habits. In Tibet this fox lives among the thorn bushes and willows fringing the edges of streams, in Kashmir and the Himalayas it is common in brushwood and cultivated lands ; this, and not forest, is its chosen habitat. In the desert zone it lives among the sand dunes, or in the broad sandy beds of dry rivers, and also in waste land covered with scrub. Its distribution within our limits suggests a preference for a dry rather than a moist climate. Red Foxes shelter in a burrow dug in the ground, or under or among rocks, and, where there is vegetation, among reeds and bushes. Like all foxes they seek their food by night, though hunger and other conditions may compel an individual to venture out by day. Foxes are not social in habit like wild dogs or wolves. They usually hunt alone or in pairs. Food varies with habitat and season. They prey chiefly on rodents. Ground birds like partridges and pheasants are killed and, in the Himalayas, their rodent fare includes squirrels, marmots, voles, and mouse-hares. In the desert, gerbilles and other sand-rats are their main prey. But winter conditions in the mountains are more rigid and many, driven by hunger, visit human dwellings to pick up scraps of discarded food and offal. The diet of meat is varied in season with fallen fruit, berries, and the combs and honey of wild bees.

Red Foxes are said to pair for life. A pair may occupy the same den year after year. Usually it is a burrow with more than one opening. Six to seven cubs are produced. In the Himalayas, cubbing time is in the spring and by the late summer the cubs are well grown and able to fend for themselves.

THE INDIAN FOX

Vulpes bengalensis (Shaw)

Plate facing p. 113

Local Names. Hindi *lomri, lom, lokri, lokeria* (central India) ; Mar. *kokri* ; Kan. *sanna nari* ; Tam. *kulla nuree* ; Tel. *konka nakka, gunta nakka.*

Size. Length of head and body, 1 ft. 6 in.-2 ft. (45-60 cm.) ; tail, 10-14 in. (25-35 cm.) ; weight, 4-7 lb. (1.8-3.2 kg.).

Distinctive Characters. This is the common fox of the Indian plains, a pretty, slender-limbed animal, smaller and slimmer in build than the Red Fox ; distinctive in the black tip to its tail. The backs of its ears are generally of the same tone as the head and nape, never jet-black and strongly contrasted as in the Red Fox. While northern animals grow a handsome winter coat, it is not as long and luxuriant as the winter pelt of the Red Fox. Its general colour is grey, purer grey in winter, contrasting with the rufous limbs.

Distribution. The whole of India from the foothills of the Himalayas to Cape Comorin.

Habits. The Indian Fox keeps to open country and rarely enters forest. It is common in the waste and scrub of our desert zone, but not in true desert. Many live in cultivated lands, bordering irrigation channels. Much the same is the habitat in the rest of India, waste land and cultivation, rocky hills and broken country. The Indian Fox lives in a burrow dug by itself in open ground or in scrub. Where land is subject to flooding a mound, natural or artificial, is chosen. The burrow always has several openings, some blind, others leading to a central chamber, 2-3 ft. (60-90 cm.) below the ground. Here the little animal sleeps by day, coming out at dusk to seek its food. In the gathering darkness its chattering bark is heard, a sharp yelp, repeated three or four times. Those living near human settlements enter compounds and gardens, yet seldom attack poultry. Small mammals, reptiles, and insects, rather than birds, are what this fox eats. By its consistent destruction of rats and land crabs it does real service to the farmer. Flights of termites or white ants, so common before the onset of the rains, attract these foxes. They gobble up the insects as they emerge from the termite mounds, or snap at them as they fly past. Melons, *ber* fruit, and the shoots and pods of *Cicer arietum* are eaten in season.

Its main defence against enemies is its speed and the dextrous way in which it twists and turns and doubles on its course, using its tail to balance its movements. The tail trails over the ground when the fox is going slow, is carried horizontal when on the run, and flicked up erect when twisting and turning.

Whether the Indian Fox pairs for life or changes partners is not known. As with most of the Canidae both male and female share in the care of the young. The main breeding season is the cold weather. The cubs, usually four in number, are raised in the burrow, but mother and young are rarely seen. Cubbing time is between February and April. The gestation period is 50-53 days and the young weigh at birth 52 to 65 gm. and have a total length of 18-19 cm.

THE DHOLE, or INDIAN WILD DOG

Cuon alpinus (Pallas)

Plates facing pp. 113, 114

[RACES IN INDIA : *dukhunensis* (Sykes), *primaevus* (Hodgson), *laniger* Pocock]

Local Names. Hindi *dhole, son, ram, jangli kutta, ban kutta* ; Mar. *kolsun, kolsa, kolsara* ; Guj. *kol kutta* ; Kan. *kadu nai, chira nai* ; Tel. *reza kutta* ; Mal. & Tamil *chen nai, kattu nai* ; Himalayas *bhaosa, bhoonsa, buansu* ; Kash. *ramkun* ; Tibetan *sidda ki* ; Bur. *tor kway*.

Size. Height, 17-22 in. (43-55 cm.) at the shoulder ; head and body, about 3 ft. (90 cm.) in length ; tail, 16-17 in. (40-43 cm.) ; weight, a big male scaled 43 lb. (20 kg.), females are lighter.

Distinctive Characters. Much like a domestic dog in general appearance, with the long, lank body of the wolf, but relatively shorter in leg and muzzle. The ears are more rounded at the tip and the tail quite bushy. Essentially it differs from wolves, domestic dogs, or jackals in having six molar teeth in the lower jaw, whereas the others have seven. Also the Dhole usually has 12 to 14 teats as against ten in true dogs (*Canis*). Very distinctive is its red coat, which varies in tone with season and locality. Trans-Himalayan animals are paler, those from the Himalayas are a deeper red, in peninsular India the coat takes on a tawnier tinge.

Distribution. Central and eastern Asia from the Altai mountain and Manchuria southward through the forest regions of India and the Malay countries. Within the limits of India three races are recognised, a trans-Himalayan, a Himalayan, and a peninsular form.

Habits. In central Asia Wild Dogs live in forests but are occasionally found in the open steppes. In Ladak and Tibet they inhabit open country. There are no forests in those bleak uplands ;

PLATE 30

Striped Hyena
(*Hyaena hyaena*)

0   20   40   60 cm.
0   1   2 ft.

Sloth Bear
(*Melursus ursinus*)

Brown Bear
(*Ursus arctos*)

Himalayan Black Bear
(*Selenarctos thibetanus*)

PLATE 31

Red Panda
(*Ailurus fulgens*)

Common Otter
(*Lutra lutra*)

Smooth Indian Otter
(*Lutra perspicillata*)

Clawless Otter
(*Aonyx cinerea*)

Himalayan Yellowthroated
Marten
(*Martes flavigula*)

Beech Marten
(*Martes foina*)

but in tropical and sub-tropical countries such as India they keep entirely to forests where there is food, shade from the sun, and water to drink or lie in, a thing Wild Dogs frequently do in hot weather. Like wolves, Wild Dogs are social animals, going about in packs. As has been explained, social life in these animals originates in the prolonged association between parents and young. The pack is a family, or a union of two or more, sometimes of several, families. Such union increases the chances of killing larger prey. Usually Wild Dogs hunt by day, rarely by night. Their prey is trailed by scent and pursued at sight, with no violent outburst of speed but in a steady, tireless canter which finally outruns the quarry. The pursuit may be silent or, in heavy cover, the directive yaps of the leaders may indicate the line of approach. Nearing their victim the dogs may break into an excited whimpering which bursts into a clamorous yapping as it comes into view. When scattered, as when pursuing separate individuals of a herd of deer or other prey, or when suddenly contacting man Wild Dogs call to each other with a peculiar ' whistling ' cry which can be exactly imitated by blowing sharply and repeatedly into an empty cartridge case of medium bore. Mr. R. C. Morris records calling up members of a pack in this way on two occasions. Food varies with locality. In Tibet and Ladak Wild Dogs hunt wild sheep and antelope. In the forests of Kashmir they may kill markhor, musk deer, or goral. Tahr are hunted in the Himalayas, but their usual prey in India are various species of deer, large and small. A large pack may attack large animals like gaur and buffalo. Their usual way is to stampede the herd and attack the calves. Wild pigs are a favourite prey. Panther and bear and even tigers have been attacked and killed by Wild Dogs. Their methods of killing and feeding have been discussed, as also their association with carnivores and other animals of the jungle, and with man.

As to breeding habits, the main breeding season in the Peninsula is between November and December, the majority of cubs, usually 4-6, are born in January and February, in a cave, under rock, or in an earth. Several females may breed in a colony. When sufficiently strong the young go out on foraging expeditions with the parents ; the family may unite with other families. These large assemblages are more frequent during the non-breeding period, i.e. during the hot weather and the rains.

8. Bears

JUDGING FROM APPEARANCES, one would scarcely suspect that there is a relationship between bears and dogs. Yet fossil remains of primitive forms reveal such relationship, and show that dogs and bears are descendants of a common ancestral stock. Different modes of life adopted by their remote forbears led to the development of those differences in structure now so apparent in the two families. The progenitors of the dogs became hunters and learned to take their prey by swift and enduring chase. They developed slender sinewy limbs and compact short-clawed feet fashioned for swift movement over the ground. The progenitors of bears chose a different way of life. They probably lived as bears live now, on grasses, roots, herbs, fruit, and insects, eating meat only when opportunity offered. The getting of such food did not require swift and agile movement, but rather legs built for climbing and digging. Hence the bear's massive limbs, which carry its heavy body up rocks and cliffs and trees, its in-turned paws which secure a better hold on branch or trunk, and its great claws which help it to climb and dig. As a family, bears are easily recognised. A big head set with small eyes and rounded ears, a heavy body carried on thickset limbs, and a tail so small that it is scarcely seen under the shaggy coat—that is a word picture which describes all bears. The paws are short and broad, five-toed and furnished with long curving non-retractile claws.

ADAPTATIONS OF STRUCTURE TO HABITS

Senses. In seeking its food a bear is led by its nose. Smell is the dominant sense in these animals. Hearing and sight are poor. The auditory bullae, those bony prominences in the skull placed just behind the ear opening, are flat and depressed in bears. They are usually swollen and well developed in animals whose hearing is keen. The eyes are usually small for so large an animal. When suspicious a bear gets up on its hind legs and looks gropingly round. It is one way of increasing a poor range of vision. But powers of scent, sight, and hearing apparently vary in these animals. The Brown Bear can pick up the wind-borne scent of a man a mile distant, while the Sloth Bear is comparatively short-scented. The Himalayan Black Bear is said to see and hear better than the Brown Bear, and better still than the Sloth Bear. As to the sense of touch, the facial vibrissae or whiskers, delicate organs of touch, so finely developed in many beasts of prey, are rudimentary and functionless in bears. Dominated by the sense of smell, dull in every other faculty, it is not surprising that bears lack the alertness and decision of animals whose lives are directed by a more balanced use of all the senses. There is no knowing what a bear will do or how it will react to set conditions. Its mental life is the mental life of the primitive mammal. Yet, with training, bears display high intelligence and become star performers in circus and zoo.

In quest of food bears tramp many a weary mile, walking with their slow and shuffling gait. Their walking is generally described as plantigrade. The footprints of a bear are much like a man's and have been mistaken for human tracks. **(Plate facing p. 115)**

But not all bears are flat-footed. When walking on all fours, a Brown Bear or Polar Bear may keep its heels raised slightly off the ground. Urged into action, the bear breaks into a lumbering gallop, going faster than one would expect from so heavy and clumsy an animal. All bears are good swimmers.

Food-getting. Much of their food bears find on the ground, or they dig for it below the surface. Their long curving claws, always longer in the forefeet, are good digging implements. They have yet another way of getting at insects which have tunnelled into trees or underground. Breaking down the shelter the bear draws its victims out by suction. Its lips are designed for such work. Unlike the lips of other carnivores a bear's lips are free from the gum. Mobile and protrusible, they are well adapted to the forceful intake and expulsion of air. This character is especially well developed in Sloth Bears. Breaking down a termite mound with its claws, a Sloth Bear with prodigious huffs and puffs blows away the dust and debris, and then sucks the termites up out of their galleries. In this process, its mobile pendulous upper lip is pressed back against its nostrils to prevent dirt from entering. This is not all ; to facilitate the intake of food by inhalation, the middle pair of incisors in its upper jaw is wanting. The gap between the teeth permits the passage of air, and the power of suction is further increased by a hollowing out of the roof of the mouth. A Sloth Bear's palate is deeply concave. It is flattened in other species. These modifications of the mouth are all designed to assist feeding by suction, a thing which Sloth Bears commonly do. They are much addicted to the eating of termites and the grubs of insects which tunnel underground or bore into the trunks of trees.

Feet and teeth. Food is also obtained by climbing, and a bear's powerful limbs, its padded feet, and great claws are designed to this purpose. But some bears are better fitted to climb trees than others. In the Arctic there are no trees for Polar Bears to climb. Their feet are adapted more for movement over the ground. They are distinctive in the hairiness of the soles. The dense mat of hair gives the foot a securer hold on slippery snow and ice. Our Brown Bears in the Himalayas spend most of the year in the higher levels, well above the tree-line, and even when they come down to the forests they seldom climb trees for their food. The soles of their feet, again, are well matted with hair. Now it was shown how the arboreal civets differ from the ground-dwelling forms in having, not hairy, but naked soles. This is a character repeated in bears. Bears which constantly climb trees, species like the Himalayan Black Bear, the Malay Bear, and the Sloth Bear, have broad naked-soled feet. The rough naked skin secures a better grip. The grip on tree trunk or branch is strengthened further by an inward turning of the front paws. An inward twist to the forepaws is especially pronounced in these tree-climbing bears. It accounts for their markedly bow-legged gait. It is an adaptation which fits these animals better for taking their food from the treetops. Different habits of life have produced such distinctive characters in the soles and pads of the feet of different bears that they have become a means of distinguishing between various genera. (Plate facing p. 126)

By inclination bears, as we have said, are vegetarians and eaters of insects, but they occasionally attack and kill other animals for food. There is a popular belief that a bear kills by hugging a victim in its massive arms. ' To hug like a bear ' is a common saying, only bears do not hug, they kill by striking. The inward turn of its forepaws compels a bear to strike with a round-arm swing, suggestive of a hug. The blow drives the great claws home causing the most terrible wounds.

To eat their varied food bears have as many teeth as their relatives the dogs, but they are modelled on a totally different plan. The low flat crowns of the cheek teeth are designed especially for the crushing of hard and fibrous vegetable matter, substances like roots and grass and hard-shelled nuts. None of the cheek teeth have cutting planes, and the ' flesh teeth ', so large and conspicuous in the jaws of a dog, are indistinguishable from the other molars.

BEARS AND THEIR SURROUNDINGS

The home of the family. There is but one species of bear found south of the Equator. This is the Spectacled Bear, a native of the Peruvian Andes. The real home of the family is the Northern Hemisphere, where every region has its characteristic species. The Arctic is the home of the Polar Bear. The Temperate Zone, south of the Arctic, is the special habitat of the Brown Bear and the Black Bear. South of the Temperate Zone the forests of India and south-eastern Asia are the home of two tropical species, the Sloth Bear of India and the Malay Bear of Assam, Burma and Malaysia. In Asia the Black Bear has extended its range some way into this tropical region. It is the only bear which has adapted itself both to temperate and tropical conditions of life. As to the type of surroundings in which bears live, Polar Bears have adapted themselves to an almost amphibious life, amidst the snowbound lands and ice floes of the Arctic. Brown Bears live equally in barren lands and on bare mountain peaks or in forests. Black Bears, Sloth Bears, and the Malay Bears are forest dwellers.

Geography and variation. With a distribution which extends over the temperate lands of both the Old World and the New, the Brown Bear is naturally represented by many forms or races in different areas of its range. The American races of this animal are believed to be the largest. A Grizzly Bear, which is but a form of Brown Bear, may scale 1000 lb. (455 kg.) ; while the giant Brown Bears of Alaska reach 1500 lb. (680 kg.) in weight. The Alaskan Brown Bear is therefore not only the largest of all bears, but also the largest carnivore in the world. Like most mammals of northern latitudes, Brown Bears living in the more southerly parts of their range are smaller in build. The Brown Bear of the western Himalayas, the most southerly latitude in which this species is found, judging from its smaller skull, is a smaller animal than the Brown Bear of Europe. A similar differentiation in size, as one travels southward, is seen in Asiatic Black Bears and Sloth Bears. Black Bears from Baluchistan or from the Malayan forests are smaller than those from central and northern Asia, and Sloth Bears from Ceylon are usually not as big as Indian Sloth Bears.

Coming now to colour, Brown Bears show much variation in colour, but speaking generally those from the western Himalayas are lighter in tone than European Brown Bears. It is suggested that the light coat of the Himalayan race is an adaptation to its surroundings. These bears live for most of the year on the bare open peaks, where a light coat is less conspicuous. The race of the Black Bear found in the arid hills of southern Baluchistan is also said to be distinctive in having a light brown coat. Such a coat would be in harmony with its semi-desert environment. But our knowledge of the Baluchi bears is based on scanty evidence. The brown colouring may be but an individual variation. American Black Bears produce both black and light-cinnamon-coloured cubs, so do Asiatic Black Bears and, more rarely, Sloth Bears. The length and density of the coat, particularly in winter, naturally depends again upon where bears live. It varies with locality. Such variation is particularly marked in the Asiatic Black Bears whose range extends from temperate into tropical forest. Black Bears from Burma or the Malay countries have much shorter and thinner coats than those living in the temperate forests. Even in winter their coats have little of that underwool which is so dense in Black Bears from the Himalayas or from more northerly latitudes.

Habits and surroundings. *H i b e r n a t i o n.* Winter presents not only the need for protection against cold, but also the problem of food scarcity. Many mammals, large and small, among them bears, escape the scarcity of food in winter by giving up active life. They retire into a cave, burrow, or some such shelter where they fall into a lethargic sleep called hibernation. In such sleep the animal is all but dead. The working mechanism of the body is brought almost to a standstill. The heart's action is reduced, and the body temperature falls much below the normal of active life. Just before this winter sleep, bears and many hibernating mammals grow exceedingly fat, eating abundantly during summer and autumn. It was generally believed that fat so accumulated nourishes their bodies during the long winter fast. This is not the case. The body can absorb but little of this fat, for during hibernation its functions are all but suspended. Besides, in the lethargic sleep, the body needs little nourishment. There is no expenditure of energy, little or no wastage, and therefore no loss to be recompensed by taking food. Bears on emerging from their winter sleep are almost as fat as when they entered it. They lose this fat quickly during their active life in the spring. It is a time when they need it most for sufficient food is then difficult to get, and they spend much energy in getting it. The need to hibernate is brought about not by the cold, but by the shortage of food, which becomes increasingly scarce as winter conditions intensify. It is only when getting enough food becomes impossible that bears retire into their retreats. The freezing temperature enables the suspension of the normal functions of the body and produces the comatose sleep. A rise in the temperature may cause a temporary awakening, and the return of the cold a relapse into lethargy. Therefore, governed as this habit is by external conditions, a bear may hibernate in one area of its range but continue active in another. In parts of Europe, Brown Bears remain active through the winter. They are able to get sufficient food. In the Himalayas, they live only in the higher and barren altitudes, and here they always hibernate, going into retirement early or late in the winter, as food conditions dictate. In the same way Black Bears, caught by the winter in high altitudes, pass the season in some shelter in a torpid or semi-torpid condition. But the great majority of Black Bears come down to the lower levels on the approach of winter, and remain active throughout the season, finding a sufficiency of food in these lower valleys. As winter conditions in warmer countries bring little change in the quantity of food available, bears living in tropical forests, naturally do not hibernate. But tropical bears have to contend against heat and rain and adapt their habits to these conditions. During the cold weather Sloth Bears usually sleep in the open, in tall grass or under the shade of trees, but during the hot weather and the rains, they take to sleeping in caves or dens. The temperature in caves remains constant, whatever the temperature of the air outside. Caves are a means of escaping the intense heat and also the swarms of flies, which are so troublesome during the hot weather and during periods of break in the rains. Yet the Sloth Bear is much more tolerant of the sun than the tiger but, like the tiger, it is a thirsty creature dependent on a constant water supply. During the hot weather these bears go long distances to find water and frequently have to dig down for it in the dried-up beds of forest streams.

Feeding habits also change with season and locality. European Brown Bears are said to be more carnivorous than those living in the Himalayas. And carnivorously inclined species like our Black Bears get more constant opportunity to satisfy their taste for flesh when living near human settlements. There is always livestock to kill. Finally, being to a great extent vegetarians, the diet of bears changes considerably with the seasonal flowering and fruiting of different trees and shrubs.

BEARS AND THEIR NEIGHBOURS

Big as they are, bears fill a lowly role in the animal community. They are night-workers, digging for their accustomed food, which consists mainly of small creatures which burrow in the ground, hide under stones, or tunnel into or conceal themselves under the bark of trees. Omnivorous in their food, these animals are not thrown into serious competition with other carnivores, nor are they ordinarily hunted as food by beasts of prey. They are too strong and powerful for that. A hungry tiger or panther or a pack of wild dogs or wolves may attack a bear, conflicts may arise from chance meetings, but ordinarily bears are left alone by other animals. Their movements attract little attention from their animal neighbours.

Bears and man. As to their association with man, bears have been exterminated or driven out by man from many parts of their former domains. Brown Bears have disappeared from most of the settled parts of Europe and North America, those living in our Himalayan fastnesses have little as yet to fear from human intrusion. Sloth Bears are no longer found in many parts of India where they were once common, they have retreated deeper into our forests. Black Bears both in America and Asia have been the most successful in surviving human encroachment into their domains, and in adjusting their ways to life near human settlements. In the Himalayas many Black Bears live near forest villages. Contact with man has naturally affected the habits of bears. Where subject to constant menace from man they become much more alert, more shy, and more rigidly nocturnal in habit. Black Bears are said to have better sight and hearing than most of their tribe. Their greater alertness and cunning has developed from more constant contact with man. Ordinarily bears fear and avoid him, except when defending their young, or when wounded. Attacks on man are usually sudden and unprovoked. Short of sight and hard of hearing, the bear is likely to be surprised at close quarters. Taken unawares, it rushes to furious attack in self-defence. As such bears are really dangerous animals. Many people are savagely mauled or killed by bears, mostly as a result of these 'sudden meetings. Naturally this is more frequent with species, like Black Bears, which take readily to living near human settlements. Contact with man also gives bears the opportunity to raid his fields and orchards, while more carnivorously inclined species, like Brown Bears and Black Bears, frequently take to cattle-killing. Individuals developing this habit may become notorious pests. ' Opportunity maketh the thief.'

FAMILY LIFE AND CARE OF THE YOUNG

Communication. There is little recorded about vocal communication amongst bears. They growl and grunt at each other, give vent to various puffing, bubbling, and whining sounds when seeking their food, and raise an appalling clamour when wounded. It is however recorded of the Sloth Bear that it gives out a long-drawn melodious note which is described as a mate call ; a pair were observed so calling to each other. Sloth Bears are particularly noisy at mating time. Mother bears call to their young.

Except when mating, or accompanied by their young, bears usually lead solitary lives. For most species mating time is in summer and the young are produced in winter, which means that in colder regions many cubs are born under snow during the time of hibernation. The period of gestation varies with different species extending from 7 to 8 months. The usual number of cubs is from 2 to 3. Newborn bear cubs are ordinarily small, hairless, and blind, remaining blind for from three weeks to a month. When strong enough and able to get about they accompany the mother on her wanderings. As the male deserts its mate after breeding the care of the young is left wholly to the mother. Assiduously she tends to them and most determined is she in their defence. At such a time she is really dangerous and prone to immediate attack. The cubs live with their mother till they are two, or even three years old, leaving her. then on reaching maturity. This probably explains why bears are sometimes seen associating in small parties. Judging from animals in captivity the length of life may extend from 40 to 50 years.

THE SLOTH BEAR

Melursus ursinus (Shaw)

Plate facing p. 130

[RACES IN INDIA : *ursinus* (Shaw). CEYLON : *inornatus* Pucheran]

Local Names. Hindi *bhaiu* (north India), *rinch* or *reech* (south India) ; Mar. *asval* ; Tamil & Kan. *karadee;* Tel. *elugu bunti* ; Mal. *puni karadi.*

Size. Height at shoulder, from 2 ft. 2 in. (65 cm.) to 2 ft. 9 in. (85 cm.) ; average length, 4½ to 5½ ft. (140 to 170 cm.). Males, usually larger, weighing about 280-320 lb. (127-145 kg.) ; females, from 140 lb. (64 kg.) upwards.

Distinctive Characters. With its elongated muzzle and lower lip, long unkempt hair and short hind legs, this is the most uncouth of all bears. Most have a whitish V-shaped breast patch, and usually the muzzle and the tips of the feet are dirty white or yellowish. The claws, always longer on the forefeet, are ivory white. The coat may have a brownish tinge, more rarely it is wholly brown.

Distribution. The forested tracts of India and Assam from the base of the Himalayas to Ceylon.

Habits. Sloth Bears live where there is sufficient forest to provide food, and favour places where outcroppings of rock and tumbled boulders offer them shelter during the hot weather and the rains. They come out shortly before sunset, hunt for food all night, and retire in the morning. In cloudy and cool weather they may be up and about by day, and in places remote from human interference they are less rigidly nocturnal. Their food consists mainly of fruit and insects, but a hungry Sloth Bear may be driven to eat carrion. To get sufficient food to support their bulky bodies Sloth Bears walk much and work hard. What they eat depends upon locality and season. Fruit in our jungles is more plentiful in the hot weather. Then banyan and other wild figs, mangoes, jambul, bael, and ebony trees are all in fruit. This is also the best time for honey. The great combs of the large rock bee (*Apis dorsata*), suspended in clusters under rocks or from a branch, and the combs of the smaller forest bee (*Apis indica*) usually hidden in tree hollows, are now loaded with honey. The bear climbs for fruit or shakes it down with its great paws. It knocks down a honeycomb and descends to eat it. In the monsoon, insect food is more plentiful, and bears now find many insects under stones and fallen logs, under bark, and in the crevices of trees. But their main insect food is termites. Ruined and dug-out termite mounds are evidence that these bears are about. Also they dig for the big white grubs of large dung and longicorn beetles, which tunnel in the earth. After the rains, bears living near human settlements have the opportunity to raid the ripening sugar-cane and maize crops and, where date palms are tapped, they climb the trees to drink the toddy from the pots. In the cold weather *ber* trees fruit and later, between March and April, *mowha* trees bloom and carpet the ground with heavy-scented flowers. There Sloth Bears and other animals gather in numbers to feed on the fallen petals.

Mating time is usually in the hot weather and most of the young are born seven months later between December and January. The cubs, when sufficiently strong to grip, are carried on the mother's back to and from her feeding grounds. She grows savage and quick· to attack in their defence. They live with her 2-3 years till they attain maturity. A Sloth Bear has lived in captivity for forty years.

THE BROWN BEAR

Ursus arctos Linnaeus

Plate facing p. 130

[RACE IN INDIA : *isabellinus* Horsfield]

Local Names. Hindi *barf ka rinch, lal bhalu, safed bhalu, siala reech* ; Kash. *haput* ; Baltistan *drengmo* ; Ladak *drin mor* ; Nepali *dub* ; English *Red Bear*.

Size. As with all bears, very variable. Males average 5 ft. 8 in. (170 cm.) in length, females a foot less. A very big male may be 7 to 8 ft. (210 to 245 cm.) long.

Distinctive Characters. Its heavier build and brown coat will suffice to distinguish it from the Himalayan Black Bear. The brown varies individually and seasonally from dark to light, white tips to the fur may give the coat a silvery tinge. Usually the coat becomes tawny or red-brown when old and worn ; a darker, richer brown when grown new in the summer, and long, luxuriant, and heavily furnished with underwool before the onset of winter.

Distribution. In our limits only in the higher levels of Waziristan, north-western and central Himalayas, and Bhutan. Beyond the range covers, or once covered, the whole of the North Tempe-rate Zone in Asia, Europe, and North America. The Indian race is said to be distinctive by its paler coat and smaller build.

Habits. The bare open peaks high above the tree-line are the usual haunt of these bears. Emerging from their winter sleep in the spring, they follow the melting snows up to their perpetual level. At this season and in the early summer they graze like cattle on the newly-grown grass, and spend much of their time turning over stones to look for insects, or hunting voles and marmots, which they dig out of their burrows. It is a time when food is not plentiful and even carrion may be eaten. When summer has set in individuals take to killing sheep and goats and ponies, which are then brought to the high pastures to graze. Developing this habit a Brown Bear may become a real terror to livestock ; but it never becomes a man-killer, fearing and avoiding man. Later in summer or early autumn the bears come down to the lower reaches. It is the fruiting season when berries and wild fruit are to be had in the forests, apricots, peaches, apples, mulberries, and walnuts in the orchards, and buck-wheat in the maize fields. Most of this fruit is taken from the ground. Brown Bears seldom climb, and much of their diet at this time is limited to grass, roots, and tubers. Great tracts over the hill-sides are ploughed up to get at them. But with the onset of winter and heavy falls of snow, there is no more food to be had and the Brown Bear goes into some shelter under rocks, in a cave or a den dug out by itself to pass the season of adversity in torpid sleep, buried deep under the snow. Females are then with young, for they mate early in the summer, in May or June. The cubs are born within the snug winter retreat. Cubbing time is usually in December and January and by May the cubs are sufficiently grown to follow their mother in her quest for food. They remain with her till they attain maturity. How long they really take to grow up is not accurately known. Some observers suggest three, others four or even five years. Brown Bears live to a considerable age ; 47 is the record of one kept in a zoo, while another captive female bore young in her 31st year.

THE HIMALAYAN BLACK BEAR

Selenarctos thibetanus (G. Cuvier)

Plate facing p. 130

[RACES IN INDIA : *thibetanus* (G. Cuvier), *laniger* Pocock, *gedrosianus* Blanford]

Local Names. Hindi *reech, rinch, bhalu* ; Kash. *haput* ; Nepali *sanar* ; Bhotia *dom* ; Assam Hills *satun, sitam, mapol, mansu bhurma* ; Bur. *wet woon.*

Size. Males vary from 4ft. 8 in. to 5 ft. 5 in. (140 to 165 cm.) ; a large male measured 6 ft. 5 in. (195 cm.) from nose to rump ;

females, about 5½ ft. (170 cm.). A male in the autumn may scale 400 lb. (180 kg.) when fat with high feeding ; average weight, 200-250 lb. (90-115 kg.).

Distinctive Characters. Its shorter smoother coat and black claws distinguish it at once from the Sloth Bear. Its build is less clumsy and more compact. General colour, typically black ; muzzle, tan or brown ; chin, white or buff : very characteristic is the V-shaped breast-mark which may be white, yellow, or buff. Animals from the Assam hill ranges have shorter and thinner coats with little or no underwool, which is well developed in west Himalayan animals, especially in winter.

Distribution. In India, Kashmir, the Himalayas, and Assam, extending eastwards into China and Japan, southwards into Burma and the Malay countries, westwards into Baluchistan.

Habits. Steep forested hills are the favoured habitat of this bear. In the Himalayas during summer they may be found near the limits of the tree-line 10,000-12,000 ft. (3050-3660 m.) above sea-level, but in winter most of them come down to the lower valleys, 5000 ft. (1525 m.) and even lower—they have been encountered in the Terai jungles. They live at even lower altitudes in the Assam hill ranges. In Baluchistan they have adapted themselves to life in an arid environment. The Himalayan Black Bear spends the day sleeping in a rock cave or in the hollow of a tree. It comes out at dusk to seek its food and retires after sunrise. However, it was noted to be "frequently active during the day" in the Dachigam Sanctuary in Kashmir. Food varies with season. In summer they live largely on wild fruit and berries and raid orchards for pears, apricots, and nuts of various kinds. Being expert climbers much of their food is taken from the treetops. This is the season when honey is to be had. The bears work hard to get at the combs of the little bee which builds its hive in hollow tree stems. Fields of ripening corn or maize are raided in the autumn. Insects, termites, and the larvae of beetles provide variety to this diet. It is the most carnivorous of the bears, and many living near villages kill sheep and goats and even larger cattle. Life near human settlements also leads to encounters with human beings. Many people are killed or mauled by these animals. The mating season is late autumn. The cubs are produced late in the winter and early in the spring, in the shelter of thick undergrowth or in a cave or hollow tree. The young, usually two or more, remain with the mother for a year or more ; which explains parties of four or more of these bears seen together. They probably include litters of two successive seasons.

The smaller Malayan Sun Bear, *Helarctos malayanus* (Raffles) occurs uncommonly on the Hills of north-east India, south of the Brahmaputra River. The smallest of the bears with a length of 104 to 140 cm. and weight of 27 to 65 kg. Jet black in colour with a pale patch on chest variable in pattern. More arboreal and has bowed front legs and inturned paws.

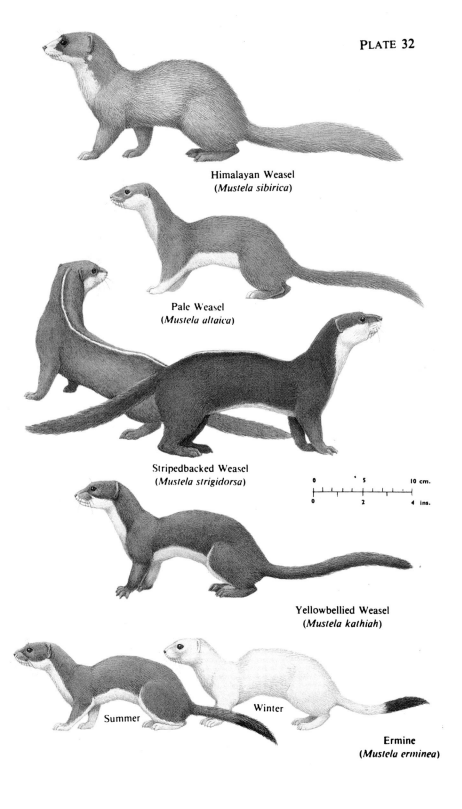

PLATE 32

Himalayan Weasel
(*Mustela sibirica*)

Pale Weasel
(*Mustela altaica*)

Stripedbacked Weasel
(*Mustela strigidorsa*)

Yellowbellied Weasel
(*Mustela kathiah*)

Summer

Winter

Ermine
(*Mustela erminea*)

PLATE 33

Marbled Polecat
(*Vormela peregusna*)

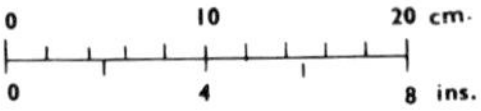

Chinese Ferret-Badger
(*Melogale moschata*)

Burmese Ferret-Badger
(*Melogale personata*)

Hog-Badger
(*Arctonyx collaris*)

Ratel
(*Mellivora capensis*)

9. Pandas

THE PLACE OF the pandas among the Carnivora is a thing about which naturalists are not in agreement. Some include them with the bears, which they resemble somewhat in external form. A panda's round head, squat heavy body, short legs and plantigrade gait are certainly bear-like. A panda is a ' Teddy Bear ' come to life. Pandas have been classed as a sub-family of the Racoons (Procyonidae), a North American tribe of Carnivores.

The Giant Panda [*Ailuropoda melanoleuca* (David)] has so far not been discovered within Indian limits, but it may well be found in the northern frontiers of Burma as it inhabits adjoining Chinese territory. In fact, a closely allied genus once lived in the mountain forests of Upper Burma, but was recently exterminated. The recent efforts to breed this rare and attractive animal in captivity have not been successful.

The smaller panda or Cat-Bear is found well within Indian limits. In general build it is much like its near relative the Giant Panda. Like the Giant Panda it is distinguishable from the bears by special characters associated with the genital organs, and by the possession of a glandular sac surrounding the anus. It noticeably differs from the Giant Panda in its long tail, quite two-thirds as long as its body and in the dense mat of wool covering the soles of its feet. So dense is this mat of hair that it completely covers the pads rendering them quite functionless. This character alone differentiates the Cat-Bear from any other tropical mammal. The only parallel is seen in the hairy soles of certain Arctic animals like polar bears—they are an aid to movement over snow and ice. Why exactly an arboreal animal like the Cat-Bear has these hairy feet has not yet been explained, but actually the Cat-Bear hunts for its food on the ground and is mainly terrestrial in habit. Trees are used for sleeping in, or as a refuge when alarmed. The animal climbs trees with ease, its toes are well formed and widely separable and furnished with strong curving semi-retractile claws, which must give it a firm grip on branches.

The massive many-cusped crowns of the molar teeth are well suited to the crushing of fibrous vegetable matter. The animals are almost wholly vegetarian in diet.

THE CAT-BEAR, or RED PANDA

Ailurus fulgens F. Cuvier

Plate facing p. 131

[RACE IN INDIA : *fulgens* F. Cuvier]

Local Names. Nepalese *wah, ye, nigalva ponva* ; Bhotia *oakdonga, wakdonga* ; Lepcha *sankam.*

Size. Head and body, about 2 ft. (60 cm.) ; tail, 16 in. (40 cm.); weight, 8½-9 lb. (3-4 kg.).

Distinctive Characters. Its rounded head, large erect pointed ears, stumpy muzzle, and short hairy-soled legs, combined with its bright chestnut colouring and ringed tail, are characters which easily distinguish this animal. The face and lower lips, white. There is a vertical red stripe from just above the eye to the gape.

Distribution. The Himalayas from Nepal and Sikkim eastwards to upper Burma and southern China. Two races are recognised : Cat-Bears from Burma and further east are said to be distinguishable by a longer winter coat, larger skull, and more robust teeth.

Habits. Cat-Bears live in the temperate forests of the Himalayas above 5000 ft. (1525 m.) or so. The animal spends its day sleeping in trees. It rests curled up in the topmost branches, with its bushy tail wrapped over its head ; or it lies along a branch with its head tucked away under its chest between its forelegs. In the evening it descends to the ground to hunt for food, climbing back to its roost in the morning. A pair will forage together or there may be a family party of parents and young. Sight and hearing are dull in these animals and their sense of smell is not specially acute.

The Cat-Bear searches for roots, for succulent grasses, for leaves and fallen fruits. Eggs, insects, and grubs may also be part of the diet—it is a question of individual taste. Some captive animals showed a particular weakness for sweetened food, taking almost any food sweetened with sugar.

Not much is known about the family life of these attractive animals. A weak whistling or squeaking note, sometimes given out and somewhat like the chirping of a bird, may be a means of communication. It has been observed that under stress of excitement they give out a strong odour produced from the anal scent glands. The odour may be a means of defence or means of sexual attraction. Cat-Bears in captivity were observed to rub this glandular area against surfaces over which they moved leaving a scent trail which might well enable one individual to find another.

The mating season and period of gestation are not known. The young, usually two, are born in the spring. The hollow of a tree or a crevice in a rock serves as a nursery. They remain with the mother or with both parents till about a year old and well able to fend for themselves. Cat-Bears are easily tamed and make charming pets.

10. The Weasel Family

WEASELS, BADGERS, AND otters differ so much from each other in appearance that it is difficult to believe that there is any relationship between them. But certain resemblances, certain details in the character of the molar teeth, indicate their common affinity. They are therefore grouped in a single family, the **Mustelidae**. In other respects, in the structure of the skull and teeth, in build and appearance, badgers, otters, and weasels show greater differences than can be found among members of any family of Carnivores. These differences arise from widely different modes of life. They provide a basis for the division of the family into a number of subfamilies. These are (1) Otters, (2) Martens, (3) Weasels, (4) Ferret-Badgers, (5) Badgers, (6) Ratels. The distinctive features of each group are best discerned by a study of structure in relation to habits.

Otters. Otters are undoubtedly the descendants of weasel-like ancestors which took to the catching of fish as their chief means of livelihood. Though not especially aquatic, many weasels enter water and swim with ease and speed. In fact, an American species (*Mustela vison*) hunts its prey on land and in water, in which it displays an otter-like prowess. Actually the webs between an otter's toes, a character always associated with swimming, are not always better developed than in some martens and weasels ; but its feet are larger and its toes longer, the webbing between them is therefore more extensive. The foot as such becomes a more powerful paddle. But apart from its feet, the otter's whole organism is adapted especially to its aquatic existence.

What are the distinguishing marks of an otter ? A close coat of waterproof fur, a thick muscular tail, paddle-like feet, the hind always larger than the fore, and a bristling array of rigid whiskers. All these characters are associated with its aquatic habits. Though it gets about clumsily yet well enough on land, it is in water that an otter shows how admirably its structure fits it for its mode of life. Its main food is fish, and its whole body is expressly designed for the capture of its prey. Its sleek coat, heavily lined with waterproof under-fur, is a protection against chill. Its streamlined, almost cylindrical, body gives it easy entry and less resisting passage through water. Its broad flattened head, scarcely showing above the surface when swimming, makes for concealment. How attractive is the ease and grace of its swimming ! Going slowly an otter merely paddles with its forepaws. In rapid swimming the large hindfeet, the body, and the tail come into action. Vigorous kicks of the hindfeet and sinuous snake-like movements of body and tail propel

PLATE 34

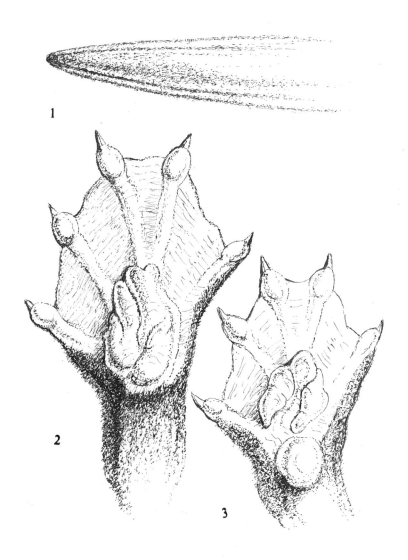

Tail (1), hindfoot (2), and forefoot (3) of Common Otter (*Lutra lutra*)

PLATE 35

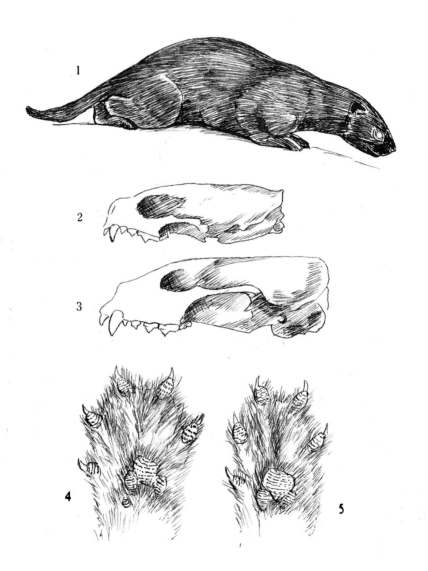

Weasel (*Mustela*) characters
1. Body-form of weasel; 2 and 3. Fore-shortened jaw and muzzle of weasel (2) as compared with those (3) of marten (*Martes*); 4 and 5. Fore- (4) and hind- (5) feet of Himalayan Weasel (*M. sibirica*) illustrating hairy soles characteristic of the Indian races of this animal

the animal swiftly through the water. Its paws are effective paddles, while the massive muscles of its tail, its length, and flattened tapering end assure its efficiency as a propeller and steering organ. An otter dives instantly after fish and follows with ease the twists and turns of its fleeing quarry. It is well fitted for such underwater work. Its small ears and valvular nostrils prevent the entry of water. When under water we discover the reason for its bristle-like whiskers. Wiry and thick they do not droop when wet but stand out rigid to effectively serve their purpose as feelers. Underwater they become an aid which reduces the disadvantage of blurred vision. With its whiskers the otter gropes or ' feels ' for fish hiding in crevices or among submerged rocks. The feet are also used as feelers. With its highly sensitive paws the otter feels for fish and other prey buried in the ooze or lying hidden under stones. The teeth of otters are well adapted for dealing with their slippery prey ; the hind teeth furnished with many sharp-pointed cusps are admirably adapted for piercing through and crunching hard scales and retaining a close grip on slippery prey.   (Plates facing pp. 127, 146)

Martens. Martens, weasels, and polecats are fitted for a life on the ground or in trees. They display none of those modifications which fit the otter for its aquatic existence. They have feet for running and climbing, and short, sharp, partially retractile claws for seizing and holding prey. These animals, typical examples of the weasel family, are grouped as : 1. the Martens (Martinae), 2. Weasels and Polecats (Mustelinae). Why becomes evident when we consider their structure and habits.

Compared with a weasel, a marten is distinctive in its longer snout, its large upstanding ears, longer limbs, and longer tail. These characters are associated with its more arboreal habits. Martens are given more to climbing and hunting food in trees, and are better fitted for an arboreal life. Longer limbs make the marten a more agile climber, a longer tail gives it better balance when running in the treetops or leaping from branch to branch, a thing which martens do with speed and precision. When hunting in the trees the marten has to rely more on vision and hearing. Its large ears help it to pick up airborne sounds better. On the ground a marten is speedy enough, but there is less ease and grace of movement. It runs with its back highly arched in an awkward cumbersome gallop.

Weasels and Polecats. Though they climb well and take readily to trees, especially when living in forested country, weasels are built more for ground work, one might say underground work. To follow a mouse or rat down into the depths of its burrow is what a weasel is especially built to do. For this it has a flattened almost snake-like head, small ears, a slim stream-lined body, short legs and tail, all designed to give it easy uninterrupted passage into holes and crevices. These are the distinctive characters of a weasel. They adapt the animal to its usual way of hunting its food. But, compared with a marten, the weasel's most distinctive feature is its short abrupt snout. Highly predatory in habit, both weasels and martens have trenchant meat-cutting teeth. But of the two the weasel is more highly specialised for the killing and eating of living prey. It has shorter jaws and fewer cheek teeth. A similar reduction in the length of the jaws and in the number of cheek teeth is seen in Cats, animals which live exclusively by hunting. Weasels are more consistent hunters and meat-eaters than martens. Their whole structure reveals a higher specialization for a predatory life. (Plate facing p. 147)

In their structure and habits of life, polecats differ little from weasels. They are fierce and persistent hunters given more to hunting on the ground than in the treetops. From weasels they differ mainly in coloration.

Badgers. With badgers we come to a group of Musteline animals which are specially fitted to earn their livelihood by grubbing in the soil. What specially distinguishes the badger from other animals in its family are its broad feet armed with great claws. They are not retractile claws. There is no device for keeping them sharp. They are not designed for striking and holding prey. They are essentially claws for digging in the ground. Distinctive again of the badger is its long projecting snout. The badger uses it to root and probe in the soil, hence its length and mobility. Adaptations to a fossorial life are more marked in true badgers and less evident in those animals known as ferret-badgers. Hence badgers are separated into: 1. Helictinae, Ferret-Badgers; 2. Melinae, Badgers.

Ferret-Badgers. A ferret-badger is a mixture of weasel and badger, hence its name. Its long projecting snout usable as a probe is badger-like. Its feet, though not as broad as a true badger's, have long non-retractile claws. They are meant for digging. But unlike badgers these animals have a fine array of whiskers and large ears, and longer limbs and tail. In this they resemble the weasels. The long limbs and tail and striated pads under its feet suggest that a ferret-badger is not completely terrestrial in habit, and like the weasel it has an aptitude for climbing. A Chinese form is known to be an agile climber.

Hog-Badgers. While ferret-badgers retain a number of weasel-like characters and to some extent a weasel-like mode of life, badgers present in their form and structure a complete departure from the weasel pattern and more complete adaptation to a fossorial life. This is seen in the badger's bear-like build, its broad squat body, short stumpy legs, and broad paws armed with strong digging claws. Its snout is long and prominent and used as a probe for rooting in the earth. Its eyes and ears are small, and its whiskers

poorly developed. True badgers are not found in India, but we
have hog-badgers which have the same general characters.

Ratels. In appearance a ratel looks much like a badger. Both
animals are well equipped to dig in the earth. A similar occupation
has produced certain similarities in build and structure, a thing
common in the world of Nature, even among wholly unrelated
animals. Like the badger, a ratel has a broad squat bear-like body,
stumpy legs, and strong large claws ; both animals are given to
digging. But here the resemblance ends. The snout of the ratel is
not prolonged and modified into an instrument for rooting in the
earth. Though omnivorous, the ratel is essentially a flesh-eater.
Its teeth are entirely unlike the broad-crowned crushing teeth of
badgers ; they are more like the teeth of a weasel. They are the
trenchant meat-cutting teeth of a highly predatory animal.

LIFE IN RELATION TO SURROUNDINGS

The home of the family. Except for some of the otters and weasels
which have spread below the Equator, the home of the Mustelidae
is the Northern Hemisphere, where the majority of genera and
species live under most varied conditions of arctic cold or tropical
heat, of extreme dryness or humidity. With such adaptability to
contrasting surroundings it is difficult to explain why so few of these
animals have colonized the Indian peninsula. Only two species, the
ratel and the Smooth Indian Otter are widely spread in India. The
rest of the family are limited in their habitat to the Himalayan region
and the hills of Assam, or to some of the higher hill ranges of south
India. The Common-Otter and the Clawless Otter live in the lower
reaches of the Himalayas and the adjoining plains, but nowhere
else in India except in the south Indian hill ranges. It is the same
with the Yellowthroated Martens. Yet these martens, an Oriental
genus, elsewhere in their range live successfully under conditions
no different from those which obtain in our main peninsular area.
As for the stone martens and weasels, they are intruders from northern lands and keep mainly to the alpine and temperate forests of
the Himalayan region and the hills of Assam. The European
badger (*Meles*) is not found in India except perhaps on the frontiers
of Tibet. Ferret-badgers and hog-badgers entering by way of our
eastern frontiers have colonized the tropical and sub-tropical zones
of the eastern Himalayas and Assam. The ratel as we have seen
has been more successful. It has established itself practically over
the whole of the Peninsula except in areas of very heavy rainfall.

Coloration and geography. One aspect of coloration in relation to
geography may be mentioned. Many weasels living in northern
latitudes change their brown summer coats for a snow-white one in

winter. In lower latitudes the change becomes less complete, and where there is no snow the brown summer coat is retained throughout the year. In India the only species of weasel, or animal for that matter, which exhibits this change is the Ermine or Stoat (*Mustela erminea*), whose lovely white winter fur is always associated with the trappings of royalty. A characteristic of weasels, particularly of those living in the alpine and temperate zones of the Himalayas, is the general hairiness of the soles of the feet, which in winter completely covers the pads. Much of this hair is lost in summer. Hairy soles are not only a provision for greater warmth but are an aid to firmer movement over snow and ice. **(Plate facing p. 147)**

Coloration and habits. We have written about the ' stink-glands ' of civets and their foetid discharge, and how this means of defence was associated with a special livery known as ' warning coloration '. Many genera of Musteline animals, badgers, ratels, martens, weasels, and polecats, are equipped with stink-glands situated in the anal region. The special defensive equipment explains their distinctive coloration. Colour and pattern in these animals is designed not to conceal but to advertise the presence of the owner. How vivid in contrasting tones is the colouring of a weasel or marten ! The pale chin and throat, the lighter underparts, stand out in bold relief against the deep dark tones of head, nape, and back. Look at a polecat, the vivid markings of its head, its display of white or buff under-fur, when the long black hairs of its coat bristle up, make the animal most conspicuous. Remarkable again is the colouring of badgers and ratels. In the ratel the colour tones reverse what is usual in Nature. The underparts are darker than the upper. Warning coloration as was explained is a reminder to other animals to keep away. The foul discharge from the stink-glands once experienced is not easily forgotten ; hence animals so equipped usually make little attempt at concealment. How characteristic of weasels, martens, badgers, and ratels is their extreme boldness, their tenacity of life, and their scant concern for the presence of other animals ! One does not mean to convey that stink-glands and ' warning coloration ' give these animals absolute immunity from attack. They obey Nature's law of tooth and fang and fall a prey to other carnivores. It is not so much a defence against habitual enemies as against new foes, who else might acquire the habit of preying on them. The range of their enemies is thus limited.

Uses. Weasels are wonderfully endowed for predatory work and are perhaps the most perfectly organised machines for killing that have been developed among mammals. In the areas where they operate they are the most deadly scourge to small mammals and birds, making up for their smallness in size by their terrifying ferocity in attack. Though very destructive to man's domestic stock they play an essential and effective role in keeping down the overwhelming number of rats, mice, and other vermin.

The value set on the fine furs of weasels, martens, and stoats has led to their steady pursuit and capture in all countries of the world. Millions of these animals fall victims annually to man's love of self-adornment. And although the various species have held their own in spite of persecution, increasing occupation of their domains by man and the growing demand for furs must lead to their ultimate decrease. Efforts are being made to establish fur farms to maintain and ensure the supply.

THE COMMON OTTER

Lutra lutra (Linnaeus)

Plate facing p. 131

[RACES IN INDIA : *nair* F. Cuvier, *monticola* Hodgson, *aurobrunnea* Hodgson, *kutab* Schinz. CEYLON : *nair* F. Cuvier]

Local Names. Hindi *ud, ud bilao, pani kutta* ; Tel. *niru kuka* ; Mal. and Tamil *neer nai* ; Kan. *neeru nai, uddra* ; Bur. *peearu.*

Size. Head and body, 2 ft. to 2 ft. 8 in. (60 to 80 cm.) ; tail, 1 ft. 6 in. (45 cm.). South Indian animals are smaller and slighter in build than those living in the Himalayas.

Distinctive Characters. The distinctive characters of otters as a group have been discussed. The present species can be distinguished from other otters found in India by its fuller, rougher coat, and by its grizzled dorsal surface due to the pale tips of the longer hairs. The grizzling is less apparent in the south Indian race (*L. l. nair*). The hairs of the muzzle terminate above the naked nose in an angular or zigzag line. In the Smooth Indian Otter (*L. perspicillata*) the marginal line of hair above the nose is straight.

Distribution. In India the Common Otter is found only in Kashmir, the Himalayas, and Assam, and nowhere in the Peninsula except in south India. Beyond our limits, Europe, North Africa, and suitable localities over the greater part of Asia. Four Indian races are recognised.

Habits. In India this is essentially an otter of cold hill and mountain streams and lakes. It makes its lair among rocks and boulders, in hollows beneath the roots of trees growing by the water's edge, or it lies up in reed beds, fern brakes, and bushes. Bones and scales of fish, and the web-footed tracks of the animal round the den show whether the owner is in residence or not. In summer in the Himalayas and Kashmir many otters go up the streams and torrents ascending to altitudes of 12,000 ft. (3660 m.) or more. Their upward movement probably coincides with the upward migration of carp and other fish for purposes of spawning. With the advent of winter they come down to the lower streams. Much of this journeying from stream to stream is done overland. Fish is their main food. Failing fish, crabs, and other crustacea, frogs, rodents, and waterfowl are eaten, and also leaves and other vegetable matter. Aquatic birds such as ducks may be attacked from below when swimming, or at the water's edge. Apart from its tracks, the presence of an otter in a stream or lake is easily detected by the excreta deposited on rocks and by the banks. As with many mammals the same spot may be used day after day. Otters hunt at night, especially where harassed by man. Where undisturbed they hunt in the evenings and stay out till late in the morning. A pair, a family, or several families may combine to surround a shoal of fish and drive them into the shallows. The fish actually eaten may form a small proportion of those killed in the lust and excitement of the hunting. Such massacres occur usually when a stream is running low and conditions wholly favour the otters.

Little is known for certain of the breeding habits of these animals. We do not know whether they have a fixed breeding season. Many young are born in the early part of the year. Mating may take place in the water. The period of gestation is about 61 days. The nursery or ' holt ' is usually a burrow dug by the water's edge. It has several entrances, one of them under water. The young remain with the parents till nearly full-grown. Otters are easily tamed. They make engaging pets, following one about like a dog.

THE SMOOTH INDIAN OTTER

Lutra perspicillata I. Geoffroy

Plate facing p. 131

[RACES IN INDIA : *perspicillata* I. Geoffroy, *sindica* (Pocock)]

Local Names. Hindi *ud, udni, ud bilao, ludra* (Sind), *pani kutta, jal manus* (central India) ; Mar. *pan manjar, jal manjar* ; Kan., Mal., and Tamil *neer nai* ; Tel. *niru kuku.*

Size. Head and body, 25-29 in. (65-75 cm.) ; tail, 16-18 in. (40-45 cm.) ; weight, 16-24 lb. (7-11 kg.). A heavily built animal about the size and proportions of the Common Otter.

Distinctive Characters. Distinguished from the Common Otter by its smooth sleek coat. Colour, blackish to rufous chocolate-brown, sometimes sandy or tawny brown ; dorsal fur not grizzled. The hairs of the muzzle terminate in a straight line above the naked part of the nose. In the Common Otter the line is angular. Otters from Sind and the drier areas of the Punjab, distinctive in their paler coats, are regarded as a separate race.

Distribution. India, from the Himalayas and Sind to the extreme south. Beyond our limits, Burma, Indo-China, and Malaya.

Habits. This is essentially a plains otter, which has adapted itself to life even in our north-western deserts, and in the dry zone of central India and the Deccan. It ascends hill ranges to low elevations. It lives, like the Common Otter, by the margins of lakes and streams and in large tanks and canals. It hunts in flooded fields, creeks, and estuaries and, on the coast, goes out after fish into the open sea. In the dry lands of central India, when pools and streams dry up, these otters show a ready adaptability to changed conditions. They take to jungle hunting like other land carnivores, and lie up in burrows in the hill-sides.

Fish is their main food, but when fish is wanting they eat whatever they can capture and kill. Though built for an aquatic life they are perfectly at home and active on land travelling long distances in search of water or food. Families may combine when fishing. Such a fishing party was seen swimming in a huge semi-circle maintaining a distance of 50 yards (45 m.) or so between each other and driving the fish before them. Every now and then one would dive and emerge with a fish in its jaws, keeping its place in the advancing line. When excited these otters give a short yelping bark. They have a sort of whistle used as an alarm note to their fellows.

Nothing is known about the breeding habits of this otter. Most cubs appear to be born early in the year. In Orissa and Sind these otters are kept by fishermen and employed to drive fish into the nets. The Muhanas of Sind use them as decoys for capturing river dolphins [*Platanista gangetica* (Lebeck)]. Two or three tame otters are let into the river and fish and prawns are thrown to them, whereupon there ensues a great mewing and splashing; the commotion attracts the dolphins which blunder into the nets set for them.

THE CLAWLESS OTTER

Aonyx cinerea (Illiger)

Plate facing p. 131

[RACES IN INDIA : *nirnai* (Pocock), *concolor* (Rafinesque)]

Local Names. As for other otters.

Size. The smallest of our otters. Head and body, 18-22 in. (45-55 cm.) ; tail, 10-13 in. (25-35 cm.) ; weight, 6-13 lb. (3-6 kg.).

Distinctive Characters. Its name indicates its distinctive character. The claws of these otters are rudimentary, no more than small upstanding spikes which, except in small cubs, do not project beyond the toe pads. Colour : dark brown above, paler below. South Indian animals (*A. c. nirnai*) are distinctive in their darker colouring.

Distribution. The Himalayan foothills from Kulu in the Punjab eastwards to the Assam hill ranges, plains of Assam, and lower Bengal. Nowhere else in India except the higher elevations of hill ranges of Coorg and the Nilgiris, the High Range, and the Palnis. Outside Indian limits, Burma, southern China, and the Malay countries.

Habits. In southern India, this otter hunts the same hill streams and lakes as the Common Otter, keeping to the higher levels. In northern India, it is found only on the lower slopes of the Himalayas and in the plains of lower Bengal where it hunts in streams, rivers, tanks, and flooded rice fields, and probably in creeks and estuaries, a favoured hunting ground of clawless otters in Java and the East Indies. Their ways and habits are similar to those of other otters ; but the Clawless Otter is said to feed less on fish and to live more on crabs, snails, mussels, and other aquatic creatures. As such it is believed to be less destructive to fish preserves and hatcheries. Its massive teeth are admirably suited to this diet. Nothing is recorded of the breeding habits of this otter in India.

THE BEECH, or STONE, MARTEN

Martes foina (Erxleben)

Plate facing p. 131

[RACE IN INDIA : *intermedia* (Severtzov)]

Size. Head and body 10 to 17 in. (25 to 45 cm.).

Distinctive Characters. A graceful slender marten, with moderately long legs, and tail about half as long as its head and body. Its build suggests a mixture of squirrel and cat. The colour of its upper side is almost uniform drab or slaty brown, dark or light and never varied with black or yellow ; nor is the white of its throat set off by dark bands running down the nape, both characters so marked in Yellowthroated Martens. In the Himalayan form the white of the throat is generally broken up by brown patches or even completely obliterated.

Distribution. In India, only Kashmir and the Himalayas as far east as Sikkim. Southern Europe, western and south-western Asia, except Arabia.

Habits. Stone Martens inhabit the temperate and alpine zones of the Himalayas and are rarely found below 5000 ft. (1525 m.). They live both in forest and on the barren heights above the tree-line, sheltering in hollows in trees, under logs, among rocks, or in holes in the ground. They hunt by day or by night, preying on any creature which they can capture and overcome. What they hunt and eat varies with season and locality. In the higher levels of the Himalayas they prey largely on voles and mouse-hares living in this treeless terrain. Forest dwellers have a wider range of food. They hunt much in trees, pursuing squirrels and stalking and pouncing on birds. This diet of flesh is varied in season with honey, nuts, and fruits. Stone Martens are said to be especially fond of cherries. Driven by hunger they take to preying on lizards, snakes, and frogs, in fact on anything they can get. Those living in or around mountain villages raid poultry yards and pigeon-coops ; and frequently do much damage. In this the Stone Marten is different from the yellowthroated species, which usually avoids the abodes of man and keeps to forests.

Mating time is about February ; four to five young are produced nine weeks later in April. The nursery, a hole in a tree, or a cranny between rocks, is made comfortable with grass or dead leaves. The young are born blind, naked, and helpless. When large enough they accompany the mother in her hunting. They leave as soon as they are able to fend for themselves ; for, except at mating time and when very young, martens are solitary creatures. A marten fiercely resents the intrusion of others of its species into its preserves. Young individuals are not difficult to tame and make attractive pets.

YELLOWTHROATED MARTENS

The Himalayan Yellowthroated Marten *Martes flavigula* (Boddaert)

Plate facing p. 131

[RACE IN INDIA : *flavigula* (Boddaert)]

The Nilgiri Marten *Martes gwatkinsi* Horsfield

Local Names. Garhwali *chitrola* (male), *chitroli* (female) ; Bhotia *shingsam, humiah* ; Tamil *murra nai.*

Size. Head and body, 18-24 in. (45-60 cm.) ; tail, 15-17 in. (38-43 cm.).

Distinctive Characters. A larger animal than the Stone Marten, with a proportionately longer tail measuring about three-fourths the length of head and body. The colour varies among individuals and with season, but it is never the uniform brown or grey-brown of the Stone Marten. The dorsal fur is usually variegated with deep brown, black, and yellow, and the yellow of the throat is emphasized by dark bands running down the nape. Variegation of the dorsal fur is less marked in the Nilgiri Marten (*M. gwatkinsi*) which is deep brown from head to rump, the forequarters being almost reddish.

Distribution. *M. flavigula* : In India, the Himalayas and the Assam hill ranges. Burma, China, and the Malay countries. *M. gwatkinsi* : Nilgiris, south Coorg, and Travancore.

Habits. The adaptability of these martens to the most varied surroundings has been commented upon. In the Himalayas they keep to forest limits and are not found above the tree-line. Here they live in the temperate forest belt between 4000 ft. (1220 m.) and 9000 ft. (2745 m.) and are also found in the sub-tropical and tropical forests below, almost down to plains level. The south Indian species keeps to the higher hill ranges and is rarely found below 3000 ft. (915 m.). Like all their family these martens are restless creatures. They hunt both by day and by night, on the ground but more commonly in trees. In the mating time a pair or a mother with her young hunt together.

Ordinarily they live and hunt alone. In the treetops they display extreme agility, leaping from branch to branch or coursing along and under boughs. Speed of movement and great boldness in attack make them a real menace to all the small creatures living in their neighbourhood. In the treetops they hunt squirrels and birds, raid nests for eggs and young. On the ground their usual quarry is rats and mice, hares, pheasants, and partridges, but they are bold enough to attack larger defenceless animals, like young deer. When pressed for food carrion, snakes, and lizards, and even insects are eaten. Their diet is varied with fruit and honey from flowers. Thrusting its pointed snout into the great scarlet blooms of the silk cotton tree, the marten sucks up the abundant nectar. It is one of the many animals which assist in the pollination of these flowers. These martens usually avoid human habitation. Nothing has been recorded of their breeding habits, they are probably similar to those of the Stone Marten. Individuals are easily tamed.

THE HIMALAYAN WEASEL

Mustela sibirica Pallas

Plate facing p. 142

[RACES IN INDIA : *subhemachalana* Hodgson, *canigula* Hodgson, *hodgsoni* Gray]

Size. Head and body, about 1 ft. (30 cm.) ; tail, 6 in. (15 cm.).

Distinctive Characters. Colour varying from bright foxy red to dark chocolate, no sharp contrast between upper and underparts, which are but slightly paler. The colour of the muzzle is dark in some forms, more or less white in others ; the extent of white on the chin and throat also varies. Paws, same tone as legs except for a few scattered white hairs, or spots. The Himalayan races are : a dark-muzzled form (*subhemachalana*), a white-muzzled form (*canigula*), and a third race (*hodgsoni*) in which the white of the muzzle does not extend as far as the eyes.

Distribution. The Himalayas. Outside Indian limits : central and eastern Asia, upper Burma, and Java.

Habits. In the Himalayas this weasel lives in temperate and alpine forests and in the open grass and scrub above the tree-line at altitudes ranging from 5000-16,000 ft. (1525-4880 m.). Elsewhere in its range it shows a remarkable adaptability to varied conditions of life, being found in dense forest, in dry sandy valleys, and even in low-lying swamps. It makes its den in any convenient shelter, among rocks, under roots of trees, in hollow stumps or logs, and quite often in the burrow of some other animal. Those living in our mountain villages shelter in holes in walls, in the roofs, or under the floors of houses. They may hunt by day, but more usually come out after nightfall. A weasel covers much ground walking slowly with back arched, or moving swiftly in a series of rapid easy bounds. It trails its prey by scent, stopping now and then to stand erect and peer about. Ever restless and on the move, it thrusts itself in and out of thickets and brushwood, holes, and crevices. Weasels hunt for rats and mice, birds and birds' eggs, reptiles, and even eat insects. Those living near villages raid chicken runs and pigeon coops, killing many more than they eat, content often with sucking the blood of their victims. Such resort to man for food increases during winter when many of them congregate about human dwellings. A weasel has all the boldness and courage of its family, attacking and killing for food animals larger than itself. The prey, paralyzed with terror, may be killed without any effort at self-defence. Should it resist, the weasel, its long neck thrust out, its head a-swaying, eyes a-glitter, awaits its chance to spring. Its attack is always aimed at some vital part, the head or the back of the neck, to bite down to the brain or spine, or to the side of the throat to sever the jugular vein. A perfect killing machine, it kills with deadly efficiency. Weasels, except in mating time or when with young, hunt alone. Nothing has been recorded of the breeding habits of our Indian species.

Another Himalayan weasel is the **Ermine**, or **Stoat** [*M. erminea* Linnaeus. Race in India : *ferghanae* (Thomas)] (Plate facing p. 142) which is found in Chitral, Hazara, and Kashmir. Its forepaws, and usually the hindpaws, are conspicuously white, contrasting with the legs. The **Pale Weasel** [*M. altaica* Pallas. Race in India : *temon* Hodgson] (Plate facing p. 142) is generally distributed in the upper levels of the Himalayas, 7000 ft. (2135 m.) to 13,000 ft. (3960 m.). Like the Ermine its paws are white, but its tail is without the black tip so distinctive in the Ermine both in brown summer and snow-white winter coat. The **Yellowbellied Weasel** [*M. kathiah* Hodgson. Races in India : *kathiah* Hodgson, *caporiaccoi* de Beaux] (Plate facing p. 142) ranges from the western Himalayas eastwards to Assam. Like the Himalayan Weasel (*M. sibirica*) it has dark paws, but is distinctive in the sharp contrast between the dark chocolate-brown of its upper parts and the sharply defined rich yellow of the under surface. Finally, there is the **Stripedbacked Weasel** (*M. strigidorsa* Gray) (Plate facing p. 142) a rare animal, distinctive in the white or whitish streak along its back and belly. It lives in temperate forests ranging between 4000 ft. (1220 m.) and 7000 ft. (2135 m.). The general habits of these animals do not differ essentially from the species described above.

PLATE 36

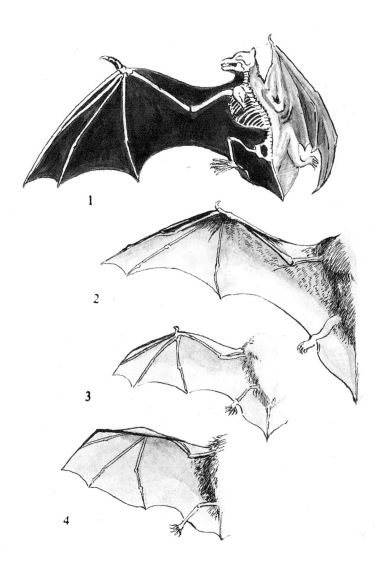

Wings of Bats

1. The long fingers of the hand help to support the wing
2. Wing of long-winged bat
3. Wing of Horseshoe bat
4. Wing of Pipistrelle

PLATE 37

Shortnosed Fruit Bat (*Cynopterus sphinx*) carrying away banana

Photo : *T.S. Lal, APSA, EFIAP*

THE MARBLED POLECAT

Vormela peregusna (Güldenstaedt)

Plates facing pp. 79, 143

[RACE IN INDIA : *alpherakii* Birula]

Size. Head and body, a little over 1 ft. (30 cm.) ; tail, 6 in. (15 cm.) ; weight, 8-12 oz. (230-340 gm.).

Distinctive Characters. Has the general build of a weasel but looks bigger and heavier on account of its longer fur and bushier tail. Colour and pattern very distinctive, especially the facial markings, the white band across the forehead and back of the head, the large ears fringed with white. Body patterned with irregular, black, yellow, and white lines and blotches.

Distribution. Within our limits, Baluchistan only. Beyond, eastern and central Europe, south-western to central Asia, and China.

Habits. The environment of this polecat in Baluchistan is open ground amongst rocks and scrub, in thorn or in dry temperate forests, and quite commonly in gardens and cultivation. Here it adapts itself to extremes of heat and cold, sheltering in deep burrows dug by itself or some other animal. A captive animal showed a great propensity to dig, using its forelimbs to scoop out the earth, and teeth to pull out roots and other obstacles. The burrow is used as sleeping quarters by day. The night is spent in quest of food, but hunger may drive an individual to come out in daylight. Though it can climb, a polecat is essentially a ground hunter. Its ways of hunting are those of the weasel. It hunts the same prey, rats and mice, birds and reptiles. It is as merciless and fierce in attack and displays the same lust and efficiency in killing. Extermination of these animals in many areas of their range is due largely to the havoc they play with poultry. In such wholesale slaughter the polecat contents itself with lapping up the flowing blood of its victims. Ordinarily, what remains of a meal is taken to the den. Like its relatives the weasels and martens, a polecat shows little concern for the presence of man and other animals and faces its adversary with growls of defiance, head flung back, teeth bared, every hair erect, and tail bristling and curved over its back. It is then that the vivid contrasts of its colouring, the facial bands, the long black hairs of its coat, the bright underwool, show up to fullest effect. The warning coloration is associated with the discharge of a foetid fluid from the anal glands. It is a means of defence not usually resorted to except under extreme necessity or provocation. Little is known of the mating habits of the polecat in India. They are solitary creatures and association between males and females is limited to the mating season. The mother, left solely to care for the young, produces them in a burrow, made more comfortable with grass and leaves. The period of gestation is nine weeks, and the young are born in March or early in April ; growth is rapid and they are able to fend for themselves by the winter. The **Tibetan Polecat** [*Mustela putorius* Linnaeus. Race in India : *larvatus* (Hodgson)] enters our territory only in Kashmir and Tibet. Its general colour is creamy white or yellowish. The hairs of its coat, dark-tipped, long, and loose, show the pale under-fur ; legs black, darker than the back. Its habits do not differ essentially from those of the Marbled Polecat. In the terrain in which it lives it must prey largely on marmots, mouse-hares, and ground birds.

FERRET-BADGERS

The Chinese Ferret-Badger *Melogale moschata* (Gray)

Plate facing p. 143

[RACE IN INDIA : *millsi* (Thomas)]

The Burmese Ferret-Badger *Melogale personata* I. Geoffroy

Plate facing p. 143

[RACES IN INDIA : *personata* I. Geoffroy, *nipalensis* (Hodgson)]

Size. Both species : head and body, about 1 ft. 6 in. (45 cm.) ; tail with hair, near 9 in. (23 cm.).

Distinctive Characters. The general appearance of ferret-badgers has been described. Two species *M. moschata* and *M. personata* are found in India ; the distinction between them is based mainly on the character of the teeth. The molar teeth are small and narrow-crowned in *moschata*, massive and wide-crowned in *personata*. Both species are similar in coloration. In general tone the coat varies from deep purplish grey to shades of brown. The bleached tips of the longer hairs give the coat a distinctly silvery tone. The facial markings, cheeks, nuchal stripes, and the underparts yellowish or buffy white. A narrow whitish stripe runs from the crown of the head down the middle of the back to the rump. In *M. moschata* this median stripe seldom extends beyond the shoulders.

Distribution. *M. moschata* : Assam, ranging eastwards into upper Burma, south China, and the Indo-Chinese countries. *M. personata* : from Nepal eastwards to Assam, Burma and Siam and Cochin China.

PLATE 38

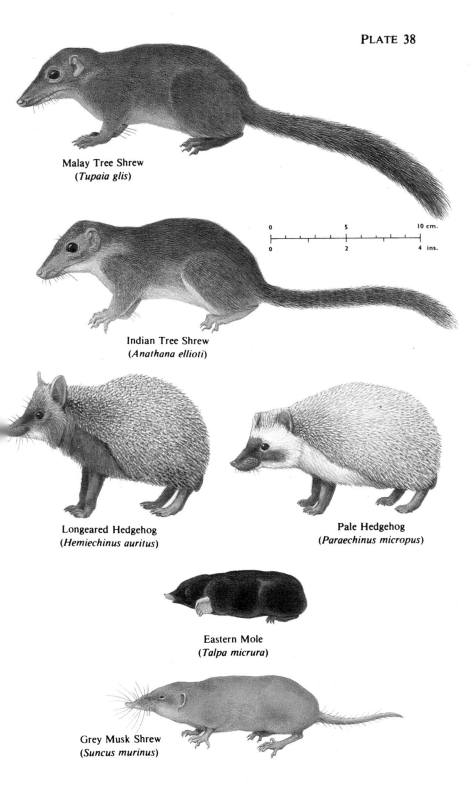

Malay Tree Shrew
(*Tupaia glis*)

Indian Tree Shrew
(*Anathana ellioti*)

Longeared Hedgehog
(*Hemiechinus auritus*)

Pale Hedgehog
(*Paraechinus micropus*)

Eastern Mole
(*Talpa micrura*)

Grey Musk Shrew
(*Suncus murinus*)

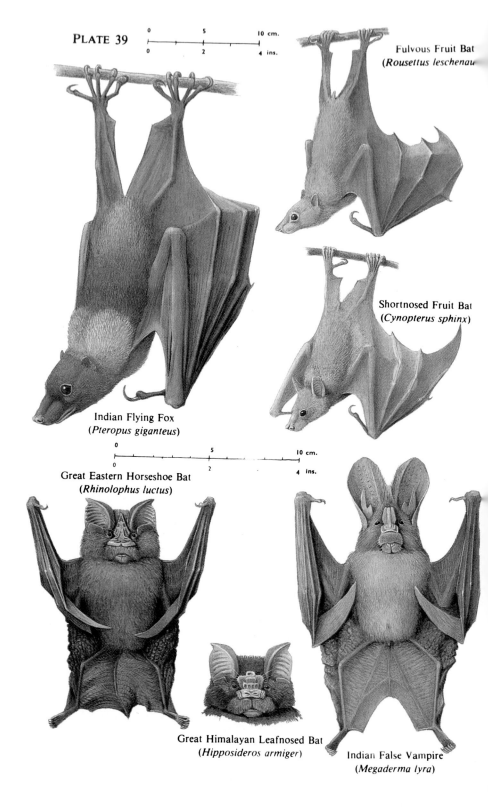

PLATE 39

Fulvous Fruit Bat
(*Rousettus leschenau*

Shortnosed Fruit Bat
(*Cynopterus sphinx*)

Indian Flying Fox
(*Pteropus giganteus*)

Great Eastern Horseshoe Bat
(*Rhinolophus luctus*)

Great Himalayan Leafnosed Bat
(*Hipposideros armiger*)

Indian False Vampire
(*Megaderma lyra*)

Habits. In India, ferret-badgers live in the tropical and sub-tropical forests of their range, and also in grassland. They are nocturnal, coming out at dusk and lying up by day in burrows of their own making, or in natural holes and crevices. They hunt their food on the ground, but their long limbs and tail and the striated pads under their feet indicate an aptitude for climbing. It is reported of a form found in Formosa that it climbs trees with agility and is frequently captured when sleeping curled up on a branch. They are omnivorous feeders, living much on fruit as well as on birds and small mammals. It is said that Lepchas and Bhotias encourage these animals to enter their huts because of their usefulness in destroying cockroaches and other insects. Roots form part of their diet and also earthworms. To get such food these animals are well-equipped with digging claws and probing snouts. The anal glands in these animals show no abnormal development. Yet the behaviour of these animals, their utter fearlessness, and tenacity of life are attributes which suggest that in common with most members of this tribe they belong to the group of nauseous, warningly coloured animals. Little is known of the breeding habits of ferret-badgers. One record states : the ' young, usually three in number, are born in a burrow '. The litter was observed in June. They apparently remain with the mother and are suckled by her till nearly full-grown.

THE HOG-BADGER

Arctonyx collaris F. Cuvier

Plate facing p. 143

[RACES IN INDIA : *collaris* F. Cuvier, *consul* Pocock]

Local Names. Hindi *bala sur* (bear-pig).

Size. Head and body, 21-28 in. (55-70 cm.) ; tail, 4-7½ in. (10-20 cm.).

Distinctive Characters. The squat bear-like body, stumpy legs, and long powerful claws of a badger. Snout much like that of a pig, long, mobile, naked towards the end, the terminal disc containing the nostrils. Ears short, rounded, small. Colour, a mixture of black and white and buff, which gives the coat a soiled grey tone. The pale throat and the dark stripe on the cheek distinguish this animal from the true badger (*Meles*), which has a black throat and no cheek stripe.

Distribution. Assam and the eastern Himalayas, Burma, Tibet. China, Indo-China, Siam, and the Malay countries.

Habits, Little is known of the habits of this animal in the wild state. Seclusive and nocturnal, it is seldom seen. Within its range in India it frequents stony ground or small hills amongst tropical jungle, and lives in fissures among rocks or in a hole dug by itself. Apparently it is dull of sight, and in its quest for food relies more on scent, in which its hunting methods resemble those of bears ; bearlike also is the habit, frequently noticed, of awkward gambolling and tumbling in play. The Hog-Badger is omnivorous but what we know of its food is known mainly from observation of captive animals. They reveal how individuals have their particular tastes. One prefers fruit and vegetables to meat ; another eats the flesh of mammals, birds, or reptiles voraciously. Some display a fondness for earthworms. A captive, fed at first on rice and water, ate it noisily like a pig, holding the bowl between its paws. This individual also ate small centipedes and the contents of reptiles' eggs, but not their leathery shells. It was however afraid of snakes, and would not touch roots, fruits, or vegetables. Hog-Badgers use their long snouts for rooting, and for the crushing of fruit. These animals display the usual savagery and boldness of their tribe. When demonstrating, a Hog-Badger arches its back, bristles its coat, and utters a grunting noise ; when attacked, one sat erect on its hindquarters and fought savagely with tooth and claw. Its boldness, the bristling of its coat, and the display of the pale under-fur are the usual attributes of animals which use the nauseous discharge of their stink-glands as a means of defence. Nothing has been recorded of the breeding habits.

THE RATEL, OR HONEY BADGER

Mellivora capensis (Schreber)

Plate facing p. 143

[RACES IN INDIA : *indica* (Kerr), *inaurita* (Hodgson)]

Local Names. Hindi *bejoo, bajra* ; *bal, bol-reencha* in north and central India ; Sindhi *gorpat* ; Cutch *ghurnar* ; Tel. *bigu khawar* ; Tamil and Kan. *tarakaradi*.

Size. Head and body, 2 ft. (60 cm.) ; tail, 6 in. (15 cm.) ; weight, 17-23 lb. (8-10 kg.) ; males heavier in build.

Distinctive Characters. Body squat and bear-like, legs short and stumpy, tail small, feet broad, claws long and blunt, snout not projecting as in the Hog-Badger. Colour, crown and dorsal surface grey, paling to yellowish or white. Underparts of face, throat and chest, belly, and undersurface of tail, deep black contrasting vividly with the pale dorsal surface.

Distribution. The base of the Himalayas to Cape Comorin. South-western Asia, Africa.

Habits. In India Ratels live in the desert and in the dry and moist deciduous zones, avoiding regions of heavy rainfall. They prefer hilly broken country where shelter is easier to find, and when living in the plains choose the banks of streams or rivers where burrows are easily dug. A Ratel may however occupy any convenient hole or be content to sleep under dense cover. In gait and movement, in their clumsy gambols and somersaults, Ratels resemble bears, bear-like again is their habit of digging great holes in the sandy beds of rivers, probably in quest of water.

The diet is substantially a diet of flesh. The Ratel preys on mammals, birds, reptiles, and insects, and varies its food with fruit and honey. Those living near villages take to raiding poultry. Like most carnivores, Ratels will feed on carrion and, being well equipped with digging claws, are believed to exhume and feed on corpses. ' Grave-digger ' is the interpretation of its name in many Indian languages. The accusation of ' grave-digging ' should be treated with caution. As F. W. Champion, a competent observer, points out no reputable naturalist has ever obtained first-hand evidence of the habit, and the majority of villagers who use the vernacular name have only the vaguest idea of the animal to which it refers. The Ratel has the boldness and fearless courage of its tribe, and will not hesitate to attack a man in self-defence, fighting gamely against odds. Besides its sharp teeth, powerful claws, and its battery of large stink-glands, the loose thick hide of the Ratel, not easily pierced by tooth or claw, is its protection. An individual may also adopt the ruse of lying prone and inert as though dead.

Little definite is known of the breeding habits of the Ratel. They are said to live in pairs. How long the association is maintained we have yet to discover. Two are usually produced in a litter and the period of gestation is believed to be six months.

11. Insectivores

THE NATURAL ORDER, the **Insectivora** or insect-eating mammals, contains the tree shrews, hedgehogs, moles, ground shrews, etc. These animals follow and are adapted to varied modes of life, the tree shrews to climbing, moles to living and finding their food underground, while hedgehogs and ground shrews seek their food on its surface. With these varying habits there is naturally great diversity of form and structure among these animals, hence it is difficult to frame a common definition by which all the members of the tribe can be recognised.

Generally it may be said that none of the Insectivora are large animals. Except for the tree shrews, all are nocturnal in their habits. A characteristic feature, very pronounced in almost all of them, is a long, pointed snout projecting far beyond the lower jaw, at times it is almost a proboscis. The limbs are as a rule short and five-toed, and their gait is more or less plantigrade. As to teeth, there is a tendency to uniformity in pattern, so much so that in many instances, among the shrews for example, it is difficult to say which are the canines, which the incisors, or the premolars, except from their position in the jaws. The true molars are studded with sharp-pointed cusps well adapted to the usual, though not exclusively, insect diet of these animals. Some ten different families of Insectivora are recognised, four of which are found in India. They are the Tree Shrews (Tupaiidae), Hedgehogs (Erinaceidae), Moles (Talpidae), and Ground Shrews (Soricidae). The distinctive characters of each of these families are made clear in the descriptions of their commoner representatives.

TREE SHREWS, OR TUPAIAS

The Indian Tree Shrew *Anathana ellioti* (Waterhouse)

Plate facing p. 160

[RACES IN INDIA : *ellioti* (Waterhouse), *wroughtoni* Lyon, *pallida* Lyon]

The Malay Tree Shrew *Tupaia glis* (Diard)

Plate facing p. 160

[RACES IN INDIA : *assamensis* Wroughton, *versurae* Thomas, *lepcha* Thomas]

Size. Head and body, 7-8 in. (18-20 cm.) ; tail, 8-9 in. (20-23 cm.).

Distinctive Characters. The word ' *tupaia* ' is a Malay name for squirrel. In appearance a tree shrew is a combination of shrew and squirrel. Its long snout is shrew-like, but its rounded ears, body, limbs, and tail suggest a squirrel. The feet again are like a squirrel's, well fitted for climbing, the soles naked, the toes long and supple, the claws sharp and moderately curved. The Malay Tree Shrew is grizzled brown or ferrugineous above, its throat and underparts buffy. The Indian Tree Shrew is similar in colouring but its throat and breast are nearly white.

Distribution. The Indian Tree Shrew is found both in the dry and moist deciduous forests of peninsular India, south of the Ganges. The Malay Tree Shrew's range extends from Burma into Assam and the eastern Himalayas where it lives from plains level to an altitude of about 6000 ft. (1830 m.).

Habits. The name tree shrew gives a wrong impression of the true habits of these animals. Though expert climbers, tree shrews take to trees mainly as a means of escape or as a shelter. Most of their food they seek on the ground, nosing for it among fallen leaves, under rocks, or in crevices, or climbing for it in and out of the undergrowth. Their busy movements on the ground are suggestive of a small mongoose or ferret. On trees, their ways are not the ways of a squirrel. They do not leap from tree to tree as squirrels do, nor jerk their tails, nor cling head downwards to the trunk, all movements characteristic of a squirrel. The resemblance to a squirrel is confined to appearance, there is little of the squirrel in their habits. Once recognised, no one can mistake a tree shrew for a squirrel. The food consists mainly of insects, but fruits are also eaten, and almost certainly small mammals and birds. One was seen making for a wounded bird with obvious intention. They are fond of water both to drink and bathe in. Little is known of their breeding habits. The female is said to have one young at a time, but as many as three have been recorded. A pair or family party establishes a territory, follows the same beat within it, and drives away intruders of its own species. They are easily tamed, and in Burma become as familiar as palm squirrels, entering houses, climbing on beds and tables, and helping themselves to such food as they fancy.

HEDGEHOGS

The Longeared Hedgehog *Hemiechinus auritus* (Gmelin)

Plate facing p. 160

[RACE IN INDIA : *collaris* (Gray)]

The Pale Hedgehog *Paraechinus micropus* (Blyth)

Plate facing p. 160

[RACES IN INDIA : *micropus* (Blyth), *nudiventris* (Horsfield)]

Size. Head and body, 6-7 in. (15-18 cm.) ; tail, about 1 in. (2.5 cm.).

Distinctive Characters. A pig-like snout gives the hedgehog its name. Its eyes and ears are well developed, the body stout and clumsy, the tail short, the legs stumpy and furnished with claws, not especially adapted for digging. Distinctive in these animals is the dense mat of spines which cover the back and sides. The loosely stretched skin covering the back and flanks is supplied with a marvellous system of muscles, which draw the spiny mantle completely over the retracted head and limbs ; rolled thus into a ball of bristles the hedgehog is well protected.

The commonest northern species are the Longeared Hedgehog (*Hemiechinus auritus collaris*), an animal with deep brown, almost black, fur on its head and underparts, and the Pale Hedgehog (*Paraechinus micropus*), a light-coloured species. Like other species of its genus the Pale Hedgehog has a parting bare of spines running from the centre of the forehead to the crown. The parting is not seen in *Hemiechinus*.

Distribution. In our area, hedgehogs are confined mainly to the dry desert zone of Cutch, Sind, the Punjab, and the former N.W.F.P. and the neighbouring tracts. A single form, *P. m. nudiventris*, is confined to the plains of south India.

Habits. As seen from their distribution, hedgehogs inhabit our dry plains and deserts. Here they shelter by day in holes in the sand, or beneath thorny bushes or tufts of grass, coming out to feed at dusk and retiring at dawn. Insects, worms, slugs, lizards, rats and mice, and the eggs of birds are their food. Their diet is varied with fruit and roots. They cover long distances in their rambles, going at a steady trot. When alarmed the animal rolls itself into a ball and lies still. If handled, it throws its back up with a sudden jerk to drive the spines into one's fingers, grunting or hissing the while in protest. The young are produced in holes usually lined with grass or leaves. They are blind and almost naked at birth. Their spines, soft and flexible at first, rapidly harden. The **Afghan Hedgehog** *Hemiechinus megalotis* (Blyth), which is found near Quetta, is known to hibernate in deep holes during the winter. No other Indian hedgehog is known to hibernate, but in Sind and northern areas of India, though common at other seasons, hedgehogs are rarely seen during the winter months, and probably become lethargic in the rigorous cold which prevails in our northern desert zone.

MOLES

The Eastern Mole *Talpa micrura* Hodgson

Plate facing p. 160

[RACES IN INDIA : *micrura* Hodgson, *leucura* Blyth]

Size. Head and body, about 4 in. (10 cm.) ; tail, rudimentary.

Distinctive Characters. Moles are distinctive in their form, which is so admirably adapted to subterranean habits, more so than any other mammal. The body is cylindrical, the neck so short that the head seems to project between the powerful shoulders and enormous forelegs. Behind, the body tapers to a short tail, which may be completely hidden under dense fur. The forepaws, backed by the muscular shoulders, are efficient digging implements. They are broad and flat, turned outwards, and furnished with large claws. The eyes are minute, and the fur is so dense and velvety that no soil adheres to it when burrowing. It is doubtful whether the European Mole (*Talpa europaea* Linnaeus) occurs within our limits. The **Indian Shorttailed Mole** (*T.m. micrura*) is velvety black, with a silvery grey gloss. Its extremely short tail is completely concealed by the fur. Its feet are nearly naked above and its minute eyes covered by skin. A second form the **Whitetailed Mole** (*T. m. leucura*) is distinctive in its longer, club-shaped tail, which is thicker towards the end than at the base and sparsely clad with white hair.

Distribution. In India the Shorttailed Mole occurs in the central and eastern Himalayas, and in the Assam hill ranges. The Whitetailed Mole has been recorded from the Khasia and Naga Hills.

Habits. The Shorttailed Mole is found at altitudes varying from 5000 (1525 m.) to 8000 ft. (2440 m.). About Darjeeling, where these moles are common, they live in the deep bed of black vegetable mould which forms wherever the original forest has been destroyed.

The mould contains earthworms and insect larvae in plenty, the chief food of these animals. In habits the Shorttailed Mole differs somewhat from the European species. The European Mole usually has its burrow under a hillock or beneath the roots of a tree. It consists of a central chamber with passages leading to two circular galleries, one higher and smaller in diameter than the other. From the larger gallery divergent tunnels, some of great length, lead in various directions. They are excavated by the mole in its quest for food and are extended daily. Small surface piles of earth or ' mole-hills ' mark the area of these operations. We have no exact know-ledge of the burrows of the Shorttailed Mole. They have yet to be studied. As with the European species the burrow is dug at the foot of a tree or beneath a bush ; runs are made from one tree to another, but mole-hills are not thrown up. In soft soil the runs may extend 40 to 50 yards (35 to 45 m.). Nothing is known of the breeding habits of our moles.

GROUND SHREWS

The Grey Musk Shrew *Suncus murinus* (Linnaeus)

Plate facing p. 160

[RACES : At least 12 in India, and 4 in Ceylon]

Local Names. Hindi *chuchunder*; Mal. *chundeli*; Mar. *chichundri*; Kan. *chundeli* ; English *Musk Rat*.

Size. Head and body, about 6 in. (15 cm.) ; tail, 3 in. (8 cm.).

Distinctive Characters. A long pointed snout, projecting consider-ably beyond the lower lip, small eyes, rounded ears not unlike the human ear in shape, body covered with soft fur, feet and tail spar-sely clad with hair. The feet are not especially designed for climbing or digging. The teeth of shrews are distinctive. The two front teeth differ from all the others. In the upper jaw they are curved and have a more or less prominent basal cusp. In the lower jaw they are long, project horizontally forward, and are sometimes slightly curved upwards at the end. The pointed snout, depressed ears, and teeth at once distinguish these shrews from rats, with which the present species is commonly confused, hence its popular, though erroneous, name ' musk rat '. The strong smell of musk given out by this and other species of the genus is derived from a gland on each side of the body. It is absent in the females of some species. The opening of this gland is surrounded by stiff hairs directed in-wards. Its secretion is produced in much greater abundance during the mating season. The soft fur of the Musk Shrew is pale grey or tipped with brown, or the coat is ashy brown or fawn. The pinkish skin of the snout, ears, feet, and tail shows through the sparse hairs.

Distribution. Shrews are the most widely distributed of the Insectivora, being found throughout the temperate and tropical regions of Europe, Asia, Africa, and North America. A large number of species are found in India, some restricted to the plains, others inhabiting the hills. Our commonest shrew is the Grey Musk Shrew which is generally distributed throughout the Peninsula.

Habits. This is the large shrew which enters our houses at dusk or after lamplight running about the rooms seeking insects. Its loud squeaking cry, usually uttered when frightened, gives away its presence. Their rat-like appearance and unpleasant musky odour cause these shrews to be killed whenever seen. Actually they are inoffensive useful animals, which help to rid a house of cockroaches and other noxious pests. They are very intolerant of rats and help in keeping away these vermin. The Plague Commission drew attention to their beneficial influence in this respect. Nor do these shrews as is popularly supposed contaminate articles, which they have touched, with their musky odour, which is always pronounced in their hides and sleeping quarters. They breed before they are adult. 2 to 3 young are born in a rough nest of straw, dead leaves, and other debris. The young are most active and follow their mother on her excursions trailing behind, each holding with its jaws the tail of the one in front.

12. Bats

BATS (CHIROPTERA) ARE perhaps the most easily recognizable group of animals. A bat is the only mammal with wings, the only mammal which can really fly. There are mammals, like flying squirrels and flying lemurs, which glide through the air supported by parachute-like extensions of skin from their bodies. But such a parachute does little more than prolong the squirrel's leap and reduce the impetus of its landing ; whereas with bats there is true and sustained flight effected by an upward and downward beat of wings. How bats came by their wings we do not know. Fossil remains found in geological deposits show that even the earliest known bats had wings and were able to fly. Unfortunately none of these fossils reveal the stages by which bats attained this power of flight. We have no clues to the origin and ancestry of bats. Certain peculiarities in their structure point to an intimate relationship between bats and the Insectivora, a group of animals which includes hedgehogs, moles, tree shrews, and ground shrews. It is believed that bats are derived from some form of tree-dwelling, leaping, insectivorous animal. It is safe to assume that bats, before they learned to fly, learned to live in trees and to leap into the air. This is how birds first mastered the art. In their early sallies into the air, bats were probably helped by their somewhat webbed forelimbs, and by parachute-like extensions of skin connecting body and limbs. The motive and urge to sally into the air was the capture of insects for food. For in the beginning all bats were insect-eaters. Fruit-eating, now the means of livelihood of a comparatively few species, was a later development. This difference in food and habits of life has led to the development of minor differences in structure now apparent between fruit-eating and insectivorous bats. Because of these differences bats are classified in two main groups: **Megachiroptera** including all the frugivorous bats, and **Microchiroptera** all the insect-eating and carnivorous species. The name Megachiroptera meaning ' large bats ' refers to the size of the fruit bats. Some like the Flying Foxes (*Pteropus*) **(Plate facing p. 161)** have a wing span of quite 4 ft. It is true that insectivorous bats are generally smaller. None of them attain the size of Flying Foxes, but some are as big as or even bigger than some fruit-eating bats.

STRUCTURE IN RELATION TO HABITS

Wings. Their wings, as we have seen, distinguish bats from all other mammals and fit them completely for life in the air. Let us consider their structure. The name *Chiroptera* given to bats is a combination of the Greek words *chieros*, a hand, and *pteron*, a wing. It describes exactly the structural plan of a bat's wing. A bat's arms and hands are the framework of its wings. They are built on the usual pattern of the vertebrate forelimb. There is the upper arm ending at the elbow, the double-boned forearm ending at the wrist, and the hand with a thumb and four fingers. The thumb is free, the fingers are enormously lengthened and embedded in the leathery wing membrane to support it. Like the ribs of an umbrella, they open and close the wing and keep it taut when expanded. The jointed finger-bones give the bat's wing its special flexibility. The facile movements of the joints adapt the wing to the twists and turns of flight, and adjust its surface to changing currents of air. A drawing together of the fingers reduces the wing expanse, ' takes in sail ' so to speak, and instantly checks speed and momentum. In its flexibility, its power of controlling momentum, the wing of a bat is the most perfect flying organ devised by Nature.

From the wings proper the flying membranes extend to the feet, and then spread between the legs forming here what is called an inter-femoral membrane, which usually encloses the tail, and is supported also by a spur of bone projecting from each foot. Besides the inter-femoral membrane there is an accessory flying membrane, the ante-brachial membrane which, rising from the region of the neck, connects up with the humerus and forearm. Thus there is, so to speak, a continuous and uninterrupted parachute of skin around the bat's body. Motive power to this parachute is supplied, as we have shown, by the forelimbs, by the arms and the hands, which have become agents for propelling the bat's body through the air. As further aids to flying, the bat has a capacious thorax, which contains a remarkably large heart and lungs, and offers space for the attachment of the great muscles which sustain the arms in flight. The large heart and powerful lungs, and the big flight muscles give these animals great staying power on the wing, many of them flying vast distances in quest of food. But the manner of flight in bats varies almost as much as it does in birds. (Plate facing p. 158)

Variation in the length and number of the bones of the hand and fingers, so evident in bats, profoundly influences the shape and size of the wing, its strength, and power of flight. Bats with long tapering wings are the swiftest fliers.   Such are the wings of our Sheath-tailed Bats (Emballonuridae) (Plate facing p. 176).   With their long, pointed wings, their speed and grace of movement, they look almost like swallows in flight.   They are among the swiftest bats in the world. Bats with short rounded wings are slower in movement. The Horseshoe Bats (*Rhinolophus*) (Plates facing pp. 158, 161) are an example. They emerge after dark and course slowly round trees and over hedges in search of insects.   They seldom fly high.   Intermediate between these extremes are the wings of many of the typical bats (Vespertilionidae), the Pipistrelle [*Pipistrellus coromandra* (Gray)] (Plates facing pp. 158, 176) for example. They hunt at no special level. But how marvellously buoyant is their flight! How they twist and turn, plunge and rise, in an ever-changing irregular course! Their extreme mobility in flight admirably displays the superiority of the bat's wing, whose perfection is derived from its skeletal structure, the flexible, many-jointed mammalian hand.

Though converted into wings, the bat's arms and hands are used, as most mammals use them, for walking and climbing. They may even be put to such purposes as the holding of food and the killing of prey. The clawed thumb, as we have seen, is free of the wing. It is used for securing a hold when walking, climbing, or resting. Fruit bats usually have two such claws to their wings, one at the end of the thumb and one at the end of the first or index finger (**Plate facing p. 161**). The additional claw must be a help in scrambling and climbing among the twigs and branches of trees, where these bats get their food. This extra claw is distinctive of fruit bats. It is never present on the index finger of insect-eating species. The wing is sometimes used like a hand for holding food. When eating a large fruit, a Flying Fox may hold it in the folds of one wing or clasp it between its wrists. This habit, suggestive of the use of the wing as a hand, is adopted also by some insectivorous species. Some of the Horseshoe Bats on capturing an insect too big to be dealt with in the air, alight and then kill the victim by pounding it against the tough membrane of the wing, which is thrust against the muzzle by an inward sweep of the arm. Some bats use their wings to strike at flying insects. The wings are, after all, arms and hands, and are used as such in special need.

In repose the wings are usually folded along the side of the body. Horseshoes completely envelop themselves in their wings; so enwrapped, they look almost like great cocoons. Different again is the way Sheathtailed Bats fold their wings. Their wings are long and tapering. To pack them away compactly, a special method of folding has been devised. With most bats the bones of the wings fold inwards, much as our fingers do, i.e. towards the palm of the hand. But with the Sheathtails the second finger folds inwards and then outwards taking a sort of double bend. This zigzag folding reduces the length of the wing. It appears to be adopted generally by all long-winged bats.

Legs. Compared with the great development of the forebody and arms, the hindquarters and legs of bats are weak. The whole structure of the animal is designed to one purpose, maximum efficiency in flight, but such efficiency has been secured only at a cost to other forms of progress. With the limbs hobbled to each other, and their free movement encumbered by enveloping flight membranes, the walking of a bat is reduced to an awkward hobble. The gait is rendered yet more cumbersome by the peculiar articulation of the knee-joints, which are directed backwards instead of forwards as in other animals. The device secures maximum spread of the flying membranes, but is of little help to other movements. Many bats are quite helpless on the ground. Others get along with some speed, proceeding backwards and forwards or crab-wise, moving their fore- and hindlimbs much as four-legged animals do. They climb with ease, using the claw on the thumb and the claws of their toes to secure a hold. But why the feet of some bats are so large and others so small requires explanation. It has been said that the feet of bats which live habitually in caves are usually larger enabling them to cling better to a flattened surface. Bats do not use their legs for holding and catching prey. The Flying Fox sometimes holds a fruit with one of its legs, not grasping it but striking its claws into it like the prongs of a fork. The claws of the hindlegs are commonly used to clean and comb their fur, or even as toothpicks. But walking and climbing and other uses to which a bat may put its legs are merely incidental. It is a creature of the air. The main purpose of its legs is as a means of securing a hold after landing. When alighting a bat usually secures first hold with its hooked thumbs and then, swinging over, grips its perch with its feet. Some species turn a somersault as they alight and take hold hindfeet first. This is what Horseshoes generally do, but they have noticeably weak thumbs ! Taking hold with its feet the bat rests and sleeps hanging head downwards. This is the usual attitude. But some bats cling with their thumbs and feet, the body slung like a hammock, or lie prostrate along a convenient surface. Most of the smaller bats creep into holes and crevices. The flattened heads of some of them seem especially designed for entry into narrow openings.

Tails. Tails are a variable quantity in bats. They may be long or short or so small as to be scarcely visible. The tails of fruit bats are distinctive. When these bats have a tail it is always very short and placed beneath the interfemoral membrane, and with this membrane it usually has no connection. In the Horseshoes the tail is distinct and reaches to the end of the interfemoral membrane in which it is embedded. The Indian False Vampires (Megadermatidae) **(Plate facing p. 161)** have scarcely a vestige of a tail. In the typical bats (Vespertilionidae) the tail is long and enclosed in the membrane spread between the legs, but its tip is often free and is then used as a hook when climbing. In the Sheathtails the tail perforates the interfemoral membrane towards the middle and appears on its upper surface or reaches considerably beyond it.

The tail when well developed serves as a strut or support for the interfemoral membrane and controls its movement, bending it inwards or upwards, stretching it full length, adjusting its surface to movements of flight. In Sheathtailed Bats, the tail slips in and out of the membrane as from a sheath, and some species are thus able to expand or contract this membrane or, to use a nautical term, to ' shake out or take in a reef ' in the stern sheet. Apart from flight, the tail and its enveloping membrane may be put to yet other uses.

Curved bellywards by the inbending of the tail, the membrane, when sufficiently developed as it is in most of the typical bats, acts as a brake to flight. It may be used as a large and capacious pouch for holding prey. An insect disabled by a blow of the wing is driven into this pouch, or cleverly 'netted' as it falls in mid-air. Thrusting its head into this pouch, the bat kills its victim. This improvised pouch is also used by some of these bats as a cradle for the reception of newborn young. When resting, the tail and connected membrane may be extended, tucked inwards, or folded over the back, the last is a habit common to many Horseshoes.

Teeth. Insect-eating bats usually swoop down on smaller insects and seize and eat them on the wing. Or the prey is eaten after alighting, which accounts for the accumulations of wing cases and other hard parts of insects which litter the floor below the roosts of these bats. Fruit bats also carry away fruit to eat at their roosts as a final *bonne bouche* (Plate facing p. 159). But food is not always taken on the wing. An insect may be snapped up from a tree or bush. Hovering above its victim the bat settles for a fraction of a second, seizes it, and flies upwards again, munching its capture. Some of the smaller fruit bats also hover over their food, biting off morsels of fruit, and eating them on the wing. The Flying Fox is too big for such agile action. It eats in the usual resting position, hanging head downwards. All bats are voracious feeders. A small fruit bat may eat more than its own weight of fruit at a single meal. But there is this about the eating of fruit bats, all that is taken into the mouth does not find its way into the stomach. All fruit bats are entirely nectar or fruit juice feeders. They live upon liquid, not upon solid food. The pulp of the fruit is chewed, but only the juice is swallowed and the substance rejected. The tough fibrous element ground into a mash lodges in the hollow of the palate and is continually removed and ejected by the tongue. But the substance of glutinous fruits which liquefy easily, like plantains or ripe guavas, may be swallowed. It is the same with flowers when large, their nectar is licked up with the finely pointed tongue. Some fruit bats have particularly long tongues. Minute flowers like those of the mango and cashew nut, favourite food of some fruit bats, are chewed and crushed to extract their nectar. Such being their food and way of dealing with it, the cheek teeth of fruit bats are little more than grinding mills. The oblong molars have quite smooth, or nearly smooth, crowns divided by a deep longitudinal groove. These grooves are channels by way of which juice crushed out of the fruit flows into the bat's gullet. Worked by powerful cheek muscles the fruit bat's molar teeth are admirably designed for their special work.

Quite different are the teeth of insect-eating bats. Their molar teeth have sharp cusps to their crowns. Shaped somewhat like the letter W, these sharp pointed teeth are well adapted for holding and piercing the hard-shelled bodies of beetles and other insects. But the hard parts of an insect's body are not eaten. The wing cases of beetles and other hard indigestible parts of the insect's body are cut away and ejected. The Vampires are bloodsuckers and have their front teeth especially modified for piercing the skin of animals they feed on—they do not occur in India. The number of teeth in different genera of bats is variable and is of great importance in distinguishing between them.

Senses. Bats feed by night. They fly in the dark with ease and swiftness. Many display an amazing faculty for avoiding obstacles in the dark. Sight must play its part in guiding some bats, especially those which come out early in the evening or in the morning. But there are many species which must depend little on vision to guide them. Bats deprived of sight were able to fly unhampered in absolute darkness. They found their way between threads stretched across a room without once touching them. In the same way, these blinded bats evaded branches and twigs set in their path and came to rest on the walls of the room. Loss of sight did not hamper their movements. What then is the faculty which enables bats to steer their way so unerringly in the dark ? Recent research has revealed their secret. It was discovered that bats use a highly developed echo-apparatus, a radar system of their own. Supersonic sounds emitted by them vibrate through the air and striking upon any object in their path are deflected back and instantly ' picked up ' by bats. These ' warning echoes ' enable bats to locate and evade obstacles in their course. By using an elaborate sound-detection apparatus, the experimenters discovered that their bats sent out signal cries at the rate of 10 per second before taking off. The rate increased to 30 per second when they launched into the air, and rose to 50 per second as ' warning echoes ' began to be received. The increased burst of sound strengthened the intensity and volume of the returning echoes. To emit these high cries bats have a powerfully developed vocal apparatus. The unusual development of the muscles of the larynx in these animals was long unexplained. Its purpose is now clearer, the transmission of supersonic sounds. That re-echoing of sounds so emitted plays an essential part in guiding these bats was made apparent in the experiment. Bats with their mouths closed tightly to prevent them from giving out sounds blundered about hopelessly.

So much for ' sound transmission '. How do bats ' pick up ' these ' warning echoes ' ? The faculty of sound perception is probably not located in any single organ. It arises from a combination of senses acting in unison and mutually assisting one another. The most important of these is perhaps the sense of hearing. It is especially acute in insectivorous bats. An insectivorous bat can be told from a fruit bat by its ears. In fruit bats the margins of each ear meet at the base to form a ringed, funnel-like opening ; in insectivorous bats they do not meet at the base. Besides, many insect-eating bats have what appears to be an additional hearing aid. This is a process called the tragus. It arises inside the anterior margin of the ear. There is also a lobe at the base of the outer margin, known as the anti-tragus, which sometimes attains considerable proportions. These accessories to the ear are never seen in fruit bats. They have neither a tragus nor an anti-tragus. Besides, the ears of fruit bats are small ; those of insect-eating bats are frequently large, very mobile, and capable of independent movement. Under stress of excitement they are set into tremulous motion. The ears of these bats seem especially attuned to pick up high-pitched supersonic sounds, sounds quite inaudible to the human ear. Loud noises like thunder scarcely disturb them, but the slightest squeak puts them on the alert. So much for the sense of hearing. Co-ordinated with hearing is the sense of touch. Few if any animals have so exquisite a sense of touch as bats. This sense, delicate enough to pick up the slightest pulsation in the air, is exercised chiefly by the flying membranes. Their wide expanse, abundantly supplied with nerves and blood vessels, makes them extremely sensitive. Besides these membranes, many insect-eating bats have yet another organ of perception. This is an expansion of skin around the nose generally called the ' nose-leaf '. The nose-leaf may be comparatively small or simple as in the False Vampires, or large and complex as in the Horseshoes (*Rhinolophus*) and the Leafnosed bats (*Hipposideros*) (Plate facing p. 161). Its intricate folds are lined with fine sensitive hairs. It is evidently an organ of special perception. When alarmed these facial crests, like the ears, are thrown into tremulous movement, the bat turns its head from side to side seeking the source of danger. The nose-leaf appears to be more specially the equipment of bats which are more rigidly nocturnal in habit, and which seek their prey among trees and bushes. Horseshoes come out after dark and hunt much in forests, flying in and out among the branches. There seems little doubt that the highly developed nose-leaf is an organ especially designed to aid such intricate movement. This does not mean that bats without nose-leaves are incapable of such movement. Temporarily blinded and with its ears stopped, a Pipistrelle not only flew around a room without hesitation, but avoided all obstacles, and skilfully dodged all attempts to capture it with a net. As stated, it is no single sense or sense organ, but a combination of senses, which guides these bats in the dark and helps them to find their prey. Fruit bats are less well-equipped than insect-eating species. They have no extra aids to hearing or sound perception. The ear of a fruit bat has no tragus and they have no nose-leaf. Yet the smaller forms emerge well after dark and find their way about easily, though it must be said they seldom hunt in forests but keep instead to open cultivated country or to the margin of forests. Flying Foxes on the contrary are early on the wing and sight must largely

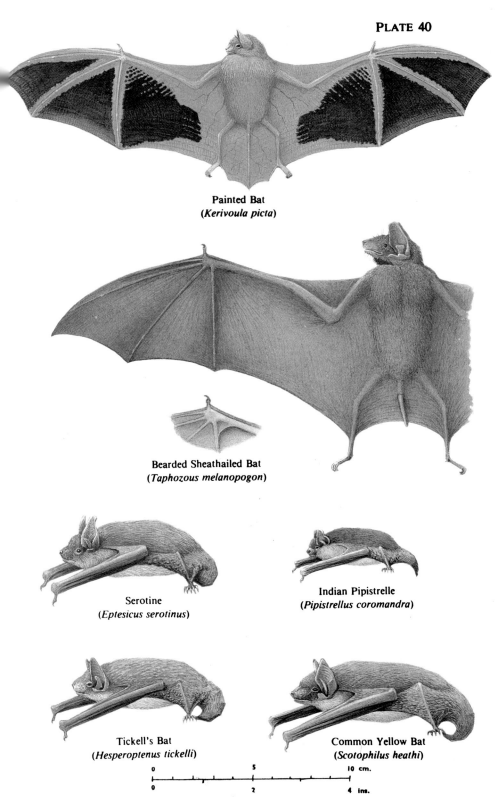

PLATE 40

Painted Bat
(*Kerivoula picta*)

Bearded Sheathailed Bat
(*Taphozous melanopogon*)

Serotine
(*Eptesicus serotinus*)

Indian Pipistrelle
(*Pipistrellus coromandra*)

Tickell's Bat
(*Hesperoptenus tickelli*)

Common Yellow Bat
(*Scotophilus heathi*)

0		5		10 cm.
0		2		4 ins.

PLATE 41

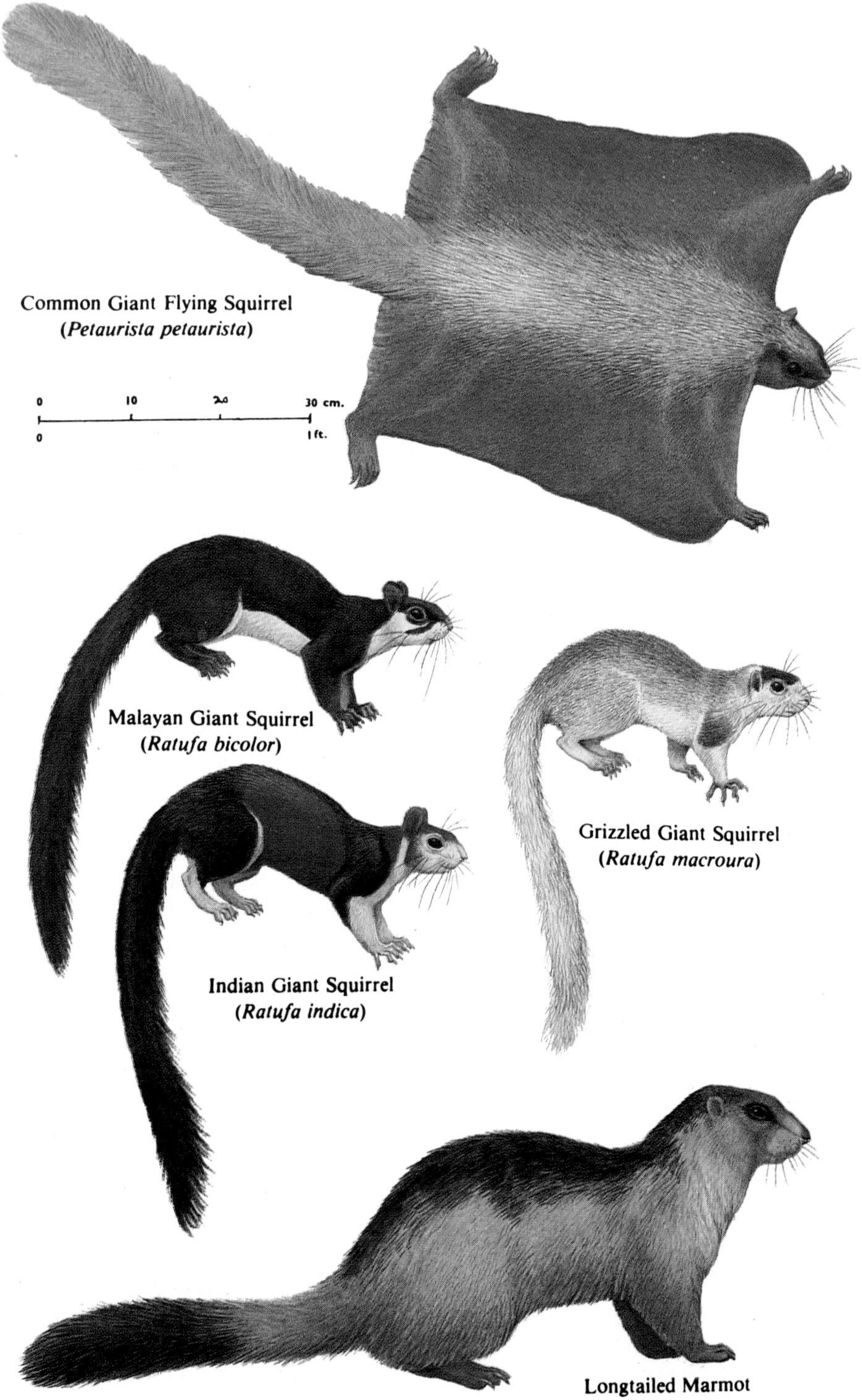

Common Giant Flying Squirrel
(*Petaurista petaurista*)

Malayan Giant Squirrel
(*Ratufa bicolor*)

Indian Giant Squirrel
(*Ratufa indica*)

Grizzled Giant Squirrel
(*Ratufa macroura*)

Longtailed Marmot
(*Marmota caudata*)

guide their flight. They are less successful in avoiding unexpected obstacles in the dark. So, many of them come to grief at night on telegraph and telephone wires, evidence of misdirected flight.

BATS AND THEIR SURROUNDINGS

Distribution. Owing to their powers of flight, it is generally assumed that bats are more easily able to cross barriers like mountains, seas, and rivers which so limit the range of terrestrial mammals. Their powers of flight should give them an advantage in establishing themselves in new territories ; but as a matter of fact there is little reason to believe that it actually does so. The majority of bats display a tendency to live or remain under particular conditions of environment. Their range is strictly limited. Flying Foxes, for example, are abundant on islands not 40 miles (65 km.) from the African mainland, yet no single species has established itself on the African Continent. Again, there are many different species of Flying Foxes inhabiting the chain of islands stretching across the Indian Ocean. Yet each species keeps to its island home. No inter-migration has been observed.

Fruit bats as a whole are confined entirely to the tropical and sub-tropical regions. In India they do not live in the temperate levels of the Himalayas except as seasonal or nightly visitors in fruiting time. They do not penetrate much into evergreen rain forests. Their main area of distribution is in the tropical, semi-evergreen, moist deciduous, and dry deciduous zones of the Peninsula. Some have colonized the desert or thorn forest zone, where life has been made possible for them as a result of the planting of fruit trees by human agency.

It is the same with the insectivorous bats. Like fruit bats their range is largely limited by physical and other factors in their surroundings. Only one species of bat, the Serotine **(Plate facing p. 176)**, has succeeded in establishing itself in both the eastern and western hemispheres, in crossing from the Old World into the New. It is believed that most bats are unable to withstand the cold of the regions about the Behring Straits, where the passage between the two Hemispheres is the shortest, and hence have failed to spread themselves as many purely terrestrial mammals, like the reindeer, the elk, and the glutton have done.

The various genera of insectivorous bats have a distribution more or less circumscribed by climatic and other factors. The majority of species live in the tropics. The Sheathtails and the False Vampires are purely tropical. The typical bats (Vespertilionidae) include the Pipistrelles some of which show an adaptability to almost any conditions. Their range reaches from the confines of the Arctic to below the Equator. Other genera are less adaptable, and are mainly temperate or tropical in their range. Races of the common European species like the Longeared Bat [*Plecotus auritus* (Linnaeus)], the Serotine [*Eptesicus serotinus* (Schreber)], and the Barbastelle [*Barbastella barbastellus* (Schreber)] are found in India only in the temperate levels of the Himalayas ; while species like the Common Yellow Bat [*Scotophilus heathi* (Horsfield)] (Plate facing p. 176) and Tickell's Bat [*Hesperoptenus tickelli* (Blyth)] (Plate facing p. 176) keep to the tropical zone of the Peninsula. The Himalayas and the foothills, where both temperate and tropical conditions prevail, are a meeting ground for both temperate and tropical species, and provide either a home or temporary shelter for a greater variety of species than can be found anywhere else in the Indian peninsula.

From what has been written it would be seen that, despite their advantage of wings to carry them across natural barriers, bats are largely limited in their range by conditions of climate, temperature, and other physical factors in their surroundings.

Let us consider the bat's reactions to its physical surroundings. How do bats react to light ? We consider them to be creatures of the dark. But many bats, both fruit-eaters and insect-eaters, come out to hunt in the bright light of the evening and, like other nocturnal animals, many hunt by day in cloudy or misty weather, and some even in brilliant sunshine. Again, some bats spend the day in roosts exposed to intense light. It would appear that bats, in common with many nocturnal animals, have no inherent objection to light. Temperature, the movements of their prey, and other factors largely influence the time of their emergence and the direction of their flight.

Conditions of temperature profoundly influence the life and habits of these animals. With the majority of species, the choice of a diurnal retreat is governed largely by prevailing climatic factors. There are species like the Flying Foxes and some insectivorous bats which sleep in open exposed roosts. But these are exceptional, and even to these hardy species such exposure is not without its risks. It is recorded how Flying Foxes fell to the ground panting and many quite dead when the moist winds prevailing over Madras suddenly changed to a hot, fierce blast. A similar incident is recorded from Ghazipur in U.P. Though inured to exposure, these bats were unable to withstand a sudden climatic change against which there was no protection in their exposed roosts. Except where their habits have been changed by living near man, whose works and dwellings offer them shelter, bats may be generally classified either as tree or as cave dwellers. Some species, particularly in cold regions, occupy trees in summer but shift to caves or more sheltered dwellings when winter sets in. This seasonal change of the diurnal retreat is less evident in tropical lands where there is less deviation between winter and summer temperatures. Again, while many tropical species are habitual cave dwellers, individuals may be found at times living in caves or in trees. Caves are however the favoured retreat of the majority of our bats. Why ? Because trees provide less protection against the vagaries of climate. The temperature within the hollow of a tree or under its leaves varies with the temperature of the surrounding air. It is different with caves. Whatever the conditions outside, the temperature within a cave remains more or less constant. It varies but little. Caves provide the uniform conditions of temperature that bats find suitable. In tropical lands, rock-cut dwellings of man, or ancient tombs and temples with their thick walls and high-domed architecture are much favoured by bats, simply because they reproduce, to some extent, the equable temperature maintained within caves. However high the temperature of outside air it is cool within these retreats. Caves are in fact essential to the existence of many species. The presence of caves has made possible their entry and existence in areas where the climate would otherwise have remained a barrier. The Rousette, or Fulvous Fruit Bat [*Rousettus leschenaulti* (Desmarest)] (Plate facing p. 161), a habitual cave dweller, has established itself at an altitude of 7000 ft. (2150 m.) in the Himalayas, a height at which no other Indian fruit bat is permanently resident. This bat, like other fruit bats, is a tropical species. It is able to exist in a temperate clime because it is a habitual cave dweller while other fruit bats live in trees. In America it has been found that bats living in caves are able to live throughout the winter in cold northerly latitudes from which other species migrate. Cold profoundly influences the habits of bats.

Hibernation and Migration. In northern countries the majority of bats hibernate in winter. With the lowering of the temperature all bodily functions cease and the bats fall into a lethargic sleep. But even in the depth of winter a warm spell restores them to activity. Their winter sleep is never very profound. Hibernation enables animals to tide over the scarcity of food which prevails wherever winter conditions are severe. In winter there are few insects about. The numbing effect of cold on insects is well known. Faced with a shortage of food supply, insect-eating bats either fall into a lethargic sleep, a condition in which they require no food, or migrate to warmer climes where food is abundant. Little is known of the hibernation or migration of bats in India. But such records as are available show that various European species, amongst these the Barbastelle, the Longeared Bat, and the Noctule [*Nyctalus noctula* (Schreber)], which have established themselves in the higher levels of the Himalayas follow the inherent habits of their kind and hibernate in winter. Whether any of the European forms migrate from the Himalayas in winter to warmer southern latitudes is not known. But apparently various tropical species which visit the temperate levels of the Himalayas in spring and summer leave this zone on the approach of winter. The Indian Pipistrelle, common at Simla at other times of the year, completely disappears in winter. The Mustachioed Bat [*Myotis mystacinus* (Kuhl)], a widely distributed Oriental species, also disappears from the hill-station in winter and does not return till the spring. So much for the Himalayas. Bats living in tropical zones of the Peninsula naturally do not hibernate, but even these animals are reduced to temporary inactivity under severe and unaccustomed cold. During an unusually cold spell in Ahmedabad Flying Foxes were found keeping to their roosts through the night. On the other hand extreme heat has been known to cause the Indian Flying Fox great discomfort. At midday on 21st May on one of the hottest days at Panvel, near Bombay, Flying Foxes were seen awake and fanning themselves hard with one wing, some using the right wing, and some the left, not one at rest. Further observations would probably multiply these examples.

So much for heat and cold. What of moisture and damp ? How do bats react to the monsoon ? Rain, unless it is heavy, seems to make little impression on bats. Many come out to hunt on wet evenings and, judging by the way they roost in caves and culverts which are almost water-logged, many species appear to be little affected by excessive damp. High winds may influence the height at which bats fly and, when these prevail, even strong-winged species like our Sheathtails come down to hunt at more sheltered levels.

BATS AND THEIR NEIGHBOURS

Fruit Bats. An animal's relationship with its neighbours is largely governed by its food. As fruit-eaters there is an intimate interrelationship between fruit bats and the various forms of plant life which provide them with food. They exert a mutual influence on each other. The distribution and local movements of these bats, the changes in feeding grounds, and the nature of their food are largely influenced by the seasonal flowering and fruiting of trees, which explains why fruit bats may be abundant in a given area at one season and absent in another. The breeding periods of these bats, and the time when the young are born are again co-ordinated with flowering and fruiting seasons, in other words with the abundance or scarcity of food supplies. Except for the Rousette, a habitual cave dweller, trees again usually provide diurnal retreats for all our fruit bats. The kind of tree selected depends much upon the locality. Wherever palms are available they become the favourite shelter of the Shortnosed Fruit Bat [*Cynopterus sphinx* (Vahl)] (Plate facing p. 161). Flying Foxes usually select wide-spreading banyan trees, various species of figs, and feathery tamarinds ; while in some localities clumps of bamboo are chosen. A particular tree or group of trees may be occupied by Flying Foxes year after year, evidence of their essentially sedentary habit. They are loath to leave a favoured locality. These are some of the ways by which the lives and habits of fruit bats are influenced by the surrounding plant life. What is the influence they exert on plants ? By their destruction of flowers and fruit, fruit bats become a factor in the control of plant life, but they also function as agents in its propagation. Their habit of carrying away fruit to their distant roosts makes them agents in seed dispersal. So great is the quantity of seed so carried that, in parts of Bengal, the ground under which large colonies of Flying Foxes habitually roosted was rented annually for the right of seed collection.

Then, as flowers form an important part of the food of fruit bats, they become fertilizing agents carrying pollen from one flower or tree to another. When drinking the nectar, the movements of the bat cause the pollen to be shed on its snout, or head, or other parts of its body, and so to be carried about. Many of the flowers visited by fruit bats are species which open only after dusk, they have a strong scent to guide bats to them and, apart from this, their shape and structural peculiarities lend themselves specially to fertilization by bats.

Insectivorous Bats. As predatory animals, the relationship of insectivorous bats with their animate environment is largely influenced by the creatures upon which they prey. From their voracity and the myriads of insects they must destroy they are perhaps Nature's most important check on nocturnal or crepuscular insect life. Almost any insect that can be caught is food for these bats. But, because of differences in the levels at which they hunt and differences in feeding grounds, there is some differentiation in prey. High-flying bats like the Sheathtails are brought more into contact with high-flying insects. The smaller less powerfully winged species prey largely on moths and flies and insects which keep to lower levels. Then again some bats, many Horseshoes for example, hunt mainly in hill forests ; others keep to open country, cultivation, or the neighbourhood of human dwellings ; and others again hunt habitually over water and become factors in the control of aquatic insect life. As with other predatory animals, these bats follow the movements of their prey. The seasonal abundance or scarcity of insects in a given area may lead to a change in hunting grounds. Tanks drying up in hot weather temporarily become the hunting ground of many insectivorous bats which swoop on the swarms of insects hovering round the decaying vegetation. Flowering trees, attracting insects, also attract bats which prey upon them. The height at which bats fly and the time of their emergence are again largely influenced by the movements of the insects upon which they feed. Insectivorous bats, particularly cave-dwelling species, indirectly become providers of food and shelter to their neighbours. The accumulations of dung and insect remains in caves and similar retreats where they roost attract and offer sustenance and shelter to many insects and small creatures.

Carnivorous bats. While the majority of bats function as a potent check on insect life, there are those specialised species, the Vampires, which have assumed a different role, and have taken to preying on other animals. The true Vampires are found only in the tropical forests of the New World. But here in India, and in the tropical lands of the Old World, we have a family of bats known as False Vampires, the Megadermatidae. The name *Megaderma*, meaning ' large skin ', alludes to the enormous ears of these bats. They stand out from the head like great flaps of skin. There is no authentic record of these bats ever attacking human beings, a habit developed by some of their American counterparts. Our ' Vampires ' prey on small animals, on smaller bats for example, on birds, on frogs, and even on fish—though how these bats capture the fish remains to be discovered. Grasshoppers and crickets are also eaten.

Bats and man. Man influences the lives and habits of these animals mainly as a provider of food and shelter. Fruit bats are habitual raiders of our plantations. They feed on almost every kind of cultivated fruit, and upon the flowers of such trees as the mango and the cashew nut. Their migrations and seasonal movements are influenced very considerably by the abundance or scarcity of food supplies made available by man, and their incursion and establishment in the arid treeless parts of India has been made possible only as a result of irrigation and the planting of fruit trees by human agency. Indirectly man also becomes a provider of food for insect-eating bats. Many species take up their abode in or near human dwelling or in cultivated areas. Human dwellings and cultivation attract their attendant hordes of insects, and the insects attract their attendant armies of bats.

The roosting habits of bats also have been considerably modified by association with man. Many species have taken to living in houses and other retreats provided by him. And in the absence of natural caves, cavernous tombs and temples built by man offer accommodation to cave-dwelling species. Such man-made shelters have undoubtedly aided the establishment and spread of species into areas in which, but for such shelters, they could not have existed.

Insect-eating bats, by their destruction of myriads of crop and other pests, must play a useful role in human economy ; the same cannot perhaps be said of fruit bats. Such good as they may do in the spread of plant life is largely offset by their enormous damage to human food resources. Yet bats are rarely molested by man. The flesh of some species, the Flying Fox in particular, is sometimes eaten. It is said to have a fine and delicate flavour. What then are the enemies of bats ? How are their numbers controlled ?

Enemies and means of defence. Little is known of the natural enemies of bats. In their exposed roosts Flying Foxes ought to become an easy prey to predatory animals, but there is little evidence of their being attacked. The smaller species are preyed upon by owls and hawks. There is a record of a stoat attacking a bat. Vampires are known to prey on their smaller brethren. A baby pipistrelle was found in the clutches of a large spider which was sucking out its juice. The real enemies of bats are the various parasitic flies, and to a lesser extent fleas and mites which feed on the fur, membranes, and blood of these animals. Various species of bats appear to have their particular insect parasites. To rid themselves of these irritating pests bats constantly comb their fur, using the claws of their feet, and even their teeth where possible.

What other means of defence have they? On the wing their extreme agility must help them to escape. When at rest one might assume that their gregarious habits are a source of mutual protection, as also the darkness of their retreats, and the penetrating stench which usually prevails wherever large colonies of bats are roosting. Many species give out a peculiarly repellent body odour. Colour must also be a source of protection.

Colour as a means of protection. The sombre coloration of most bats, so much in keeping with the darkness of their diurnal retreats must have its protective value. This applies even to such brightly coloured species as the Painted Bat [*Kerivoula picta* (Pallas)] (Plate facing p. 176). Despite its bright orange fur and startling vermilion and black wings the bat is most difficult to detect, its colour so matches the deep reds and yellows of fading leaves, a favourite roost. On a different plane is the colouring of Flying Foxes. Here there is no concealment or camouflage. The bright golden colouring of the bat's head and neck glows in contrast with the sombre tones of its body and wings. Far from concealing, the bold colour pattern attracts attention. One may class these bats with those animals whose coloration is known as ' warning coloration '. The meaning of ' warning colours ' has been explained. It will be seen that animals which exhibit warning colours always have some repellent means of defence, e.g. they possess stinkglands and use nauseous fumes and discharges to divert attack. Also such boldly-coloured animals do not fear exposure. These attributes are seen to some extent in Flying Foxes. All the species have so strong an odour that any of their enemies, man or animal, can easily detect them with closed eyes ! They do not fear exposure, make no attempt at concealment, but sleep in open roosts, exposed to the gaze of all who pass by.

INTERRELATIONSHIPS BETWEEN BATS

We have discussed the relationship of bats with their animal neighbours, their enemies, and means of defence and protection. Let us consider the interrelationships between animals of their own kind, between bats and bats. Food is again one of the most important factors governing such interrelationship. The influence of numbers on these animals, the relationship between population and food supplies, and the control exerted by this factor on over-population are all matters which remain to be investigated. Flying Foxes, as we know, congregate in suitable areas in teeming numbers. With their capacity for feeding one can well imagine the quantity of food required to support such large populations. We have yet to learn whether there is any division of territory or of feeding grounds among Flying Foxes and other fruit bats.

Among insectivorous bats, equally voracious in habit, some division of food supply is brought about by differences in hunting habits, and the surroundings or the strata of the air in which different species customarily hunt their prey. There is also a division of territory among individuals of many species. Individual bats may have their own ' beats ' which they guard against intrusion by wandering members of their own species. Writing of Tickell's Bat Mr. Phillips in his MAMMALS OF CEYLON says : ' a paddy field may be divided into three or four territories each bat keeping more or less strictly within its own territory. Should a stranger intrude it is at once driven off '. Common Pipistrelles (*P. coromandra*) also have their special beats. An individual may be seen keeping to the same round evening after evening, occasionally varying it by sporting in mid-air with comrades of adjacent beats. Many Horse-shoe Bats also display this habit.

Social Life. Most bats are gregarious. Individuals of a species tend to live together in large or small colonies. The rule is not invariable. A number of Indian bats are commonly found living alone or in pairs. But many species congregate in vast colonies. There is no apparent social organisation in these colonies. In the common roost the individual exhibits some toleration for the presence of others. This tolerance appears to be the limit of social life. There is no prolonged association between parents and young, no sustained family life, no organisation or leadership. Each individual fends for itself. Members of a colony of Flying Foxes leave their roosting trees at about the same time, fly in the same general direction, but each bat steers its own course. Arrived at the feeding tree each bat does its best to get the better of its neighbour. There is incessant wrangling. Late comers endeavour to dislodge earlier arrivals from good feeding places. It is the same when they return to their roosts. They fight for sleeping places, snap viciously at each other, or strike out with the great claws on their thumbs, shrieking and cackling incessantly. The Rousettes also are highly gregarious. Thousands roost together in caves and tunnels. The smaller fruit bats (*Cynopterus* etc.) do not assemble in such numbers. The colonies are comparatively small.

It is the same with insect-eating species. The Painted Bat and some of the Horseshoe and other species live singly or in pairs. Pipistrelles assemble in comparatively, small numbers. But many species, such as some of the Sheathtails etc., congregate in vast colonies. Different species occupying the same roost generally roost apart, and in such roosts individuals keep their distance. Sometimes different kinds of bats share the same cave or retreat. But even then there is no intermixing. Each species keeps to its own quarter. The 'hide-outs' of Vampires are usually shunned by smaller bats. Their predatory habits make them unwelcome neighbours. Apart from sex, the causes which lead to the congregation or segregation of bats remain obscure. As to means of communication bats are rarely silent, and probably have a keen perception of the voices of their fellows. Young bats call to their mothers as persistently as the young of any other animal.

FAMILY LIFE AND CARE OF THE YOUNG

Except for scattered notes and observations on a few species little is known of the breeding habits and family life of Indian bats. The life histories of all the commoner European species have been studied by Continental and British naturalists. Their writings offer some indication of the family life of these interesting animals and provide a model for comparison with Indian forms. Breeding season and habits naturally vary with climatic and other conditions. In northern latitudes the breeding season and time when young are produced are profoundly affected by cold and other factors. The general mating season is at the end of autumn. Most of the females are impregnated at this time. But while the sperms are active in the uterus through the winter, the ovaries remain quiescent till the spring when hibernation ends and active life is resumed. Then the ovum is fertilized, and gestation and the actual development of the embryo commences. Thus while mating takes place in the autumn, the birth of the young is postponed till the spring or early summer. Similar conditions may apply to various northern species which have colonized the temperate levels of the Himalayas. It is a matter for investigation. In the Indian peninsula, some of the Pipistrelles apparently produce their young in any month of the year. What other Indian bats do so is not known. Such records as are available show that our insect-eating bats have two main breeding seasons. The Horseshoes, the Leafnoses, and the False Vampires (*Megaderma*) produce their young mainly at the commencement of the hot weather (March-May), while the majority of the typical bats (Vespertilionidae) and Sheathtails are born in the second half of the year. Both for the early and the late breeders the peak periods of production coincide with peak periods of insect activity. Horseshoes hunt their food mainly about trees and the young produced between March and May are just in time for our main flowering season and its corresponding abundance of insect life. For the young of other bats which are not especially tree hunters there is an abundance of insect food during and just after the rains.

It is the same with fruit bats, the majority of young are produced just before the main flowering and fruiting season. On the west coast, near Bombay, Flying Foxes usually mate between October and December. The majority are born between March and April.

There are practically no records of the period of gestation for the majority of Indian bats; usually one young is produced, some species like the Pipistrelles may have two. The process of giving birth has been observed in one or two captive European species, the Noctule and the Common Pipistrelle. A Noctule was seen to reverse her usual resting position. Hanging by her thumbs, head up and feet down, she gave birth to her young which, squeaking lustily, passed into and was cradled in her interfemoral membrane. Fully expanded and tucked upwards the membrane formed a perfect ' pouch ' for the reception of the offspring. In the case of the Pipistrelle the mother hung head downwards and received her offspring in her right wing which she held partially extended for the purpose. The process varies with different species. To continue the story of the baby Noctule, thrusting her head into the interfemoral pouch the mother licked her offspring clean, and then resuming her normal head down position tucked it away under the membrane between her thigh and shoulder where it had easy access to the nipples on her breast. Bats have two pectoral teats.

The young are born blind and are generally naked. Some newborn Horseshoes and Flying Foxes have a coating of downy hair. The baby bat clings tightly to its mother's body, its feet and claws buried in her fur, its mouth holding one of her teats in a permanent grip. The great majority of bats are born with a complete set of milk teeth, all of one pattern. There is no differentiation between incisors, molars, or canines. Their sole function is to fasten on the mother's teats and so obtain secure hold of her body during movements or flight. The teats, besides being a channel of nourishment of the offspring, are a means of gripping on to the parent. Horseshoes and False Vampires actually have ' false teats ' for this express purpose, two long nipple-shaped prominences springing from the region of the pubis. No milk is drawn from them. The baby bat clings to them with its teeth when not feeding. When hungry it turns round and transfers its hold to the true nipples on its mother's breast. The mothers have at first no difficulty in carrying their young about with them, but they grow rapidly and may become an embarrassment. In some species the females leave the young at home and return at frequent intervals to feed them. In others the young are put together in swarms and feeding is communal, each female feeding the first that gets at her and sometimes even two at a time.

Certain species, such as Rousettes and Flying Foxes, carry their young continuously till they are able to fly.

With most European species females after fecundation live in separate colonies from which the males are generally excluded. We have no information as to whether such segregation takes place in India. It is practised by every European species whose life history is known. Males and females of some Indian bats occupy separate sleeping quarters during the non-breeding season. Two separate colonies of Bearded Sheathtails (*Taphozous melanopogon* Temminck) were found to consist exclusively of males. This was in April when nursing of the young was long over. Males and females of the Longarmed Sheathtail (*T. longimanus* Hardwicke) occupied separate sleeping quarters on the same tree. Colonies of Flying Foxes consisting exclusively of males have also been observed. How far the segregation of the sexes during the non-breeding season, as also the establishment of separate roosts of gravid females and separate nurseries for females with young, applies to Indian bats remains to be investigated.

Family life is not prolonged. As soon as they are able to fend for themselves, which is within a brief span of a few months or weeks after birth, the young fend for themselves and lead a separate existence.

FLYING FOX

Pteropus giganteus (Brunnich)

Plate facing p. 161

(RACES IN INDIA: *giganteus* (Brunnich), *leucocephalus* Hodgson)

Local Names Hindi, *Gadal, Badur ;* Mar. *Watwagul;* Kan. *Sikat Yella;* Tel. *Sikurayi;* Tamil & Mal. *Vowval.*

Size. Head and body, about 9 in. (229 mm.); wingspread about 4 ft. (122 cm.); Weight 20 to 22 oz. (568-625 gm.).

Distinctive Characters. The large size of this bat makes it unmistakable. Head usually reddish brown with a darker, sometimes blackish, snout. Hind neck and shoulders pale brownish yellow to straw; behind shoulders dark brown or black. Ventrally yellowish brown. Chin, neck, vent and flanks darker. Wings black.

Distribution. India, Ceylon, Burma. Rare in West Rajasthan, Cutch, and Sind. Does not occur as a resident species in the higher hills.

Habits. The largest of Indian bats, usually seen flying with slow wing beats at dusk. Roosts during the day in large, noisy, squabbling colonies on trees, often in the midst of busy towns and villages. Creatures of habit, the bats usually leave the roost within half an hour after sunset, flying the same route regularly in single file for considerable distances which may include crossing substantial arms of the sea. They have an uncanny memory for the location and fruiting time of trees and are very destructive in orchards. Feeds only on the juice of fruits, extracted by chewing dry the fleshy pulp, which is spat out. Breeds once a year, a single young being born in early February after a gestation of 140 to 150 days. The young are carried by the mother for a considerable time. Many methods have been tried, though not very successfully for eradicating these bats from places where they are serious pests of orchards. The flesh is eaten in many parts of the country.

FULVOUS FRUIT-BAT

Rousettus leschenaulti Desmarest

Plate facing p. 161

[RACE IN INDIA: *leschenaulti* Desmarest]

Size. Head and body, 5 in. (127 mm.); tail, 0.7 in. (18mm.); forearm 72 to 86 mm.

Distinctive Characters: Medium sized bat, uniformly light brown, occasionally yellowish in colour. Older males with dull grey flanks. Completely hairless individuals may be seen during the spring and summer moults. The bats have an odour like that of fermented fruit.

Distribution. Indian peninsula and south-east Asia.

Habits. Gregarious while roosting. Roosts in noisy colonies of 10 to 2000 in caves and man-made structures such as tunnels, rock-cut caves, wells, and rooms in old ruins, not necessarily dark. If disturbed may move elsewhere. There is also movement between different roosting sites depending on the availability of food in the surrounding country. Colonies can be readily distinguished from those of insectivorous bats by the large brilliant eyes. There is usually no sexual segregation in the colonies; however separate roosts of the sexes have also been reported. The juveniles once independent of the mother live in exclusive colonies of their own. Most members of a colony leave at dusk, flying heavily with slow wing beats in search of fruit bearing trees. They have a very good sense of smell, as well as a good memory of fruit trees in their area and may travel fairly long distances. As among other fruit bats only the fruit juices are swallowed.

The mating season is probably between November and March. Two discrete birth seasons, one in March and the second in August, are reported. The young, pink and naked at birth, are carried by the mother for two months during her nocturnal flights. The adult size is reached after an year.

SHORT-NOSED FRUIT BAT

Cynopterus sphinx Vahl

Plate facing p. 161

[RACES IN INDIA: *sphinx* Vahl, *gangeticus* Andersen]

Size. Head and body, 4.4 in. (112 mm.); tail 0.4 in. (10 mm.); forearm 69-75 mm.

Distinctive Characters. The white margined, nearly naked ears and divergent nostrils are distinctive. Brown of varying tints, ferruginous or yellowish or dull grey brown in colour. Males often with a bright reddish brown or rusty brown collar.

Distribution. Peninsular India and south-east Asia.

Habits. A common species but not as easily seen as the Flying Fox and Fulvous Fruit-bat as it roosts singly or in small groups among palm leaves, aerial roots of banyan, tree hollows, and similar situations, and only exceptionally in ruins and caves. Leaves quite early in the evening for foraging, flying to fruit bearing trees or to sip honey from flowers, flitting from flower to flower without settling. Often flies off with ripe fruit to roost and eat at leisure. Its usefulness as a cross-pollinator and seed dispersal agent is perhaps offset by its destructiveness in orchards.

Information on breeding habits is scanty. Pregnant females have been obtained in February and young probably born in March and September have been collected, suggesting two birth peaks. Young carried by the mother have been seen in September. The period of gestation is said to be 115 to 125 days.

BEARDED SHEATH-TAILED BAT

Taphozous melanopogon Temminck

Plate facing p. 176

[RACE IN INDIA: *melanopogon* Temminck]

Size. Head and body 3.1 in. (79 mm.); tail 1 in. (25 mm.); forearm 63-69 mm.
Distinctive Characters. Male sandy yellowish-grey with a black beard of long and thick hairs. Female brown with reddish tint. Young dull dark grey, the males growing a beard after five or six months of age. During rut the beard is drenched by a thick secretion produced by small glands under the chin.

Distribution. Peninsular India and south-east Asia.

Habits. Gregarious, living in colonies varying in numbers from 150 to 4000. Original habitat rock clefts, now largely ruins and underground temples. The same haunts are occupied throughout the year. The bats do not hang by their hind limbs but cling to the walls and ceilings by all four limbs and move with facility in all directions when disturbed. Sexes not usually segregated, but the males stay on the periphery of the colony. The bats fly out to feed about half an hour after sunset in batches of three to a dozen. Lactating females leave about a quarter hour earlier than the males. The flight is swift. Feeds on insects.

Ruts in January-February and a single young is born between 20 April and 15 May in Western India. The young, which is carried in a lateral position under the wing of the mother, separates permanently after a month but is apparently suckled for another month.

INDIAN FALSE VAMPIRE

Megaderma lyra Geoffroy

Plate facing p. 161

[RACES IN INDIA: *lyra* Geoffroy, *caurina* Andersen & Wroughton]

Size. Head and body 3.4 in. (86 mm.); forearm 65-68 mm.; tail absent.

Distinctive Characters. A dark ash grey or slaty grey bat; paler below with large rounded ears united for more than one-third their length. The nose-leaf has a truncated appearance.

Distribution. Peninsular India and south-east Asia.

Habits. Gregarious, usually in small colonies not exceeding 30 in number. However, one colony of 1500-2000 bats was noticed in March in Aurangabad. Roosts in old buildings, wells, and caves. Emerges well after sunset when it is completely dark. In addition to larger insects like the Tussar Silk Moth, other moths, and grasshoppers, the Indian False Vampire feeds on small vertebrates and has been recorded to take smaller bats like pipistrelles, young rats, birds like crag martins, geckos, and frogs. These are picked off as it flies close to the ground or along the face of rocks and walls. It is also said to take fish but whether from water or those stranded on shore is not known.

The rut is apparently at its peak in October and November, and young are born in late April. The large colony at Aurangabad mentioned earlier dispersed after the breeding season. The females carry the young till they are nearly as large as the adults.

GREAT EASTERN HORSESHOE BAT

Rhinolophus luctus Temminck

Plate facing p. 161

[RACES IN INDIA: *perniger* Hodgson, *beddomei* Andersen]

Size. Head and body 3.55 in. (90 mm.); tail 2.6 (66 mm.); forearm 2.6 to 3 in. (66-76 mm.).

Distinctive Characters. The largest species of the genus. The body fur is long and woolly and slightly curly. Jet black in colour; hairs with ashy tips. Occasionally reddish brown. Ears large with tapering blunt tips, the outer margin of the ear concave below the tip and separated from the large antitragus by a deep notch. The 'horseshoe' of the nose leaf large, projecting over the lip and deeply incised in the middle. Lower lip with a median groove. Tail within the large interfemoral membrane.

Distribution. Himalayas, Western Ghats, and hills of Ceylon and south-east Asia.

Habits. Uncommon. Roosts alone or in pairs in secluded corners of caves and old buildings. In the Himalayas commences its evening hunt early in the evening, flying noiselessly and rather heavily around houses and trees, rarely flying above twenty or thirty feet. Hibernates in winter in the Himalayas. Little information is available on its breeding habits. Females with young have been seen in May in the Western Ghats.

The **Great Himalayan Leafnosed Bat** (*Hipposideros armiger* Hodgson) is equal, if not larger than the Eastern Horseshoe Bat. It is light to dark brown in colour and is restricted to the Himalayas in India.

Leafnosed bats (*Hipposideros*) are distinguished from the Horseshoe bats (*Rhinolophus*) by the absence of a notch separating the antitragus from the outer margins of the ear and in all toes having two joints only.

SEROTINE

Eptesicus serotinus (Schreber)

Plate facing p. 176

[RACE IN INDIA: *pachyomus* (Tomes)]

Size. Head and body 2.85 in. (72 mm.); tail 2 in. (51mm.); Forearm 2.1 in. (53 mm.)

Distinctive Characters. In colour dark smoky brown above and yellowish brown to white below. Head flat with moderate sized ears.

Distribution. A palaearctic species, which occurs in Indian limits in the Himalayas from Kashmir to Assam.

Habits. The Serotine is not uncommon in Kashmir. It appears late in the evening. The flight is slow and fluttery. Hibernates in winter, singly or in small groups in hollows of trees and similar situations. Though a very well known bat in Europe little information is available on the species in India. In Europe mating occurs in autumn and the implantation of the ova is delayed till spring when development commences. Normally one young is born at a time.

INDIAN PIPISTRELLE

Pipistrellus coromandra (Gray)

Plate facing p. 176

[RACE IN INDIA: *coromandra* (Gray)]

Size. Head and body 1.8 in. (46 mm.); tail 1.4 in. (36 mm.); forearm 27-31 mm.

Distinctive Characters. Usually dark brown in colour, slightly paler below. Muzzle blunt, without fur up to the eyes in the adult. Crown of head and forehead between eyes densely furred. Ears subtriangular, rounded at the tips.

Distribution. India, south-east Asia.

Habits. The bat most frequently noticed from its habit of roosting in the roof of houses and other buildings. It has also been collected from below the bark of trees. This bat is apparently the earliest to fly and appears to remain out throughout the night retiring a quarter of an hour before dawn. The flight is fast and erratic and it may enter houses in search of insects such as small flies, which it eats in large quantities. Hibernates in the northern areas of its range.

Very little information is available on its breeding habits. Young have been collected in May and a heavily pregnant female in September, suggesting two birth seasons. Two young at a birth seem to be the usual number.

TICKELL'S BAT

Hesperoptenus tickelli (Blyth)

Plate facing p. 176

Size. Head and body 2.6 in. (66 mm.); tail 2 in. (51 mm.); forearm 54-58 mm.

Distinctive Characters. A pale yellowish grey bat, with grey head and a tuft of whitish hairs at the base of the ears. Wing long, the 3rd finger having a third phalange. Tail tip free.

Distribution. India and Ceylon.

Habits. Very little is known of its habits. It is thought to roost in hollows of trees. An early flier its flight is slow and is limited to its territory. A single young is born in May.

COMMON YELLOW BAT

Scotophilus heathi (Horsfield)

Plate facing p. 176

[RACES IN INDIA: *heathi* (Horsfield), *belangeri* (Geoffroy)]

Size. Head and body 3 in. (76 mm.); tail 2 in. (51 mm.); forearm 56-64 mm.

Distinctive Characters. The canary yellow of the underparts is distinctive. A reddish variety is also known. Yellowish brown above. Size and colour varies considerably.

Distribution. India and south-east Asia.

Habits. Gregarious. Roosts in small colonies in crevices or cracks on roofs, rafters and in holes in ceilings. In between hunts they spends a large part of the night at the diurnal haunt in noisy quarrels among themselves. Appears quite early in the evening and usually flies around in company. The stomach of one specimen held a large quantity of flying ants. Hibernates in the northern areas of its range.

Usually two young are born in June-July.

PAINTED BAT

Kerivoula picta (Pallas)

Plate facing p. 176

[RACE IN INDIA: *picta* (Pallas)]

Size. Head and body 1.5 in. (38 mm.); tail 1.7 in. (43 mm.); forearm 32-35 mm.

Distinctive Characters. The bright orange or ferruginous colour makes this bat unmistakable. The orange colour extends to the wings along the fingers and the flanks. Wing membranes black with orange spots. Interfemoral membrane bright orange. Ears funnel-shaped; tragus very long, narrow and transparent.

Distribution. India and south-east Asia.

Habits. Inspite of its startling coloration, the Painted Bat is rarely seen, its colour matching perfectly with the dry leaves among which it roosts during the day, singly or in pairs. The flight is moth-like. No information is available on its breeding habits.

13. Rodents

SQUIRRELS, MARMOTS, RATS and mice, porcupines, and their kinsfolk are classified as **Rodentia,** the rodents or gnawing animals. Both in species and in numbers this is quite the largest single group of mammals. There are more than a thousand different species of rodents, many of them swarming in vast hordes. They are all comparatively small animals, earning a livelihood in diverse ways. Some live on the surface of the ground, others below it, some in trees, and some in water. With such diversity in habits and modes of life, rodents naturally display great diversity of form and structure. But there is one character by which any rodent can be distinguished from all other mammals, viz. its teeth. Their distinctive structure is associated with their food and the way in which they eat it.

STRUCTURE IN RELATION TO HABITS

Teeth. All rodents are essentially herbivorous animals. There is probably no edible vegetable substance that a rodent will not eat. The mode of eating is peculiar to the tribe. A rodent first breaks up its food by gnawing, scraping, or nibbling at it with its front or incisor teeth, which are especially designed for such work. They are sharp, chisel-shaped cutting implements. Rodents have four such incisors, two in the upper jaw and two in the lower. These incisor teeth are implanted in sockets reaching far into the jaw bones, and there is a remarkable provision to prevent their being worn away from long use and to keep them always sharpened to a fine chisel-like edge. Actually a rodent's incisors are built much like a chisel. A chisel is made of soft iron and faced in front with a thin layer of hard steel. In much the same way a rodent's incisors are built of soft dentine and faced with a fine layer of hard enamel, usually bright orange or yellow in colour. In use, the softer iron composing the back of the chisel wears quicker than its facing of steel. A fine bevelled edge is thus maintained. The same thing happens with the incisor teeth of a rodent. In process of gnawing, the soft dentine composing the body of the tooth wears quicker than its facing of hard resistant enamel. Thus, as with the chisel, the incisor teeth constantly maintain their sharp cutting edge. There is no risk of these teeth being worn away through long use. They grow through life. So much for the incisors. They are the most distinctive attribute of rodents, and are marvellously adapted to their food and their way of eating it. As for canine teeth, rodents have none. There is always an empty gap in the jaws between the front and back teeth. This gap serves a special purpose. It enables the inner surfaces of the cheeks to be brought closer together inside the mouth. This inward constriction of the cheeks divides the mouth into two chambers, a front chamber containing the incisor teeth and a rear chamber containing the grinders. The passage from the outer to the inner chamber of the mouth is thus reduced to a narrow opening by a drawing inwards of the opposing cheeks. As their inside surfaces are wholly or partly lined with hair, the cheeks with their hairy lining act as a sort of sieve. Through this sieve only finer well chopped-up particles of food enter the inner cavity of the mouth. Coarser material is excluded. Food cut up roughly by the incisor teeth is thus strained before it reaches the molar teeth which crush and grind it. Rodents usually have three true molars or grinders on each side of each jaw. Their broad surfaces are in most instances furnished with cusps, which with wear grind down to transverse ridges of hard enamel. The whole structure of the rodent's mouth is distinctive and intimately related to its special way of dealing with its food. (Plate facing p. 192)

RODENTS AND THEIR SURROUNDINGS

There are rodents living in every part of the Globe except in the extreme Polar regions. High altitudes are equally no barrier to some of the Order. Marmots live all the year.round on the bleak plateaux of Tibet, 18,000 ft. (5500 m.) and more above sea-level. They are among the highest-dwelling mammals in the world. Other rodents display the most remarkable adaptability to the most varied surroundings. Wandering or carried by human agency, the Common House Rat (*Rattus rattus*) and the Brown Rat (*R. norvegicus*) have adapted themselves to life in every part of the world. A study of variations in the Common House Rat shows how readily these animals respond to the requirements of their surroundings. If necessary the colour and quality of the coat are modified. Changes in diet soon produce changes in the ' set ' of the muscles of masti-cation, which in turn remould the form of the skull or lead to the lengthening or shortening of the rows of cheek teeth.

Colour and surroundings. Changes in surroundings have produced the distinctive variations in colour seen in the Common House Rat (*R. rattus*). Those which live in the open, in field or forest, have retained the bright rufescent coat and white belly believed to be the original livery of the species. But those which have become parasitic on man and live more or less indoors have lost their bright colouring and have assumed the dull coat and dingy underparts so characteristic of these rats when they live in human dwellings. How variable again is the colouring of other rodents. Squirrels living in the same area may show marked individual differences in colour. Their colouring may also vary with season or with locality. Dryness or humidity are generally believed to be one of the factors which produce these local forms. In peninsular India, the darkest form of Giant Squirrel (*Ratufa indica*) is found in the moist evergreen forests of Malabar, the palest in the dry open forests of the Dangs; forms intermediate in colour inhabit our dry deciduous and mixed deciduous forests (Map between pages 24 and 25). All of which seems to suggest that these differently coloured geographical races are in some way correlated with local physical and climatic differences. Whether this is actually the case remains to be investigated. Other factors than climate may influence such colour variation. Pale, dark, and intermediate colour forms of mice and other rodents may be found living in close proximity under identical climatic conditions. In a single valley in the deserts of Mexico, pale forms of Pocket Mice and other rodents are found living in areas where the soil is light and sandy, and intermediate and dark-coloured races of the same species live in near-by areas where the soil is intermediate in colour, or dark. Since climatic conditions are the same in both areas they could not account for these variously coloured races. Colour variation in such instances is explained not in terms of climate, but in terms of its protective value. In each of these areas individuals whose colouring was not in harmony with the background were more conspicuous. They fell an easier prey to enemies. Thus, the more conspicuous dark-coloured individuals may have been gradually eliminated from areas where the soil was light and light-coloured animals from areas where it was dark. It was thus the concealment value of the colour, the protection it gave against enemies, which led to the preservation and establishment in each area of only those forms whose colouring was correlated with the soil, i.e. to the production of dark- and light-coloured races among these particular rodents. Colour variation in animals may be the result of climatic conditions, or it may be produced as a result of its protective value, or by a combination of both these factors. But among the smaller rodents, which are the natural prey of so wide a range of enemies, concealment must be the more important factor influencing coloration.

Hibernation. Among rodents, hibernation in winter is well instanced in the case of the marmots which are perhaps the most thoroughly hibernating of all mammals. They live at high altitudes where in winter their food is buried under great depths of ice and snow. As they hoard no food in their burrows to tide over this season of scarcity, a thing which many rodents do, marmots can only escape death from starvation by passing the whole of the winter in profound sleep. The freezing cold makes this lethargic sleep possible. Voles (*Microtus*), like marmots, live at the higher levels of the Himalayas. Probably, like the Alpine

Vole, they remain active through the winter. The Alpine Vole [*M. nivalis* (Martins)] makes regular runs through the snow along which it travels in search of food, when the supply hoarded for winter is exhausted. In the Himalayas one finds the remains of such runs, made by voles, deposited on the ground after the snow has melted. Apparently, the runs are lined with earth to strengthen them. The earth carried down by the melting snow is deposited in the form of long ridges, some little distance below the mouth of the burrows. In the higher Himalayas, flying squirrels are believed to hibernate in holes in trees. But Red Flying Squirrels (*P. p. albiventer*) have been observed fully active in the depths of winter at altitudes of 10,000 ft. (3050 m.) and more. If they hibernate at all, it may be that their winter sleep is never very profound, and that they are restored to activity during the warm spells. This happens with many hibernating animals. But many of these squirrels probably remain active wherever food is still available.

Seasonal movements. Probably there is some winter migration of Himalayan squirrels from higher to lower levels. Such movements also take place in summer. But these seasonal migrations are regulated directly, not so much by climatic conditions, as by the prevailing abundance or scarcity of food, by such factors as the fruiting of trees etc. In Sikkim the Parti-coloured Flying Squirrels (*H. alboniger*) move up and down the higher and lower valleys according to the availability of food supplies. They may be abundant in a particular locality at a certain time and absent at another.

In peninsular India, the habits of rodents must vary considerably during the dry and wet seasons. Changes in the nature and abundance of food affect the distribution and diet of rodents. For instance, in south India when the paddy is in ear the burrows of the Southern Mole-Rat (*Bandicota bengalensis kok*) abound in the bunds of the paddy fields and are filled with ears of paddy stored by it. In the off season, however, the burrows are confined to the bunds near the water channels, probably to facilitate access to water and contain accumulations of grasses and roots and, sometimes, the remains of landcrabs. In areas subject to the monsoon the need for shelter may bring about a change of abode. With the advent of the monsoon there is a partial migration of Common House Rats (*R. rattus*). During the dry season, the outdoor population increases, as many take to living in fields, compounds, and gardens ; when the rains set in, the indoor population rises as a result of rats seeking shelter from the wet.

The risk of flooding during the monsoon also influences the selection of sites for burrows. In areas subject to inundation many field rodents choose high ground, mounds of earth or ' bunds ' between fields, for their burrows. Nevertheless, in low-lying areas, thousands of young rats and mice are destroyed annually by monsoon floods.

Periodic rises in numbers. Nature employs many means of keeping the numbers of these highly prolific animals in check. Accidents, disease, predatory animals, and parasites are all powerful checks on over-population, but climatic conditions are perhaps the most potent of all. Actually the rate of breeding depends largely on food supply and the competition for it. But when food supply, climatic conditions, and other factors are favourable rodents may multiply at an amazing rate. Periodically, great plagues of gerbilles, metads, and other field rats occur in the Deccan. This frequently happens in the second year following a prolonged period of drought. The suggested explanation is that when there is a drought there are no floods to destroy the rats, especially their newborn young. Also there are fewer ticks and fleas, parasites which require favourable conditions of humidity for their increase and well-being. In the absence of these normal controls, a great surplus population of rats is raised. During the period of drought, alternative foods available are sufficient to keep much of this surplus alive. When the drought ends and food becomes abundant, the increased numbers breeding rapidly produce in the following year vast hordes which overflow their territory and devastate great areas of the country. This is the suggested explanation, but much more study is required before we can arrive at a true understanding of the factors which produce or end these great plagues of field rats. The high breeding rate of smaller rodents has undoubtedly been developed to enable them to overcome the many risks and the many enemies to which they are exposed.

Rodents are a 'feeble folk' comparatively insignificant in size and strength, yet through the Age of Mammals they have held their own against legions of natural enemies. Their defence is their wariness, their cunning, their timidity and agility, their secretiveness, and above all their amazing fecundity, the rapidity with which they breed. Some rodents are protected by an armament of spines. There are many spiny rodents, but in all the Order this means of defence is best developed in the porcupine. The porcupine's bristling armature of sharp piercing quills gives protection to this otherwise defenceless animal. In the Indian forests even large animals like tigers and panthers have been killed by porcupines, their vital organs pierced by the powerful spines. Rodents are, as we have said, a weak and timid folk, but hunger may make them exceedingly bold. Hungry rats have been known to attack man and the larger animals. Mice and rats gnaw the feet of captive elephants and attack domestic pigs. Young animals, and the eggs and young of wild and domestic birds are items in their diet.

PLATE 42

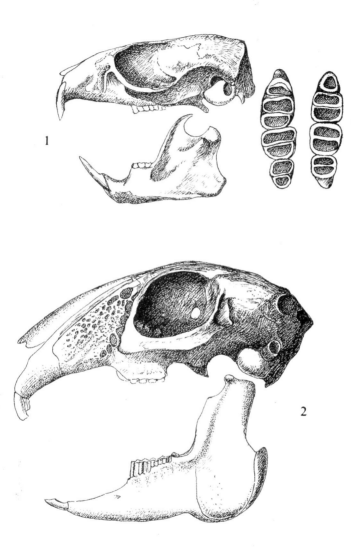

Teeth and jaws of Rodents and Hares

1. Teeth and jaws of Indian Mole-Rat (*Bandicota bengalensis*)
2. Teeth and jaws of Indian Hare (*Lepus nigricollis*)

PLATE 43

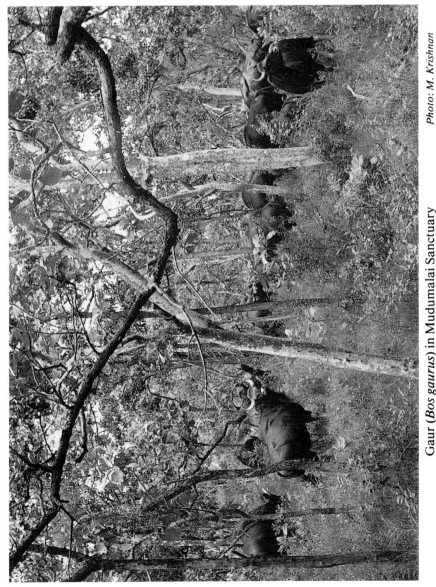

Gaur (*Bos gaurus*) in Mudumalai Sanctuary

Photo: M. Krishnan

RODENTS AND THEIR NEIGHBOURS

In the economy of Nature rodents because of their large numbers play a most important role. Being mainly herbivorous they provide a potent control on plant life. But their very habits make them the easiest prey of carnivorous animals. In fact they form the staple food of most of the smaller carnivores. But for the check provided by the smaller cats, mongooses, weasels, birds of prey, snakes, larger lizards, and parasites, life would become impossible for man over vast areas of our country. Ill-considered extermination of these natural controls is fraught with danger to man and has frequently led to the most disastrous consequences.

The burrows of rodents provide shelter for a number of animals. Hyenas often live in enlarged porcupine earths. Many of the smaller carnivores take advantage of such shelter ; even bats find in them a suitable roosting place. Desert Gerbilles (*Meriones hurrianae*) share their burrows with toads, beetles, and other small creatures. McCann suggests that the Sawscaled Viper (*Echis carinata*) also occupies their burrows. The Viper probably kills and eats the owners, and from these quarters visits neighbouring burrows to prey on other gerbilles. In North America Rattle Snakes occupy the burrows of prairie marmots and victimise the owners and the colony in much the same way.

As to relationship with their own kind, though rats will attack and eat a sick or injured comrade, they usually live on good terms with each other. As with other animals, food supply and the competition for it are the primary factors governing interrelationship between smaller rodents. Overcrowding and competition produced by an undue increase in numbers bring in their wake starvation and disease, which is another factor which helps to restore the normal population. Competition between two species has led to extermination of the one or the other. In England the Common House Rat (*R. rattus*) has been practically displaced by the Brown Rat (*R. norvegicus*). To England the Common House Rat came as an immigrant from the tropics, the Brown Rat as an immigrant from the temperate lands of Asia ; better able to withstand cold, a stronger and more formidable animal, the Brown Rat killed out its weaker rival wherever it came into contact with it. Thus the Common House Rat is now reduced in England to a few isolated and dwindling colonies.

Rodents and man. Of all the mammals which have become parasitic on man, none are greater pests and more destructive than rats and mice. The magnitude of the havoc they cause is due not so much to any peculiar viciousness, as to the sheer weight of their numbers. Their high rate of breeding usually defeats attempts at extermination. It would be difficult to estimate the damage done to agriculture alone in India by rats and mice. It must run to several crores of rupees. Grain of all sorts is their chief and favourite food. Before the grain is sown, in every stage of its growth and, after the harvest, wherever it is stored and in whichever form it is used, it is subject to the attacks of these animals. Great havoc is also wrought to all kinds of fruit and vegetables and to poultry and other domestic stock. While the quantity of food eaten is considerable, far more is ruined than devoured. Rat-tainted food, though it appears wholesome, sometimes entails disastrous consequences to the health of man and animals.

Rodents and Disease. However great the loss caused by rats to man from damage to his food stocks, more grave still is the risk of disease caused by the presence of rats in our midst. Bubonic plague, the dread disease which has caused the death of millions of human beings in India and other countries of the world, is a disease which belongs essentially to rats and the peculiar species of fleas infesting them. The disease is one of Nature's unfailing methods of periodically reducing the rat population to reasonable proportions. Plague-smitten rats die and the fleas which have fed on their infected blood leave their hosts and seek other animals to feed on. They choose other rodents, but may also infect horses, dogs, pigs, and monkeys. Very often they attack man, and in the process of feeding on his blood infect him with plague germs with which their bodies are gorged from feeding on plague-stricken rats. The species usually instrumental in the spread of plague in India are the Common House Rat (*R. rattus*) and the Brown Rat (*R. norvegicus*). The House Mouse (*Mus musculus*) and bandicoots (*Bandicota*) may spread the disease. Palm Squirrels (*Funambulus*), which have become almost as parasitic on man as rats, can also become agents in the spread of plague. There are yet other diseases spread by rats, among them there is rat-bite fever which is caused by the bite of a rat. It is a progressive wasting disease which may persist for long periods. Rats, emboldened by familiarity with man, frequently attack babies or sleeping persons. Influenza in an acute form occurs among horses. It is conveyed from stable to stable by rats.

The great and numerous group of rodents has been variously classified by various naturalists. An account of the principal families inhabiting India follows.

The first family of Rodents comprises the squirrels and marmots (**Sciuridae**).

FLYING SQUIRRELS

Among other rodents a squirrel is easily recognised by its slender build, its long bushy tail, and arboreal habits. Some of these animals have acquired the power of sailing or gliding through the air and are known popularly as Flying Squirrels.

Distinctive Characters. Flying Squirrels are distinctive in having their limbs connected by a membrane or parachute. While on the ground or when climbing about in the treetops, Flying Squirrels differ little in their movements from·ordinary squirrels. They are perhaps less agile because of their ' hobbled ' limbs. When at rest, the parachute is scarcely noticeable. It tucks in close to the body by its own elasticity. But when the animal leaps into the air, as squirrels leap from tree to tree, the outspread limbs expand the parachute to its fullest extent. Supported by its parachute the squirrel glides smoothly and swiftly downwards. An unfinished glide of 100 yards by an alarmed squirrel down a steep valley has been observed. There is no true continuous flight as with bats or birds. The aerial progress is little more than a prolonged leap. There is no sudden change of direction. Progress is in a flat curve from a higher to a lower level. The body is steered by altering the position of the limbs and the membrane connecting them. Nearing its objective, another tree, the squirrel swerves upwards, speed of movement is checked; it alights softly on bough or trunk and scampers upwards to the summit of the tree.

Our Flying Squirrels may be divided into two groups according to size, the Large Flying Squirrels, with head and body 1 ft. 6 inches (45 cm.) and tail 2 ft. (60 cm.) and more, and the Small Flying Squirrels with head and body 10 to 12 inches (25 to 30 cm.).
Except for the **Kashmir Woolly Flying Squirrel** (*Eupetaurus cinereus* Thomas) which is found only in Hunza, Gilgit, and Sikkim, all our Large Flying Squirrels belong to a single genus *Petaurista*. Two races of the **Common Giant Flying Squirrel** [*P. petaurista* (Pallas)] **(Plate facing p. 177)** occur. The **Large Brown Flying Squirrel** [*P. p. philippensis* (Elliot)] inhabits all the larger forests of the Peninsula south of the Ganges. North of the Ganges, in the western Himalayas, the commonest Large Flying Squirrel is the **Red Flying Squirrel** [*P. p. albiventer* (Gray)]. It has a bright chestnut or bay-coloured coat and salmon-buff underparts. In the eastern Himalayas and Assam the Red Flying Squirrel is replaced by **Hodgson's Flying Squirrel** [*P. magnificus* (Hodgson)]. In its summer coat this beautiful squirrel has a bright yellow line down the middle of its deep maroon coat. The body is always darker than the parachute ; tail black-tipped ; underparts rufous. Another east Himalayan species is the **Lesser Giant Flying Squirrel** [*P. elegans* (Müller) Races in India : *caniceps* (Gray), *gorkhali* (Lindsay)]. The **Greyheaded Flying Squirrel** (*P. e. caniceps*) is recognisable by its ashy grey or grey speckled head.
Our smaller Flying Squirrels are confined mainly to the Himalayas and the hill ranges of Assam and Burma. A single species the **Small Travancore Flying Squirrel** [*Petinomys fuscocapillus* (Jerdon) Races in India : *fuscocapillus* (Jerdon). Ceylon : *layardi* (Kelaart)], inhabits the forests of Travancore and the Nilgiris. The

common species of Small Flying Squirrel in the western Himalayas is the **Kashmir Flying Squirrel** [*Hylopetes fimbriatus* (Gray) Races in India : *fimbriatus* (Gray), *baberi* (Blyth)] **(Plate facing p. 196).** Its fur is light and buffy brown more or less suffused with black. It is found at elevations ranging from 6000 ft. (1830 m.) to the limits of the tree-line. In the eastern Himalayas and Assam its place is taken by the **Particoloured Flying Squirrel** [*Hylopetes alboniger* (Hodgson) Race in India : *alboniger* (Hodgson)] **(Plate facing p. 196)** a hoary or blackish squirrel with white underparts. The **Hairyfooted Flying Squirrel** [*Belomys pearsoni* (Gray) Races in India : *pearsoni* (Gray), *trichotis* Thomas] is also found in these parts. It can be recognised by the pencil of long chestnut hairs growing from the base of each ear-conch.

Habits. The general habits of Flying Squirrels are somewhat similar. Essentially they are forest animals. Various species inhabit our tropical and temperate forests from plains level to an altitude coinciding with the limits of the tree-line. The single exception is the Kashmir Woolly Flying Squirrel which is found even in the treeless parts of Hunza and Gilgit among barren rocks and cliffs.

Unlike other squirrels, Flying Squirrels are nocturnal. They emerge from shelter at dusk and retire before dawn. The usual roost is a hole in a tree or a sheltered place among the branches. The small Kashmir Flying Squirrel sometimes roosts under the roofs of forest bungalows. In such a site numbers may roost together. Flying Squirrels sleep curled up in a ball, either on their sides or belly downwards. The head is tucked between the fore- or even the hindlegs and the tail is curled about the body. The Large Brown Flying Squirrel, during the hot weather, may sleep on its back with legs and parachute outspread. It is one way of keeping cool in the tropical forests in which it lives.

The food of the Flying Squirrels consists of the fruits and nuts of various trees. They eat the bark, the lumps of gum and resin exuding from it, and also insects and their larvae which shelter beneath. The smaller Flying Squirrels of the Himalayas feed commonly on the leaves and buds of various conifers. The ground is often strewn with thousands of green cones destroyed by these animals. When eating, the Flying Squirrel may sit up on its haunches, as squirrels do, holding and turning the food round with its forepaws. Food may be held even by the hindlegs and brought forward to the mouth. The jaws move continuously. The grating of the chisel-like front teeth on a hard-shelled nut sounds like the rasping of a small saw, and may be heard a long way off. Food is usually sought in the treetops, more rarely on the ground.

Flying Squirrels call to each other at night with a low monotonous note quickly repeated. The sound gives away their presence, but it is ventriloquial and difficult to locate. The Large Brown

PLATE 44

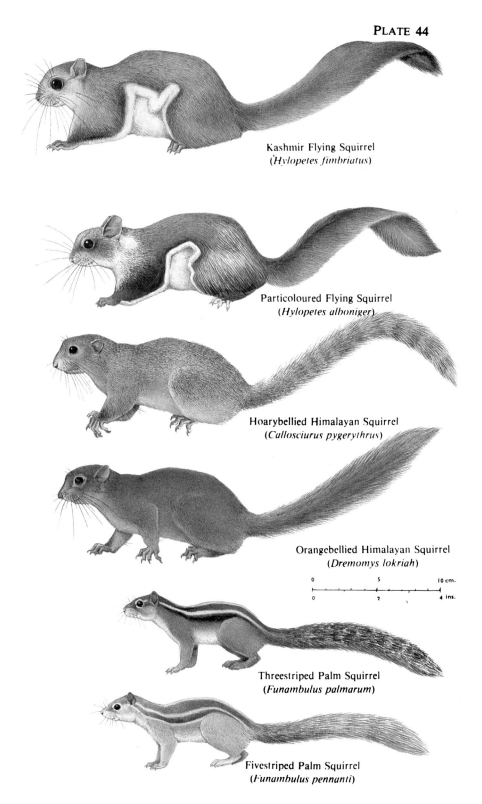

Kashmir Flying Squirrel
(*Hylopetes fimbriatus*)

Particoloured Flying Squirrel
(*Hylopetes alboniger*)

Hoarybellied Himalayan Squirrel
(*Callosciurus pygerythrus*)

Orangebellied Himalayan Squirrel
(*Dremomys lokriah*)

Threestriped Palm Squirrel
(*Funambulus palmarum*)

Fivestriped Palm Squirrel
(*Funambulus pennanti*)

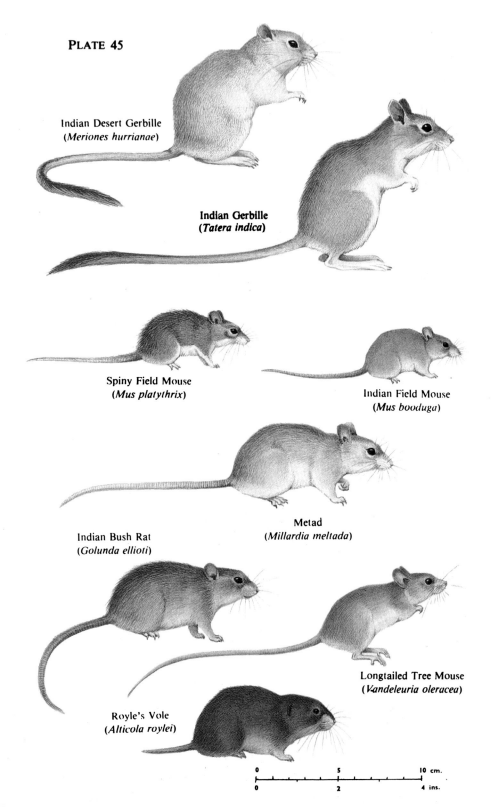

PLATE 45

Indian Desert Gerbille
(*Meriones hurrianae*)

Indian Gerbille
(***Tatera indica***)

Spiny Field Mouse
(*Mus platythrix*)

Indian Field Mouse
(*Mus booduga*)

Indian Bush Rat
(*Golunda ellioti*)

Metad
(*Millardia meltada*)

Royle's Vole
(*Alticola roylei*)

Longtailed Tree Mouse
(*Vandeleuria oleracea*)

0   5   10 cm.
0   2   4 ins.

Flying Squirrel of the Peninsula has a loud alarm call and also the sharp chattering cry usual among many squirrels.

Very little is known about the breeding habits of our Flying Squirrels. Their usual habit is to nest in holes in trees. The mother previously lines the hollow with leaves, moss, fur, and other soft material. A pair of Large Brown Flying Squirrels (*P. p. philippensis*) were found occupying such a nest. How long the association between the sexes lasts is not known. When the young are born the nest hole is occupied solely by the mother and her offspring. Apart from nesting in holes in trees, Flying Squirrels have been observed occupying large leaf nests, such as other squirrels build, and in the Himalayas a young Red Flying Squirrel (*P.p. albiventer*) has been taken off such a nest in May. The nests are made of sticks and vegetable matter and are big as that of a crow and similar to the English squirrel's dray. The number of young produced at birth by various species is not recorded. A baby Large Brown Flying Squirrel taken from its nest was still blind though grown to quite a foot in length. Very striking was the size of its head which seemed out of all proportion to its body, as also a curious flattening of the terminal portion of the tail, a character sometimes seen even in adults. The parachute was not fully developed. The cartilaginous 'spurs' which grow from the outside of each wrist and help to support the parachute were not in evidence, the wing flaps ended at the elbow and not at the wrists. When handled the baby squirrel made a series of whistling noises ending in a squeak.

Flying Squirrels are easily tamed but they are delicate animals and do not live long in confinement.

GIANT SQUIRRELS

The Indian Giant Squirrel *Ratufa indica* (Erxleben)

Plate facing p. 177

[RACES IN INDIA : *indica* (Erxleben), *maxima* (Schreber), *bengalensis* (Blanford), *dealbata* (Blanford), *superans* Ryley, *centralis* Ryley, *elphinstoni* (Sykes)]

The Grizzled Giant Squirrel *Ratufa macroura* (Pennant)

Plate facing p. 177

[RACES IN INDIA : *dandolena* Thomas & Wroughton. CEYLON : *dandolena* Thomas & Wroughton, *macroura* (Pennant), *melanochra* Thomas & Wroughton]

The Malayan Giant Squirrel *Ratufa bicolor* (Sparrmann)

Plate facing p. 177

[RACE IN INDIA : *gigantea* (McClelland)]

Local Names. Hindi *karrat, rasu* ; Mar. *shekra* ; Kan. *keshalilu* ; Tamil *anil.*

Size. Head and body, 14 to 16 in. (35 to 40 cm.) ; tail, about 2 ft. (60 cm.).

Distinctive Characters. All the Indian squirrels of these dimensions belong to a single genus *Ratufa.* Three species are described from our limits. The **Indian Giant Squirrel** (*R. indica*) inhabits the deciduous, mixed deciduous, and moist evergreen forests of peninsular India south of the Ganges ; a number of local races have been described (Map between pp. 24 and 25). In some hill ranges of south India and in Ceylon there is a second species, the **Grizzled Giant Squirrel** (*R. macroura*). It is distinctive in having the dorsal surface and tail grey or brownish grey, more or less grizzled with white. North of the Ganges in Nepal, Sikkim, Bhutan, and Assam there is a third form. This is the **Malayan Giant Squirrel** (*R. bicolor*). It has a deep brown almost black coat with buff-coloured underparts. This squirrel ranges eastwards into Burma and the Malay countries.

Habits. Giant Squirrels live only in forests. They keep to the summits of the higher trees, and seldom if ever come to ground. They move from tree to tree taking amazing leaps with limbs outspread, covering as much as twenty feet in a single bound. They are active and agile animals, most active in the early hours of the morning and in the evening. As with most animals, midday is a time of rest. It is not unusual at this time to see one of these squirrels sleeping spread-eagled on a branch, its long tail drooping over the side. Or the animal takes its siesta in its nest, especially if the weather is cold or wet.

They are shy, wary animals not easy to discover. Despite its brilliant colouring the Indian Giant Squirrel is sooner heard than seen. Its loud rattling call, oft repeated, usually reveals its presence. Any unusual sound, any unfamiliar sight, sets these squirrels calling in all directions. They share with monkeys the habit of scolding, barking, and raising a general alarm when any suspicious object is sighted. When frightened these squirrels do not always dash away ; quite a common habit is to lie flattened against a branch or to slip behind a heavy bough or trunk. It is said that the Indian Grizzled Squirrel at times seeks escape by sliding down a tree and slipping away into the dense undergrowth.

The Indian Giant Squirrel usually lives alone, or in pairs. These animals build large globular nests of twigs and leaves, placing them for greater security among the slimmer twigs and branches of trees, where heavier predators cannot get at them. In deciduous forests these nests become conspicuous objects when the trees are bare. An individual may build nests in several trees within a small area of jungle. They are used as sleeping quarters, and one of them as a nursery. In captivity the Malayan Giant Squirrel has given birth in March, April, September and December. The young weigh on an average 74.5 gm. and have a total length of 27.3 cm. at birth. In Kanara they were found with young in March.

HIMALAYAN SQUIRRELS

The Orangebellied Himalayan Squirrel *Dremomys lokriah* (Hodgson)

Plate facing p. 196

[RACES IN INDIA : *lokriah* (Hodgson), *macmillani* Thomas]

The Hoarybellied Himalayan Squirrel *Callosciurus pygerythrus* (Geoffroy)

Plate facing p. 196

[RACES IN INDIA : *lokroides* (Hodgson), *blythi* (Tytler), *stevensi* (Thomas)]

Local Names. Nepalese *lokria* ; Bhutan *zhams*.

Size. Head and body, about 8 in. (20 cm.) ; tail, a little longer.

Distinctive Characters. The Orangebellied Squirrel is a dark rufous-brown animal, sometimes slightly speckled with dark yellowish brown. The dorsal fur is leaden brown at the base ; the longer hairs have a single yellow ring and a long black tip. Lower parts more or less orange varying from pale to rusty red. These characters and its long pointed snout distinguish it from the Hoarybellied Himalayan Squirrel ; also distinctive is its greyish, isabelline, or pale rufous belly ; besides, the longer dorsal hairs in this species have two light rings instead of one as in *D. lokriah*.

Distribution. Nepal, Sikkim, Bhutan, and Assam eastwards into Burma.

Habits. In Sikkim the Orangebellied Himalayan Squirrel is common in all forests at levels between 5000 (1525 m.) and 9000 ft. (2745 m.). It lives in holes in trees, generally low down in the trunk. It frequently comes to the ground to feed on fallen fruit. As a rule, it is silent but occasionally gives vent to a loud cackling call.

The Hoarybellied Squirrel occupies lower elevations in Sikkim. It may be found from almost plains level (500 ft., i.e. about 150 m.) up to an altitude of 5000 ft. (1525 m.). It lives in dense forest, and also about villages, and is given to raiding orange groves to which fruit it is said to be especially partial. For its small size its call is astonishingly loud. The nest or ' dray ' of this squirrel is a collection of grass and sticks placed high up in a tree.

STRIPED SQUIRRELS

The Fivestriped Palm Squirrel *Funambulus pennanti* Wroughton

Plate facing p. 196

The Threestriped Palm Squirrel *Funambulus palmarum* (Linnaeus)

Plate facing p. 196

[RACES IN INDIA : *palmarum* (Linnaeus), *bellaricus* Wroughton, *robertsoni* Wroughton. CEYLON : *brodiei* (Blyth), *kelaarti* (Layard), *matugamensis* (Lindsay)]

Local Names. Hindi *gilheri* ; Ben. *beral* ; Mar. *khadi khar* ; Tamil *anna pilli.*

Size. Head and body, 5 in. (13 cm.) to 6 in. (15 cm.) ; tail, slightly longer.

Distinctive Characters. *F. pennanti* is distinctive in having five pale stripes on its back, three median, pale, dorsal stripes flanked on each side with a supplementary pale stripe. These supplementary stripes are wanting in *F. palmarum*, which has only three dorsal stripes. A number of local races of these squirrels are recognised, the differences being based on the lightness or darkness of the coat or variations in the tone of the dorsal stripes.

Distribution. Both species inhabit the Indian peninsula from the base of the Himalayas southwards. The Fivestriped Squirrel is commoner in northern India, particularly in the drier and more arid portions and extends into the dry plains of the South. It is essentially more commensal with man. The Threestriped species predominates in the South, and in the moister parts of western and eastern India. Both species may however be found living in the same area.

Habits. The Fivestriped Squirrel is the commonest and most familiar of all Indian wild animals. It is not found in forest, but has forsaken forests to live with man in and about his dwellings and fields. It has become almost as dependent on man for food and shelter as house rats and mice, and lives in crowded towns and cities, or in villages ; it shelters in houses, gardens, groves, and hedges, and on roadside trees. Lively active sprites, frisking about on the ground, or scampering about the house or in the trees, their antics are always pleasing to watch. But like most squirrels they are noisy creatures. The Threestriped Palm Squirrel on the other hand is a forest animal. It has a particularly shrill bird-like call which it repeats again and again, accompanying its music with quick jerks of its tail. Their food is the usual food of all squirrels, fruits, nuts, young shoots, buds, and bark. When the silk cotton trees are in bloom these squirrels visit the flowers to drink the nectar and so probably help in their pollination. They also eat the pods. They are partial to ' prickly pears ' and, in fruiting time, may be seen in the thorny cactus hedges, their mouths and feet stained red with the juice of the ripe fruit. Insects are eaten at a pinch, as also the eggs of birds. They are persistent egg robbers.

The male and female come together for only a day or two during which period it is probable that the female mates with more than one male. The period of gestation is about six weeks. When about to bring forth her young, the female builds an untidy nest of grass and leaves and fibres. This is placed in a tree, or in the rafters of a house, or in holes in the walls. Two or three young are produced. They are born blind and remain in the nest till able to fend for themselves.

There is a third species in the forests of south India and Ceylon. This is the **Dusky Striped Squirrel** [*Funambulus sublineatus* (Waterhouse) Races in India : *sublineatus* (Waterhouse). Ceylon : *obscurus* (Pelzeln & Kohl)]. It has a coat speckled with dull greenish grey. It has four dark brown longitudinal stripes with three intervening pale ones. It is found in the south Indian hill ranges. It is a shy and secretive creature keeping to damp gullies in densest forest where it is most difficult to discover among the tangled creepers and dense undergrowth which are its hunting ground. It feeds largely on the fruit of the wild raspberry (*Rubus*). In the eastern Himalayas there is a small striped squirrel. This is the **Himalayan Striped Squirrel** [*Callosciurus macclellandi* (Horsfield) Race in India : *macclellandi* (Horsfield)]. It measures about 5 inches (13 cm.) from nose to base of tail. It has a greyish brown coat with black, brown, and buff stripes on its back. It lives in forests above 5000 ft. (1525 m.). It is common but difficult to detect because of its small size, its colouring, and its habit of keeping to densest cover. In Assam and Burma this species is found at lower elevation, almost at plains level. It has the same seclusive habits as the Dusky Striped Squirrel of the South.

MARMOTS

The Himalayan Marmot *Marmota bobak* (Müller)

[RACE IN INDIA : *himalayana* (Hodgson)]

The Longtailed Marmot *Marmota caudata* (Jacquemont)

Plate facing p. 177

[RACES IN INDIA : *caudata* (Jacquemont), *aurea* (Blanford)]

The squirrel family (**Sciuridae**) includes the marmots. They are all burrowers living in holes in the ground.

Distinctive Characters. Marmots are distinctive in their stout, squat build, short or moderate tails, and very small ears. Our two common marmots are the **Himalayan Marmot** and the **Longtailed Marmot.** The Himalayan Marmot is about 2 ft. (60 cm.) long with a 5 in. (13 cm.) tail. Its body and limbs are pale tawny much mixed with black on the upper parts. The face and terminal third of the tail are dark brown. The Longtailed Marmot is handsomer and more richly coloured. Its fur is yellowish tawny, deep orange, or rufous ; the back is chiefly black, sometimes wholly black. In size it is about as large as the Himalayan Marmot ; but very distinctive is its longer tail, which is quite 1 ft. (30 cm.) or more long.

Distribution. Within our limits marmots are confined to the higher levels of the Himalayas and the highlands beyond. The Himalayan Marmot is found in Nepal, Sikkim, Garhwal, Kashmir, and Ladak. The Longtailed Marmot inhabits the mountain ranges to the north of the valley of Kashmir extending into Gilgit and Ladak and onwards into the Central Asian highlands.

Habits. The Himalayan Marmot lives at altitudes ranging from 13,000 (4000 m.) or 14,000 (4300 m.) to 18,000 ft. (5500 m.). The Longtailed Marmot is found at levels between 8000 (2400 m.) and 14,000 ft. (4300 m.). They live in large colonies excavating deep burrows in which they hibernate through the winter. With the coming of spring they emerge, and till the autumn find food enough to sustain them, roots, leaves, grasses, and the seeds of various plants. On fine days one may see marmots feeding outside their burrows. When disturbed, one or more sit up on their haunches to look around. Scenting danger they utter a loud whistling scream which sends their comrades headlong into shelter. In the Alps marmots are said to crowd together in their winter quarters. Ten to fourteen may occupy a single burrow, sleeping closely packed together. They are born in the spring when the snows have melted and food is once more available. Two to four appears to be the usual litter.

GERBILLES, OR ANTELOPE-RATS

The Indian Gerbille *Tatera indica* (Hardwicke)

Plate facing p. 197

[RACES IN INDIA : *indica* (Hardwicke), *cuvieri* (Waterhouse), *hardwickei* (Gray). CEYLON : *ceylonica* Wroughton]

The Indian Desert Gerbille *Meriones hurrianae* (Jerdon)

Plate facing p. 197

Distinctive Characters. The gerbilles form a subdivision of the greatest and most numerous family of Rodents, the **Muridae**, or Rats and Mice. A gerbille is at once distinguishable from a rat by its tail. It is not bare or naked, but clothed with hair, and usually ends in a tassel. Also the hind feet of a gerbille are very long, much longer than those of any rat of equal size. This character is associated with the gerbille's mode of progress. When moving quickly, it moves in a series of leaps and bounds. A number of species are found in India mostly in the desert zone. The commonest are the **Indian Gerbille** (*T. indica*) and the **Indian Desert Gerbille** (*M. hurrianae*). The Indian Gerbille is the larger of the two, head and body 6 to 7 in. (15 to 17 cm.). Its colour ranges from reddish brown to fawn or greyish fawn. A band of light brown colour runs along each side of the tail. Variation in colour and other minor details has led to the recognition of a number of Indian species. These so-called species are nothing more than geographical races of a single species, *Tatera indica*, which inhabits the whole Peninsula. The Indian Desert Gerbille is a smaller squatter animal measuring about 5 in. (13 cm.) from nose to base of tail. Its body and limbs are a sandy yellow ; underparts dirty white.

Distribution. The Indian Gerbille (*T. indica*) is found throughout India from the Himalayas to Cape Comorin. Its range extends westwards to Persia and Mesopotamia, and southwards to Ceylon. Within our limits the Indian Desert Gerbille is found in the desert and semi-desert zones of north-west and central India.

Habits. The Indian Gerbille (*T. indica*) inhabits open plains and downs and is commonly found on the borders of cultivation. It builds its burrows near hedges and thickets or under bushes, but sometimes quite in the open. In areas subject to floods, high level ground is chosen for security. These burrows are quite noticeable. Beaten paths lead from the mouth of one to the other. Males and females are said to live in separate burrows and to build them on a slightly different plan. The male burrow has a single entrance, the female's more than one. The entrance leads downwards to a central chamber, a foot or more below the ground. Depth is however dependent on the hardness of the soil. There is always a 'bolt hole', an exit passage leading from the sleeping chamber to the surface. The exit is usually concealed with a thin crust of earth, which the gerbille easily breaks through in hurried flight. Gerbilles sleep by day in their burrows and come out at dusk. The slightest alarm sends them bolting back. When frightened they move with leaps and bounds, and can clear 4 (1.2 m.) or 5 ft. (1.5 m.) in a single jump.

Their food consists mainly of grain, roots, leaves, and grass. When in great numbers they can be exceedingly destructive to crops and cultivation of all kinds and at every stage of growth, from seeds and seedlings to the grown plant and its grain. Harvest time is their season of plenty. Then they collect in their burrows large stores of grain to be eaten in the dry season which follows. When this store is consumed, the gerbilles turn to other food, to the roots and fruits and leaves of wild plants. They are, for instance, very partial to the fruits of the prickly pear, a dry season stand-by for many small rodents. They also eat insects and their grubs, the eggs and nestlings of ground birds, and quite probably kill and eat smaller rodents.

As for breeding, the exact relationship between the sexes requires study. The males and females are said ordinarily to live apart. Whether mating takes place below or above the ground is not known. Chambers sometimes communicate with one another below the ground. Surface paths leading from burrow to burrow suggest an alternative means of communication. The nesting chamber is usually lined with leaves and grass. Whether it is a specially built apartment we do not know. Usually it is a mere widening of the entrance tunnel set a foot or more below the ground. The usual number of young produced at a birth is said to be four. But as many as 8 to 12 young have been found in a burrow. These may have included more than one brood.

The Indian Desert Gerbille (*M. hurrianae*) has the same general habits. It is much more gregarious than the Indian Gerbille and lives usually in small colonies. It abounds in desert and semi-desert country, where in some parts the ground is honeycombed with its burrows.

The burrows go down to a depth of a foot or more and have the usual 'bolt holes'. Living in the desert they are less parasitic on man, and their burrows, though sometimes built near cultivation, may be found far away in waste lands, thorn forests, and open desert. Sand-dunes, banks, and cuttings are favourite sites, as also the wind-built mounds of sand which usually collect and consolidate beneath desert shrubs and plants.

Unlike the gerbille of cultivation, these desert animals are thoroughly diurnal in habit. They are seen up and about at all hours of the day, in all seasons. They are most active in the early hours of

PLATE 46

Indian Mole-Rat
(*Bandicota bengalensis*)

Bandicoot Rat
(*Bandicota indica*)

Whitetailed Wood Rat
(*Rattus blanfordi*)

Bay Bamboo Rat
(*Cannomys badius*)

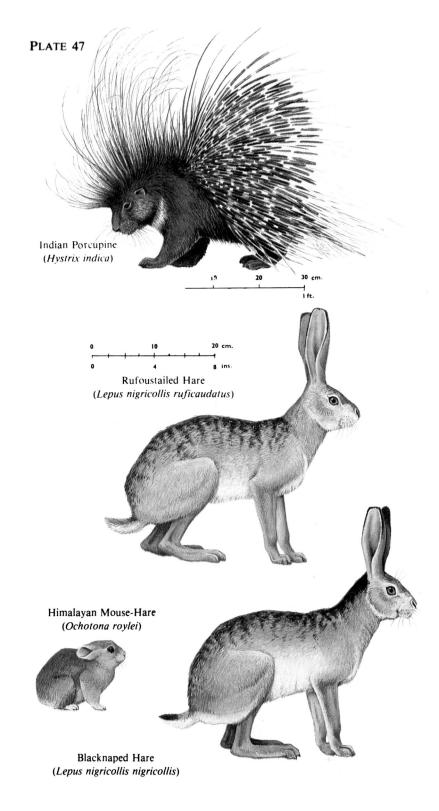

PLATE 47

Indian Porcupine
(*Hystrix indica*)

10   20   30 cm.

1 ft.

0   10   20 cm.

0   4   8 ins.

Rufoustailed Hare
(*Lepus nigricollis ruficaudatus*)

Himalayan Mouse-Hare
(*Ochotona roylei*)

Blacknaped Hare
(*Lepus nigricollis nigricollis*)

the morning. When alarmed or suspicious these gerbilles make a curious drumming sound by stamping on the ground with their hindlegs. An upward whisk of the tail is the usual prelude and signal to flight. The little fellows scamper into their burrows, but do not stay below for long. First one head pops out, then another, till one bolder than the rest sits up or stands on its hindlegs to get a better view. Reassured it ventures out, presently followed by its companions.

Indian Desert Gerbilles feed mainly on seeds, supplemented by bulbous roots, grass, leaves, flowers and the nuts of *Salvadora*. They breed throughout the year with two peak birth seasons in February and July. The gestation period varies from 28 to 30 days and litter size ranges from 1 to 9.

RATS AND MICE

The second division of the **Muridae** includes the Rats and Mice. They are represented in India by numerous species. Their naked, scaly tails, sometimes sparsely clothed with hair, distinguish them from the gerbilles. For convenience, Indian rats and mice may be divided into three groups according to their habits. Firstly there are the field rats, by which is meant rats which are habitual and common pests of crops and cultivation. Our second group includes wild species which live in scrub and forest and which are more or less arboreal, namely bush and tree rats, and lastly come those which are habitual household pests. The commoner species generally distributed in the peninsular area are described in the pages which follow.

MOLE-RATS

The Indian Mole-Rat *Bandicota bengalensis* (Gray & Hardwicke)

Plate facing p. 204

[RACES IN INDIA : *bengalensis* (Gray & Hardwicke), *kok* (Gray), *wardi* (Wroughton). CEYLON : *gracilis* (Nehring)]

Local Names. Beng. *tenkrai* ; Kan. *kok, heggana* ; Tel. *golatta koku* ; Mar. *ghus*.

Size. Head and body, 6 to 9 in. (15 to 23 cm.) ; tail, 5 to 7 in. (13 cm. to 18 cm.).

Distinctive Characters. The Mole-Rat was classified under a separate genus (*Gunomys*). It is now included in the genus *Bandicota* (the Bandicoots). It has the bandicoot's robust form, its rounded head, rounded ears, and short broad muzzle, and the bandicoot's habit of erecting its piles of long hairs and grunting when excited. It is easily distinguished from other Indian bandicoots by its smaller size. Its giant relatives are a foot and over in body length. The general colour of its coat is dark greyish brown speckled with buff, undersides paler.

Distribution. Practically the whole of peninsular India from the Himalayas to Cape Comorin, more common in the moist alluvial tracts. In the desert and semi-desert zone of north-west India there is another genus of mole-rat. This is the **Shorttailed Bandicoot** [*Nesokia indica* (Gray & Hardwicke) Races in India : *indica* (Gray & Hardwicke), *huttoni* (Blyth)]. It is a densely furred yellowish brown animal, with a shorter tail measuring 3-5 in. (8-13 cm.).

Habits. The Indian Mole-Rat commonly lives in cultivated plains and gardens and pasture land, but is found even in waste lands, and in forests, both deciduous and evergreen. Its presence is always made known by a pile of fresh earth resembling a large molehill, hence its name ' mole-rat'. The entrance hole leads downwards to a circular chamber some 2 ft. (60 cm.) or so below the ground. This gallery may extend as much as 20 yards (18 m.) or more, or as many feet, or it may be quite short—it all depends where the burrow is dug. On bunds between fields, a common site when crops are growing, it is usually short. On open ground it is more extensive. When very extensive, the excavated earth is thrown up in small piles at intervals along the course of the tunnel. But there are no external indications to show the origin of such midway piles. Their temporary openings are sealed and the gallery continues unbroken. Small circular chambers are excavated along its path, or to one side of it, not far from the sleeping chamber. These are store rooms, which in harvest time are stocked with much grain. The burrows of mole-rats and gerbilles are often dug up by hungry people for these hoards of food. The sleeping apartment gives off a number of exits or ' bolt holes'. Their surface openings are usually concealed with loose earth which the rat breaks through in flight. This is one of the most destructive rats to crops and cultivation.

Usually one mole-rat is found in each burrow or it is occupied by the female and her young. The mother lines her nursery with straw and leaves. As many as 10 or 12 young may be produced at a birth. They are born blind and naked, but within a month are well covered with fur. They mature rapidly and within three months are able to produce young of their own.

Recent studies by Spillett show that the mole-rat forms 98% of the total rodent population in Calcutta. The Calcutta mole-rat weighs over 200 gm., has an average life expectancy of 200 days; is sexually mature 58 days after birth for the male and between 90 to 100 days for the female, which may have 11.32 pregnancies per year with a break of 32.3 days between pregnancies and may produce nearly 70 young per year.

METADS

The Metad, or Softfurred Field Rat *Millardia meltada* (Gray)

Plate facing p. 197

[RACES IN INDIA : *meltada* (Gray), *pallidior* Ryley. CEYLON: *meltada* (Gray)]

Size. Head and body, 5 to 6 inches (13 to 15 cm.) ; tail, nearly as long.

Distinctive Characters. The dense soft fur and large rounded ears distinguish these rats from others commonly found in cultivation. The general colour is pale brownish grey, greyish white on the underside. The palest coloured forms are found in the desert zone.

Distribution. The peninsula of India from the Punjab and U.P. southwards to western and southern India.

Habits. Metads live chiefly near cultivated fields. They may be found sometimes in heavy scrub surrounded by forest, or living among rocks and in tumble-down walls. In the Deccan they specially favour the plains of black cotton soil. They live in pairs or in small colonies. The ' burrow ' is a very slight hole at the roots of a bush, or under a hedge ; prickly-pear hedges are favoured. Some make no burrow and are content to hide under a heap of stones. In black cotton soil they quite commonly make a home in the deep cracks and fissures which form in the hard baked ground during the hot weather. When in large numbers they do some damage to paddy and other food crops ; in cotton fields, which they favour so much, metads can become a serious pest. Two breeding periods have been noticed, March to May and August to October. The number of litters per female ranges from 2 to 7 in a year, and young per litter 1 to 8. The minimum period between consecutive litters was 20 days.

FIELD MICE

The Indian Field Mouse *Mus booduga* (Gray)

Plate facing p. 197

[RACE IN INDIA : *booduga* (Gray)]

The Spiny Field Mouse *Mus platythrix* Bennett

Plate facing p. 197

[RACES IN INDIA : *platythrix* Bennett, *ramnadensis* Bentham, *sadhu* (Wroughton), *bahadur* (Wroughton & Ryley), *gurkha* (Thomas)]

In addition to the common field rats of peninsular India, there are numbers of field mice. One of the commonest is the **Indian**

Field Mouse (*Mus booduga*). It is about 2 to 3 in. (5 to 8 cm.) in body length, with a tail slightly over 2 inches (5 cm.). The dorsal fur varies from pale sandy in the desert and thorn forest zone to brown or dark greyish brown in moister country. Underside white. It is common in our fields, is also found in compounds and gardens, and may even venture into a house. A second equally common species is the **Spiny Field Mouse** (*Mus platythrix* Bennett). The fur in this mouse, both above and below, is composed almost entirely of flattened spines, those on the back stiffer and coarser than those on the lower parts. The spiny nature of the coat is apparent on examination through a magnifying glass or if the hand is passed over it against the lie of the hairs. The colour above is sandy or dark brown, white below. The separation of the two colours is sharp and well defined. In the Deccan these spiny mice live in burrows of moderate depth. On going in, the mouse closes the entrance with small pebbles, a quantity of which are usually collected outside the burrow. The sleeping chamber may also be furnished with a bed of pebbles.

TREE AND BUSH RATS

There are a number of wild rats and mice which are less habitual pests of cultivation and which live mainly in scrub and forest. Among these are :

The Indian Bush Rat *Golunda ellioti* Gray

Plate facing p. 197

[RACES IN INDIA : *ellioti* Gray, *myothrix* (Hodgson), *watsoni* (Blanford), *paupera* Thomas, *gujerati* Thomas, *coenosa* Thomas. CEYLON : *ellioti* Gray, *nuwara* (Kelaart)]

This rat measures some four inches (10 cm.) in length and has a tail about as long. Its distinctive features are a short, rounded head, rounded ears, and a rather hairy tail. The coat is yellowish brown above, not uniform, but finely speckled with black and fulvous. It is found throughout the greater part of the Indian peninsula. It is essentially a rat of jungle and forest, but many venture into cultivated lands. A favourite habitat is bush and scrub jungle, where this rat chooses some thick bush in which to build a densely woven nest of stalks and fibres and grass. Sometimes the nest is placed on the ground. It is a slow-moving creature, which in its quest for food follows regular beats and makes little paths or ' runways ' from its nest to its feeding grounds. The food consists of roots, grass stems, and seeds. It is partial to the seeds of the

PLATE 48

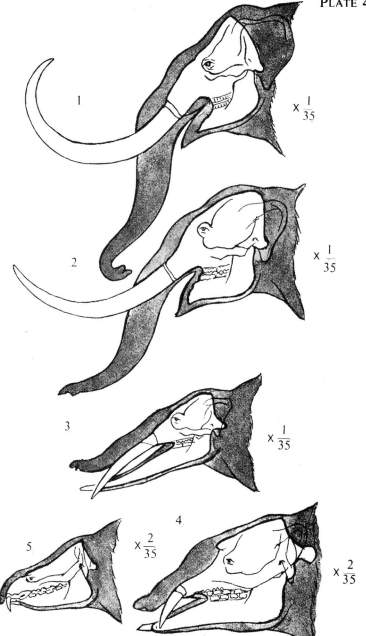

$\times \frac{1}{35}$

$\times \frac{1}{35}$

$\times \frac{1}{35}$

$\times \frac{2}{35}$

$\times \frac{2}{35}$

Evolutionary changes of Proboscidea

1. *Elephas columbi* (early and middle Pliocene); 2. *Mastodon americanus* (late Pleistocene);
3. *Trilophodon angustidens* (middle and upper Miocene); 4. *Palaeomastodon* (Lower Oligocene);
5. *Moeritherium* (upper Eocene)

(After R.S. Lull, *Ann. Rept. Smithsonian Inst.*, 1909)

PLATE 49

Elephant (*Elephas maximus*) in Bandipur Sanctuary, Karnataka

Photo : E.P. Gee

Lantana, a plant now widespread in most parts of India. In Ceylon this rat was once a great pest of the coffee plantations. With the abandonment of coffee planting, the species exists on the island in much reduced numbers.

The Whitetailed Wood Rat *Rattus blanfordi* (Thomas)

Plate facing p. 204

This rat is about 6 (15 cm.) to 7 (18 cm.) inches long, its tail a little longer. Very distinctive in this species is the colouring of the tail. It is brown for three quarters of its length, but the terminal portion is clothed with longer white hairs. Its soft long fur is grey brown above, and white on the underside. This wood rat inhabits dry or moist deciduous and evergreen forest zones in southern, central, and eastern India as far north as Bengal. In southern India it lives mostly in forest, but in the more open parts of Mysore it has colonized scrub jungle ; whilst further north in Madhya Pradesh, it lives among rocks on bare hill-sides. In forests, this rat is to a great extent arboreal. It makes a large untidy nest, usually in a hole or crevice in a tree. In open treeless country it has changed its normal habits, and makes a home in caves or under rocks and bushes, and the nest may be flat and rudimentary, made of sticks, dry leaves, etc., or there may be no nest at all. Litters of 2 to 3 young are born in June and October. It has also been recorded from Ceylon.

The Longtailed Tree Mouse *Vandeleuria oleracea* (Bennett)

Plate facing p. 197

[RACES IN INDIA : *oleracea* (Bennett), *dumeticola* (Hodgson), *nilagirica* (Jerdon), *spadicea* Ryley, *rubida* Thomas, *modesta* Thomas. CEYLON : *nilagirica* (Jerdon), *nolthenii* Phillips]

This is a beautiful soft-furred mouse, with a very long tail, a chestnut-red coat, and white underparts. Head and body, 2 to 3½ inches (5 to 9 cm.) ; tail, 3 to 4½ inches (8 to 11 cm.). Its completely arboreal habits are revealed in its feet. The first and fifth toes on all four feet are partially opposable and furnished with a flat nail and not a claw.

The species is found almost throughout India.

It is a pretty and attractive creature, very active and nimble in trees and bushes, where it finds most of its food, fruit, buds, and tender shoots. When climbing it uses its long tail to get a better hold. Trees and shrubs are its natural haunt ; its movements on the ground are less facile.

When about to produce her young the female builds a large nest much like that of a dormouse. The material she uses depends upon what is available. In bamboo jungle, dry bamboo leaves are used ; elsewhere, she may use the broad blades of ribbon grass, or make her nest of grass and dead leaves. The nest is usually placed in a hole or crevice in a tree, sometimes among the branches. It has been found even in the thatched roof of a house. Like the dormouse, our tree mouse sometimes uses the nests of other animals. McCann found one occupying the mud nest of a swallow built under a rock. Another was found bringing up her young in the great untidy mass of cobwebs which formed the nest of a social spider (*Stegodyphus sarasinorum*) ; the spiders and the mice lived sociably together.

The nest is occupied solely by the mother and her young, which may number from 3 to 6. The males have separate nests, rougher and less tidy in structure, which they use as sleeping quarters. Whether females build such separate structures during the non-breeding time is not recorded.

HOUSE RATS, BANDICOOTS, MICE

The habits of house rats, the damage they cause to human property, and the deadly role they play in the spread of disease have already been discussed. An account of the common species inhabiting peninsular India follows.

The Common House Rat *Rattus rattus* (Linnaeus)

[RACES : About 13 in India, 2 in the Andamans, and 3 in Ceylon]

This is our common species. It is believed that its original home was somewhere in India and Burma, whence this animal has been conveyed by human commerce to all parts of the world. We have already referred to the variable colouring of this rat. There are three main types. In *R. r. rattus* (Linnaeus) the dorsal fur is black and the belly smoky grey. This colour form is characteristic of the cold and temperate countries of Europe, where this rat, an immigrant from the tropics, is compelled to shelter indoors. The second form known as the **Alexandrine Rat** [*R. r. alexandrinus* (Geoffroy)] is brownish grey above and dingy below. This is the common form in the Mediterranean countries, where with a warmer climate these rats are less dependent on indoor shelter. In these countries again there is a third prominent colour form [*R. r. frugivorus* (Rafinesque)], in which the back is yellowish or reddish brown and the belly pure white. This form is essentially a wild-living rat which seldom takes to indoor shelter. A parallel colour variation is seen in many parts of India. The all-black type of *R. rattus* is seldom found except perhaps in seaports. It is an immigrant or a descendant of immigrants from the North brought in by ships. The brown dingybellied type is largely restricted to the towns and cities of the Peninsula, and to places where there are substantially built houses. Finally, we have the whitebellied form of *R. rattus*, which usually lives wild in open country and forest areas both in the hills and the plains. These whitebellied rats display more or less marked variation in colour and other details in different parts of India and have been split up into a number of geographical races.

The Brown Rat *Rattus norvegicus* (Berkenhout)

[RACE IN INDIA AND CEYLON : *norvegicus* (Berkenhout)]

, The original home of the Brown Rat is believed to be in the temperate lands of central Asia whence this animal has spread or been carried to all parts of the world. As an immigrant from temperate lands it has been more successful in establishing itself in cooler countries, where it became a successful rival of the House Rat. The House Rat (*R. rattus*), a creature from the tropics, found greater difficulty in acclimatizing itself to conditions of cold. It had to limit itself largely to living in places where it was able to obtain suitable shelter. In India the House Rat faced its rival on more equal terms. Here in its warm and native climate, the House Rat has held its own. It remains the dominant species, established everywhere, while the Brown Rat is limited largely to seaports, where it has been introduced by ships, and to larger towns and cities in the interior, where it has been transported by rail, road, or navigable rivers. The Brown Rat is a larger and more robust-looking animal than the Black Rat and can be distinguished immediately from the latter by its shorter tail, which is shorter than its head and body. The general colour is brown, darkest on the back ; lower parts, white or whity brown, or light brown ; head and body, 7 to 8 inches (18 to 20 cm.) ; tail, 6 to 7 inches (15 to 18 cm.). In large cities this rat is found chiefly in drains and sewers. The propinquity of water seems essential to its existence in our warm climate.

The Bandicoot Rat *Bandicota indica* (Bechstein)

Plate facing p. 204

[RACES IN INDIA : *indica* (Bechstein), *nemorivaga* (Hodgson).
CEYLON : *indica* (Bechstein)]

The distinctive characters of bandicoots (*Bandicota*) have been given in the description of the Indian Mole-Rat (*B. bengalensis*). This bandicoot is largely a creature of field and forest, but the other bandicoot (*B. indica*) found in India is essentially parasitic on man, living in or about human dwellings. They are creatures of large size measuring about 12 to 15 inches (30 to 40 cm.) from nose to base of tail, the tail about equally long. They weigh from 2 to 3 lb. (0.9 to 1.4 kg.). Their large size is sufficient to distinguish bandicoots from other house rats. *B. i. indica* is widely spread throughout peninsular India. Nepal to Assam and Burma is given as the range of a separate race, *B. i. nemorivaga*. *B. i. indica* has also been recorded in Ceylon.

Bandicoots are seldom found far from villages and towns and, though not as common or numerous as House Rats (*Rattus rattus*), in parts of India, especially in the south, they are quite as domestic. They chiefly occupy the outskirts of human dwelling such as compounds and gardens, stables and outhouses. Here from their burrowing habits they do much damage to grounds and floorings, or by tunnelling through bricks and masonry. Their large burrows are always an indication of their presence. Like other rats they are omnivorous and feed on household refuse, on grain and vegetables, and occasionally attack poultry.

House Mouse *Mus musculus* Linnaeus

[RACES : Five in India and one in Ceylon]

This is the common house mouse of the plains of India. In general build and appearance it is a miniature replica of the Common House Rat (*R. rattus*). It measures about 2 to 3 inches (5 to 8 cm.) in body length and has a tail about equally long. The general colour varies from dark to light brown, paler below. The House Mouse is believed to be of Asiatic origin and has spread or been carried to all parts of the world. It is found over the greater part of the Indian peninsula from the Himalayas to Cape Comorin. It lives chiefly in houses, but sometimes in gardens and fields near villages and towns. Excessively active, it climbs well, scaling vertical walls and taking considerable leaps. Like other rats, it shows the tendency to follow its beaten tracks, and in a house will usually follow the same daily beat keeping close to the walls. It is omnivorous, and feeds on any food that it can get. It builds a nest of soft materials which is tucked away in any convenient recess, under floors or steps, or in bookcases and other articles of furniture. It breeds 3 to 5 times in a year and produces at each birth from 4 to 8 young. They are born blind, but quickly attain full growth and are capable of producing young of their own within one month of their birth.

PLATE 50

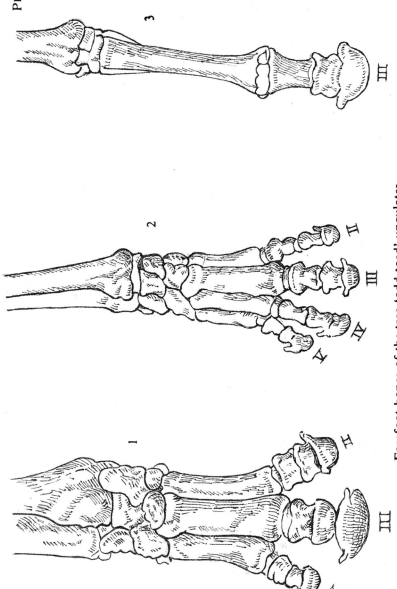

Forefoot bones of the tree 'odd-toed' ungulates

1. The **Rhinoceros** (three digits); 2. the **Tapir** (four digits); 3. the **Horse** (one digit)

In all the feet the third or middle digit is symmetrical in itself and more developed than the other digits

PLATE 51

Asiatic Wild Ass (*Equus heminonus*) in the Rann of Cutch
Photo : E.P. Gee

VOLES

Royle's Vole *Alticola roylei* (Gray)

Plate facing p. 197

[RACES IN INDIA : *roylei* (Gray), *blanfordi* (Scully),
montosa (True), *albicauda* (True), *glacialis* Miller,
cautus Hinton, *acmaeus* Schwarz]

Size. Body length, 3 to 4 inches (8 to 10 cm.).

Distinctive Characters. We have dealt with two sub-divisions of
the great Rodent Order, the Gerbilles (Gerbillinae) and the Rats
and Mice (Murinae). The Voles (Microtinae) form yet another
division. Voles are not exactly rat-like. They are mainly burrowers,
and have bodies adapted to this purpose. The muzzle is short,
the head rounded, and the ears small ; the body more or less cylindrical. The tail in all the Indian species is less than half the length
of the body. The thumb is short, sometimes clawless, more often
it bears a little compressed claw. The teeth are distinctive. The
grinders have flat crowns, and in most genera these teeth are rootless and grow through life. Their grinding surfaces, except when
quite unworn, present a curious pattern somewhat like alternating
triangles.   They are well adapted to the hard diet of coarse grasses
and roots upon which Voles live.

Distribution. In India, voles are found only in the higher levels of
the Himalayas, Kashmir, Ladak, and Tibet. They are colonists
from the highlands of central Asia, whence these creatures also
migrated by way of the Behring Straits into the New World and
colonized the whole of North America.

Royle's Vole (*A. roylei*) is fairly common at elevations above
10,000 ft. (3000 m.) in Kumaon and Kulu, where it lives in open
uplands and rocky ground covered with coarse grass. It is
a rufous-brown animal, paler and yellowish on the sides, pale brown
below, tail coloured like the back, ears projecting above fur.

A second species, the **Sikkim Vole** [*Pitymys sikimensis* (Hodgson)]
has a dark brown coat with a yellowish tinge, underparts pale
brown.   This vole is found in Sikkim at elevations ranging from
7000 to 12,000 ft. (2100 to 3700 m.). It inhabits forests and breeds
in hollow decayed trees, or amongst the roots, making a nest of
soft moss and grass. The **Murree Vole** [*Hyperacrius wynnei* (Blanford)] is better specialised for a burrowing life. The ears are small
and completely buried in the fur, the head very blunt and rounded,
the body more cylindrical, and the foreclaws considerably lengthened. The fur, very close and dense, is a rich dark brown with a
soft greyish tinge.   Further west in Baluchistan there is yet another

species the **Quetta Vole** [*Ellobius fuscocapillus* (Blyth)]. It is even more specialised for a fossorial life. The head is very blunt, the ears vestigial, the body almost cylindrical. The feet are broad, though the claws are not much enlarged. The colour is pale sandy, except the head, which is dark brown. This vole makes long horizontal galleries marked by heaps of earth thrown up at intervals.

BAMBOO RATS

The Bay Bamboo Rat *Cannomys badius* (Hodgson)

Plate facing p. 204

[RACE IN INDIA : *badius* (Hodgson)]

The Hoary Bamboo Rat *Rhizomys pruinosus* Blyth

[RACE IN INDIA : *pruinosus* Blyth]

Size. Bay Bamboo Rat : head and body, 7 to 8 inches (18 to 20 cm.). Hoary Bamboo Rat : head and body, 11 to 14 inches (28 to 36 cm.).

Distinctive Characters. Bamboo Rats are included in a separate family of rodents, the **Rhizomyidae.** These strange creatures are especially adapted to a subterranean life. Except for their large projecting incisors, which at once proclaim them as rodents, bamboo rats look very much like gigantic moles. The eyes are small and rudimentary, the limbs short and armed with large claws, the tail is short or vestigial, the body is cylindrical and not marked off from the head by any distinct neck. Two species are found within Indian limits, the Bay Bamboo Rat, distinctive in its smaller size and chestnut or dark brown colouring, and the Hoary Bamboo Rat, a larger animal distinguished by its dark brown, grizzled coat.

Distribution. The Bay Bamboo Rat ranges from the base of the Himalayas in Nepal through Sikkim and Bhutan to the Assam hill ranges, Burma, and Siam. In India the Hoary Bamboo Rat has been recorded only from the Khasia and other hill ranges of southern Assam. It ranges eastward into south China and Siam.

Habits. The two species of animals, as far as is known, have the same general habits. They live in burrows which they excavate with their powerful teeth and claws. The burrow may be dug in the side of a bank, at the base of a tree, or in open grass-covered ground. The excavated earth is piled high at the entrance and is thrown up at intervals along the course of the tunnelling. The gallery runs horizontally at a depth of 2 ft. (60 cm.) or so below ground and ends in a roomy sleeping chamber. It is usually continued a short distance beyond the chamber and ends in what looks like a blind alley. This may be a bolt hole with its exit concealed with earth. When the burrow is occupied its mouth is closed with earth.

Bamboo Rats come out at dusk to feed on young grass and leaves, and on roots which they persistently dig for. Their movements are slow and their sight weak, permitting of easy capture. But they bite fiercely. When cornered the rodent turns round and faces its opponent, baring and grinding its huge incisor teeth and making a loud hissing noise. The flesh of these animals is eaten by the hill tribes. Nothing is known of their breeding habits.

THE INDIAN PORCUPINE

Hystrix indica Kerr

Plate facing p. 205

[RACE IN INDIA AND CEYLON : *indica* Kerr]

Local Names. Hindi *sayal, sahi* ; Mar. *sheval, salendra, saloo* ; Kan. *yed, moolu handi* ; Tel. *yedu pandi* ; Mal. & Tamil *moollam punni* ; Bur. *hreeu.*

Size. Head and body, 28-35 in. (70-90 cm.) ; tail, 3 to 4 inches (8 to 10 cm.), with its spines 7 to 8 inches (18 to 20 cm.) ; weight 25 to 40 lb. (11 to 18 kg.).

Distinctive Characters. Porcupines (**Hystricidae**) form a separate family of rodents, easily recognised by their hair, modified more or less completely into spines. Other rodents have spines, but never so long or formidable. They reach their highest development in the Indian Porcupine (*H. indica*). Its neck and shoulders are crowned with a crest of bristles 6 to 12 inches (15 to 30 cm.) long. The quills on the back are very profuse. Here the under-armature of short thick quills is more or less hidden by a bristling mantle of longer and thinner spines. Each quill is ornamented with deep brown or black and white rings. The white ' rattling quills ' on the tail are large and well open, and attain their greatest development in this porcupine. A colour phase of the Indian Porcupine referred to as the **Red Porcupine** has been observed in some of the southern hill ranges in Mysore, Coimbatore, and Kerala, in which bright rusty red or orange more or less replaces the white bands on the quills. It is said to be smaller than the typical race and local people prize it more highly as food and recognize a distinctive odour emanating from its burrows. The richness of the colouring is said to decline in captivity or ill health. A second species **Hodgson's Porcupine** [*H. hodgsoni* (Gray) Races in India : *hodgsoni* (Gray), *subcristata* Swinhoe] is found only in the central and eastern Himalayas, Assam, and lower Bengal, at elevations up to about 5000 ft. (1500 m.). In this porcupine the crest is either very small, less than 6 inches (15 cm.) long, rudimentary, or wanting.

Distribution. The Himalayas to Cape Comorin and Ceylon. Westwards through Persia and Baluchistan to Syria, Asia Minor, and Palestine.

Habits. The Indian Porcupine favours rocky hill-sides. It adapts itself to any type of country, moist or arid, and inhabits both open land and forest. In Kumaon and the western Himalayas, it is found at an altitude of 8000 ft. (2400 m.) and more. It shelters by day in caves, amongst rocks, or in a burrow dug by itself, or it uses and, if necessary, enlarges one dug by some other animal. Burrows are not always essential for its shelter. In the crop season, porcupines lie up in thick scrub near cultivation and in the Terai they commonly shelter in the tall grass, making regular runs and tunnels through it.

When a burrow is dug, a great quantity of earth is thrown up at its mouth. The entrance is usually strewn with bones ; porcupines gnaw these bones just as they gnaw the dropped horns of deer. Horn and bone contain calcium and lime which helps the growth of their quills. Besides the main entrance, there are usually two or three bolt holes or emergency exits near the mouth of the burrow. The entrance gallery runs deep into the earth. A burrow excavated in Madhya Pradesh had a gallery 60 ft. (18 m.) in length. It led to a chamber about 4 ft. (120 cm.) square and 18 inches (45 cm.) high, lying some 5 ft. (150 cm.) or so below ground level. Porcupines come out after dark. They have a keen sense of smell and display high intelligence in evading traps. Vegetables of all kinds, grain, fruit, and roots are their main food. They can be very destructive in gardens and cultivation, tunnelling under walls and hedges to make an entry. When irritated or alarmed, porcupines erect their spines, grunt and puff, and rattle their hollow tail quills. Their method of attack is peculiar. The animal launches itself backwards with incredible speed and, clashing its hindquarters against an enemy, drives its erect quills deep into it with painful, or even fatal, results. Mr. R. C. Morris records how a panther was slain by a porcupine, its head pierced by the thrusting quills. There is yet another record of an almost full-grown tiger meeting its death by leaping on a porcupine. Its lungs and liver were riddled with quills, and it could do little more than crawl away, to die a few yards from its victim. In its backward rush the real damage is done by the compact mass of short white quills, solid and strong, set above its hind quarters. If the object struck is large, the longer quills also take effect. They are more easily dislodged and are left embedded in the victim. The popular belief that porcupines ' shoot ' their quills can be disregarded. Quills damaged in action or from other causes are replaced. A new quill grows up under the old one and dislodges it. Individuals may be quite fearless. There is a record of a porcupine attacking a panther at a drinking pool.

Porcupines were found with young in Madhya Pradesh in March. Both parents usually occupy the burrow with their offspring, which may number 2 to 4. They are born with their eyes open and the body covered with short soft spines.

In lower Bengal and Assam southwards to the Malay countries there is a third species, the **Brushtailed Porcupine** [*Atherurus macrourus* (Linnaeus) Race in India : *assamensis* Thomas], distinctive in its long tail ending in a thick tuft of bristles. It is an uncommon animal and nothing is known of its habits.

14. Hares, Mouse-Hares

THE ORDER LAGOMORPHA comprises two families, the **Leporidae** (hares and rabbits) and the **Ochotonidae** (mouse-hares). These families, formerly classed as a subdivision of the rodents, the Duplicidenta, can be distinguished from the rodents by having four incisors in the upper jaw instead of two, a large anterior pair and a smaller pair behind them. At birth there are six upper incisors, but the two outer ones are soon lost. The skull is distinctive, and the testes are permanently external unlike the rodents in which they are retained in the abdomen except in the breeding season when they become greatly enlarged.

Mouse-hares are small and tailless, with short, broad, rounded ears and short legs, the front pair a little shorter than the rear one. They are restricted to the Himalayas, the mountains and steppes of central Asia, and the mountains of western North America.

In hares and rabbits the ears and hind legs are long, being considerably longer in hares than in rabbits. Hares are born in ' forms' in growing grass and at birth are well furred and have open eyes. Rabbits, on the contrary, are born in burrows, blind and nearly naked, but in two weeks' time are able to run, and by a month can fend for themselves. The Leporidae have a worldwide distribution being originally absent only from Australia and the Oceanic Islands.

Several species besides the Indian Hare (*Lepus nigricollis*) occur in the Indian region. A race of the widespread Cape Hare (*Lepus capensis tibetanus* Waterhouse) is found in Kashmir and the North-West Frontier Province, a race of the Arabian Hare (*Lepus arabicus craspedotis* Blanford) in Baluchistan, and the Woolly Hare (*Lepus oiostolus* Hodgson) at higher elevations in Sikkim, Nepal, and Ladak. The true rabbits do not occur in India, but the closely related Assam Rabbit or Hispid Hare [*Caprolagus hispidus* (Pearson)] is found along the foot of the Himalayas from Uttar Pradesh to Assam. The Hispid Hare, as it is more commonly known on account of its coarse bristly fur, is equal to the Indian Hare in the length of its body, but it has a much shorter tail (1 in. against 4 in. including the terminal hair). Above it appears dark brown as a result of the intermingling of black and brownish white hairs ; brownish white below with the breast a little darker than the abdomen ; tail brown throughout, paler below ; ears brown on the outside. Very little is known of the habits of this species though it has been reported sporadically from the grass jungles of the Terai and the Duars of the foothills areas of the Himalayas. The last record was in 1951 from Kheri on the U.P.-Nepal border. It is not known whether the young are born blind and naked though it is reported that they burrow like rabbits.

THE INDIAN HARE

Lepus nigricollis F. Cuvier

Plate facing p. 205

[RACES IN INDIA : *nigricollis* F. Cuvier, *ruficaudatus* Geoffroy, *dayanus* Blanford, *simcoxi* Wroughton, *mahadeva* Wroughton & Ryley, *rajput* Wroughton, *cutchensis* Kloss. CEYLON : *singhala* Wroughton]

Local Names. Hindi *khargosh* ; Mar. *sasa* ; Kan. *mola* ; Tamil *musal* ; Tel. *choura pilli* ; Mal. *moilu*.

Size. The **Rufoustailed Hare** (*L. n. ruficaudatus*) : head and body, 17 to 19 in. (40 to 50 cm.), weight, 4 to 5 lb. (1.8 to 2.3 kg.). The **Blacknaped Hare** (*L. n. nigricollis*) is larger and scales 5 to 8 lb. (2.2 to 3.6 kg.).

Distinctive Characters. The Blacknaped Hare (*L. n. nigricollis*) is distinctive in having a dark brown or black patch on the back of its neck from the ears to the shoulder, upper surface of tail black. In the northern parts of its range this nape patch is grey instead of black. These hares are recognized as a separate race, the Rufoustailed Hare (*L. n. ruficaudatus*). They have a rufous-brown coat much mixed with black on back and face, breast and limbs rufous, chin, upper throat and lower parts white, upper surface of tail rufous-brown. In the Desert Hare (*L. n. dayanus*) the coat is yellowish sandy grey, paler in coloration than that of the Rufoustailed Hare. It has no black patch on the nape ; upper surface of tail blackish brown. The other races mentioned, which are of limited occurrence, are distinguished by minor characteristics.

Distribution. The Blacknaped Hare ranges from southern India to the Godavari on the east, and in the west as far north as Khandesh and Berar and the adjoining districts of Madhya Pradesh. The Rufoustailed Hare ranges from the Himalayas southwards to the Godavari River. In the desert zone, the south-west Punjab, Sind, Cutch, Rajasthan, and Kathiawar it is replaced by the Desert Hare. *L. n. simcoxi* and *L. n. mahadeva* occur in Madhya Pradesh and Vidarbha district of Maharashtra and *L. n. cutchensis* in Cutch.

Habits. Where the country is suitable hares are numerous. Large tracts of bush and jungle alternating with cultivated plains afford them ideal conditions. They are less numerous in forests. They ascend the hills to some height. *L. n. ruficaudatus* is found in Kumaon at levels nearing 8000 ft. (2400 m.) ; while *L. n. nigricollis* is common in the Nilgiris and other south Indian hill ranges. The Desert Hare (*L. n. dayanus*) has adapted itself to life in the most arid terrain.

Many hares live in the neighbourhood of villages and cultivation. Here they become unclean feeders. During the hot weather, when grass is scanty, hares come to roadsides or even enter compounds to feed on the grass growing there. Driving by night, the lamps of a car or carriage give a fleeting glimpse of these animals. They are nocturnal but not exclusively so. By day a hare usually makes itself comfortable in some patch of grass. Scraping the blades this way and that with its paws, it scoops out a hollow. In this ' form ' it settles down to sleep. Sometimes they lie up in fallow fields. They have many enemies, foxes, mongooses, wild cats, even village pie-dogs prey upon them. Lying still the hare is not easily detected and remains safe, unless stumbled upon. Then it bolts wildly or goes off at an easy canter, usually stopping at the end of its run to sit up and look around. A common refuge in flight is a fox hole or some such burrow.

The Rufoustailed Hare is said to have one to two young at a birth. Its particular breeding season is not recorded. The Black-naped Hare breeds chiefly between October and February. Two young born in captivity (in Kanara) were produced early in November. Their eyes were open at birth and they were able to move about within twelve hours.

THE HIMALAYAN MOUSE-HARE

Ochotona roylei (Ogilby)

Plate facing p. 205

[RACES IN INDIA : *roylei* (Ogilby), *wardi* Bonhote, *baltina* Thomas]

Local Names. Bhotia *gumchi pichi* ; Lepcha *cumchen*.

Size. Head and body, 6 to 8 inches (15 to 20 cm.).

Distinctive Characters. Mouse-hares belong to the same Order as the hares. They are placed in a separate family the **Ochotonidae.** A mouse-hare is somewhat like a guinea-pig in build. It has a short muzzle, small rounded head, rounded ears, and no tail.

PLATE 52

Great Indian Onehorned Rhinoceros (*Rhinoceros unicornis*)

Photo : E.P. Gee

PLATE 53

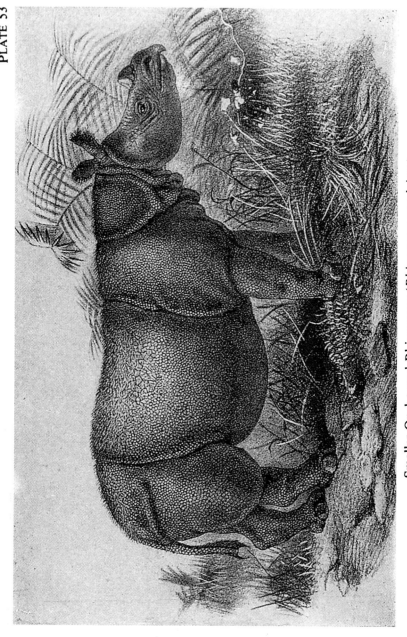

Smaller Onehorned Rhinoceros (*Rhinoceros sondaicus*)
Courtesy : Zoological Society of London

The hair is exceedingly fine, straight, and glossy. Several species are found in the Himalayan region. The common species of the Himalayas is *O. roylei*. The 'typical form of this species, inhabiting Kumaon, has a reddish brown coat with a pale band over the nape. There is a considerable seasonal change in colour in these animals.

Distribution. The home of the mouse-hares is central and northern Asia, whence they have spread into eastern Europe and North America. *O. roylei* ranges through the Himalayas from Kashmir to Moupin at elevations ranging usually from 11,000 to 14,000 ft. (3400 to 4300 m.). In the eastern Himalayas they come down to lower levels and have been taken as low as 8000 ft. (2400 m.).

Habits. Himalayan Mouse-Hares usually live on open rocky ground above the tree-line. In the eastern parts of their range where they inhabit somewhat lower levels they are found both in open ground, and in the pine forests of the steep slopes. In open ground they make no burrows but live under rocks and piles of stones. In forest, they burrow under the roots of trees. In the higher Himalayas, mouse-hares are perhaps the most popular and fascinating animals. Their timid interest in the traveller is sometimes the only cheerful incident during long marches over the desolate boulder-strewn wastes. When approached, they seek immediate shelter in the piles of rocks. But soon one or more reappear to peep over the top of a rock, or sit motionless deciding whether the intruder is dangerous or not. Reassured, they re-commence their play racing over and around the rocks, springing from one projection to another, vanishing and as suddenly popping up in unexpected places. Their food must vary considerably with the season. They feed on coarse grasses. A captive specimen ate alpine flowers, strawberry leaves, berries, cabbage, and carrots. During winter their homes lie buried under many feet of snow. Whether they hibernate, or live on gathered stores of food is not exactly known. At Thangu in Sikkim, 12,000 ft. (3700 m.) above sea-level, they are common in summer, but disappear completely during winter. It is suggested that there may be some movement to lower levels. Breeding habits, unrecorded.

15. The Elephant

THE PROBOSCIS OR trunk of the elephant gives the name **Proboscidea** to this order of mammals. There are but two species of elephant in existence, the Indian and the African. They are the sole survivors of a great assemblage of species which once inhabited the Earth. No fewer than seven species of elephant and eight different mastodons are known to have existed in India during remote geological periods.

STRUCTURE IN RELATION TO HABITS

With its pendant trunk, its curious dentition, and its great size, the elephant presents distinctive characters which differentiate it from all other mammals. However remarkable these characters may be, they are the ultimate result of a gradual deviation from a standard type of mammal, a hairy creature of no great size walking on the soles of its five-toed feet and carrying in its jaws the typical complement and number of incisor, canine, and molar teeth. The earliest known proboscidean, *Moeritherium*, a creature of the upper Eocene, was about 3½ feet (110 cm.) in height.

A comparison of existing and extinct forms of elephants and their allies has helped to indicate the great physical changes which the elephant has undergone during the long ages of its history. These changes have been brought about largely by migrations to new countries and the new conditions of life which they imposed. These migrations were impelled not only by the natural urge of the creature to extend its territory, but also by actual changes in the Earth's surface, which brought about a difference in climate and vegetation, and forced the ancestral forms to migrate into areas where conditions of life were more congenial. **(Plate facing p. 208)**

The physical modifications which elephants display are seen firstly in a great increase in size. This necessitated the development of pillar-like limbs to support the enormous weight of the body, which again implied the straightening of the limb bones and a change in the angle of their articulation. The foot itself changed its posture from the primitive plantigrade or ' soles to the ground ' position. The heel and ankle bones were elevated above the ground, and a thick pad of gristle developed beneath each foot and so formed a cushion to receive its share of the weight. The toes were embedded in the common mass of the cylindrical foot and encased in a common skin. Their position is indicated externally by broad flat nails which may be fewer than the number of toes. Thus, the limb bones gradually developed into vertical shafts through which the weight of the body was transmitted.

The shortness of the neck and the height of the head from the ground necessitated the development of a proboscis or trunk, a combined and lengthened nose and upper lip, as a device for securing food and water. Its development was accompanied by marked changes in the character and form of the skull. The skull of an elephant shows no ' snout '. The bony part of the face is almost straight. But it would appear that the ancestral elephants had a prolonged bony snout, which is seen to some extent in the skull of the American mastodon (*Mastodon americanus*), and to a more remarkable degree in a yet more ancient form of mastodon, the *Trilophodon angustidens*. This creature had a greatly lengthened lower jaw furnished with two horizontal tusks, and also a downward bent pair in the upper jaw. Its ' trunk ' rested horizontally on its lower jaw between these tusks in the form of an elongated upper lip. It is believed that the elephant's trunk originated in this way. Firstly the great elongation of the lower jaw produced a corresponding lengthening of the proboscis ; then owing to the shrinkage of the lower jaw and the straightening of the bones of the face, the long proboscis losing its support developed in the course of successive ages into a pendant trunk.

Teeth. Other physical changes undergone by elephants are seen in the increase in the size and complexity of the teeth, their consequent diminution in number, and the development of a peculiar method of tooth succession. All the canine teeth have been lost, and all the incisors except the second pair in the upper jaw. These have developed into tusks. As to the grinding teeth, an elephant develops six molars in each jaw during its lifetime. But there is never room for more than two, one entirely and the other partly exposed above the gums. The new tooth forms in the rear of the jaw. Pushing forward, it gradually replaces the preceding tooth which, as it wears away, is crowded out of the jaw. The first milk molar is shed at the age of 2 years, the second at 6, the third at 9, the fourth (or first adult tooth) between the 20th and 25th year, the fifth at 60, and the sixth lasts for the remainder of the creature's life.

Each molar is larger than the one which preceded it. It is made up of a series of plates composed of a flattened mass of dentine invested by a layer of enamel, bound together in a solid mass by cement. As the dentine wears the harder enamel appears in a series of transverse ridges across the crown of the molar. In the Indian Elephant the last or sixth molar may show 27 of these ridges. In the African species the number never exceeds 11.

The Proboscidea form a single family the **Elephantidae** which includes but two living genera, *Elephas* the Asiatic elephant and *Loxodonta* the African elephant.

THE INDIAN ELEPHANT

Elephas maximus Linnaeus

Plates facing pp. 193, 209

[RACES IN INDIA: *indicus* G. Cuvier: CEYLON: *maximus*
Linnaeus, *ceylanicus* Blainville]

Local Names. Sanskrit *hasti*, *gaja* ; Hindi *hathi* (male), *hathni*
(female) ; Mar. *hatti* ; Tamil *anai* ; Mal. *ana* ; Kan. *ane* ; Bur. *tor
sin.*

Size. The Indian Elephant rarely exceeds 10 ft. 6 in. (3.20 m.)
at the shoulder. The average height of an adult male is 9 ft. (2.75
m.). The female is a foot (30 cm.) lower. A pair of tusks in the
Royal Museum at Bangkok, Siam, taped 9 ft. 10½ in. (3.01 m.).
A pair in the possession of King George VI measured 8 ft. 9 in.
(2.67 m.) and 8 ft. 6½ in. (2.60 m.) and weighed 160 lb. (72.57 kg.)
and 161 lb. (73.03 kg.) respectively. Few tusks weigh more than
100 lb. (45.5 kg.) the pair.

Distinctive Characters. Smaller than the African Elephant. It has
not the enormous ears and hollow back of the African species.
Further it has four nails on each hindfoot, the African has three.
The trunk ends in a single ' lip ' in contrast with two equal-sized
' lips ' in the African species.
    Generally only the males have large tusks. The tusks of females
scarcely protrude or perhaps protrude a few inches. The contour
of the tusks varies. They may be widespread, curved, straight, or
pointed downwards. In some males the tusks are no longer than
in females. Many of these tuskless males or *makhnas* are very large
in build, with extraordinarily well-developed trunks.

Distribution. Western Ghats, from Mysore southwards, Orissa,
Bihar, Himalayas in U.P., West Bengal, and Assam in India, Ceylon,
Burma, Siam, Cochin-China, the Malay Peninsula, Borneo, and
Sumatra. The elephants found in Ceylon are regarded as races,
distinct from that found in India. The males carry quite normal
tusks. The females are tuskless. Introduced into the Andamans.

Habits. Elephants chiefly frequent areas covered with tall forests
where the ground is hilly or undulating, and where bamboos grow
in profusion. They are extremely adaptable and will live in steamy
humid jungle or in cool elevated forests. In Burma they wander
at all seasons of the year into bamboo forest at a height of 10,000
ft. (3050 m.) ; while in Sikkim their tracks have been seen in the
snow 12,000 ft. (3660 m.) above sea-level. In the dry season the

PLATE 54

Smaller Onehorned Rhinoceros (*Rhinoceros sondaicus*)

Photo : A. Hoogerwerf

PLATE 55

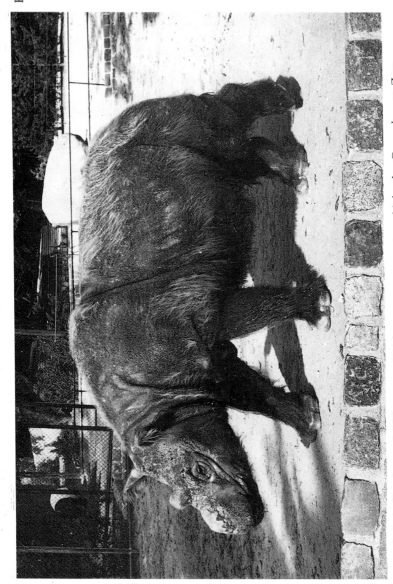

Asiatic Twohorned Rhinoceros (*Didermocerus sumatrensis*) in the Copenhagen Zoo

Photo : E. P. Gee

herds generally keep to the denser forests, but during the rains they come out into open glades and frequently enter cultivation. Individuals of various sizes and ages associate in herds which may vary from 5 to 60 or more animals. Herds are believed to be composed of single families. Different herds do not mix, but stray females and young males may migrate from one herd into another. When fodder is scarce, the larger herds break up into small parties, which reunite when conditions are favourable. The big tuskers are usually seen feeding at some distance from the main herd. The bulls when they arrive at a certain age live as solitaries, or two males of equal age may associate together. A solitary bull will graze with a herd when it happens to be in the same patch of jungle, and will seek the herd when the urge to mate is on him and desert it again when his desire is appeased.

When undisturbed, the herd pursues a regular and ordered routine, drinking and feeding in accustomed places and lying up to rest in its usual retreat. Elephants sleep during the hot hours of the day, being intolerant of the sun, feed early in the morning and evening, and come out after nightfall to feed in open forest or to raid crops, retiring to sleep after midnight. An elephant rests standing or stretched out on its side. The food consists of various kinds of grasses and leaves, stems and leaves of wild bamboos and plantains, all species of crops, and the bark of particular kinds of trees. A full-grown elephant will eat from 600 to 700 lb. (270 to 320 kg.) of green fodder a day.

Male elephants, very rarely females, both tame and wild, on attaining maturity are subject to peculiar periodical paroxysms of excitement. At such times they are spoken of as being *musth*. The condition seems to have some connection with the sexual functions. It is probably analogous to the ' rut ' in deer. It occurs most frequently during the cold season and may be due to ungratified sexual desire. This is not always so, since the society of a female will by no means quell or pacify the animal. At other times a *musth* elephant will seek a mate.

The exact breeding season is uncertain but, as most of the young are dropped in late autumn and the period of gestation lasts about 20 months, it is probable that the main breeding season is during the hot weather and at the commencement of the rains. One calf only is born at a time though, in rare instances twins, and once even triplets, were produced. The mother of a young calf is invariably assisted in caring for her young by another female, who takes on the duties of a guardian and is as assiduous in her care of the calf as the parent.

Elephants have very poor sight ; the senses of smell and hearing are highly developed, more so than in most animals.

16. Horses, Rhinoceroses

THE UNGULATES OR hoofed animals of India may be divided into two natural orders : (1) the **Artiodactyla** or even-toed ungulates ; (2) the **Perissodactyla** or odd-toed ungulates. The salient feature which distinguishes the even-toed ungulate lies in the arrangement of its toes. The axis of the foot, a line drawn down its middle, passes between the third and fourth toes. These two toes are large and equal in size. The hooves which encase them appear like a single hoof cleft in two. This prominence of the third and fourth toe is accompanied by the diminishing in size of the second and fifth and the complete disappearance of the first toe. This is the general plan of structure in the feet of oxen, sheep, goats, deer, and pigs.

The feet of horses, rhinoceroses, and tapirs are built on a different plan. The number of toes varies. A tapir has four and a rhinoceros three toes on each forefoot. Both have only three on the hind. The foot of a horse has but one functional toe. But in all these animals it is the third or middle toe of the foot which is most prominent. It is always symmetrical in itself and always larger than other toes, when these are present. This pre-eminence of the third and middle digit of the foot gives this group of animals its name, Perissodactyla or odd-toed ungulates. With them, excepting in the case of the tapirs, the number of toes in each foot is usually odd, either one or three. **(Plate facing p. 212)**

The odd-toed ungulates are further marked by having their molar and premolar teeth in one unbroken series, the posterior molars resembling the premolars in shape and size.

The odd-toed ungulates are poorly represented at the present day. Horses, rhinoceroses, and tapirs are the only surviving members of a group of animals which flourished in great variety during the early Tertiary period. With the exception of the tapirs which are found also in Central and South America, all the existing odd-toed ungulates are Old World animals.

THE ASIATIC WILD ASS

Equus hemionus Pallas

Plate facing p. 213

[RACES IN INDIA : *khur* Lesson, *kiang* Moorcroft]

Local Names. Hindi *ghor khar.*

Size. Height at shoulder, 3 ft. 8 in. (110 cm.) to 4 ft. (120 cm.).

Distinctive Characters. The Horse family (**Equidae**) includes the horses, asses, and zebras. In all these animals each foot has a single complete toe encased in a large solid hoof. It is supported by a long bone known as the ' cannon ' bone. Small splint bones on each side of the ' cannon ' bone represent the vestiges of the second and fourth toes. The cheek teeth are large, quadrangular, and complex, the enamel foldings being numerous as compared with the simpler ones of the rhinoceroses and tapirs. In peninsular India the horse tribe is represented by the **Indian Wild Ass** (*E. h. khur*). The general colour of its coat varies from reddish grey to fawn or pale chestnut. The erect dark brown mane is continued as a dark brown stripe extending along the back to the root of the tail ; lower parts, white.

Distribution. The deserts of the Rann of Cutch and Baluchistan. Present population is below 1000.

Habits. Dr. Sálim Ali writing of the wild ass in Cutch says that their headquarters lie in the Little Rann. Here they are attracted by the flat grass-covered expanses known as *bets*. These *bets* form ' islands ' or oases of coarse grasses which spring up vigorously with monsoon inundations. When the *bets* are so flooded, the herds keep to the higher and drier portions of the *bets*, wading freely from one ' island ' to another. As the grass in these *bets* withers in the dry weather, the asses shift to other *bets* in some of which there is a perennial supply of water and some green grass. In the dry weather, from March onwards, wild asses may concentrate in such places in enormous numbers. During this time the stallions are scattered about either solitary or in twos and threes. They graze between dusk and sunrise and spend the day roaming over the barren sun-scorched desert in troops of 10-30, or in twos and threes, or as solitary individuals. Sometimes the asses consort with straggling herds of blackbuck. As to speed, tested against a motor car it was found that the wild asses maintained a speed of 30-32 miles (48-51 km.) per hour over a considerable distance.

Writing of their breeding habits Dr. Sálim Ali says : ' Mating takes place in August, September, October. A mare on heat separates from the troop with a stallion who fights viciously with interlopers for her possession ; the combatants, rearing up on their hindlegs, use hooves and jaws in attack. After a few (?) days of isolation the couple rejoin the herd, and thereafter the female actively resists advances by the other stallions. The period of gestation is eleven months. Fcals (only one at a birth) are dropped in July, August, and September. Until the foal is about three months old the sexes live apart in separate herds or troops.' Such a herd, seen in the plains of north-west Afghanistan, was computed to number over a thousand animals.

Wild asses are readily tamed when young. Recalcitrant and vicious when grown, they ordinarily cannot be trained to harness. Their stature and sturdiness and speed suggest that an experiment to breed mules from these animals would be well worth consideration.

The **Tibetan Wild Ass** (*E. h. kiang*) is regarded by some as a distinct species, and by others as a race of the Asiatic Wild Ass. It is darker and redder than the Indian Wild Ass, and has a narrower dorsal stripe and larger horse-like hooves. It occurs in Ladak and Tibet and the high open plateaux of the regions further north.

RHINOCEROSES

The various species of rhinoceros, all now confined to the Old World, differ remarkably from one another in structure. As a result of migrations during past epochs into different habitats and climates, and into new feeding grounds to which they became adapted, the various species appear to have become distinct at a very early period of their history.

A comparison of the remains of numerous extinct forms with those now living indicates seven main lines of descent and evolution from which lesser branches have diverged. Though these animals are externally similar they are thus really very far apart both in history and anatomy : even the two living African rhinoceroses probably separated from each other and became distinct species a million years ago.

Three species of rhinoceros are found within our limits. The Great Indian Onehorned Rhinoceros (*Rhinoceros unicornis*) and its relative the Smaller Onehorned, or Javan Rhinoceros (*R. sondaicus*) have an obscure genealogical history. No representatives of these true and typical rhinoceroses have been discovered anywhere but in south-eastern Asia. Their remains are not found in the more ancient Siwalik beds. But they appear with relative suddenness in the uppermost and more recent beds in the form of two species known as the Siwalik Rhinoceros (*R. sivalensis*) and *R. paloeindicus*, the ancient rhinoceros of India.

The Asiatic Twohorned Rhinoceros (*Didermocerus sumatrensis*) was on the other hand widely distributed in the past. It was quite abundant in the Siwalik Hills in Pliocene times. It was a geological period when these animals, favoured by a genial climate, inhabited a broad forest belt which stretched from the east coast of England southward and eastward across southern France and northern Italy to India.

All the living rhinoceroses are included in a single family. Their massive build, the thickness and solidity of their bones, their short stumpy legs each furnished with three toes are some of the family characters. The skin in all the living forms is either thinly clad with hair or naked, and in all the Indian species the heavy hide in places is thrown into deep folds. The nasal bones are enlarged to serve as a support for a single horn or double horns. When two horns are present they are situated one behind the other in the middle line of the snout. The horn is formed of a closely-matted mass of horny fibre issuing from the skin. It has no connection with the skull, although a boss of bone in the skull may serve as its foundation.

The horns grow throughout life and if lost are re-produced.

With the increase in the use of firearms, the exaggerated value attached to rhinoceros horn, and the superstitious beliefs entertained regarding the magical power of the blood and other parts, and even the urine, of the animal (see p. 230 below) all the three species stand in danger of extinction unless they are strictly protected and the duty of protection is entrusted to men equipped with the knowledge and zeal necessary for the successful performance of their duty.

THE GREAT INDIAN ONEHORNED RHINOCEROS

Rhinoceros unicornis Linnaeus

Plate facing p. 220

Local Names. Hindi *gainda, gargadan* ; Mar. *genda*.

Size. One of the largest of all existing rhinoceroses. A male may reach over 6 ft. (180 cm.) at the shoulder. The average height is about 5 ft. 8 in. (170 cm.) with a girth of 11 ft. (335 cm.) behind the withers. It is smaller than the African White Rhinoceros but larger than the African Black. The horns do not compare in length with the African species. The record from Assam measures 24 in. (61 cm.); 8 in. (203 mm.) at the present day is a good average.

Distinctive Characters. The skin of this massive creature is divided into great shields by heavy folds before and behind the shoulders and in front of the thighs. The fold in front of the shoulders is not continued right across the back, a distinctive character of this rhinoceros. On the flanks, shoulders, and hindquarters, the skin is studded with masses of rounded tubercles. With its grotesque build, long boat-shaped head, its folds of armour, and its tuberculated hide, the animal looks like a monster of some bygone age.

Distribution. Formerly extensively distributed in the Gangetic plain today it is restricted to parts of Nepal and West Bengal in the north, the Dooars, and Assam. In Nepal it is found only in the country to the east of Gandak River known as Chitawan, in Assam in isolated areas of the plains.

Habits. Though it prefers swamp and grass the Great Indian One-horned Rhinoceros is also found in wood jungle up ravines and low hills.

The animal is solitary as a rule, though several may occupy the same patch of jungle. Its food consists chiefly of grass. In Nepal during the rains they frequently enter cultivation. Along the numerous rivers which flow through the jungles of the Nepal Terai the rhino has particular places for dropping its excreta ; so mounds accumulate in places. In approaching these spots a rhinoceros walks backwards and falls an easy victim to poachers. Breeding takes place at all times of the year. From observation of animals in zoos it would appear that the male undergoes a period of ' heat ' as does the female, and these periods must coincide before mating can take place. Mr. E. P. Gee gives four records of these animals observed mating in the wild state. All four incidents occurred between the end of February and the end of April. He also records the instance of a newly born female found dead on the 22nd of April. The period of gestation is about 16 months and the young at birth is 105 cm. in length and 60 kg. in weight. The female attains sexual maturity in 4 years and the male when 7 years old. The majority of the rhinoceroses in India occur in the Kaziranga Sanctuary in Sibsagar/Nowgong district in Assam.

Many legends and beliefs are attached to this animal. In Europe, during the Middle Ages, its horn was generally believed to have peculiar medicinal virtues.

In Nepal the flesh and the blood of the rhinoceros is considered highly acceptable to the *manes*. High caste Hindus and most Gurkhas offer libation of the animal's blood after entering its disembowelled body. On ordinary Sraddh days the libation of water and milk is poured from a cup carved from its horn. The urine is considered antiseptic and is hung in a vessel at the principal door as a charm against ghosts, evil spirits, and diseases. These beliefs connected with the rhinoceros are prevalent in varying forms in Burma, Siam, and China. They set a great value upon the animal and provide the main reason for its persecution.

THE SMALLER ONEHORNED, OR JAVAN RHINOCEROS

Rhinoceros sondaicus. Desmarest

Plates facing pp. 221, 224

Local Names. Hindi *gainda* ; Mar. *genda.*

Size. Smaller than the Great Indian Onehorned Rhinoceros but still very bulky. Old bulls measure about 5 ft. 10 in. (180 cm.) at the shoulder. The single horn is never very long ; 10¾ in. (27.3 cm.) is the record.

Distinctive Characters. In distinction to the Great Indian One-horned Rhinoceros the fold of skin before the shoulder is carried right across the back in this animal. The hide is marked all over with a curious mosaic-like pattern. The horn does not appear to be developed in the females or, if developed at all, it is only a low boss.

Distribution. The Smaller Onehorned Rhinoceros was once believed to range from Bengal and Assam, south of the Brahmaputra, through Burma and the Malay Peninsula to Sumatra. As far as can be ascertained the Javan Rhinoceros is now extinct in India and Burma. What was believed to be the last surviving animal in Malaya was shot for the preservation of its entire remains in a museum in America. It is possible though not very likely that the species may still exist in some of the more remote and ill-explored tracts of the Malay Peninsula.

Today, the Udjung Kulon Sanctuary in the western extremity of Java is the main place where this species exists. As the animals hide so well and the forest is so dense it is difficult to take a census. In 1960 the number of animals living in this Sanctuary was estimated at ' between two dozen and four dozen'.

Habits. The Smaller Onehorned Rhinoceros is more an inhabitant of tree forest than of grass land. Its low-crowned grinding teeth indicate that it is a browser, indulging less in grazing than the Great Indian Onehorned Rhinoceros, whose armoury of high-crowned grinding teeth are peculiarly adapted to the mastication of grass. Its usual habitat is forested hill country where it has been found at elevations as high as 7000 ft. (2135 cm.) above sea-level.

The feeding habits of this rhinoceros and of the twohorned rhinoceros described below have profoundly affected their distribution. Being able to live on a great variety of forest trees and shrubs these animals have extended their range through the great forest tract reaching from Assam and Bengal through Burma and the Malay countries. The Great Indian Onehorned Rhinoceros is on the other hand limited by the nature of its food to living in the grass jungles of the alluvial plains of north India. Similar factors have limited the range of the grazing White Rhinoceros and facilitated the distribution of the browsing Black Rhinoceros on the African Continent.

THE ASIATIC TWOHORNED RHINOCEROS

Didermocerus sumatrensis (Fischer)

Plate facing p. 225

[RACE IN INDIA : *lasiotis* (Buckland)]

Local Names. Burmese *kyan, kyan-shaw.*

Size. Male: height at shoulder, 4 ft. 4½ in. (135 cm.) ; girth behind the withers, a little over 7 ft. (215 cm.).

Distinctive Characters. This rhinoceros differs from the two other Asiatic rhinoceroses in possessing two horns. On this account it is considered to represent a distinct genus. It is further distinguished by having a single pair of lower front teeth instead of two pairs as in the Great Indian Onehorned and the Javan Rhinoceroses. Other distinctions are seen in the structure of the skull and in the anatomy of the intestines. The greater part of the body is covered with bristles varying from red-brown to black. The hairy fringes of the ears and the body are lost with age.

Distribution. Till the end of the last century the range of this species extended from the hill tracts of Assam, through the hill ranges of Tippera and Chittagong, into Arakan and Burma ; and thence into French Indo-China, Siam, Malaya, Sumatra, and Borneo, but not Java. At the present time its survival in India is doubtful. The upheaval of the war and the unrest which followed it have left a few survivors in Burma, in Shwe-U-Daung, Arakan, the Pegu Yomas, Kahilu, Yuzal in the Uyu drainage, and the Tenasserim peninsula. The estimated number of these is given as between twenty-one and forty-five.

Habits. The Twohorned Rhinoceros, like the Smaller Onehorned has a preference for forested hill tracts where it wanders up to considerable elevations. A sufficiency of shade and a good supply of water are essential to its habitat. A pair will frequent a given area for a time and then move off, their movements being affected by the water supply. They enter streams by night and also during the hot hours of the day. In suitable spots there are regular wallows or mud-baths in which the huge creatures roll much as buffaloes and pigs do. As a result of this habit their bodies are always well coated with mud. Tracks lead off in all directions from these wallows. They present the appearance of large tunnels hollowed through the dense undergrowth. Unlike the elephant, a rhinoceros does not break through the jungle but burrows its way through the dense tangle. They visit the wallows singly, or a bull and a cow may be found together. The night and early morning are spent in wandering about and feeding, the hot hours of the day in rest in some cool and shaded spot. In the cold weather and rains they visit the low country coming down in search of particular foods. They are not grazers but browse on twigs and shoots, and are very partial to fallen fruit, wild mangoes, citrous fruits, and figs.

The sense of smell and hearing is acute, but sight is poor. Collections of dung found in particular places reveal a habit similar to that noticed with the Great Indian Onehorned Rhinoceros.

Little is known about their breeding habits but it is known that the young remain with the mother to a fairly advanced age.

17. Wild Oxen, Sheep, Goats

OXEN, SHEEP, AND goats, antelopes, deer, and pigs, all belong to the second order or division of hoofed animals, the **Artiodactyla** or even-toed ungulates. Giraffes, camels, hippopotami are included in this order, which contains the great majority of living hoofed animals. This varied assemblage is divided into a number of families, the largest of which is the **Bovidae**. The family includes all oxen, sheep, and goats, domestic or wild, and also the antelopes and gazelles.

The points of resemblance and distinction between these animals are best revealed in considering their structure.

STRUCTURE IN RELATION TO HABITS

Feet. Our wild oxen include the Gaur or Indian Bison, the Banteng or Tsaine, strictly speaking a Malayan animal which may just occur within Indian limits on the frontiers of north-eastern India, the Yak, and the Wild Buffalo.

Wild oxen are easily recognizable by their massive build and their general similarity in form to domestic cattle. Wild sheep and goats again are built much like their tame kindred. But despite their heavy build, wild oxen are active and nimble creatures. Gaur and yak are admirable climbers ascending the steepest slopes with speed and facility. Of the climbing powers of wild goats and sheep there is little need to speak. Few animals are so quick and sure-footed on precipitous ground.

Now, unlike the clawed limbs of beasts of prey, which serve as weapons of attack, or the grasping hands and feet of apes and monkeys, the limbs of all hoofed animals are suited to one purpose only, which is carrying and moving the body. Their feet, shod with horny hooves, are built to withstand the roughest wear, while speed and surety of movement are attained both by their mode of progress and by the special structure of their limbs. All hoofed animals walk on the tips of their toes. Thus the full extent of the limbs is brought into action and the length of the stride and speed are increased. A moving body moves faster when resistance to its movement is reduced. In hoofed animals such resistance is reduced not only by progress on the tips of the toes, but also by a reduction in their number ; so that the part of the body brought into contact with the earth is reduced to the narrowest limits and resistance is proportionately diminished. No typical hoofed animal has more than four functional toes. Some as we have seen have three, the majority two, horses only one. With these animals Nature's plan has been to lengthen and strengthen the bones of one or more toes and to dispense completely with the others.

This reduction has been effected in different ways in different groups of hoofed animals. In rhinoceroses, horses, and tapirs, as was shown, it is the third or middle toe of the foot which has increased in size at the expense of the others. But in the great majority of hoofed animals, in oxen, sheep, goats, antelopes, deer, camels, pigs, and the hippopotamus, it is not the third toe alone but the third and fourth which are greatly developed. The other toes are dispensed with or reduced in size. In all these animals the first, the innermost toe, is wanting. The second toe and the fifth or outermost toe are either absent or reduced in size ; they form the ' petty toes ' seen in cattle, antelopes, deer, pigs, etc. The third and fourth toes, i.e. the two middle toes of the foot, are fully developed ; they are large, equal in size, and perfectly symmetrical, and the centre line of the limb passes between them. The two hooves which encase these toes present a flat surface to each other, and look like a single hoof cleft in two. Hence the name ' cloven-hoofed ' applied to these animals. Coupled with this reduction in the number of toes is another distinctive character. The two bones of the foot attaching to the two middle toes are fused together to form a single bone, the ' cannon bone '. There is also a corresponding development in the length and method of articulation of the bones of the wrists and ankles. These modifications in the bony structure ensure greater firmness to the foot during rapid movement. Thus reinforced and strengthened, it is less likely to give under pressure. The cloven hooves provide a better hold on rough ground and, as they expand when sunk into soft soil and close on extrication, they help movement in marsh and swamp. The size and set of the hooves are adapted to the habits of the animal. Our wild buffalo, a creature of swamps and marshland, has large, wide-splayed hooves well suited to movement in marshy soil ; while the hooves of the Gaur, a hill dweller, are small and close-knit and better adapted for use on hard stony ground.

From what has been written it will be seen that the limbs and feet of bovines and their kin are perfect running organs meant to ensure speed and surety of movement. To most of these large, yet timid creatures, a capacity for rapid flight is their chief means of escape from beasts of prey, their numerous and habitual enemies. Apart from this, their sturdy, hoofed limbs, designed for continuous and rough usage, are well adapted to carry them for long distances over difficult ground. Most wild cattle, sheep, and goats seasonally travel many weary miles in search of food.

Teeth. The food of cattle, sheep, and goats, and their kin, consisting mainly of grasses and other coarse vegetable matter, requires

long mastication before it becomes digestible. Their grinding teeth
are specially suited to such a diet. They have broad crowns complicated by folds and ridges of hard enamel. These ridges are
braced on either side with layers of softer dentine. An effective
grinding surface is constantly maintained by the persistence of the
harder enamel and the quicker wear of the softer dentine ; a similar
device, as we have seen, keeps the teeth of rodents in good grinding
order.

Their front teeth are equally adapted to their food and way of
eating it. All the members of the family have no incisor teeth in
the upper jaw. Their place is taken by a soft pad. Again, the
canine teeth in the upper jaw are rudimentary or absent. In the
lower jaw, on the other hand, incisors and canines are present.
But the canines are brought into close contact with the incisors.
They can scarcely be distinguished from them. They have become
part of the grass-cropping apparatus. The grass is drawn into the
mouth by the tongue, its surface covered with rough points all
directed towards the throat.

These bulky animals require a great amount of food. Their food,
as we have said, consists mainly of tough fibrous grass which has
to be long and continuously chewed before its nourishment becomes
available. Now to animals, which have so many enemies to prey
upon them, long exposure on open grazing grounds implies grave
risk. Their food, however large its quantity and however difficult
to digest, has to be eaten quickly during limited grazing hours.
Nature has provided them with the means to do this without harm
to themselves. They can take and swallow large quantities of food
during comparatively short feeding hours, and chew and assimilate
it later when resting in safety and seclusion. Their stomachs are
expressly designed for this purpose.

Stomach. The stomach consists of four separate chambers. The
first and largest, the paunch, serves to contain quantities of hastily
chewed food. In the paunch it undergoes a softening process and
is then returned to the mouth in small boluses. Each bolus is
thoroughly chewed in a slow and deliberate manner. It is a familiar
process known as ruminating or ' chewing the cud '. As each
mouthful is reduced to pulp it is swallowed and replaced by another
sent up from the paunch. The food when pulped enters the second
chamber of the stomach, called the *reticulum* or ' honeycomb '
bag because its walls are celled like a honeycomb. Here the food
is pressed and shaped and sent up to the gullet, whence it
passes downwards again into a third, and then into a fourth
chamber. Actual digestion takes place in the last chamber. Antelopes and deer have similar complex stomachs. Like oxen, sheep,
and goats, they are true ruminants. Camels and chevrotains also
ruminate, but they are distinctive in other ways. The special features
of true ruminants, as we have seen, are the absence of incisors in the

upper jaw, a four-chambered stomach, and the presence of horns. No other hoofed animal has true horns.

Horns. The horns of all the **Bovidae** consist of two parts, a core of bone arising from the skull and an outer sheath or cap of true horn. The outer sheath is hollow and can be removed whole from its bony core. This is why these animals are called hollow-horned ruminants. It is a character which distinguishes them from the deer (**Cervidae**) which are ruminants with solid horns. Unlike in deer, the horns of the Bovidae persist through life, though the upper layers of horn may wear and flake off as new horn grows below. Deer shed their antlers periodically. The horns of oxen are present in both sexes and of nearly equal dimensions in both males and females. Usually they arise near or from the summit of the skull, whence they generally sweep in a more or less outward direction and then curve upwards, sometimes inwards, near the tips. They are never spirally twisted or ornamented with prominent knots or ridges, a feature so common in the horns of sheep and goats. In sheep and goats also both sexes are horned, but the horns of the females are usually smaller and less massive.

LIFE IN RELATION TO SURROUNDINGS

The home of the family. Oxen are believed to be descendants of ancestors whose original home was northern Asia. From this centre the family spread into Europe, and by way of the Behring Straits into North America. Later they extended their range into tropical countries, where the majority of species now live. Of our Indian species, the gaur, the tsaine, and the buffalo are tropical. The yak alone is found in the temperate zone. As to sheep and goats, like oxen their original home was central Asia where the majority of species are still found. Within Indian limits they are confined mainly to the temperate forests or the alpine levels of the Himalayas. One species of wild sheep, the urial, has adapted itself to a life in the barren sun-scorched hills of Sind, Baluchistan, and the Punjab. And a single species of wild goat is found in the Peninsula ; this is the Nilgiri tahr which lives on the heights of the Nilgiris and some of the adjoining hill ranges. This is the lowest latitude at which any wild goat lives.

Habits and surroundings. Seasonal changes in climatic conditions and consequent changes in vegetation naturally influence the habits of these animals. Writing of gaur in the Central Provinces, Mr. Dunbar Brander says : ' During the cold weather they frequent the grass maidans on the hill-tops and the bamboo and creeper-clad slopes of the hills. As the hot weather advances, shortage of food and water forces them down and they can be found at low elevations frequenting grassy glades by the banks of streams. In the rains they wander much, but during other seasons they frequent the same places at the same time of the year.' In the bamboo jungles of Mysore the movements of these animals are somewhat different. Between January and May they seek the evergreen valleys watered by perennial streams. With the coming of the rains in May, they roam forth to feed on the succulent grass which springs up on the summits of the hills. About September when the grass grows too rank for their liking many gaur move down to the forest tracts at the foot of the hills. Wild buffalo in the riverain plains of Assam, where grazing is always to be had, are less given to wandering. But in parts of Orissa and Madhya Pradesh the jungles are dry, the green cover withers during the hot weather, and many water-holes and wallows cease to exist. Buffaloes then wander much in search of grazing and frequently resort to village tanks to drink and wallow. Where swamps and water persist they spend much of the day lying almost completely submerged in pools. The yak, an inhabitant of the bleak Tibetan plateau, lives in continuous struggle with the fiercest elements of Nature. In the bitter cold of these silent, snow-bound altitudes many die of starvation during winter and many come down to comparatively lower levels, to 14,000 ft. (4270 m.) or so, in quest of food. Similarly rigid are winter conditions for wild sheep and goats in the Himalayan highlands.

In the Peninsula, not winter, but the hot weather, is the time of adversity. In the Punjab and Sind hills, where the heat during summer is intense, urial seek shelter under shady rocks or even enter forest and come out to feed only in the comparative cool of the evening or before sunrise. But in the cold or cloudy weather they are on the move at all times.

Bovines and their neighbours. The role of ruminants in the economy of Nature is the general role of grazing animals. They are a check on the superabundant growth of various types of grasses, the most quick-spreading of all vegetation. At the same time, ruminants are the basic food of a wide range of carnivores. Wild oxen because of their large size are naturally at the very end of the food chain and fall a prey only to the largest carnivores. In our forests, tigers alone can deal with gaur or buffalo. Leopards, wolves, wild dogs prey on wild sheep and goats in their mountain fastnesses and help to keep down their numbers. As for the larger bovines, gaur and buffalo, the main control on their over-increase are diseases carried by various parasites which periodically decimate the herds.

Many writers have commented upon the association between gaur and elephants. Both, having much the same habits as regards food and type of shelter, are frequently found feeding together. Gaur apparently derive some benefit from this association. They feed on high bamboo shoots and such foliage as would be out of their reach unless pulled down by the elephants. Apart from elephants, tolerated companions, and the tiger, an inveterate foe, gaur have little or no relationships with other forest animals. But like other game animals they are persistently worried by biting flies, particularly during the hot weather and dry spells of the monsoon, when they may have to leave the shelter of the forest and take to the open to escape these swarming pests. For the same reason tsaine lie out in open grassy *kwins*. They do this to avoid the swarms of insects in the forest. Various blood-sucking and parasitic flies become an intolerable nuisance to them during the hot weather and the rains.

As to relationship between their own kind, the existence of a dominance hierarchy is apparent among Gaur bulls, the ranking being established more by conventions such as threat displays rather than actual fights. The hierarchy based largely on size and age ensures that high ranking males have first call on females in season. The Gaur and other bovines are largely non-territorial and live within ranges in their habitat which they share with other members of their species.

Interrelationships between different species of Bovidae are tolerant. Gaur and tsaine may occupy the same hill forests. Markhor are sometimes found grazing near ibex. Bharal and ibex have been observed in the same ground, and bharal and tahr actually seen grazing in company.

Relationship with man. Gaur, timid animals by nature, fear and avoid man. A wounded gaur may charge, and a solitary bull may attack without provocation, but their usual impulse on the approach of man is immediate flight. Except for rare stragglers, gaur keep away from human habitation, do not enter cultivation, or feed on crops. Tsaine are less afraid than gaur of approaching human dwellings and sometimes enter crops. Wild buffaloes on the other hand do not shun the neighbourhood of man ; they are usually defiant and will, if not much molested, permit a close approach. These animals may cause great havoc in fields, from which they can scarcely be driven. They are easily the boldest and most savage of Indian bovines. As with all animals, man is the most serious enemy of the family. In many parts of India where they were once common, gaur have retreated before the advance of cultivation into the innermost fastnesses. The wild buffalo's domains have also been considerably reduced. The great herds which once inhabited Midnapore and the coastal tracts of Orissa and the adjoining parts of Madhya Pradesh are now no more. Man influences the habits of these animals. His presence or absence near their haunts induces wariness or indifference, and affects their habits and times of grazing.

Human interference with these animals is manifested in yet other ways, one of which is the spread of disease. Gaur and other bovines contract diseases through feeding in jungles where infected domestic cattle are left to graze. Great herds are periodically decimated by rinderpest and foot-and-mouth disease induced by contact with domestic cattle.

Origin of domestic breeds. Of man's use of oxen for food, as beasts of burden, and in so many other ways, there is little need to speak. From time immemorial these animals have been brought into the service of man. All our wild species, the gaur, the tsaine, the yak, and the wild buffalo, have made their contribution to Indian domestic breeds of cattle. It is said that the humped bullocks of India, generally referred to in European literature as the 'zebu', have been derived from the banteng or tsaine of Burma and the Malay countries, or from some nearly allied extinct type. The conclusion rests on similarities in the structure of the skull, the development of the dewlap, and on the banteng's tawny coloration. Also, it is suggested that the elevated ridge on the banteng's withers may have been the origin of the zebu's hump. Against this theory there is the more recent belief that both Indian humped cattle and the straight-backed European cattle are descended from the aurochs or wild ox of Europe. Both theories require further proof before either one or the other can be established. This much is certain, both humped and humpless cattle were known in India from remote times. We find both types figured on seals recovered from the excavations at Mohenjo-Daro. These seals were the products of a civilization which flourished more than 3000 years before the Christian era. While the tsaine has been domesticated successfully in parts of Borneo and Java, all attempts to domesticate the Indian gaur, the most magnificent of all the bovines, have failed. Nevertheless it has made its contribution to our domestic stock. Both tsaine and gaur have been known to breed with domestic cattle. With the gaur such interbreeding has given rise to a handsome breed of cattle kept in a partially domesticated condition by the hill tribes of Assam and the Indo-Burmese hill ranges. These hybrid cattle are generally called *mithan* or *methne*. In the Assam hill ranges, where gaur are still plentiful and where opportunities for interbreeding are frequent, *mithan* retain their massiveness and show many points of resemblance to the gaur but in the Chin Hills, where gaur are more scarce and wild blood less frequently introduced, they soon lose their massive proportions and other gaur-like characters. *Mithan* are smaller in stature, shorter in limb, and generally have a well-developed dewlap, a thing very unusual in gaur. If breeding with domestic cattle is continued, the high dorsal ridge which lends so much to the imposing stature of the gaur disappears, the horns become cow-like, and the domestic cow's varied colourings begin to appear. If *mithan* are not to deteriorate, frequent interbreeding with wild gaur is essential.

The wild yak of the high plateaux of Tibet and central Asia has

PLATE 56

Wild Buffalo Bull (*Bubalus bubalis*) in Manas Sanctuary

Photo: E.P. Gee

PLATE 57

Goral (*Nemorhaedus goral*)

Photo : E. P. Gee

been domesticated. The pure-bred domestic yak is a magnificent beast which has lost nothing in strength and stature. Such are some of the yak kept by the Tartar tribes of the Rupsu plateau. They thrive only at high levels. Interbreeding of yak with Ladaki cattle has however produced a strain known as the *zo* which is a cross between a male yak and a domestic cow. These hybrids are of two kinds, horned and hornless, and each form breeds true, the horned producing horned young, the hornless young without horns. These cross-bred animals are generally smaller in build and frequently display a tendency to piebald colouring. They are able to stand much higher temperatures than pure-bred yak and provide transport for men and merchandise between Ladak and Kashmir. Without the yak as a beast of burden travel and trade in the desolate regions of the trans-Himalaya would be impossible.

As to the buffalo, Indian domestic buffaloes are the descendants of the wild species. The tame buffalo differs but little from the wild one. Domestication has scarcely changed it. Selection and elimination have produced numerous well-defined domestic breeds.

As for sheep and goats, it is generally believed that the Persian Wild Goat (*Capra hircus aegagrus* Erxleben) is one of the sources, probably the principal one, from which domestic goats are derived. The urial or shapu breeds freely with tame sheep and has undoubtedly influenced the production and improvement of domestic breeds.

FAMILY LIFE AND CARE OF THE YOUNG

Means of communication. Among gaur and other wild oxen the sense of smell is perhaps the most keenly developed. The strong body odours given out by many of these animals must be a means by which members of a herd keep together, and many of them are equipped with special scent glands which serve this purpose.

Scent Glands. All the more typical sheep have a face gland situated in a shallow depression of the skull, just below the eye. They also have a pair of glands in the groin, known as inguinal glands, and a gland between the two main toes of the feet. In this character sheep differ from oxen, which have no such glands, and also from goats. In the urial the foot glands give out a clear semi-fluid secretion ' with a pleasant scent like toffee, slightly infused with acetic acid '. The secretion of these foot glands by scenting the ground over which sheep and goats pass enables members of a scattered flock to ascertain the whereabouts of their fellows. In like manner the groin glands of sheep are brought into contact with the ground when they sit down to rest and their scent must serve as a guide. Typical goats (*Capra*) have no face glands and no inguinal glands. Glands may or may not be present in the forefeet, but are always absent in the hind.

Calls. The family have various calls by which members of a herd communicate with each other. Dunbar Brander distinguishes no less than five different sounds made by gaur. He describes two distinct alarm calls, one prefaced by a loud hissing sound caused by the expulsion of air from the lips before the sound is produced, the second a loud ' bhaying ' which, though a cry of alarm, is more in the nature of an interrogation, a call to which a reply is expected. Angry bulls bellow in rage and mothers low to their young. The breeding bull gaur utters an absurd piping or whistling sound more like the call of a bird than anything else. It is an astonishing and ridiculous note coming from so large an animal. The calls of wild sheep and goats are not unlike those of their domestic kin. When frightened, urial utter a shrill whistle and drum the ground with their forefeet, a drumming which sends the whole herd bolting.

Family life. Gaur ordinarily live in small herds of 8 to 12 animals. Such a herd is essentially a family party. In quest of pasturage or from other causes, several families may unite to form large assemblages. Except during the mating season, bulls of all sizes herd together with the cows in perfect amity. Bulls, when mature, are given to wandering usually in quest of grazing, either alone or in company with other mature males. But ordinarily they do not stray far. According to Schaller, during the breeding season bulls, particularly black bulls, roam extensively through the forests stopping at intervals and calling musically in "a clear resonant *u-u-u-u* about one to three seconds long, either constant in pitch or slightly rising and falling". The call is repeated in a descending scale, and though not loud, carries for over a mile in the forest. Frequency of calling is more at dawn and dusk but during the height of the season is heard throughout the night. The roaming males in search of females in heat. locate the herds and are themselves located by the call and when successful defend the female from other males until they have mated; no effort is made to hold herds exclusively and no territory is established by the rutting male. Really old bulls past the urge or capacity to mate lead permanently solitary lives. When about to calve the cow gaur moves away from the herd and drops her calf in some secluded spot. The newborn calf lies crouched in the grass with its neck stretched out, a position in which it is well concealed, its light colouring blending with the dry grass. The mother remains in the vicinity of the calf, but may desert it and rejoin the herd if disturbed.

Observations on the family life of other Indian bovines suggest that their social life is based on similar principles. Older males live away from the cows except during the rutting season. The care and upbringing of the young and leadership of the herd is left entirely to the cows.

PLATE 58

0 1 m.
0 1 2 3 ft.

Gaur
(*Bos gaurus*)

Banteng
(*Bos banteng*)

Yak
(*Bos grunniens*)

Wild Buffalo
(*Bubalus bubalis*)

PLATE 59

Shapu
(*Ovis orientalis*)

Marco Polo's Sheep
(*Ovis ammon polii*)

Nayan
(*Ovis ammon hodgsoni*)

Bharal
(*Pseudois nayaur*)

THE GAUR, or INDIAN BISON

Bos gaurus H. Smith

Plate facing p. 242

[RACE IN INDIA : *gaurus* H. Smith]

Local Names. Hindi *gaur, gaur gai* ; Mar. *gaviya, gawa* ; Kan. *kadu yethu, kartee* ; Tamil *kattu erumai* ; Mal. *katu poth* ; Bur. *peeoung.*

Size. A bull may stand 6 ft. 4 in. (195 cm.) at the shoulders. The average is between 5 ft. 8 in. (175 cm.) and 5 ft. 10 in. (180 cm.) ; cows are about 4 in. (10 cm.) shorter. Gaur appear to attain their finest development in the south Indian hill ranges and Assam. The spread of the horns taken together with their girth is the test of a good head. Average spread 33 in. (85 cm.), 40 in. (100 cm.) exceptional. Cows have smaller, less sturdy horns. They are rounder and have a narrower sweep. An old bull may scale over 2000 lb. (900 kg.).

Distinctive Characters. With its huge head, deep massive body, and sturdy limbs the Gaur is the embodiment of vigour and strength. Very striking in the Gaur is the muscular ridge upon its shoulders which slopes down to the middle of the back where it ends in an abrupt dip. A newly-born Gaur is a light golden-yellow which soon changes to fawn, then to light brown, and so to coffee or reddish brown, the colour of young bulls and cows. Old bulls are jet black, their bodies almost hairless. An ashy forehead and yellowish- or white-stockinged feet complete the livery. The Gaur has no white patch behind the thighs, a character well marked in the tsaine. The colour of the eyes is brown. In certain lights, as a result of reflection, they appear blue.

Distribution. Western Ghats southwards from south Maharashtra. Hill forests of central and south-eastern Peninsula and West Bengal eastwards to Burma and Malay Peninsula.

Habits. Though Gaur come down to low levels at certain seasons in quest of pasture, they are essentially hill animals. In the hill ranges of the Peninsula they climb to levels of 6000 ft. (1830 m.) or more. In the Himalayas, they are seldom found at this height and keep mainly to the foothills. Forests are essential to the existence of Gaur. They come out to graze early in the mornings and feed till about 9 a.m., or later if the weather be cool or cloudy, and graze again in the afternoons. During the hot hours of the day Gaur retire to the shelter and seclusion of the forest. Their food is chiefly grass, they also browse on leaves and eat the bark of certain trees.

In common with many other animals Gaur have the habit of visiting ' salt-licks ', spots where the ground is impregnated with salts and other minerals. It is believed that such earth acts as a purgative and rids animals of internal parasites. Gaur are by nature shy and timid animals. Their defence is their massive size and an acute sense of smell. As with most wild cattle, hearing and eyesight are comparatively poor.

The composition of the herds, social life, and breeding habits of Gaur have been discussed. The time of mating apparently varies as calves are born at all seasons. In Madhya Pradesh according to Schaller, new born young are seen mainly from November to March and the peak of the rut is in March, April, May. The period of gestation is not accurately known It is said that the cow separates from the herd when her calf is born and remains with it for a few days feeding near by. The herd remains in the vicinity and she rejoins it as soon as the offspring is able to accompany her. But the calf is not necessarily helpless. Morris records how a calf walked ten minutes after it was born, and when disturbed galloped off with its mother twenty minutes later.

THE BANTENG, or TSAINE

Bos banteng Wagner

Plate facing p. 242

[RACE IN INDIA : *banteng* Wagner]

Local Names. Bur. *tsaing* ; Malay *sapi utan.*

Size. The Banteng, the wild ox of Burma, is a smaller animal than the gaur. Nevertheless it is massively built, standing quite 5 ft. 6 in. (170 cm.) at the shoulder or even higher.

Good average horns measure about 24 in. (60 cm.) in length, with a girth of 14 in. (35 cm.) and a spread of 25 to 30 in. (60 to 75 cm.). Anything over 25 in. (65 cm.) may be regarded as a good head. Young bulls and cows have cylindrical horns ; those of cows grow almost straight upwards and are smooth throughout with but little girth.

Distinctive Characters. The Banteng is longer in the leg than the gaur, and its dorsal ridge is less prominent. The high concave forehead and ' roman ' nose of the gaur are wanting in the Banteng. The horns are connected by a hairless mass of horny substance as hard as the skull beneath. Cows and young bulls are a bright chest-nut with a white face, white stockings, and a distinctive white patch on the buttocks. Young bulls sometimes show white spots on the flanks, which in time merge and turn dirty grey. Older animals are described as being yellowish brown, sometimes turning into a soiled grey on the sides. Old bulls usually have the face down to the muzzle dirty white, almost approaching grey. The coat may be entirely grey or khaki, sometimes dark chocolate-brown, more rarely quite black like the Javanese Banteng. Ordinarily, in Burma, the older the bull, the lighter in colour it becomes.

Distribution. The range of the Banteng includes Burma, Siam, the Malay peninsula, Borneo, and Java. About five races have been described within this area. It is said to be found in the hills of Manipur, but whether any herds exist in these hills at present is not known. There is no evidence of its occurrence in Manipur.

Habits. The Banteng, unlike the gaur, prefers flat or undulating ground covered with light deciduous or mixed deciduous and evergreen forests, where there are glades of grass and bamboo. In parts of their territory in Burma they have however retreated with the advance of cultivation, and deserted their favoured grounds for the seclusion of denser hill forests, the accustomed habitat of the gaur. Their habits are much like those of the gaur, but they are less timid of approaching human habitation, and sometimes enter cultivation. Like gaur they feed in the morning and again in the afternoon, and spend the hotter hours of the day at rest. Their food consists of various kinds of grasses, and the leaves and shoots of bamboos and various plants and trees. They have the same liking for ' salt-licks '. The herds wander about visiting different grounds at different seasons in quest of pasturage. In April, the under-growth of grass, a feature of the low level forests, is usually burnt away by forest fires and the herds visit these areas to graze on the new grass which springs up. During the early rains they visit bamboo jungles to browse on the young shoots.

The Banteng is a more wary animal than the gaur. It lives in greater peril from tigers than the gaur and is therefore more alert. Scent, sight, and hearing are all acutely developed in these animals. As to sounds, Banteng bellow like domestic cattle, but much less frequently. They are more silent animals than gaur. When alarmed a loud snort is the usual prelude to a stampede.

The herding and mating habits of the Tsaine are those of the family. The main rutting season is not recorded. As many calves are seen with the herds in April and May, and as the period of gestation is about nine months, the main rut is probably between September and October. Usually one, sometimes two, young are produced.

THE YAK

Bos grunniens Linnaeus

Plate facing p. 242

[RACE IN INDIA : *grunniens* Linnaeus]

Local Names. Tibetan *dong, brong dong* (wild), *pegu* (domesticated) ; Hindi *ban chour*.

Size. An adult bull Yak stands about 5 ft. 6 in. (170 cm.) at the shoulder and may reach about 6 ft. (185 cm.). A bull weighs about 1200 lb. (545 kg.). Good horns measure 25 to 30 in. (65 to 75 cm.).

Distinctive Characters. The wild Yak is a massively built animal with a drooping head, high humped shoulders, a straight back, and short sturdy limbs. Shaggy fringes of coarse hair hang from its flanks, cover chest, shoulder, thigh, and the lower half of the tail, and form a bushy tuft between its horns and a great mane upon its neck.

The Yak receives additional warmth through the rigorous winters from a dense under-coat of soft closely matted hair. In the spring the under-fur comes away in great masses and, though completely separated from the skin, adheres in untidy scattered patches to the hairy body. The long hair fringes are not noticeable in the calves until the second or third month.

The colour of a wild Yak is a uniform blackish brown with a little white about the muzzle. The wild bull's horns are much more massive than those of any domestic Yak. Besides tame Yaks usually have patches of white on the chest and tail. This tendency to piebald colouring is never seen in the wild species. On the other hand tame Yaks are at times wholly black and, like wild Yaks, wander to great heights in search of food. Distinguishing between the wild and tame animals is sometimes less simple than is popularly believed.

Distribution. Northern Ladak, the plateaux of Tibet, and part of the Kansu Province in China. Within Indian limits proper, Yak only occur in the Changechenmo Valley in Ladak. They sometimes stray into the Sutlej valley, and into some of the passes in east Kumaon.

Habits. An inhabitant of the coldest, wildest, and most desolate mountains, where both arctic and desert conditions prevail, the wild Yak's existence is one of continuous struggle against the adverse forces of its environment. It is one of the highest dwelling animals in the world. In summer time Yaks are found at elevations ranging from 14,000 to 20,000 ft. (4270 to 6100 m.) and even in winter they do not descend much below this level. They live in small herds, except during the spring when the newly sprouting grass attracts large assemblages. In summer their food consists mainly of wiry tufts of grass and small shrubs which clothe the barren plateau. They also eat much of the ' salt '-encrusted earth, which in spots covers the ground with a white crust. Winter is a time of great privation, when many die of starvation and exposure. Streams and pools are frozen hard, and in lieu of water Yak eat the frozen snow, even in summer. When grazing at extreme heights, melting snow is their usual liquid nourishment. Like other bovines Yak love to stand or wallow in running water. Their wallows are the icy streams which spring from the snout of a glacier. The herd moving together in search of pasture travels at a rapid pace. They are in their element in the snow, in which their usual way is to travel in single file, each animal carefully placing its feet in the imprints left by the hoofs of the one preceding it. As with most bovines smell is their acutest sense, sight and hearing are less keenly developed.

The rutting season is limited to the late autumn, and the young are produced in April when the new-grown grass ensures a good food supply

THE WILD BUFFALO

Bubalus bubalis (Linnaeus)

Plates facing pp. 240, 242

[RACES IN INDIA : *bubalis* (Linnaeus), *fulvus* (Blanford)]

Local Names. Hindi *arna* (male), *arni* (female) ; Mar. *jungli mhais* ; Kan. *kadu kona, kartee.*

Size. A large bull stands 5 ft. 6 in. (170 cm.) at the shoulder, and may reach even 6 ft. 6 in. (200 cm.) and scale some 2000 lb. (900 kg.) and over. Heads are measured from tip to tip across the forehead ; 108 in. (275 cm.) is a good head. The record horn measurement of a cow is 77¾ in. (197.6 cm.).

Distinctive Characters. Though it has a finer carriage the Wild Buffalo differs little in general appearance from the tame one, except perhaps that it is sleeker, heavier, and more robust-looking. Like the domestic buffalo, the Wild Buffalo is a slaty black. The legs are dirty white up to just above the hocks and the knees. The newborn calf is light coloured, almost yellow. As to horns, Wild Buffalo usually exhibit two types. In one, the horns curve upwards in a semicircle, the tips being separated by a small interval. In the second, the horns spread outwards almost horizontally from the head and curve slightly upwards and inwards near the tips. Both types may be found in the same herd and there is much intergrading between the two forms. The horns are flat and triangular in section; those of the cows are less massive and vary less in shape.

Distribution. The grass jungles of the Nepal Terai and the plains of the Brahmaputra in Assam; a few herds survive in parts of Orissa, adjoining Bastar District of Madhya Pradesh. and in the Bastar district of Madhya Pradesh.

Habits. Tall grass jungles and reed brakes in the neighbourhood of swamps provide the ideal habitat for buffaloes, offering them both food and shelter, pools of water to lie in, and mud wallows in which to roll and cake themselves with earth. Such is their habitat in the riverain flats of Assam and the Terai. In the southern parts of their range they live on drier harder ground, well broken up into nullahs and scattered with trees and open expanses of grass. They associate in small herds which may combine to form large assemblages. They feed chiefly on grass, grazing in the mornings and in the evenings and sometimes at night, lying up by day in high grass or dense patches of cover, or submerged in a marsh or pool. In the drier areas of their range they are given to wandering, and during the hot weather sometimes cross the low hills in search of grazing. Unlike gaur, Wild Buffalo do not shun the neighbourhood of man, and given opportunity enter cultivation. During the rains when crops are growing Wild Buffalo sally forth into the fields and can scarcely be driven from them. They are described as being the boldest and most savage of the Indian Bovidae. A bull may attack without provocation. This depends much on the individual; one will show no fight when approached, another will charge at once. A cow with a newly born calf is dangerous. Even tame buffaloes retain this courage ; they will face a tiger and are frequently used to drive out wounded tigers from cover. Except for man, the tiger is the only enemy the Wild Buffalo has to fear, and against a vigorous bull even the tiger stands little chance. Scent is keenly developed in these animals, they have good powers of hearing, their sight is moderate. As to sounds, members of a herd grunt to each other when moving along. Bellowing is rare. A bull charges with a preliminary snort, or stamps the ground with its feet under excitement. The main pairing season is at the end of the rains. Calves are usually dropped in March, April, and May, but have been observed in other months of the year. Wild Buffaloes not infrequently mate with domestic ones. These interbreeders are generally young, though mature, bulls driven from the herd during the rut.

THE SHAPU, or URIAL

Ovis orientalis Gmelin

Plate facing p. 243

[RACES IN INDIA: *vignei* Blyth, *blanfordi* Hume, *punjabiensis* Lydekker]

Local Names. Punjabi *urial* ; Baluchi & Sindhi *kar* (male), *gad* (female) ; Ladaki *sha, shapo* (male), *shamo* (female).

Size. The Ladak Urial stands about 3 ft. (90 cm.) or more at the shoulder ; animals from the Punjab hills are smaller, about 2 ft. 8 in. (80 cm.). Average horns measure 20 to 30 in. (50 to 75 cm.) round the curves and have a girth of about 10 in. (25 cm.) at the base. The maximum recorded length in the Ladak Urial is 39 in. (99.1 cm.) ; Afghan 41½ in. (105.4 cm.) ; Punjab 38 in. (96.4 cm.).

Distinctive Characters. Its smaller size distinguishes the Urial from other species of wild sheep. In summer coat, the Ladak Urial is rufous-grey or fawn, in winter a mixture of grey and brown. The Punjab Urial is redder in colouring. The adult ram wears a great black or grizzled ruff growing from either side of the chin which meets below and extends down the throat. In older rams the ruff is grey or white in front passing into black behind. In the shorter summer coat much of the ruff is shed. It is best developed in the Punjab race. The horns are strongly wrinkled. They are set close together and curve round in a circular sweep. In the Ladak Urial the horns turn inwards at the tips. In the Afghan race they tend to turn outwards and form an open spiral. In the Punjab race the horns tend to form a circle. But there is much variation, and divergent types may be seen in the same herd within the same area.

Distribution. Gilgit, Astor, and Ladak, eastwards to northern Tibet; southwards and westwards, the Punjab, Sind, and Baluchistan, and south Persia.

Habits. In Ladak this wild sheep inhabits steep grassy hill slopes above forest. In Astor, it keeps to open grassy mountain slopes at moderate elevations, below the tree-line. Its environment in the Punjab is rocky scrub-covered hills, and in Sind and Baluchistan it is found in barren stony ranges, all of which shows the adaptability of the species to the most varied conditions of life. Living as they do in open ground Urial are ever wary and alert. Though they avoid the precipitous cliffs which are the home of wild goats, they get over the steepest hill-sides with remarkable ease. In summer, the ewes and young rams live together in small herds, at this season the rams will be found living apart. In the Punjab, the main rutting season is between September and October, when the rams rejoin the ewes, and the herds break up into small parties, a ram with a following of 3 or 4 females. In Ladak and Astor the breeding season must be considerably later than September, as the young are produced in summer. The period of gestation is not accurately known. It is believed to be between 4 to 6 months. One or two young are produced at a birth.

THE NAYAN, or GREAT TIBETAN SHEEP

Ovis ammon hodgsoni Blyth

Plate facing p. 243

Local Names. Ladaki *nayan* (male), *nayanmo* (female) ; Tibetan *nyang*.

Size. This is the largest of all wild sheep, standing $3\frac{1}{2}$ to 4 ft. (110 to 120 cm.) at the shoulder; horns, 36 to 40 in. (90 to 100 cm.). The record horn measures 57 in. (144.8 cm.).

Distinctive Characters. *O. a. hodgsoni* is a race of the **Argali** *Ovis ammon* (Linnaeus). Another race *O. a. polii* Blyth, which occurs in India, is described in the next section. Long in the leg, graceful and light, the Nayan suggests an antelope in build. The horns in the male never exceed a single circle, as they do in *O. a. polii*. The ram is light brown, darker on the withers ; its rump, the caudal disc surrounding the tail, throat, chest, belly, and the insides of the legs are white. Old rams develop a white ruff about the neck, much of which is shed in the summer coat. Females have little or no mane, the white of the undersides is less pure, and the caudal disc indistinct. The winter coat in both sexes is paler.

Distribution. The plateau of Tibet from northern Ladak eastwards to the country north of Sikkim. In quest of grazing they occasionally cross into Spiti, Nepal, and Kumaon and are found near Tso Lhama Lake in the extreme north of Sikkim and in Bhutan.

Habits. The Tibetan plateau, where Nayan live, presents a wilderness of desolate plains and low undulating sand hills, scorched in summer and swept by icy winds through the freezing winters. In this desert terrain the sheep are naturally migratory and wander to wherever food and water is to be got. In the spring, when melting snows cause the scanty herbage to sprout, Nayan frequent the borders of the snow-line or enter the ravines, some of which hold trickling streams whose banks are covered with low bushes and herbage. They summer in the higher levels above 15,000 ft. (4575 m.), and in winter descend to the shelter of the lower valleys. They feed early in the morning and again in the evening, climbing some bare hill-sides to rest during the day. They avoid damp snow and select some dry spot on the stony slopes, kicking out with their feet a shallow ' form ' in which to lie down. Their coloration is highly protective. When lying down Nayan usually keep their heads erect, but they sleep with outstretched necks, the big rams resting their great curling horns on the ground.

In the spring, the sexes separate. Through the summer the older rams herd together in small parties and usually live away from the ewes and yearlings. They rejoin them in the late autumn, when the mating season begins. The young are born in May and early June, when the ewes seek the shelter of the more secluded valleys to lamb.

MARCO POLO'S SHEEP

Ovis ammon polii Blyth

Plate facing p. 243

Local Name. Wakhan *kuchan* (male), *mesh* (female) ; Turki (east Turkestan) *gulja* (male), *arkar* (female).

Size. An adult ram is about 44 in. (110 cm.) at the shoulder and scales some 250 lb. (115 kg.). Females are about one-third smaller. Horns, average length 52 in. (130 cm.), with a girth of 15 in. (38 cm.) at the base. The record pair is 75 in. (190.5 cm.) in length.

Distinctive Characters. Marco Polo's Sheep is not a distinct species but is the northern race of the **Argali** *Ovis ammon* (Linnaeus). Like the nayan it is long in the leg, light and graceful in build. The magnificent horns of the rams are deeply wrinkled, and the colour of old ivory. They curve in a complete circle and then extend outwards in a bold sweep. In winter, the adult ram has a creamy white head, legs, and belly. His flanks are grey, merging into the darker brown of the back. The general colouring is that of the bare boulder-strewn lands in which this sheep lives. The colour makes the animal almost invisible, except in movement. Young lambs are uniform dark grey, yearlings a lighter mouse-grey. The heavy winter coat is replaced about the end of May by the short paler summer pelage.

Distribution. Within our limits, *O. a. polii* are found only in Hunza. They exist in more or less reduced numbers in most of the side valleys of the Tagdumbash Pamirs. In the Russian Pamirs they still seem to be plentiful.

Habits. Rolling boulder-strewn plateaux, cut up by broad stony nullahs, set against a sky-line of snow-capped mountains, this is the dead and desert region in which *O. a. polii* live. In the spring the little patches of grass along the snow-line or in the nullahs, where a small lake or a winding stream produces herbage, form their habitual resort. Their food is then limited to the bunches of wiry grass. Later they feed on a species of wild onion which springs up in the sandy tracts. After a hard winter, conditions are most arduous and many die of starvation. In the summer, when there is a fair growth of grass over the Pamirs, the veteran males ascend into the higher and more remote nullahs. They feed morning and evening, and go up some bare hill-side to rest during the day ; always moving in single file, the big ones leading. Excellent of sight and wonderfully keen of scent, when alarmed they stand stock-still or crowd together stamping the ground with their forefeet, even advancing nearer. All at once one bounds away and the herd follows, heads held high, galloping with long easy strides ; but, intensely curious, they go a short distance, then turn and stop to see what disturbed them.

In their breeding habits they differ in no way from the Tibetan nayan. The rams fight for the ewes as sheep do, a frontal attack with lowered head, the horns meeting in a clash which can be heard a long way off, or they charge alongside to strike sideways at the ribs and flanks.

THE BHARAL, OR BLUE SHEEP

Pseudois nayaur (Hodgson)

Plate facing p. 243

[RACE IN INDIA : *nayaur* (Hodgson)]

Local Names. Hindi *bharal, bharar, bharut* ; Ladaki *na, sna* ; Nepali *nervati* ; Bhotia *nao, knao.*

Size. 3 ft. (90 cm.) high at the shoulder ; scaling 120 to 150 lb. (55 to 70 kg.). Horns average 23 to 24 in. (58 to 61 cm.) ; record head from Gyantse, Tibet, 33¼ in. (84.5 cm.).

Distinctive Characters. In structure and habits the Bharal holds a place intermediate between sheep and goats. Its horns are rounded and smooth, and curve backwards over the neck. It has no face glands. Their position is however marked by a small bare patch of skin. In these characters the Bharal approaches the goats. But a Bharal ram is not bearded, nor has he that unpleasant ' goaty ' odour. Again, Bharal may have glands between the hooves in all four feet ; in goats these are always absent in the hind limbs.

The general colour of the head and upper parts is brownish grey, suffused with slaty blue, browner in summer and more distinctly slaty grey in winter. The colour in any season blends perfectly with the blue shale and rock of the open hill-sides where Bharal live. The face and chest in old rams is black. A black stripe runs along the middle of each flank and down the front of the legs. All these black markings are absent in ewes. The horns are smooth and marked with fine striations, lines of growth. They curve outwards and downwards and in well-grown rams, curl backwards at the tips.

Distribution. Though typically a Tibetan animal, the Bharal is also found in Ladak, Kumaon Himalayas, Nepal, Sikkim, and Bhutan.

Habits. To find Bharal one must seek the higher altitudes, neighbouring on 16,000 ft. (4880 m.) in summer and rarely below 12,000 (3660 m.) in winter. In the main Himalayan range they are found at levels between the tree- and snow-line, where there is rich and abundant grass. They never enter scrub of any kind. In the Zaskar and Ladak ranges, the slopes above the tree-line are bare, and Bharal find their food in the occasional patches of coarse grass, moss, and dwarf shrubs. In habits, as in structure, Bharal are a mixture of goat and sheep. Like sheep they graze on open undulating grassy slopes, but like goats they climb well and do not hesitate to take to precipitous cliffs, ascending to the most difficult and inaccessible places when disturbed. They never enter forest or scrub. Bharal feed and rest alternately during the day. They lie down to rest in their grazing grounds, where they are difficult to distinguish, the colour and forms of these sheep blending completely with scattered boulders and outcroppings of rock projecting from the turf.

In summer they live in flocks of 10 to 40 or 50 animals, but sometimes as many as 200 may assemble. These mixed flocks of rams and ewes may contain well-grown males, but the mature rams keep somewhat to themselves. In spring and summer, the really old rams seek the higher levels; they rejoin the females and younger males in September when the rutting season commences. The large flocks now break into small parties consisting of a ram and his harem of wives accompanied by immature males.

Unlike the urial the Bharal will not cross with domestic sheep nor is it as easy to tame.

THE IBEX

Capra ibex Linnaeus

Plate facing p. 254

[RACE IN INDIA : *sibirica* (Pallas)]

Local Names. Ladaki *skin* or *sakin* (male), *dabmo* or *danmo* (female) ; Kash. *kail* ; Kulu *tangrol.*

Size. Height of male at shoulder, 40 in. (100 cm.) ; female, smaller. Good horns of males measure 40 to 45 inches (100 to 115 cm.) around the curve. The greatest recorded length is 58 inches (147.3 cm.) (Tian Shan), 55 inches (139.7 cm.) (Gilgit). A male in good condition weighs about 200 lb. (90 kg.).

Distinctive Characters. A sturdy, thick-set goat, the male with a great beard and a coat of coarse brittle hairs. In winter, a dense under-fur of wool helps it to withstand the intense cold of its native mountains. The colour is variable. In general, the winter coat is yellowish white, more or less tinged with brown and grey. In summer, the general hue is dark brown with irregular white patches. The female is yellowish brown and insignificant to look at. The great scimitar-shaped horns of the buck are flat, and bossed with bold ridges in front. The various races of Asiatic ibex, said to be distinguishable by the form of the horns and differences in general colouring, cannot be satisfactorily separated by these characters which vary considerably in the same areas.

Distribution. Mountain ranges of central Asia from the Altais to the Himalayas, from Afghanistan to Kumaon. Within this area a large number of doubtful races have been described on characters which are not constant. The Himalayan Ibex inhabits the western Himalayas on both sides of the main Himalayan range, and the mountain ranges which lie beyond in Kashmir and Baltistan. Its eastern limits are set by the upper reaches of the Sutlej river, east of which it does not occur.

Habits. The favourite grounds of Ibex lie in the higher elevations above the tree-line. In the spring they are found low below the snow-line, attracted by the new grass sprouting in patches on the steep slopes of the nullahs. They graze early in the morning, and again in the evening. Above their grazing grounds Ibex have the shelter and security of precipitous cliffs and ridges. To these heights the herd retires to rest or takes refuge when alarmed. Here it is safeguarded not only by the inaccessible nature of the retreat, but also by ever watchful individuals, usually females, whose keen eyes

PLATE 60

Wild Goat
(*Capra hircus*)

Ibex
(*Capra ibex*)

Markhor
(*Capra falconeri*)

Nilgiri Tahr
(*Hermitragus hylocrius*)

Himalayan Tahr
(*Hermitragus jemlahicus*)

0   1 m.
0   1   2   3 ft.

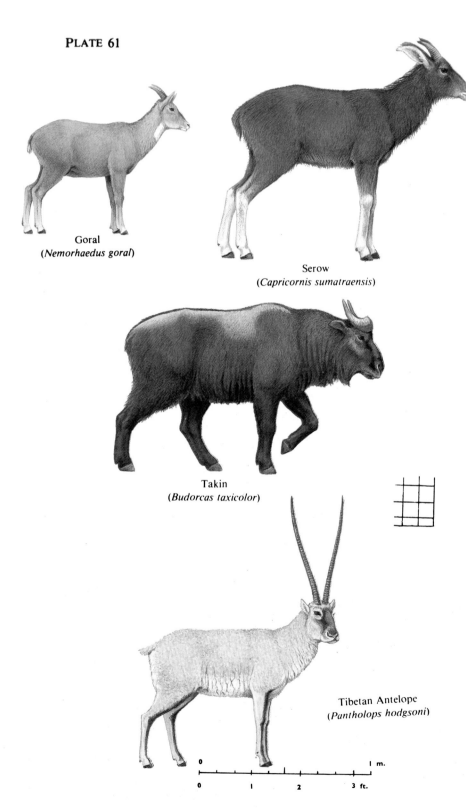

PLATE 61

Goral
(*Nemorhaedus goral*)

Serow
(*Capricornis sumatraensis*)

Takin
(*Budorcas taxicolor*)

Tibetan Antelope
(*Pantholops hodgsoni*)

0   1 m.

0   1   2   3 ft.

and scent detect any movements or approach of an enemy from below. A shrill whistle of alarm uttered by any one of the ' sentinels ' sends the flock dashing down, and then upwards again to the shelter of the steeps.

Ibex live in herds numbering from a dozen to 40 or 50 animals, but much larger assemblages are sometimes seen. In the early spring and summer the old males are usually with or near the herds of females and young, but later in the summer the patriarchs retire to the more inaccessible fastnesses where they live alone or in small groups of 3 and 4. They rejoin the main herds in October when the rut commences. As with most Himalayan animals the young are born in May and June when food is abundant. Protected by an investure of dense underwool, Ibex are little affected by cold, and even in winter do not descend to the lower levels, but resort to the steeper slopes where the snow does not lie so deep. They are hunted for their soft woolly under-fur. It is used for lining shawls and making stockings and gloves. No wool is so rich, so soft, and so full. From the long hairs of the coat blankets and ropes are made. The skin provides the best leather for the sock-like boots worn in Kashmir and the Pamirs.

THE WILD GOAT

Capra hircus Linnaeus

Plate facing p. 254

[RACE IN INDIA : *blythi* Hume]

Local Names. Sindhi *ter, sarah* ; Baluchi *pashin, pachin* ; English *Sind Ibex.*

Size. A full-grown male is about 37 in. (95 cm.) high at the shoulder ; females are less. Good horns measure 40 inches (100 cm.) round the curve. The record measurement is 52.5 in. (134.4 cm.), with a girth of 7 in. (17.8 cm.).

Distinctive Characters. A handsome bearded goat, brownish grey in winter, short-haired, yellowish or rufous-brown in summer. The underparts are whitish. Old males are lighter coloured. Well-grown bucks have a dark stripe running from the nape of the neck along the back to the root of the tail, and a cross stripe down each shoulder. The face, the chin with its beard (developed only in the male), the throat, the tail, the front of the legs except the knees, and a stripe along the flanks are dark brown. The horns of the male are long and scimitar-like. They sweep back in a graceful curve.

Unlike the flat and regularly knobbed horns of the ibex, they are compressed in front into a narrow jagged keel. Horns of females ribbed, much smaller, erect, and curving slightly backwards.

Distribution. Hills and mountains of south-western Asia from the Caucasus to Sind. Within our limits, the Wild Goat is found on the barren hills of Baluchistan and western Sind, but not east or northeast of the Bolan Pass and Quetta, where it is replaced by the markhor. The Sind-Baluch race, the **Sind Wild Goat** (*C. h. blythi* Hume), is distinguished by its smaller size.

Habits. The Sind Wild Goat lives in small or large herds. In the arid hills of the Khirthar range their environment is one of jagged rock and loose stones, thorn and cactus with little or no water, a furnace of heat in summer, freezing cold in winter. Like all goats, they are active, agile, and sure-footed, leaping from ledge to ledge, stopping short to balance on a pinnacle of rock where there is scarcely a foothold. They go to rest on some commanding ridge whence the sentinels of the flock can obtain a view of the surrounding slopes.

The ' bezoar stone ', formerly famed in Europe and regarded in the East as an antidote to poison and a remedy in many diseases, is a hard concretion found in the stomach of this goat. The young are produced between January and March.

The species is of special interest as being the chief ancestral stock from which the various breeds of domestic goats are derived.

THE MARKHOR

Capra falconeri (Wagner)

Plate facing p. 254

[RACES IN INDIA : *falconeri* (Wagner), *megaceros* Hutton, *jerdoni* Hume, *cashmiriensis* Lydekker, *chialtanensis* Lydekker]

Local Names. Punjab and south Kashmir *markhor* ; Ladaki *raphoche* (male), *rawache* (female).

Size. Height at shoulder of old males, 38 to 41 in. (95 to 100 cm.). Record horn measurements : Astor and Pir Panjal, 65 in. (165.1 cm.) ; Suleman, 48½ in. (123.2 cm.) ; Kabul, 39⅝ in. (100 cm.).

Distinctive Characters. An old male, with his great horns and flowing beard, and his mane falling from neck and shoulders to the knees, has a dignified and patriarchal appearance. The winter coat is a rusty iron-grey ; in summer, the hair is shorter and reddish brown in tinge. Old males become more or less white. Young males are not as copiously bearded as the veterans. Females are dark fawn and about half the size of a well-grown male. Some wear a scanty beard. Markhor carry magnificent horns. These show more or less constant variation in form in different areas. Otherwise there is nothing to really distinguish the five known races. The typical Markhor (*C. f. falconeri*) inhabits Astor. Its horns diverge widely and form an open spiral. Horns of this type are also seen in Baltistan and Gilgit. Markhor from the Pir Panjal and Kaj-i-nag Mountains (*C. f. cashmiriensis*) have horns which diverge less and, in fine heads, show two complete twists or spirals. This type is also common in Baltistan, Gilgit, and Chitral. In the hills on the northern edge of Peshawar, the horns assume the straight corkscrew pattern, typical of Markhor living in the mountains of north Afghanistan. The race is known as the **Kabul Markhor** (*C. f. megaceros*). The straightening of the horns and the accentuation of the spiral twist reaches its extreme in the **Suleman Markhor** (*C. f. jerdoni*), which is found in the Suleman Mountains in the trans-Indus districts of the Punjab. The Markhor of the mountain ranges of Baluchistan, curiously enough, show two forms of horns, one resembling the wide-spanned Astor type, and the other the Pir Panjal form with its more modified sweep. In the Markhor of the Chialtan Range near Quetta (*C. f. chialtanensis*) the horns form an open spiral of rather more than one complete turn, with the front and hind keels ascending so that at the completion of the first turn the hind keel is situated on the inner border of the horn.

Distribution. Himalayas from the Valley of Kashmir westwards, and Hindu-Kush.

Habits. Markhor live under varying conditions. The **Astor Markhor** with widely diverging horns although living where there is much forest keeps mainly to the open. In the Pir Panjal and Kaj-i-nag ranges, where their horns are less divergent, this goat is an inhabitant of the dense pine and birch forests, whose grassy glades form their grazing grounds. In the Suleman Range, Markhor live on the barren and bare slopes, exposed to intense cold in winter and to the fiercest heat in summer. Their habitat here is similar to the habitat of the urial in the arid hills of the Punjab and Sind. Like the urial, this wild goat shows a remarkable adaptability to the most contrasting conditions of environment.

Markhor seldom go higher than the snow-line. Their sensitiveness to cold is attributed to the absence of underwool, with which ibex, snow-loving creatures, are so well provided. In winter they descend to comparatively low levels. The ground they like best is precipitous crag and rock where they are more secure from attack even when lying up for the day.

Like other goats, they live in herds which haunt particular nullahs and particular bits of ground in such nullahs. Early in the year Markhor are to be found low down near the side entrances of the nullahs, later they inhabit the highest precipices near the head of a nullah. No wild goat excels the Markhor in climbing difficult and dangerous ground. They live, like other goats and sheep, in mixed herds, but in summer the veteran males live apart, either alone or 4 or 5 of them together. In the Himalayas the old males rejoin the herds between October and December when the rut takes place. The young, one or two in number, are born in May and June.

THE HIMALAYAN TAHR

Hemitragus jemlahicus (H. Smith)

Plate facing p. 254

[RACES IN INDIA : *jemlahicus* (H. Smith), *schaeferi* Pohle]

Local Names. Western Himalayas *tehr, jehr* ; Kash. *kras, jagla* ; Nepali *jharal.*

Size. Height of male at shoulder, 36 to 40 inches (90 to 100 cm.) ; weight about 200 lb. (90 kg.). Horns 12 to 15 inches (30 cm. to 40 cm.) ; record, 16½ inches (41.9 cm.) with a girth of 10 inches (25. 4 cm.). Females, smaller in build with horns seldom exceeding 10 inches.

Distinctive Characters. A wild goat with a finely formed head, narrow erect ears, a heayy body, and long, robust limbs. The hair on head and face is short. The body is covered with tangled masses of coarse, flowing hair. On the neck and shoulders it grows in a mane which sweeps down to the knees. The colouring is very variable. Generally it is a deep reddish brown, and there is a dark mid-dorsal streak, not always distinct. Old males are darker, particularly about the back and quarters. Ewes and young males are lighter brown ; kids much paler.

The horns are short and close-set. They are stout at the base, keeled in front, and wrinkled except towards the tips. They curve backwards, and in old bucks continue downwards.

Distribution. Throughout the Himalayas from the Pir Panjal to Sikkim and Bhutan.

Habits. Of all wild goats, Tahr perhaps select the most inaccessible ground to live in. They are found in several vegetation types between 2500 and 4400 m., their favourite habitat is a precipitous terrain of towering cliffs, rocks, dense scrub, and forest. Ibex and markhor ascend equally difficult ground as nimbly when driven to, but the Tahr makes such terrain its natural home. Few Himalayan animals so tax the skill and endurance of the hunter. Their love of shade and shelter gives them further protection. Females frequently come out to graze in open clearings, but not the old males. They bury themselves in the forests of oak and ringal and cane. From such shelter they emerge only in the evening and are never found outside it after the sun has well risen. Like all true goats, Tahr live in herds. About March and April, before the snows have melted, they crowd into the bottoms of the valleys, and at this time of the year are more accessible to the hunter. Later they ascend to higher and more unattainable retreats. In the late summer, the old males live away from the herds ; they rejoin the females late in the autumn. They rut in the winter and fight savagely for the possession of the females. Combats on such precipitous ground, where an animal can scarcely obtain a foothold, sometimes end in one or the other of the contestants crashing down the crags. Many are said to be killed in this way. The young are born in May and June. No offspring was produced as a result of Tahr crossing with tame goats. The flesh of the female Tahr is excellent, but that of old males is rank with a strong ' goaty ' scent. Nevertheless it is much relished by local people.

THE NILGIRI TAHR

Hemitragus hylocrius (Ogilby)

Plate facing p. 254

Local Names. Tamil and Kan. *Varai ádoo* ; Mal. *mulla átu* ; English *Nilgiri Ibex.*

Size. Slightly larger than the Himalayan Tahr, standing 39 to 42 in. (100 to 110 cm.) at the shoulder. The record buck horns measure 17½ in. (44.5 cm.) with a girth of 9⅞ in. (25.1 cm.) ; the record doe, 14 in. (35.6 cm.).

Distinctive Characters. The Nilgiri Tahr is a near relative of the Himalayan species. Its short crisp coat, the rounded outer surface of its horns, and the presence of only a single pair of teats are distinguishing characters.

The general colour of the animal is a dark yellowish brown, paler on the undersurface. Does and young bucks are grey. With age the bucks get a very deep brown, almost black, coat with a distinctive light ' saddle patch ' on the loins. From a distance the saddle looks almost white. In build, bucks are far heavier and stockier than the does.

The horns, almost in contact at the base, rise parallel for some length, then diverge and curve downwards in a bold sweep. They are deeply wrinkled. The knotted keel in front, so distinctive in the horns of the Himalayan Tahr, is absent.

Distribution. From the Nilgiris to the Anaimalais and thence southwards along the Western Ghats at elevations from 4000 to 6000 ft. (1220 to 1830 m.). The isolated distribution of this wild goat so far south of the usual range is taken to indicate the existence, at some remote epoch of the Earth's history, of temperate conditions which enabled Tahr to inhabit the country now lying between the Himalayas and their present-day refuge in the temperate levels of the south Indian hill ranges.

Habits. The preferred habitat of Tahr in the Nilgiris is the scarps and crags which rise above forest level. Occasionally Tahr graze in those grassy upland downs so characteristic of the south Indian hills. Like all goats they associate in flocks of half a dozen or more animals, which may at times assemble to form much larger herds. They graze early in the mornings and again in the late afternoons. During the hottest hours of the day Tahr retire to rest in the shelter of the crags and rocks. They are quick and sharp-sighted, quite as wary as Himalayan Tahr or the markhor, and just as active and sure-footed on precipitous ground. During hours of rest one or more does stand ' sentinel '. It is a common habit among all wild goats. As with ibex and other wild goats which retire to rest above their feeding grounds trusting to the inaccessibility of their shelter, Tahr are exceedingly watchful against any danger approaching from below but less conscious of an enemy which may descend upon them from above. Many are killed by panthers, a few by tigers, and some probably fall victim to roving packs of wild dog. Excessive shooting considerably reduced their number but strict preservation has since helped somewhat to restore the population. In a census taken by the Nilgiri Wild Life Association in May 1975 as many as 334 animals were seen and the total number on the Nilgiri plateau was estimated as at least 450. As to the main rutting season there is nothing recorded. The old bucks desert the herds during the hot weather and at this time, more often than not, are found solitary. Kids are seen with the herds in most months of the year. Sometimes two are produced at a birth, but one is more usual. The majority are born at the commencement of the hot weather.

An old male Tahr has the usual strong odour of a goat, and its flesh is rank and unpalatable, but that of the does and young males is excellent. The total population is about 1000.

18. Goat-Antelopes

THE GOAT-ANTELOPES, a general name for Serow, Goral, and Takin, form the third division of the Bovidae, which is known as the **Rupicaprinae.** They are said to hold an intermediate position between 'goats' on the one side and that heterogeneous assemblage of animals on the other which is collectively known as 'antelopes'. All of them are mountain animals. Most have a more or less goat-like build, goat-like teeth, and short tails. Relatively small cylindrical horns are present in both sexes. The group also includes the Chamois (*Rupicapra rupicapra*), the type from which the name of the group is derived, and the Rocky Mountain Goat, *Oreanus americanus*, of North America.

Distinctive Characters. Serow and Goral have distinctive conical horns. They curve backwards and have not the terminal hook seen in the straight horns of the Chamois. Though there is a superficial resemblance between them, Serow and Goral differ much in the structure of the skull. Further, unlike Goral, Serow have well-developed face glands which rest in a depression in the skull. The gland opens by a small orifice in front of the eyes. At times the opening looks like a small sore. It exudes a whitish secretion which, when dry, has the consistency and smell of gum arabic. Serow have a strong 'goaty' odour — a characteristic which they share with sheep and goats. This odour appears to come from the surface of the skin and not from any special glands.

Goral are much smaller animals than Serow. They have no face glands, but are furnished with foot glands similar to those found in sheep. These glands open by a small orifice in front of the pastern, above the hoof. It is not known whether Serow have them. Strangely enough, in the structure of its skull, the Goral approaches the Takin. This resemblance suggests a kinship which one would not easily have suspected taking into consideration the widely different appearance of these two animals.

The Takin is a large heavily-built aberrant form of goat-antelope. It lacks that lightness of limb and body to which Serow and Goral owe their agility. The horns, which are thick and nearly in contact at the base, grow outward, downward or forward, and then take an abrupt curve upward or backward in the same direction as the plane of the face.

THE SEROW

Capricornis sumatraensis (Bechstein)

Plate facing p. 255

[RACES IN INDIA : *thar* (Hodgson), *humei* Pocock, *rodoni* Pocock, *jamrachi* Pocock]

Local Names. NW. Himalayas *sarao* ; Kash. *ramu, halj, salabhir*; Sikkim *gya* ; Bur. *taut tshiek* ; Malay *kambing utan.*

Size. Old males, 39 to 42 inches (100 to 110 cm.) at the shoulder ; weight, over 200 lb. (90 kg.) ; horns, 9 to 10 inches (23 to 25 cm.) in length, 5 to 6 inches (13 to 15 cm.) in girth.

Distinctive Characters. With its large head, donkey-like ears, thick neck, and short limbs the Serow is an ungainly creature. Its habit of standing with its forelegs astraddle, the hoofs widely splayed and its head thrust downward, adds to its awkward appearance. Both sexes are similar in build.

The coat is coarse and rather thin in Serow which live at lower elevations ; its colour varies so much that it is difficult to describe. It ranges from grizzled black or blackish grey-roan to red. In the darker animals the head, the neck, and the mane which covers the nape and . withers are grizzled black. The black passes into rusty red on the shoulders, flanks, and lower thighs, and turns a dirty grey on the inside of the limbs and belly. There is a varying amount of white on the muzzle, throat, and chest. In the Himalayan races the limbs are chestnut above and dirty white below. From this there is a transition to the Malay Serows in which the limbs are wholly black.

Horns are common to both sexes. They are black, conical, and closely wrinkled for three quarters of their length.

Distribution. The Himalayas from Kashmir to the Mishmi Hills in Assam, eastwards through the hill ranges of Yunan and Sze-chuan, the hills of Burma, Siam, Malay Peninsula, and Sumatra. From this wide area several races have been described.

Habits. In the Himalayas Serow favour an elevation between 6000 to 10,000 ft. (1850 to 3050 m.). In the Burmese hill ranges they may be met with at a height which varies from 700 to 8000 ft. (200 to 2450 m.).

Serow live in the recesses of thickly-wooded gorges whose boulder-strewn slopes and shallow caves give shelter from the weather. In the mornings and evenings they come out to feed on the rank herbage of the more open slopes. They are more or less solitary creatures, though four or five may be seen feeding on the same hill. Their movements belie their awkward appearance. They are exceedingly active animals, not only on rock but also on flat ground. When disturbed, Serow dash away with a hissing snort. Their call is a whistling scream. The female usually has one kid at a birth, sometimes two. In the Himalayas the rut commences at the end of October, and the young are born in May and June. In Burma the young are born about the end of September. The period of gestation is said to be about seven months.

THE GORAL

Nemorhaedus goral (Hardwicke)

Plates facing pp. 241, 255

[RACES IN INDIA : *goral* (Hardwicke), *hodgsoni* Pocock]

Local Names. NW. Himalayas *goral* ; Kash. *pij, pijur, rai, rom* ; Sikkim Bhotia *ra giyu* ; Assamese *deo chagal*.

Size. Height at shoulder, 26 to 28 inches (65 to 70 cm.) ; weight, from 58 to 63 lb. (25 to 30 kg.) ; horns, about 5 inches (13 cm.).

Distinctive Characters. A stocky goat-like animal. Hair coarse, forming a small crest on the neck.

Two races of goral are found within Indian limits : the **Grey Goral** [*N. g. goral* (Hardwicke)] of Kashmir and the western Himalayas, and the **Brown Goral** (*N. g. hodgsoni* Pocock) of Nepal and Sikkim.

The general colour of the Grey Goral is a yellowish grey suffused with black. Individuals differ, but no Grey Goral has the pale area of the hairs tinged with rufous or brown. The chin, upper lip, underside of the jaws, and throat patch are white. The dark spinal stripe, if present, does not pass beyond the withers. There is no stripe down the middle of the tail, and none up the back of the thighs.

The Brown Goral is distinguished by its golden or rufous-brown coat, speckled with black. The black spinal stripe reaches to the root of the tail, but tapers away and is indistinct on the croup. The tail is black above. A dark ill-defined stripe runs up the back of the thigh from the hocks.

Goral have short insignificant horns. They diverge slightly, curve backwards, and are marked with rings or ridges for the greater part of their length.

Distribution. Grey Goral, western to eastern Himalayas. Brown Goral, eastern Himalayas to Assam.

Habits. In the Himalayas, Goral favour an elevation of 3000 to 9000 ft. (900 to 2750 m.) ; though they may ascend to and have been observed at 13,000 to 14,000 ft. (3950 to 4250 m.). In the Arakan and Chin Hills, Goral are found above 3000 ft. (900 m.). This is one of the best known of Himalayan animals, frequently seen near hill-stations. Where one is seen others are not far off. They usually associate in small parties of four to eight feeding on rugged grassy hill-sides, or rocky ground in forest, usually in the mornings and evenings, and in cloudy weather at all hours. The loud ' hiss ' given when one is alarmed is repeated by the others. In the Himalayas young are born in May and June.

THE TAKIN

Budorcas taxicolor Hodgson

Plate facing p. 255

[RACE IN INDIA : *taxicolor* Hodgson]

Size. Height at the shoulder, 3½ ft. (110 cm.).

Distinctive Characters. The Takin is a clumsy heavy animal, which from the shape of its horns looks as if it might be some relation to the gnu, or to the musk ox, though there is no structural affinity between them. Its most striking feature is its immense convex ' face ', heavy mouth, and tremendously thick neck. The muzzle, except for a bare spot at the extremity, is covered with hair. It is a character seen also in the yak and is associated with life at high altitudes, where the snow in winter has to be scraped away to get at the vegetation beneath. The Takin's heavy body is supported by exceptionally short, thick legs, thicker than those of the gaur. Its withers are slightly raised and its narrow back arches in the centre and slopes downward to the root of the tail.

There is a great variety of colour in Takin, ranging from dark brown to golden yellow. The withers are conspicuously lighter in tone. Adult males of the Mishmi Takin are golden-yellow merging into dark brown or black on the flanks and quarters. There is a dark dorsal stripe. Young males are reddish brown in front merging into black. Calves all black. Females are greyer than the bulls with no trace of yellow. The dark dorsal stripe is inconspicuous in females and young males.

The horns of a young Takin grow straight up from the head with an outward tendency. Later they grow outwards and downwards. In the final stage the horns grow forward and bend downward and outward with the points growing up.

Distribution. There are said to be three forms. The **Mishmi Takin** (*B. t. taxicolor* Hodgson) is found in the Bhutan Himalayas, the Mishmi Hills, and in the mountains of the Salween-Irrawaddy divide.

Habits. Takin live in the steepest and most thickly wooded declivities of their native mountains. In the Mishmi Hills they have been seen in tropical forest as low as 3000 to 4000 ft. (900 to 1200 m.). They are usually found in dense bamboo and rhododendron jungle at an elevation of 7000 to 10,000 ft. (2135 to 3050 m.). In the summer months they collect in herds of considerable size ; as many as 300 have been observed congregated about a hot spring to drink—they went into cover at midday and came out in the late afternoon. In the winter the herds break up into smaller parties. In western China, the rut takes place in July-August. The calves, usually one, are dropped towards the end of March or early in April.

19. Antelopes, Gazelles

ANTELOPES AND GAZELLES form other sub-divisions of the family Bovidae. As a group they cannot be classified either with the oxen or with the sheep and goats. They bear characters common to both. As in point of evolution they are the earliest known ruminants and in structure the most generalised, it is believed that antelopes represent the original stock from which oxen on the one hand and sheep on the other were derived. If this be the case it is easy to see how in their general structure they present affinities to both. These animals, so varied in size and form, are classified in a number of sub-families, two of which, the Pantholopinae and the Antilopinae are considered here. The **Pantholopinae** contains a single genus the Chiru or Tibetan Antelope, remarkable for its swollen nose and elegant horns. Though very unlike in appearance, the Chiru is a relative of the Saiga Antelope of the Russian Steppes. Both the Saiga and the Chiru have the same curious trunk-like development of the muzzle. The snout of the Chiru is however not as trunk-like as the Saiga's. It is but slightly bent downward and not so inflated at the sides. The **Antilopinae** contains the other antelopes and gazelles.

Structure and Habits. In their general structure antelopes and gazelles resemble other members of the Bovidae. As a whole antelopes are characterised by their graceful build. The horns, which may or may not be present in the females, are generally long, more or less cylindrical, and often lyre-shaped. They are commonly marked with prominent rings. The bony cores of the horns instead of being honeycombed with air spaces as in oxen, sheep, and goats are nearly solid throughout. Antelopes generally have a gland under the eyes, a character in which they differ from the oxen and goats. The swollen gland below the eyes of the Indian Antelope or Blackbuck attracts attention. Outwardly this gland takes the form of a vertical slit of black, nearly hairless skin. The slit opens into a deep hair-lined, perforated pocket into which the secretion of the underlying gland exudes. Large inguinal glands are present ; as also large glands between the hooves. The purpose of these glands as a means of communication has been indicated.

If antelopes are elegant in build, gazelles are the *élite* of the family. They are characterised by their sandy colouring and a distinctive white streak on each side of the face. The facial markings are absent in the Tibetan Gazelle. Horns are present in both sexes. They are completely ringed throughout. Characteristic of gazelles are the tufts of hair growing from the knees.

Of Indian species, two live in the Temperate Zone. They are the Tibetan Antelope (*Pantholops hodgsoni*) and the Tibetan Gazelle (*Procapra picticaudata* Hodgson) which inhabit the Tibetan plateau. The remaining species are tropical. Antelopes and gazelles are essentially creatures of open plains and grassland. Constant persecution by man has sadly reduced their number, and the vast herds which once roamed the plains of north India, where antelopes thrive best, are now no more. The social life of these animals as regards the composition of the herds and breeding habits differ in no essential respect from that of other members of the Bovidae.

THE CHIRU, or TIBETAN ANTELOPE

Pantholops hodgsoni (Abel)

Plate facing p. 255

Local Names. Tibetan *tsus* (male), *chus* (female), *chiru*, *chuku*.

Size. The male Chiru stands 32 in. (80 cm.) at the shoulder. Horns measure between 24 and 26 in. (60 and 65 cm.). The record pair is 27¾ in. (70.5 cm.).

Distinctive Characters. The Chiru is remarkable for its swollen snout. The muzzle is peculiarly swollen in the male. It is suggested that this inflation of the nose may have some connection with the high altitudes at which Chiru live. Each nostril is furnished inside with a large lateral chamber or sac whose function may assist in breathing the rarified atmosphere of high altitudes.

Another peculiarity of the Chiru is the unusual development of the inguinal or groin glands. Perhaps the function of these glands, which are possessed also by other ruminants, is to scent the ground, and so indicate to other individuals of a herd the place where one of them has rested. Chiru are known to lie concealed in shallow pits which they scrape out for themselves in the sand. Large scent glands are also present between the fore and hind hooves of the Chiru. It has no face glands. Its body is covered with dense wool. The colour is variable. Generally it is pale fawn above and white below. The whole of the face and a stripe down the front of each leg is black or dark brown in the bucks. The horns of the bucks rise close together ; they diverge towards the tips and curve slightly forward. The long slender horns seen in profile may well suggest a one-horned animal. The Chiru is classed among the animals which gave origin to the belief in the fabled unicorn. Females are hornless.

Distribution. Chiru inhabit the great desert of northern Tibet. The only spot in Indian territory in which they are found is the Chang Chen Mo Valley, into which they cross from Tibet by way of the Lanak La pass at the head of the valley.

Habits. Chiru live in vast herds in the Chang Tang desert of northern Tibet. Some straggle into the Chang Chen Mo Valley in northern Ladak, but they are not found there in any numbers till mid-summer, when their favourite haunts are the grassy flats bordering the plains of the Chang Chen Mo River, and also the ravines which lead from the higher ground to the river valley. In the summer, the river flats carry an abundant crop of grass on which Chiru graze. In the early summer the herds frequent the higher plains and more exposed slopes but, as the snow in the river flats melts, Chiru descend lower to feed on the sprouting grass. They are usually seen in small parties which may consist exclusively of bucks, or of bucks and does. After grazing in the morning, a herd retire to rest in some higher and more exposed situation from which ' sentinels ' secure a good view. Like all game animals in these exposed heights, Chiru depend as much on sight as on smell to warn them of the approach of an enemy. When resting Chiru excavate deep hollows in which they lie. Towards evening they come down to feed again. The rut takes place during the winter and the young are produced in May or June.

THE CHINKARA, or INDIAN GAZELLE

Gazella gazella (Pallas)

Plate facing p. 272

[RACE IN INDIA : *bennetti* (Sykes)]

Local Names. Hindi *chinkara, kal punch* ; Tel. *burra jinka.*

Size. A full-grown male measures about 26 inches (65 cm.) at the shoulder and weighs about 50 lb. (23 kg.). The horns average 10 to 12 inches (25 to 30 cm.) and rarely exceed this length in southern India. The best heads are seen in Rajputana and the arid tracts of the North-West. The record is slightly over 16 inches (40 cm.). Horns of does, usually 4 to 5 inches (10 to 13 cm.).

Distinctive Characters. A small gazelle of slender graceful build. The body above is light chestnut, the colour deepening where it joins the white of the underparts on the flanks and buttocks. The white disc around the tail, so prominent in the Tibetan Gazelle, is absent. There is the usual white streak down each side of the face, so characteristic of all gazelles, and a dusky patch above the nose. The horns of the male appear almost straight when seen from the front; in profile they take a slightly S-shaped curve. They have 15 to 25 rings. Horns of female, smooth. Hornless females are not uncommon.

Distribution. The plains and low hills of north-western and central India extending through the open lands of the Deccan to a little south of the Krishna River.

Habits. Wastelands broken up by nullahs and ravines, scattered bush, and thin jungle are the usual haunts of Chinkara. They are common in the sand-hills of the desert zone, and in the Salt Range, Punjab, ascend to levels of about 4000 ft. (1200 m.). They are shy of man, and are not so frequently seen in cultivation. In all this they differ from blackbuck, which prefer level plains and un-dulating country and commonly enter fields. Chinkara lie up earlier in the day and come out later in the evening. When alarmed the herd goes off at a wild pace, and then stops some 200 or 300 yards (180 or 275 m.) away to discover the cause of the alarm. Sight, scent, and hearing are all equally developed in these animals.

The food consists of grass, of various leaves, crops, and fruits, such as pumpkins and melons. They go without water for long periods, and do without it completely in desert country, deriving such moisture as they need from herbage and dew, but drink when there is water to be had, particularly in the hot weather.

Chinkara are less gregarious than Blackbuck and live in smaller herds. The average group size is 3 but occasionally herds of up to 25 animals are seen. They do not have a particular breeding season but there are two birth peaks, the major one in April and a minor one in autumn. The males are territorial and hold territories of about 200 m. diameter demarcated by fecal stations used repeatedly by the male. The gestation period is 5½ months.

Reference must be made here to the **Tibetan Gazelle,** *Procapra picticaudata* Hodgson (Race in India : *picticaudata* Hodgson), which inhabits north-eastern Ladak, the Tibetan plateau, and Shensi. Its pale coat, short and slaty grey in summer, dense and pale fawn in winter, and white rump patch are distinctive. The horns rise vertically and curve sharply backwards. A good head tapes 12 inches (30 cm.) ; the record is 15½ inches (39.4 cm.).

THE BLACKBUCK, ÒR INDIAN ANTELOPE

Antilope cervicapra (Linnaeus)

Plate facing p. 272

[RACES IN INDIA : *cervicapra* (Linnaeus), *rupicapra*
Müller, *rajputanae* Zukowsky, *centralis* Zukowsky]

Local Names. Sanskrit *ena* (male), *harina* (female), *mriga* ; Hindi
harna (male), *harni* (female), *kalwit* (female), *mrig* ; Mar. *haran,*
kalwit (male) ; Tamil *moorukoo marn* ; Kan. *hoola kerra* ; Tel.
jinka.

Size. A well-grown buck stands about 32 in. (80 cm.) at the shoulder
and on the average weighs about 90 lb. (40 kg.). Horns seldom
exceed 20 in. (50 cm.) in the South but may reach 25 in. (65 cm.)
or more in north India.

Distinctive Characters. The Blackbuck is the sole representative in
India of the genus *Antilope.* Its striking colour and its beautiful
spiralled horns, which may reach the shoulder height of the animal,
give it an elegance hardly equalled by any antelope. This exclusively
Indian animal is perhaps the most beautiful of all its kind.
   When young, its coat, like that of the does, is a yellowish fawn.
When three years old it commences to turn black. This darkening
of the coat varies in intensity. In south India the adult buck is
rarely black, his coat remains a dark brown. Well-matured brown
bucks may again be seen in all parts of the country. In general there
is a fading in the richness of tone during the hot weather and an
increase in its velvety lustre after the rains.
   In the yearling buck the horns are without a spiral. In the second
year a large open spiral is developed. It is believed that the full
number of spiral twists is attained with the dark coat about the end
of the third year. Horned females are occasionally, but rarely, met
with. Females attain sexual maturity between the age of 19 and
23 months.

Distribution. Blackbuck used to occur in practically all the plains
area except along the Indian coast southward from the neighbourhood of Surat. They avoid forest or hill tracts.

Habits. Blackbuck are usually seen in herds of 20 or 30, though in
Rajputana and the Punjab gatherings may number several hundreds.
These antelopes live in open plains covered with scrub or cultivation.
They enter open forests which contain wide expanses of grass, and
where much persecuted seek refuge in such cover. They feed on
grass and various cereal crops. Usually Blackbuck graze till near
noon, and again in the late afternoon, lying down to rest during the

hot hours of the day. Their sense of hearing is moderate, scent fair. Keen eyesight and speed are their protection. When alarmed the herd moves off in a series of light leaps and bounds, and then breaks into a gallop. The leadership of a herd is usually vested in an old and vigilant female. Blackbuck breed at all seasons, but the main rut takes place between February and March, when the bucks fight each other for the possession of the does. They are particularly pugnacious at this time. A buck then struts about with a peculiar mincing gait, uttering short challenging grunts, with its head thrown upwards so that its horns lie along its back and with its face glands widely open. During this time a buck may desert his harem taking a favoured doe with him. One or two young are produced at a time. These the mother usually conceals in the grass. But they gain strength rapidly and soon rejoin the herd.

THE FOURHORNED ANTELOPE, or CHOWSINGHA

Tetracerus quadricornis (Blainville)

Plate facing p. 272

Local Names. Hindi *chowsingha, chowka, doda ;* Tamil *narl komboo marn ;* Kan. *koondoo kooree poki.*

Size. Height of male at shoulder, 25 in. (65 cm.). The posterior horns are usually 3 to 4 inches (8 to 10 cm.) long, the anterior ½ to 1 in. (1 to 2.5 cm.). The maximum recorded length is posterior 7¼ in. (18.40 cm.) and anterior 3 in. (7.60 cm.).

Distinctive Characters. The Fourhorned Antelope or Chowsingha and the Nilgai are distinguishable from the true antelopes (Antilopinae) by several characters. Among the more obvious points of distinction is the structure of the horns which are not ringed as in true antelopes. They are keeled in front. The females are hornless. These animals are grouped in a separate sub-family the **Boselaphinae.**

The Fourhorned Antelope or Chowsingha is the only member of this group with two pairs of horns. Of these the front pair are always the shorter. At times they are no more than horn-covered studs or mere bony knobs under the skin.

One of the most interesting features in the Chowsingha is the presence of a pair of well-developed glands between the false hooves of the hindlegs in both males and females. This is the only member of the group which has such glands.

The colour of its coarse coat is dull red-brown above and white below ; old bucks are yellowish. There is a dark stripe down the front of each leg. It is broader and more defined on the forelegs.

Distribution. Peninsular India south of the Himalayas where the country is wooded and hilly, but not too densely forested. Not found on the Malabar Coast.

Habits. The Chowsingha lives in undulating or hill country, and shelters in tall grass and open jungle, a terrain more usual to deer than to antelope. In this environment it has developed some of the habits of deer. It has a low whistling call, which the bucks repeat frequently in the hot weather. The alarm note is like a Muntjac's but lower in tone.

These little animals drink regularly. They are much more dependent on water than others of their kind and seldom live far from it. The edge of the jungle round a village tank is a favourite resort. Again, unlike antelopes, they do not gather in large herds. Chowsingha are usually seen alone or in pairs. In the early part of the year, before the rains, the female may be accompanied by one or two fawns. Sometimes two old animals and two young will be seen together, or even a buck with four or five does. They have a habit of defecating in one place.

The breeding season is in the hot weather and rains and young are born from October to February. The period of gestation is 8 to 8½ months. Taken young the Chowsingha is easily tamed.

THE NILGAI, or BLUE BULL

Boselaphus tragocamelus (Pallas)

Plate facing p. 272

Local Names. Hindi *nil, nilgai, rojh, roz, rojra;* Mar. *rohu, nilgai, nil* (male).

Size. Males, usually 52 to 56 in. (130 to 140 cm.) high ; may reach 58 in. (150 cm.). Females, much smaller. Horns average 8 in. (20 cm.) ; the maximum recorded length is 11¾ in. (29.8 cm.).

Distinctive Characters. A great ungainly animal somewhat horse-like in build, with high withers and low rump.

The adult bull has a coarse iron-grey coat, a white ring below each fetlock and two white spots on each cheek. His lips, chin, the inside of his ears, and the undersurface of his tail are white. Young bulls and the cows are tawny. Both sexes have dark manes and the males wear a distinctive tuft of stiff black hairs on the throat. The bulls have stout cone-like horns. They are distinctly keeled, triangular at the base and circular towards the tips.

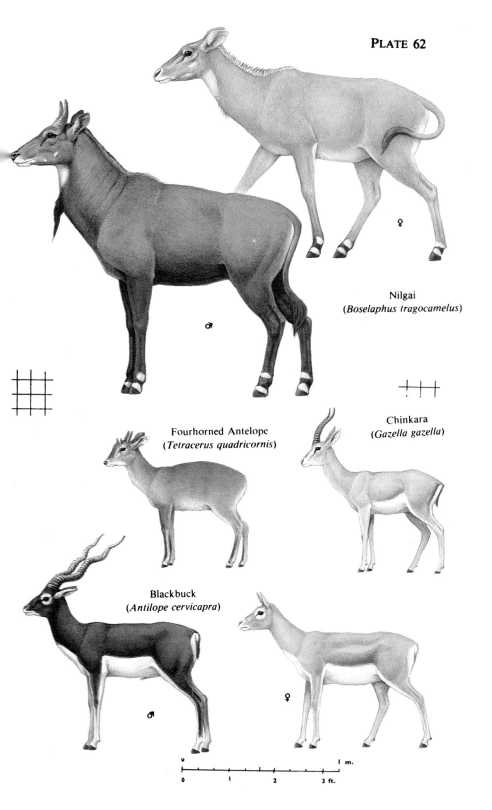

PLATE 62

♀

Nilgai
(*Boselaphus tragocamelus*)

♂

Fourhorned Antelope
(*Tetracerus quadricornis*)

Chinkara
(*Gazella gazella*)

Blackbuck
(*Antilope cervicapra*)

♂

♀

0   1   2   3 ft.

0   1 m.

PLATE 63

Sambar
(*Cervus unicolor*)

Kashmir Stag
(*Cervus elaphus hanglu*)

Thamin
(*Cervus eldi*)

Swamp Deer
(*Cervus duvauceli*)

Chital
(*Axis axis*)

Distribution. The Nilgai is found only in the Indian peninsula from the base of the Himalayas to Mysore. It does not occur in eastern Bengal, or Assam, or on the Malabar Coast.

Habits. Nilgai avoid dense forests. Their usual haunts are hills sparsely dotted with trees, or level or undulating plains covered with grass and patches of scrub. They freely enter cultivation and are a source of damage to crops. They feed till late in the morning, and again early in the evenings, caring little about the sun, seeking the shade only during the hottest hours of the day. They both graze and browse, feeding on the leaves and the fruit of the *ber* (*Zizyphus*) and other trees. The fleshy fallen flowers of the mohwa tree attract Nilgai, as they attract so many other animals. Nilgai can do for long periods without water, and even during the hot weather do not drink regularly. A grunting sound, which is the alarm cry, sends the herd away in the ungainly slouching gallop, heads held up as if gazing at the stars. Smell and sight are good in these animals, hearing moderately developed. Their chief means of escape is speedy movement. It would take a good horse to catch up with a bull, especially with its ability to cover the most difficult ground at speed. Nilgai like antelope have the habit of resorting to the same spot to deposit their droppings, forming in this way considerable accumulations. Such a rendezvous may be a means of re-assembling scattered members of a herd.

Four to ten is the usual number seen together, sometimes as many as twenty or more. Cows, calves, and younger bulls associate together. As with other members of the Bovidae, old bulls keep to themselves, or a few may associate together. The young are produced at all seasons. The period of gestation is eight to nine months. The female attains sexual maturity at the age of 25 months. Few sportsmen care about shooting Nilgai. In many parts of India they enjoy complete immunity, being regarded as a near relative of the cow and therefore sacred

20. Deer

THE GENERAL STRUCTURE of deer is in conformity with the structure of Bovine ruminants. Among the points of distinction is a large fissure or opening in the skull below each eye called the 'lachrymal fissure'. Tushes or canine teeth are usually present in the upper jaw and, since these teeth always develop in deer, they offer a ready means of distinction from the ox family, none of which have upper tushes or canines. Moreover, with the single exception of the musk deer, no member of the group has a gall bladder so constantly present in the Bovidae. The lateral digits on all four feet are more fully developed than in the Bovidae. But the most pronounced difference is to be seen in the character of the horns. Deer are ruminants with solid horns. This character alone is sufficient to distinguish them from the Bovidae. The horns of oxen, of sheep, goats, and antelopes consist of two parts, a hollow sheath or outer cover of horn and a core of bone. A deer's antlers, except for a temporary covering of skin during growth, are nothing but solid bone. Again, with the Bovidae the horns are permanent; deer on the other hand shed and regrow their antlers periodically.

STRUCTURE IN RELATION TO HABITS

Horns. The budding antlers of a deer grow from upright bases or pedicels which are part of the skull. They first appear as velvety knobs which increase rapidly in length by the accretion of more bony matter. In young deer the antler is a simple spike. With the growth of the animal, in the process of periodic renewal, it throws out tines or branches and eventually takes the familiar form of an antler. For example a sambar stag in its first year has simple spikes. These spikes are shed, and in the second year the newly-grown antler throws out a branch or tine from near its base. In the third year a terminal tine is added. The number of tines produced varies in different species. Adult sambar, spotted deer, and hog-deer normally have but three tines to each antler. Much more complex and many-branched are the antlers of the hangul or Kashmir stag, the swamp deer, and the brow-antlered deer. The main stem or beam of a hangul's antler has a tine just above its 'burr'. This is called the 'brow tine' from its position just above the brow or forehead. Above the brow tine there are two other prominent tines, the 'bez' and higher up the 'trez' or 'royal'. In addition the summit of the antler bears a number of tines collectively known as the 'crown'. Usually each antler of a hangul has a total of five points. More remarkable for their many branches are the antlers of the swamp deer, which may show 20 points and more. The antlers after completion of the branching increase in size with each renewal. They attain a maximum development and then decline. Thus the oldest stags do not necessarily have the largest antlers.

The newly-grown antler is encased in a thick soft skin called 'velvet'. Its softness and its dense covering mat of fine hairs give it the feel and the look of velvet. This skin, fed by numerous blood vessels, is highly sensitive and easily injured. When their horns are growing, deer which live habitually in dense forests take great care to avoid any harm coming to them. Sambar to avoid any risk of damage to their growing antlers may retreat from forest to more open grass plots. Here they lead the most secluded lives moving only short distances in quest of food. Again, while their antlers are in 'velvet', deer naturally do not use them in attack or defence. Stags 'in velvet', when compelled to fight, rear up and strike with their forefeet after the manner of hinds.

When a deer's antlers have reached the limits of growth a ring of bony matter, the 'burr', forms just above the point where the antler unites with its base or pedicel. The ring gradually constricts and so cuts off the flow of blood. As its blood vessels dry up, the velvet shrinks, dries, and commences to peel off. It is eventually rubbed away by the deer. Sambar have their favourite rubbing trees for cleaning their antlers, and stags may return to a favoured tree night after night. Any tree with a smooth bark is used. Swamp deer rarely use trees for ridding their antlers of peeling velvet; the long grass of their habitat serves this purpose. Stripped of velvet all that is left is the solid hard bony structure which we call horn.

The cleansing and hardening of the antlers usually coincides with the approach of the rutting season, for the antlers of deer are weapons both for defence against beasts of prey and for use at mating time when stag fights stag for the possession of the hinds or, as with sambar, to secure territory where hinds can be acquired. In such combats the stags close in with lowered heads. The trial of strength which follows is more in the nature of a shoving match. Antlers clash or interlock with all the body's force behind them. The rivals strain and push at each other, stopping from sheer exhaustion, only to fight again. The bout goes on till one or the other acknowledges defeat and retires. Wounds from antler thrusts in such combats may be severe, but more often they are of little account and seldom mortal. There is more show and noise than deadly purpose in these combats. Death, if it comes, comes from a chance though mortal thrust. Sometimes fighting stags get their antlers so interlocked that they are unable to extricate them and so perish miserably. In the collection of the Bombay Natural History Society there is a pair of chital skulls which were picked up in a forest in Madhya Pradesh. The antlers are irremovably interlocked, evidence of a duel with this strange and tragic ending.

Antlers are however not absolutely indispensable in fights between stag and stag. Hornless Red Deer stags, known as 'hummels' in Scotland, have little difficulty in overcoming an antlered rival and acquiring a harem. These 'hummels', usually in better condition than horned stags, are able fighters. A blow in the ribs from such a polled head may discomfit an opponent as much as a thrust from the point of an antler.

Shedding of Horns. Stags wear their antlers for a period after the rut and then shed them. The time of shedding varies with age. Young stags shed them earlier than the older animals. The time of shedding may also vary with locality. Among other factors, it is said that good feeding conditions influence early shedding. This suggests some connection between food and horn-growth. The period of horn-growth everywhere coincides with the season when food is most abundant. The food itself consists mainly of grass, and grass contains an abundance of calcium which enters largely into the making of bone. It may be that this periodic shedding and growth of antlers is but an outlet for the excess intake of calcium. With the hornless hinds this excess finds its outlet in the need for providing for the developing embryo and the protracted nursing of the young. That the larger species of deer have larger antlers, that the antlers decline with age, or become defective in sickness, or as a result of wounds, may be conditioned by a larger or smaller intake of food, in other words by a higher or lower absorption of calcium. Again, irregularity in the shedding of the antlers may be associated equally with the same factor, lime deficiency. The production of antlers, where there is a deficiency of lime in the soil and therefore in the food content, certainly implies a great physical drain on the stag. In lime-deficient soils stags have been known to eat shed antlers, and even the peeling velvet from their horns, wasting nothing which might make up for the deficiency in calcium. Whatever the explanation the antlers of deer and their periodic shedding are a puzzle. Why Nature should in the case of deer alone build up a large bony structure only to destroy her handiwork year after year is difficult to understand. Stags use their antlers in fighting each other, but we have seen that hornless stags are quite as able to overcome a horned rival. Antlers again are a means of defence against carnivorous enemies and certainly provide some protection. A sambar runs with its head thrust forward. Its neck and shoulders, a common focus of attack for a leaping tiger or leopard, lie between the upturned points of its antlers. The standing stag endeavours to ward off its adversary by sweeping thrusts of its horns. These weapons may delay a conclusion, but are scarcely effective against determined attacks by tigers, leopards, or a pack of wild dog. Acute scent, hearing, and sight and speed of movement are the deer's essential means of escape.

DEER AND THEIR SURROUNDINGS

Deer are perhaps the most ancient of all the typical ruminants, making their appearance in the lower Miocene, where the species were of small size and for the most part unprovided with antlers.

Deer are for the most part inhabitants of forests or grass jungles. They are never found in desert. In the Old World deer are found over the great part of Europe and Asia, but are unknown in Africa south of the Sahara. Three of the Old World species of deer have extended their range into North America. But the other New World species which range as far south as Chile belong to quite a different type from those inhabiting the eastern Hemisphere.

Structure in relation to surroundings. Variation in size in relation to different geographical areas in which they live is seen in some of our deer. Chital attain their finest proportions in the Madhya Pradesh, the Terai, and the Himalayan foothills. With sambar on the other hand, speaking generally, the largest animals with the finest horns come from central India. North of the Ganges their antlers average smaller and are comparable with those of south India and Ceylon. Eastwards, in Assam, Burma, and the Malay countries, the antlers of sambar, though massive, are rarely more than 30 inches (75 cm.) in length. These variations in size may be associated with the nature of food conditions. But the size of the animal and its antlers may be that best suited to the nature of its habitat. The smaller, more close-set antlers of sambar in Assam and Burma are better adapted to movement in the dense forests of those countries. It is a factor which could have led to the elimination of individuals with big wide-spreading horns and to the establishment of a race with small close-set horns.

Differences in the nature of the habitat may give rise to more or less marked structural differences. Swamp deer in the Terai live in water-logged marsh lands ; in Madhya Pradesh they inhabit grass maidans where the ground is dry. This difference in habitat has led to the establishment of two distinct forms of swamp deer. Among other points of distinction are the hooves. Swamp deer in Madhya Pradesh have the small, hard, well-knit hooves of animals accustomed to gallop over hard ground, while the spongy, large, and out-splayed hooves of swamp deer in the Terai are better adapted to movement in this marshy terrain.

Another structural character associated with the surroundings is seen in the size of the ears. Both sambar and swamp deer have large, spreading ears. Much smaller and compact are the ears of the chital. Sambar live in dense forest and swamp deer conceal themselves in high grass, conditions in which range of visibility is limited, and in which hearing becomes an important factor. The larger ears of these animals are designed to pick up as much sound as is possible. Hearing is much less imperative to the chital, which inhabits more open country on the fringes of forest where visibility is less limited. Speaking generally it might be said that deer which live in dense forests have a keen scent and hearing and moderate sight, while those living in more open terrain display a more uniform development of these faculties.

Again, of all our deer, sambar have the largest and best developed facial glands. The reason again is the sambar's forest habitat, surroundings in which it is well-nigh impossible for a stag to collect a following of hinds during mating time. A sambar stag attracts hinds by his call and by the powerful odour of his scent glands which attain their maximum development during the rut. Spotted deer and swamp deer have less well-developed face glands. They have no such difficulty in securing hinds, the stags fighting in the presence of the hinds to acquire a harem.

Colour and surroundings. Seasonal changes in the colour of the coat are very marked in most deer. They exchange a light-toned summer coat for a darker winter dress. The darker coat harmonises with subdued light in forest and grass. jungle, obscured during the cold weather by a luxuriant post-monsoon vegetation. The lighter summer coat is in keeping with the excessive light of the hot weather, when forests and grass jungles are sere and dry.

Summer coats are usually spotted. Hangul fawns, hinds, and young stags are spotted in summer, so are those of swamp deer and hog deer. Their coats are dappled with white or show flecks of paler hairs, more noticeable in certain lights. A dappled coat is probably protective and makes for better concealment. The dappled markings, it is explained, break up the contours of the body. They harmonize with the broken flecks of light and shade made by sunshine filtering through leaves. In cold countries when the leaves fall in the autumn, fallow deer and other northern species, including the Kashmir hangul, change their spotted summer coats for a uniform livery more in keeping with the uniform light of the winter landscape. Their coats in summer and in winter are protective. They make for better concealment in the distinctive conditions which obtain during the two seasons. How far this applies to deer living under tropical conditions remains to be investigated. A broken background of light and shade is more or less constant in the forest surroundings where sambar habitually live. Yet the sambar's coat is without spots in summer and in winter. The chital wears its bright rows of spots at all seasons. Its coat is certainly protective in forest, it so exactly repeats the flecks of light and shade filtering through the leaves. But chital seldom live under dense cover ; they prefer the fringes of forest where their bright dappled coats draw attention and are in little harmony with their evenly-lit surroundings. It is the same with swamp deer. In the Terai where they are so common, they conceal themselves in the tall grass, but during the hot weather, when their coats are spotted, they come out

PLATE 64

Swamp Deer (*Cervus duvauceli*) stags in Kanha Sanctuary

Photo : E. P. Gee

PLATE 65

Sambar (*Cervus unicolor*) stag

Photo : M. Krishnan

to feed in the open expanses where the grass has been burnt and new grass is growing, or they wade into open stretches of water to feed on aquatic plants. A spotted coat under such conditions scarcely makes for concealment. Alike in habit is the hog-deer, it feeds among reeds and bushes by river banks where there is but little of dappled light and shade. Spots in deer, so pronounced in the young of most species, whatever their protective quality, are apparently an ancestral livery now in process of being discarded, a process already complete in the sambar and other species.

Habits and surroundings. What are the effects of the weather, of heat and cold and snow, of dryness and humidity, and of rain on the life and habits of deer? Seasonal changes bringing an abundance or scarcity of food must materially influence their habits. We know that hangul in Kashmir spend the winter on the lower slopes of the mountains and the summer on the heights. Studies made of the behaviour of deer in temperate lands may help to explain the seasonal movements in hangul, where such movements are influenced by temperature. In Scotland, it has been found that Red Deer, close relatives of the hangul, do not mind the cold as such. Their movements in response to temperature, whether seasonal or daily, are always towards equable conditions. The differences between daily minimum and maximum temperatures is less great on the summits of the mountains than it is in the sheltered glens and valleys. This is suggested as the reason for deer remaining on the heights during summer. Again, the daily up- and downhill movements of deer range wider in summer, when the difference between day and night temperatures is more marked, than in the more even day and night temperatures of winter. A sharp alteration in temperature exerts a considerable influence on the movements of deer. A sudden access of cold will bring the Red Deer down. It has also the effect of causing them to flock.

Interesting is the peculiar behaviour of sambar under the influence of cold. Dunbar Brander writing of these animals in Madhya Pradesh says : ' In winter in districts where frost and severe cold are common one will often find a whole herd of sambar lying in the water. The heavy mist rising off the stream shows that the water is warmer than the surrounding air and, strange as it may appear, the animals are actually lying in the water to keep themselves warm.'

The state of wetness or dryness of the atmosphere is a potent influence on the movements of deer. Speaking generally, it has been found that humid atmospheric conditions tend to restrict day-to-day movement, and a dry atmosphere to induce it. But on the other hand scent carries better under conditions of humidity than when it is cold and dry. Under conditions of high humidity a herd of deer, reacting more to the stimulus of scent, may be more disturbed and restless.

Again it is shown that among Red Deer, sexual activity is stimu-
lated by cold. During cold dry nights the glens are full of the sound
of roaring stags but, when cloud and mists cover the sky and the
air is humid, there is little roaring to be heard and stags are visibly
not so active with their harems. Writing of the hangul, Stockley
says that in some years ' stags seem hardly to call ; after heavy rain
most stags will call '. But such calling may have little to do with
sexual activity. It is perhaps merely the expression of an exuber-
ance of spirits induced by sunshine after the gloom and depression
of clouds and rain. Many birds and animals react in the same way.

Rain does not appear to exercise much influence on the movements of Red Deer. Steady rain tends to restrict them. If the rain
is very heavy and accompanied by high temperature, these deer
move uphill to the drier slopes. These observations on the behaviour
of Red Deer in response to weather conditions are recorded here to
indicate how intimately the habits of these animals are influenced
by vagaries of weather. Few such observations have been made in
relation to Indian deer. There is need for such study if we are to
understand the life of these animals, which cannot be studied apart
from the surroundings in which they live.

Deer and their neighbours. The role of ruminants in the scheme of
Nature has already been discussed. They are a check on the exuberant growth of grass and other herbage. Each species plays its
role in its special niche, sambar in forest, chital on its fringes,
swamp deer in marsh or grass plains, hangul in temperate forests
and on alpine slopes. In common with other ruminants deer provide a basic food for a long range of carnivores. In India the principal enemies of the larger species are tigers, leopards, and wild
dogs. Of chital it is said many are seized and killed by crocodiles.
Newborn fawns fall victims to the smaller beasts of prey.

A deer's means of escape are alertness, a premonition of danger,
quickened by a keen sense of scent, hearing, and sight. Protection
is also derived from their gregarious habits. Gregariousness is best
developed in tropical species which are more liable to attack by
carnivorous enemies, witness the enormous herds in which swamp
deer and spotted deer sometimes gather. These animals when in a
large group are more immune from attacks of beasts of prey.
Solitary animals or straggling twos or threes become easier victims.

Apart from beasts of prey, deer and other ruminants have weaker
but no less persistent foes in the wide range of parasites which
subject them to attack. Besides swarms of blood-sucking species
like horse flies and clegs (Tabanidae), forest flies, and keds (Hippo-
boscidae), there are species like botflies and warble flies (Oestridae)
which are not blood-suckers but seek to lay their eggs on their hairs
and other parts of the body. The movements of deer are often
directed to escape these swarming pests. Sambar for instance will
leave the shelter of the forest and take to the open during the dry

steamy days of the monsoon when Tabanids and other flies are particularly active.

Relationships with other animals which are not their enemies vary with different species. Chital are perhaps the most tolerant and sociable of all our deer. Where they inhabit the same country, chital will be seen associating with swamp deer, nilgai, blackbuck, and even pigs. Sambar hinds may associate with swamp deer but not the stags. Langur monkeys appear to be the special friends of chital. Deer and wild cattle gather under trees where monkeys are feeding, to eat the leaves and fruit they wastefully drop. Mynas and other birds are often seen in attendance on deer and cattle. They settle on their backs and remove the ticks with which they are usually infested, or pick up insects disturbed in the grass by the movements of these animals.

Deer and man. Man's influence on deer has been mainly that of an exterminator. From time immemorial he has hunted deer, and his ever extending usurpation of forests and wastelands is steadily reducing their means of existence. In India deer survive in reduced numbers, or have disappeared from territories where they were common. From the very nature of their breeding habits, horned animals, where over-hunted, are particularly exposed to risk of extermination. With these animals the bulk of the females are sired by the biggest and strongest males who acquire their harems by right of conquest. These big animals are the usual mark of the hunter. Their persistent killing or wounding—wounded animals seldom breed—results in mating being left increasingly to younger males. Now the older animals come into season first—the time of the rut and the time of calving are so aligned that the bulk of the young are produced when climatic, food, and other conditions are propitious. In India the majority of deer begin life during the monsoon or immediately after, when optimum conditions of food and cover prevail. But these optimum conditions are not attained when breeding is left to the young. The younger males come into rut later and get the opportunity to mate only when the big males have left their harems. Their offspring are produced out of season when conditions are less favourable, and newborn animals have to face the adversities of winter or the dry torrid conditions of the hot weather. Unfavourable conditions at birth imply higher mortality among the young and therefore a decline in population, which becomes serious when increasingly large numbers of young are so produced. The extermination of deer and other game has its adverse reaction on human interests. They provide the basic food of the larger carnivores which, deprived of their natural prey, take to cattle-killing as an alternative.

FAMILY LIFE AND CARE OF THE YOUNG

Means of communication. Deer have various ways of communicating with one another. All species of deer have alarm calls, sharp staccato barks, whistles, etc., which they utter when suspicious and continue to repeat until reassured. Yet another way of attracting attention is stamping with the feet. With some species this drumming with the feet is the preliminary to the alarm call.

Quite different is the impressive roar or bellow of the stags before or during the mating time. The call is described as the embodiment of lust, a vent to anger and jealousy. A challenge to rivals, it is one of the most thrilling and awe-inspiring sounds of the forest. With some species, e.g. the chital, the challenge of the stag serves equally to attract the hinds to its neighbourhood. Communication between mother and young is effected by low murmuring calls and also by stamping with the feet.

Scent glands. Other aids to mutual recognition are the scent glands with which deer are so abundantly provided. Most deer have a scent gland below each eye. Muntjac have, in addition, a frontal gland on the forehead. These scent glands, especially active at mating, are a means of attracting the hinds. This is particularly the case with deer which live in dense forest. Their facial glands are large and highly developed. In addition to face glands, the majority of deer have glands between the hooves. There may be one or two glands on each hindleg, some distance above the hooves and, less commonly, on the inner surface of the hocks. Their position is usually indicated by a tuft of hair distinctive in length and colour. Foot glands, as already stated, leave a trail of scent where deer have passed. The various glands, emitting a powerful scent, are an important means of communication among deer. Writing of the swamp deer, Dunbar Brander says : ' They have a fairly strong smell and a herd can be detected when lying down in long grass at quite a distance. Their smell much resembles that of the European deer.'

Social organization. Most of the larger deer are gregarious. A highly developed social organization is exhibited by the Red Deer (*Cervus elaphus* Linnaeus) of Europe. The social life of this species has been the subject of intensive study in Scotland, and is elaborately described by F. Fraser Darling in his book A HERD OF RED DEER. His book shows how the problem should be studied. The social system of the Red Deer is essentially matriarchal. The leadership of the herds, the protracted care and training of the young are exclusively the role of the hinds. In the economy of the species the stag is solely an agent for procreation. Immediately it attains maturity, the stag leaves the family group. Thenceforward it associates only with other stags and displays no further interest in the hinds, except during the brief mating season. Otherwise,

PLATE 66

Barking Deer (*Muntiacus muntjak*)

Photo : E. P. Gee

PLATE 67

Indian Pangolin (*Manis crassicaudata*)

Photo : O. C. Edwards

throughout the year, the stags live apart. They may associate in small groups. Newly matured stags show a tendency to group together. Sometimes an old stag is accompanied by one or two younger animals which act as sentinels, or old stags may become entirely anti-social and live either alone or with a companion of similar morose inclinations. When past the capacity to breed a stag may live in permanent solitude. Wounded stags again may become solitary until they die or are healed of their wounds.

These stag groups have no apparent leadership. If disturbed the group scatters or runs in single file, chance giving any individual the lead.

Very different is the social organization of the hinds. They live in family groups. The young remain with the mother till they attain maturity, which is not till they are three years old. As such the group may contain newly born young, and others from one to three years old. The young follow the leadership of the parent hind. Even when several family groups assemble to form a single unit, leadership is assumed by one of the leader hinds and her supremacy is never challenged. The leader may be assisted by another hind, who takes up her position in the rear when there is any considerable movement of the herd. When feeding or resting the leader hind is constantly raising her head to smell, to hear, and to see. Even as fawns the females are more alert and inquisitive. Male calves are as alert, but from the time they are a year old they take little part in the general watchfulness of the group. It is only when they leave the family and are thrown on their own resources that the stags become wary and alert. The leadership of the hind is maintained even during the rut. The sole preoccupation of the stag is to keep his harem from straying and being acquired by a rival. He shows at this time little concern for his safety, let alone the safety of his hinds. Should an alarm be raised, the group gets together behind the hind leader and follows her in retreat. In flight the stag may keep with the hinds or steer his own course.

Jealous and intolerant of rivals, the males are a disruptive element in the social life of the species. The governance of the herd by the males would limit it to such small following of hinds as a stag can keep together. The segregation of the males on the other hand makes for greater gregariousness and family cohesion. The hinds exhibit no intolerance to each other. They permit the assemblage of families. They are selfless, their main concern is the care and upbringing of the young. Their protracted parental care, continued till maturity of the young, makes for their better protection and more intensive training. As such the matriarchal system, which is the governing principle in the social life of these deer, exerts a powerful influence on the survival of the species.

Territory. The hinds of Red Deer and their following of young graze in small groups or family parties. Various factors, climatic, requirements of food, etc., may bring these groups together in a single unit. Each such unit with its component groups has its grazing territory, a low level winter territory which gives more or less direct access to a high level summer territory. The winter territory is really the 'home ground'. It is the area from which the hinds leave for their summer grazing, and to which they return for the rutting season, and where the calves are born.

Like the hinds the stags have their summer and winter territories, but they are given to wandering much more over their domains. When the rut approaches they assemble in the winter or 'home' territory of the hinds. They now become quarrelsome and roar in challenge to each other. These stag companies slowly break up as each stag comes into rut and trots away from his fellows to secure his following of hinds.

A stag, early on the scene, may secure by conquest over rivals as many as 50 hinds. He endeavours to keep them together in as large a territory as he can maintain. Such territory is held by the intensity of the stag's sexual jealousy, by his wits and activity. For the hinds have no special link with their master, they are prone to wander and to accept any 'sultan'. As the rut increases in intensity and more stags come in, those which have come in earlier invariably lose some of the hinds and part of their territory. Harems and territories are at their smallest at the height of the rut. The rutting territories are in a state of flux because spent stags leave or are driven out by the challenge of fresh arrivals. Besides a rutting stag is not continuously active during the whole period of the rut. It may retire for brief intervals to recuperate. During such periods resting stags display no pugnacity towards each other. As the rut declines the territories disintegrate. The younger stags which have so far occupied the fringes of the rutting territories come in ; but they have neither the desire nor the finesse to establish a harem or territory in which to keep it. The bulk of the hinds are by now impregnated by the master stags. The younger animals couple with hinds which have not mated and which are coming into season a second or third time.

No such intensive study of the social and family life of Indian deer has been made. Such knowledge as is available indicates that the social organization of the hangul or Kashmir stag, the swamp deer, and the brow-antlered deer is based on the same general principles. It is matriarchal ; mature stags live apart from the hinds except during the rut, the care of the young is left entirely to the hinds.

A close approach to the Red Deer is naturally exhibited by the hangul or Kashmir stag. It is a near relative of the Red Deer, living like the Red Deer in a temperate climate and a mountainous terrain. Hangul hinds and immature young live in small family groups which may assemble to form large units. After attaining maturity, i.e. when three years old, the stags live alone or in small parties. Stags and hinds have their winter or 'home' territories on the lower slopes of the mountains, and their summer territories on the heights. There is a brief and well-defined rutting season, at the approach of which the stags assemble in the 'home' territory of the hinds. After the rut the big stags leave and the younger mature males enjoy a brief association with the hinds. Owing to the greater number of hinds and the larger areas which they inhabit, harems and rutting territories of the hangul are probably less limited, even at the height of the rut.

Coming now to the Swamp Deer, Schaller reports that in Kanha Sanctuary, Madhya Pradesh, they are found in mixed herds for the first eight months though after the rut many stags leave to form exclusive stag herds, the only stable association being of the hind and its young. The onset of the breeding season varies in different parts of the country, April at Kaziranga, September at Kheri, and December at Kanha. In the former two areas it is prolonged and lasts for about eight months, but at Kanha it is brief, January being the peak month. The swamp deer of Kanha form a breeding herd during the rutting season, the stags in the herd have a dominance hierarchy and high ranking males do most of the mating.

Sambar display some difference in their mating habits, a difference associated with their dense forest environment. In forests where sambar live visibility is limited and the collection of a harem of hinds is usually an impossibility. As such sambar stags generally do not fight in the presence of the assembled hinds or for their possession. They fight for territory, for the possession of a favoured valley, and for the right to summon the hinds living in it. The females seek the stag attracted by his call and the powerful odour of his scent glands. For the rest, the social organization is similar to that of other deer. There is the same segregation of the sexes but because of a protracted breeding season, young stags will be found in association with the hinds for longer periods.

Among the Chital living as they do in herds outside the obscurity of forests the stags roam widely from herd to herd in search of does in heat and stay with the doe till mating is accomplished defending her from rivals. No territory is established.

Stags and hinds will be found living together at all times of the year and, while there is a marked period of breeding activity, young are produced at any season.

Coming now to the smaller deer, hog-deer, muntjac or barking deer, and musk deer, they are far less gregarious than the larger species. It is rare to find more than two or three hog-deer together, as a rule individuals of both sexes are solitary. Barking deer are usually seen singly or in pairs or in small family parties. Leadership in a group of muntjac rests apparently with the stag. His mate and her fawn or a yearling follow. The buck is pugnacious and will fight at any season. The young mature in a year and leave or are driven from the family. The stags do not tolerate the presence of another mature male. In these animals the matriarchal principle is substituted by intolerant male governance which, as we have indicated, is adverse to the development of gregariousness.

When about to calve a hind leaves the herd and seeks some sheltered spot to drop her young. A Red Deer calf lies alone for from two to five days, and is fed by the mother twice a day. Once the calf is strong on its legs, it follows its mother closely, and within a few days the hind, the calf, and other young of previous years still with her rejoin the main hind groups. The period of lactation is long, both the calf and yearling have been observed sucking the mother. The young reach maturity when three years old.

Little that is precise is known about the young of Indian deer. Apparently the mother leaves the herd when about to calve ; she drops it in some favourable spot ; there is apparently more attempt at concealment. In the case of a chital kept in captivity, the hind so concealed her fawn that it was impossible to discover where it actually lay. The hind was seen with the fawn every morning, but without it in the afternoon. At about 4 o'clock every evening she appeared to ' put the fawn to bed '. This went on for 8 to 10 days. Indian deer apparently reach maturity earlier than the European Red Deer. Two years is the period recorded for sambar, swamp deer, and chital, whereas it is three years before a Red Deer comes of age.

THE KASHMIR STAG, or HANGUL

Cervus elaphus hanglu Wagner

Plate facing p. 273

Local Names. Kash. *hangal, honglu* (male), *minyamar* (female) ; Hindi *barasingha* ; English *Kashmir barasingh.*

Size. 48 to 50 in. (120 to 125 cm.) high at the withers. A well-grown stag scales a little over 400 lb. (180 kg.). Horns in adults average 40 in. (100 cm.) in length. The maximum recorded is 50½ in. (128.3 cm.), being the length on the outside curve.

Distinctive Characters. The Red Deer (*Cervus elaphus* Linnaeus) of Europe typifies a group of large deer consisting of several species and races distributed over Europe, Asia north of the Himalayas, north Africa, and North America. Of the two races which occur within our limits the Hangul is the commoner and better known. Its coat ranges from light to dark brown, fading to dingy white on the lips, chin, underparts, and buttocks. The white rump patch does not extend much above the tail and is divided by a broad median stripe extending down to the base of the tail and sometimes to its extremity. The colour fades during the summer but tones up with the denser winter coat, which in a big stag is very dark or rufous-brown. Fawns are spotted. Old hinds may show white flecks. The fine spreading antlers assume great variety in form. Normal heads have five points on each antler. Heads with 16 points have been obtained, 14 points are rare, 13 and 11 more common.

Distribution. Limited to the north side of the Valley of Kashmir and some of the adjacent valleys.

Habits. Essentially a forest animal, the Hangul is found singly or in small parties, which seldom remain long in one area but roam from forest to forest to find good grazing. Winter is spent in the lower levels, summer on the heights. After shedding their antlers between March and April most stags go uphill and congregate about the snow-line. They spend the summer at an elevation of 9000 to 12,000 ft. (2750 to 3650 m.). About the end of September the stags' new antlers have hardened. They commence to roar and challenge. They join the hinds at the beginning of October and, as the rut develops, engage in conflict. The master stags collect a number of hinds whose possession is disputed by rivals. In November, when the dry leaves cover the ground, the stags desert the hinds and go to the upland meadows or into the horse-chestnut forests. In hard winters the deer descend to yet lower levels. They come to the lower elevations in the early spring to feed on the new sprouting grass and the budding larches. The fawns are born late May.

The Chumbi Valley in Tibet and some of the adjacent valleys of Bhutan are inhabited by the other race, the **Shou** (*C. elaphus wallichi* Cuvier). The Shou is much larger than the Hangul, standing from 4½ to 5 ft. (140 to 150 cm.) at the shoulder. Its antlers are longer and more massive, and the beam is strongly bent forward above the trez line.

THE THAMIN, or BROW-ANTLERED DEER

Cervus eldi McClelland

Plate facing p. 273

[RACE IN INDIA : *eldi* McClelland]

Local Names. Manipur *sangai* ; Bur. *tamin*.

Size. This beautiful deer is nearly 4 ft. (120 cm.) high at the withers. The hinds are smaller. The maximum length of the antlers is 42 in. (107 cm.). Heads over 35 in. (90 cm.) are good. Horns are usually measured from tip of brow-antler to tip of main beam. The record (in Burma) is 44½ in. (113 cm.). Very occasionally a spatulated type is found with the main beam flattened and broadened, and 12 or more points in place of the usual 6.

Distinctive Characters. The coat is coarse and sparse. In stags it is dark brown or nearly black. Hinds are light fawn. The young are spotted. There appears to be a seasonal colour change, the dark brown Thamin of the cold season developing into the yellowish brown animals of the hot weather. The Thamin of Manipur (*C. e. eldi*) regarded as a distinct race is distinguished from the Thamin of Burma [*C. e. thamin* (Thomas)] by the great development of the hind pasterns which are horny instead of hairy and applied to the ground when walking, a development suited to progress over marshy ground. The antlers, arising from close-set almost erect pedicels, are very handsome and distinctive in this species. In profile the outline of the horns is almost circular. From the tip of the brow tine to the point of the beam the antler sweeps in one continuous, graceful curve. The number of terminal tines varies from two or three to as many as eight or ten. Stags are believed to acquire their horns in the second year and reach their prime when seven years old.

Distribution. Within the area of its range three races are recognised : *C. eldi eldi* McClelland from Manipur, *C. eldi thamin* (Thomas) from Burma, Tenasserim, Siam, and possibly the Malay Peninsula, and *C. eldi siamensis* Lydekker from Siam, Anam, and Hainan.

The present population of the Sangai, the Manipur race of the Browantlered Deer, is only about 100 and is restricted to the Keibul Lamjao Sanctuary on the shore of Logtak Lake in Manipur.

Habits. Thamin avoid hills and heavy forest. These deer prefer open scrub jungle, or flat or undulating land between rivers and hill ranges. They live in small herds, lying up in cover during the heat of the day and feeding in the mornings and evenings. After nightfall they come out to graze in the large *lwins* and *kwins* or to raid crops in their vicinity. Their speed and sharp sight is their main protection.

Stags shed their antlers in mid-August and are clear of velvet by the end of December, when the horns are at their best. The rut develops between March and April. The fawns, usually one, are dropped mostly in October. The period of gestation is 239 to 256 days. After the rut the master stags go off either alone or attended by one or two hinds. Big stags are seldom seen with the herds after May.

PLATE 68

Indian Chevrotain
(*Tragulus meminna*)

Hog-Deer
(*Axis porcinus*)

Musk Deer
(*Moschus moschiferus*)

Muntjac
(*Muntiacus muntjak*)

0   10   20   30 cm.
1 ft.

Indian Wild Boar
(*Sus scrofa*)

0   20   40   60 cm.
0   1   2 ft.

PLATE 69

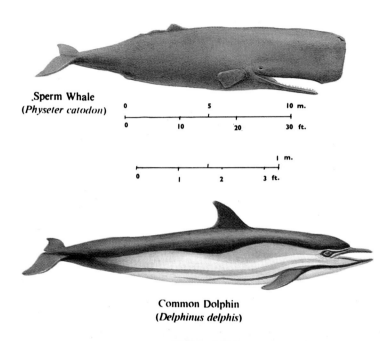

Blue Whale
(*Balaenoptera musculus*)

.Sperm Whale
(*Physeter catodon*)

0   5   10 m.

0   10   20   30 ft.

1 m.

0   1   2   3 ft.

Common Dolphin
(*Delphinus delphis*)

Gangetic Dolphin
(*Platanista gangetica*)

Dugong
(*Dugong dugon*)

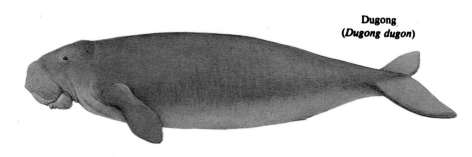

THE SWAMP DEER, or BARASINGHA

Cervus duvauceli Cuvier

Plates facing pp. 273, 278

[RACES IN INDIA : *duvauceli* Cuvier, *branderi* (Pocock)]

Local Names. Hindi *barasingha, maha* ; Nepal Terai *gonda, gonr, ghos* ; Central India *goinjak* (male), *gaoni* (female), *sal samar, nerwari.*

Size. This splendid deer attains its finest development in Madhya Pradesh. A good stag stands 54 in. (135 cm.) at the shoulder and scales 370 to 400 lb. (170 to 180 kg.). Average horns measure 30 in. (75 cm.) round the curve with a girth of 5 in. (13 cm.) at mid-beam.   The record is 41 in. (104.1 cm.).

Distinctive Characters. The coat, almost woolly in texture, shades from brown to yellowish brown. The stags are maned and darker in colour. The summer coat of stags and hinds is paler, some develop spots, not always distinct, of lighter tone. The young are spotted.
There is much variation in the form of the antlers. Two distinct types are recognised with a wide range of intermediary patterns. In the first form, the beam takes a backward and then forward curve bringing the points of the horns in line with the top of the head. Half way up the beam, tines are given off at intervals, the first usually having a shoot of its own. In the second and far handsomer type, the brow tine is set at right angles to the beam, which grows with an outward curve giving the antlers a wider spread. At the point where it branches, the beam takes an almost horizontal curve and gives off a number of vigorous vertical tines each of which throws out shoots. 10 to 14 is the usual number of points, though there may be as many as 20.

Distribution. Limited to India. Two races are recognised: the swamp-dwelling *duvauceli* of the Terai, U.P., Assam, and the Sunderbans distinguished by its splayed hooves and larger skull, and *branderi* found in the hard open ground of Madhya Pradesh with smaller well-knit hooves.

Habits. In the Terai the Barasingha lives on marshland and is seldom out of water. In Madhya Pradesh these deer inhabit grassy maidans in the proximity of forest where they appear to be less dependent on water than spotted deer. Their habitat in Assam is high ground in the proximity of water. Swamp Deer are highly gregarious. In parts of the Terai a few miles of swamp may contain thousands of these magnificent animals. Swamp Deer are less nocturnal than sambar. They feed till late in the morning, again in the evening, and lie up during the day. Their eyesight and hearing are moderate, the sense of smell acute. When alarmed the whole herd sets up a shrill baying sound which is continued in flight. They live more or less in amity till the rut develops.

Both races of the Swamp Deer are considerably reduced in number, and less than 200 of the central Indian race and not more than 4000 animals of both races are believed to exist. Strict protection is necessary if extinction of the species is to be prevented.

THE SAMBAR

Cervus unicolor Kerr

Plates facing pp. 114, 273, 279

[RACES IN INDIA : *niger* Blainville, *equinus* Cuvier.
CEYLON : *unicolor* Kerr]

Local Names. Hindi *sambar, samar* ; Mar. *sambar* ; Tamil *kudoo marn* ; Mal. *kullay marn* ; Kan. *kudawe, kaddama* ; Bur. *sut.*

Size. The Sambar is the largest Indian deer and carries the grandest horns ; height at shoulder nearly 5 ft. (150 cm.), average about 55 in. (140 cm.). A full-grown stag scales from 500 to over 700 lb. (225 to over 320 kg.). The finest heads come from the forests about the Narbada and Tapti and from Madhya Pradesh generally. The record from Bhopal tapes 50⅞ in. (129.2 cm.). Nowadays 38 in. (95 cm.) is good in N. India and 36 in. (90 cm.) in the South. The horns of the Malay Sambar are close-set, more rugged, and massive ; the average length is 26 in. (65 cm.) — a head over 30 in. (75 cm.) is good.

Distinctive Characters. The typical forest deer of south-eastern Asia. The coat is coarse and shaggy. In stags it forms a mane about the neck and throat. In the hot weather much of the hair is shed. The general colour is brown with a yellowish or greyish tinge. The underparts are paler. Females are lighter in tone. Old stags tend to become very dark, almost black. The antlers are stout and rugged. The brow tine is set at an acute angle with the beam. At its summit, the beam forks into two nearly equal tines. In some heads the outer, in others the inner, tine is longer. The full number of points are developed in the fourth year.

Distribution. The wooded districts of India, Burma, and Ceylon, extending through the Malay countries and eastwards to the Philippines and beyond. The typical race *C. u. unicolor* is from Ceylon. The Indian race *C. u. niger* is confined to India. The Malay race *C. u. equinus* extends from Assam eastwards.

Habits. Forested hill-sides, preferably near cultivation, are the favourite haunt of the Sambar. Their food consists of grass, leaves, and various kinds of wild fruit. They feed mainly at night and retire into heavy cover at daybreak and do not usually come out till dusk. Their powers of sight are moderate, their scent and hearing acute. The capacity of so heavy an animal to move silently through dense jungle is amazing. Sambar take to water readily and swim with the body submerged, only the face and the antlers showing above the surface. In central and southern India the majority of stags cast their antlers between the end of March and mid-April. The horns commence to grow in May and are in velvet during the rains and clear of velvet by November. The stags clean their horns by rubbing them against trees. The males fight for territory. Each stag fights to obtain sole rights over some favoured valley. The victor becomes the master of the hinds which enter it. Pairing takes place in November and December. The stag's harem is limited to a few hinds. After the rut he deserts them and lives a solitary life till the return of the mating season. The young are born at the commencement of the rains, in late May or early June. Young stags remain with the hinds. Sambar are rarely found associating in large numbers. Four or five to a dozen are what one usually sees. Both stags and hinds are seen singly or a party of hinds and fawns without a stag.

THE HOG-DEER

Axis porcinus (Zimmermann)

Plate facing p. 288

[RACE IN INDIA AND CEYLON : *porcinus* (Zimmermann)]

Local Names. Hindi, Sindhi, & Punjabi *para* ; Bur. *day ay.*

Size. The height at the shoulder is 24 in. (61 cm.), average horns measure 12 to 15 in. (30 to 38 cm.). Burmese stags carry better heads than Indian. The record is 24 in. (61 cm.).

Distinctive Characters. The name Hog-Deer has probably been suggested by the squat pig-like appearance of this animal and by its hog-like movements. When running it keeps its head low down, and moves without that bounding action so characteristic in deer.

The Hog-Deer is a relative of the chital and interbreeding between the two species is known to take place. The Hog-Deer is smaller and stouter in build. The body is long and the legs relatively short. The fur is brown, dark brown in the old stags, with a yellowish or reddish tinge. The white tips to the individual hairs give the coat a speckly appearance. The underparts of the body are paler and the inside of the ears and the underside of the tail are white. The young are spotted. Some young stags and hinds show these spots, particularly in summer though they are not always discernible. The summer coat is generally paler.

The small antlers are set upon very long bony pedicels. After giving out a short brow tine the beam is almost straight till it divides into a longer fore and shorter hind tine.

Distribution. The low alluvial grass plains of north India from Sind and the Punjab to Assam, whence its range extends into Burma and Tenasserim. It is not found in the Indian peninsula; but occurs in parts of Ceylon.

Habits. Hog-Deer favour grass jungles by the banks of rivers, grass-covered delta islands, or open grass plains ; always where the grass is not too high. On the banks of the Indus in upper Sind they live in scrub jungle, and in Burma they were once common in mangroves. Hog-Deer are generally solitary creatures. A pair will continue to frequent a particular stretch of grassland. Sometimes small parties up to 18 or so may be found grazing together. They come out to feed early in the mornings and in the evenings, and shelter in long grass during the hot hours of the day. They are wary creatures ; their sense of sight, smell, and hearing is acute. Persecution has made them almost nocturnal in many parts of their range.

The main pairing season is believed to be in September and October and the young are dropped in April and May. Pairing must also take place earlier in the year as young are often born during the rains. The period of gestation is eight months.

THE CHITAL, or SPOTTED DEER

Axis axis (Erxleben)

Plate facing p. 273

[RACE IN INDIA : *axis* (Erxleben). CEYLON : *ceylonensis* (Fischer)]

Local Names. Hindi *chital, chitra, jhank* ; Mar. *chital* ; Tamil & Mal. *pooli marn* ; Kan. *saranga jinke.*

Size. The Spotted Deer is at its best in the Himalayan foothills, in the jungles of the Terai, and in Madhya Pradesh. A well-built stag from these parts stands 36 in. (90 cm.) at the shoulder and weighs about 190 lb. (85 kg.).

The record head measures 39¾ in. (101 cm.). A 34 in. (85 cm.) antler would be good anywhere, 31 in. (80 cm.) in south India.

Distinctive Characters. The Chital is perhaps the most beautiful of all deer. Its coat is a bright rufous-fawn profusely spotted with white at all ages and in all seasons. Old bucks are more brownish in colour and darker. The lower series of spots on the flanks are arranged in longitudinal rows and suggest broken linear markings.

The graceful antlers have three tines, a long brow tine set nearly at right angles to the beam and two branch tines at the top. The outer tine, the continuation of the beam, is always longer. It may be noted that old bucks often have one or more false points on the brow antler where it joins the main beam.

Distribution. In India Chital are found in the forests at the base of the Himalayas and practically throughout the Peninsula and Ceylon, wherever there is jungle combined with good grazing and a plentiful supply of water. It is unknown in the arid plains of the Punjab, Sind, in a large portion of Rajputana, and the countries east of the Bay of Bengal. It is found in Assam in the Goalpara, Kamrup, and Darrang districts.

Habits. One always associates Chital with beautiful scenery, with grassy forest glades and shaded streams. They are seen in herds of ten to thirty, which may contain two or three stags ; but assemblages numbering several hundreds have been met with. They do not shun the proximity of villages, but enter cultivation, and frequently associate with many forest animals, particularly with monkeys. They are less nocturnal than sambar and feed till late in the morning and again in the afternoon, and lie down in the interval in some shaded spot.

The time at which the stags shed their antlers varies in different localities. In Madhya Pradesh and south India, it is usually in August and September. The new antlers are in velvet till the end of December. But stags carrying horns in various stages of development have been seen at all seasons. In Madhya Pradesh the pairing season is at its height in May. The rutting stag has a loud harsh bellow and combats between the males for the possession of the hinds are fierce and frequent. In north India the pairing is said to take place during the winter months. Fawns may be met with at any season. Usually the mother gives birth to a single fawn. Chital are prolific breeders ; an interval of six months may see the production of a new family.

THE MUNTJAC, or BARKING DEER

Muntiacus muntjak (Zimmermann)

Plates facing pp. 282, 288

[RACES IN INDIA : *vaginalis* (Boddaert), *aureus* (H. Smith), *malabaricus* Lydekker. Ceylon : *malabaricus* Lydekker]

Local Names. Hindi *kakar* ; Mar. *bhekad* ; Tamil *kart ardu* ; Kan. *kard koorie* ; Bur. *jee* ; English *Ribfaced Deer*.

Size. Height at the shoulder of an adult male is from 20 to 30 in. (50 to 75 cm.) ; its weight about 48 to 50 lb. (22 to 23 kg.). Excluding the pedicel, which may be up to 3 to 4 in. (8 to 10 cm.) long, the horn rarely exceeds 5 in. (13 cm.). The best Burmese head is 7 in. (17.8 cm.). Average Indian antlers measure 2 to 3 in. (5 to 8 cm.), the pedicel 3 to 4 in. (8 to 10 cm.). The maximum length obtained in the old C.P. is 7 in. (17.8 cm.), 6¾ in. (17.1 cm.) in south India.

Distinctive Characters. The antlers are small, consisting of a short brow-tine and an unbranched beam. They are set on bony hair-covered pedicels which extend down each side of the face as bony ridges, hence the name Ribfaced Deer. In does tufts of bristly hair replace the horns. Old males are browner in colour. The upper canines of the male are well developed and are used by the animal in self-defence.

Distribution. Muntjacs range over the greater part of the Indo-Malayan countries and are found also in China, Formosa, and Japan. Various races are recognised over this wide range. The Muntjac of north India is *M. m. vaginalis*. The southern form is *M. m. aureus*. A third race (*M. m. malabaricus*) is found in Malabar and extends to Ceylon. The Muntjac of Tenasserim [*M. feae* (Thomas & Doria)] is regarded as a distinct species. The coat of the north Indian race is bright chestnut. A bright red form is equally common in Burma.

Habits. The haunts of the Muntjac are thickly wooded hills. In the Himalayas and S. India it occurs up to levels of 5000 to 8000 ft. (1500 to 2450 m.), sometimes even higher. They are seen singly or in pairs or in small family parties. Muntjac keep to more or less thick jungle and come out to graze in the outskirts of forest or in open clearings. They are fairly diurnal in habit. The food consists of various leaves and grasses and wild fruits. The call from a distance sounds much like the bark of a dog. It is given out at intervals, usually in the mornings and evenings, sometimes after nightfall.

When alarmed and in flight these deer give out a series of short cackling barks. A sharp rattle likened to the sound of castanets heard when Muntjac are bounding away is a vocal noise. Muntjac appear to breed at all seasons. The rut mainly takes place in the cold weather. The young, usually one, sometimes two, are born at the beginning of the rains.

Horns are shed during May and June.

THE MUSK DEER

Moschus moschiferus Linnaeus

Plate facing p. 288

[RACE IN INDIA : *moschiferus* Linnaeus]

Local Names. Hindi *kastura, mushk* ; Kash. *raos, rons.*

Size. A little creature not more than 20 in. (50 cm.) high at the shoulder, slightly higher at the croup.

Distinctive Characters. The Musk Deer holds a place between the deer and the antelopes. It is regarded as an undeveloped form of deer which has not progressed with the rest of its family. It is hornless and has no face glands. These are generally present in all deer, and it has a gall bladder which no deer possesses. In some ways it has taken a special line of development of its own. This is seen in its possession of a caudal gland and a musk gland. The tail of a Musk Deer is peculiar. It is completely buried in the long hairs of the anal region and is for the most part naked except for a large tuft at the tip and a tuft at the base which covers its upper surface and sides. The lateral surface of the tail bears in its flaccid skin a narrow slit which is the opening of the caudal gland. The musk gland is situated beneath the skin of the abdomen of the males. When fresh its secretion has an unpleasant, pungent, urinary odour ; when dry it acquires the scent of musk. Valued as a commercial product, it induces the persecution of the species. From the great development of the caudal and musk glands it is inferred that in this deer the females seek out the males in the breeding season. Finally, Musk Deer have specially mobile feet, the long pointed central hooves and unusually large lateral hooves being well adapted to give it a foothold on snowy slopes and slippery rocks. The absence of horns is compensated for by the great development of the canine teeth, particularly in the males.

The Musk Deer wears a coat of thick and bristly hairs, almost pithy in structure. The general colour is a shade of rich dark brown speckled with grey.

Distribution. Musk Deer range over a wide area in central and north-eastern Asia. The typical form *M. m. moschiferus* is found in Kashmir, Nepal, and Sikkim.

Habits. Musk ʼDeer live singly or in pairs and are generally met with in birch forest above the zone of the pines ; at times they come down to lower levels, but always keep in thick cover. They scrape out a shallow form in which they lie concealed and come out to feed in the mornings and evenings.

The food consists of grass, lichens, leaves, and flowers. The breeding season is believed to be in January and the young are born in June.

THE INDIAN CHEVROTAIN, or MOUSE-DEER

Tragulus meminna (Erxleben)

Plate facing p. 288

Local Names. Hindi *pisura, pisora* ; Mar. *pisori, aheda* ; Bur. *yun* ; Kan. *koor andi, kooray* ; Tamil *sarugoo marn, kur, kooran panni.*

Size. Height at shoulder, 10 to 13 inches (25 to 30 cm.).

Distinctive Characters. The cloven-hoofed animals which we have considered so far all belong to the **Pecora**, an infra-order of **Ruminantia** (Ruminants). The Mouse-Deer represent a second infra-order the **Tragulina**. Like other ruminants, Mouse-Deer have no front teeth in the upper jaw. But they differ in having a three-chambered stomach in place of one with four divisions. They have four well-developed toes on each foot, the bones of the petty or side toes being complete. In other ruminants some of these bones are imperfect and wanting. Antlers are not developed. Mouse-Deer, like musk deer, are furnished with tusks. These are better developed in males. Mouse-Deer are included in a family, the **Tragulidae**, which contains : (1) the Indian Chevrotain, and (2) the Malay Chevrotains, *T. napu* (F. Cuvier) and *T. javanicus* (Osbeck). The Asiatic Chevrotains are distinguished from the African by having true cannon bones developed.

The Indian Chevrotain or Mouse-Deer is, like all mouse-deer, a tiny little creature with very slender limbs and high hindquarters.

Because of its small size, shy habits, and very protective colouring it easily escapes observation. Its coat is olive-brown minutely speckled with yellow. The flanks are marked with rows of buff or white spots which elongate and pass into longitudinal bands. The lower parts are white. The throat has three white stripes.

Distribution. Forested areas of Ceylon and southern India at elevations up to 6000 ft. (1850 m.). The 24° latitude is approximately the limit of its northerly range in the peninsular area. It has been recently reported from Nepal.

Habits. The Indian Mouse-Deer shelters in grass-covered rocky hill-sides or in forest. It conceals itself in the crevices of rocks or among large boulders. Pursued by dogs, it shows an amazing ability in climbing up the inside of a hollow standing tree. They come out to feed in the mornings or at dusk, and never venture far out into the open, bolting into a ' hide ' when alarmed. In these ' hides' the female brings forth her young, generally two in number, at the end of the rains or the commencement of the cold season. The males live solitary except during the pairing season. A timid and gentle creature, easily tamed.

The two Malayan species are the **Larger Malay Chevrotain** (*T. napu*) and the **Lesser Malay Chevrotain** (*T. javanicus*). The former is about 28 in. (70 cm.) long and 13 in. (33 cm.) high, the latter is no longer than 18 in. (45 cm.) from the tip of the nose to the root of the tail. The smaller animal has three white stripes on its throat, the larger five. Both species are common in the forests of Tenasserim.

21. Pigs

THE CHEVROTAINS REPRESENT, as was shown, a group of animals somewhat distinct from typical ruminants. Pigs, peccaries, and hippopotami are a stage further removed from typical ruminants. They form a third section of the Artiodactyla. Their feet, like the feet of the chevrotains, have the bones of the four toes complete. All these pig-like animals have incisor teeth in the upper jaws. Their molar teeth when unworn are capped with small hillock-like columns which do not wear down to the crescentic patterns seen in the grinding teeth of ruminants. As they are not ruminants their stomachs are much less complex and may, as in the pigs, consist of a single chamber. Finally, cannon bones are not developed in the feet; the bones which fuse to form the cannon bone in true ruminants remain distinct in these animals. These pig-like animals represent a more primitive type which existed at a time when ruminants were unknown and which formed the ancestral stock from which they have descended.

Peccaries are exclusively American in their distribution. Hippopotami are now limited to Africa but many species once inhabited India. They were probably contemporary with the Stone Age man in this country.

Pigs (**Suidae**) are the only representatives of the section in our area. There are two sub-genera: (1) the wild boar (*Sus*) and (2) the pygmy hog (*Porcula*). An elongate head with an abruptly truncated mobile snout ending in a flat disc containing the nostrils is distinctive in pigs. Their feet are narrow. The petty toes are completely developed but do not reach the ground when walking. The upper canines curve upwards and outwards.

The pygmy hog is closely related to the typical pigs. Because of its small size and short tail and the presence of three pairs of teats instead of four it was formerly regarded as a separate genus. Though a single species of wild boar is now found in India, in the Eocene Period six or seven species inhabited the country, one of them a monster form, the largest known of its kind.

THE INDIAN WILD BOAR

Sus scrofa Linnaeus

Plate facing p. 288

[RACES IN INDIA : *cristatus* Wagner. ANDAMANS :
andamanensis Blyth. NICOBARS : *nicobaricus* Miller.
CEYLON : *cristatus* Wagner]

Local Names. Hindi *suar, barba, bad janwar, bura janwar* ; Mar.
ran dukkar ; Tamil *punni* ; Kan. *hundi* ; Mal. *kartu punni* ; Bur. *wet.*

Size. A well-grown male stands 36 in. (90 cm.) high at the shoulder
and its weight may well exceed 500 lb. (230 kg.). Record measurements of lower tusks, 12⅝ in. (32.1 cm.) on the outside curve.

Distinctive Characters. Allied to the European boar *Sus scrofa
scrofa* Linnaeus, but distinctive in its sparser coat and in its fuller
crest or mane of black bristles reaching from the nape down the
back. The colour of the animal is black mixed with grey, rusty
brown, and white hairs. The young are browner and old boars
greyer. Newborn wild pigs are brown with light or black stripes.
The tushes are well developed in the males. Both the upper and
lower tushes curve outwards and project from the mouth.

Distribution. Widely distributed. It ranges over nearly the whole of
India, Burma and Tenasserim, Siam, and part of the Malay Peninsula. It is very common in Ceylon.

Habits. Indian Wild Boar live in grass or scanty bush jungle, sometimes in forest ; after the rains, quite commonly in high crops.
They are omnivorous, living on crops, roots, tubers, insects, snakes,
offal, and carrion. They feed in the early morning and late in the
evening and, where much disturbed, chiefly at night. No animal is
more destructive to crops and, in cultivated areas, it is impossible
to make a plea for its protection.
  Wild Boar display great intelligence and few animals show greater
courage and determination. The sense of smell is acute, the eyesight and hearing moderate. Wild Boar are highly prolific. They
apparently breed at all seasons. In central India the majority of
young are born at two periods, shortly before and shortly after the
rains. Boars and sows are known to collect in large assemblies
when pairing. A herd of 170 or more was seen by Mr. Dunbar
Brander. They were collected in a circle, the master boars in the
centre. Two males were fighting, two others had fought ; the rest

were passive though interested spectators. The period of gestation is said to be four months; four to six young are born at a time. The mother shelters them in a heaped-up mass of grass or branches which she builds before she litters.

After breeding the big boars live alone or in company with another of equal size or with one or two sows.

The **Pygmy Hog** [*Sus salvanius* (Hodgson)] which is scarcely 10 in. (25 cm.) high inhabits the forests at the base of the Himalayas in Sikkim, Nepal, Bhutan, and Assam. Its habits are similar to those of the Wild Boar.. It is said to live in herds of 5 to 20. It is nocturnal and rarely seen.

22. Pangolins

THE PANGOLINS OR scaly anteaters of the Old World compose the Order **Pholidota,** which has only one genus (*Manis*). They were formerly classed in the Order **Edentata,** meaning without teeth, along with the sloths and armadillos of America. Though they differ greatly in form and appearance none of these animals has teeth in the front of the jaw. Some, as is the case with the pangolins, have no teeth at all. Cheek teeth when present as in the sloths and armadillos are rootless, destitute of enamel, and similar to each other in shape. The absence or presence of teeth is probably associated with differences in food. Sloths are herbivorous, while the armadillos, besides feeding on ants, feed also on snails, slugs, and earthworms. The deterioration and loss of teeth in the pangolins is due probably to their exclusive diet of ants and termites. To capture these insects pangolins have a long protrusible and glutinous tongue. When feeding, the tohgue is thrust out and rapidly withdrawn into the mouth with the ants adhering to its sticky surface. The lower or pyloric region of the pangolin's stomach functions as does the ' gizzard ' in birds, containing a quantity of small stones.

The Indian Pangolin *Manis crassicaudata* Gray

Plate facing p. 283

The Chinese Pangolin *Manis pentadactyla* Linnaeus

[RACE IN INDIA: *aurita* Hodgson]

Local Names. Hindi *bajra kit, bajra kapta, suraj mukhi, silu, sal sala* ; Mar. *thirya, khauli mah, khawala manjar, kassoli manjar* ; Tel. *alawa* ; Tamil & Mal. *alangu* ; Bur. *thing wegyat.*

Distinctive Characters. The most distinctive character of a pangolin is its armour of protecting scales. The upper part of the head, the back and sides of the body, the whole tail, and the outside of the limbs are covered with large overlapping scales. In defence the animal curls itself into an armoured ball, exhibiting an enormous muscular power which defies any ordinary attempt to unroll it. The scales of the pangolin may be regarded as hairs or rather as spines enormously enlarged and flattened. Coarse bristle-like hairs scantily clothe the undersurface of its body and a few grow between the scales.

Pangolins usually live in burrows made by themselves and feed on ants and termites, which commonly have to be dug out of the earth. In association with these habits their feet, furnished with long, somewhat curved and blunted claws, are built for digging. As a pangolin digs with its forelimbs, the claws are longer on its forefeet. Either forefoot is employed for scooping out the earth. Excavation is interrupted from time to time to remove the debris, which is shot backward between the hindlimbs and cast out by a vigorous kick. In walking the front toes are bent under the soles. The whole sole of the hindfeet is however applied to the ground. The animal walks slowly with its back well arched and tail held off the ground. Like other low-bodied animals the pangolin stands upon its hindlegs to get a better look around.

Though terrestrial in habit, pangolins climb well and easily. They are often seen in trees probably in quest of tree ants. They climb somewhat like bears and grip a bough tightly with the forelimbs and claws, and if need be with a curl of the tail. Curled around a branch the animal is most difficult to dislodge, displaying an amazing gripping power. Except for the bear-cat, the pangolin is the only Indian animal with a prehensile tail. In seeking its food the animal is guided largely by its sense of smell. When digging up a termite mound it sniffs rapidly from place to place seeking the right spot to commence operations. Sniffing continues during the digging and the direction of excavation is sometimes changed. Sight and hearing are apparently poor. The eyes are small and the ear conch rudimentary.

Two species are found in India, the Indian Pangolin (*M. crassicaudata*) and the Chinese Pangolin (*M. pentadactyla*). The former measures : head and body, 2 ft. to 2 ft. 6 in. (60-75 cm.) ; tail, 18 in. (45 cm.), and has 11 to 13 rows of scales round the body. The latter measures : head and body, 19 in. to 23 in. (48-58 cm.) ; tail, 13 in. to 15 in. (33-38 cm.), and has 15 to 18 rows of scales round the body.

Distribution. The Indian Pangolin inhabits the plains and lower slopes of hills of India south of the Himalayas, and Ceylon. The Chinese Pangolin ranges westwards through Assam and the eastern Himalayas to Nepal, Burma, and south China.

Habits. The Indian Pangolin is commoner than is generally believed, but as it usually moves about only at night it is seldom seen. The animal spends the day curled up in a burrow dug by itself, or it shelters among rocks and boulders. It sleeps with its head between the forelegs and its tail firmly folded over all. A burrow dug up in Madhya Pradesh was about 8 ft. (240 cm.) in length and ended some four feet (120 cm.) underground in a circular chamber about 2 ft. (60 cm.) in diameter. The depth of the burrow varies with the nature of the soil. In rocky ground 5 or 6 ft. (150 or 180 cm.) is enough, in loose soil it may go down 20 ft. (600 cm.) or more. As the entrance to the burrow is closed when the animals are in, it is difficult to discover but for the peculiar tracks they leave round and about their ' earth '.

The food of the pangolin consists of the eggs, the young, and the adults of termites and ants. Tearing down a breach in a termite mound with the powerful claws of its forelimbs and thrusting its long narrow head inside, the animal reaches for the buried comb-like fungus ' gardens ' which usually lodge swarms of these insects, eggs, young, and adults. They are rapidly licked off by its glutinous tongue and swallowed. When such a comb is found, digging stops till its inhabitants are eaten. The ' comb ', which may hold a few survivors, is ejected with the debris, and excavation and search for other combs is resumed. A pangolin kept in semi-captivity would grub about, finding ants to eat under flower-pots and barrels. It burrowed into termite mounds but, curiously enough, would not eat those termites which live under logs and stones, or touch the small red ants commonly found in gardens, but black ants were licked up. It relished ants' eggs more than the ants themselves. It was particularly attracted by the large leaf nests of the big red tree ant which hold swarms of adults, young, and eggs.

Pangolins living in desert areas must go without water. But where water is available they drink freely. Their way of drinking, as observed in captive specimens, is to lap up water with a rapid in-and-out shuttling of the tongue.

The only sound produced by the animal is a loud hiss, usually under stress of excitement.

Little definite is known of the breeding habits of the pangolin. The young appear to be produced at different times of the year. In the Deccan the season is given as between January and March. In south India there is a record of one born in July. A large female from Ceylon, killed early in July, contained a medium-sized embryo. A single one is produced, more rarely two. The young when newly born have soft scales. Growth is apparently rapid. A baby pangolin, some 18 in. (45 cm.) long, fed on a diet of milk, doubled its weight in four months. The mother carries her baby about on her tail. It usually sits across the tail, which is held clear off the ground, gripping tightly. When alarmed, the mother curls up and the baby finds protection under the ventral part of her body sheltered by the all-covering tail. What part, if any, the male plays in the care of the young is not known. Both sexes have been found occupying a burrow with the young.

A pangolin lived in captivity for two years. As captives they eat a variety of food, such as milk, custard, sago and tapioca puddings, and raw eggs. Various legends and beliefs surround the pangolin. The flesh is eaten by some of the hill tribes, and the scales are made into rings as a charm against rheumatic diseases.

23. Marine Mammals

THE CETACEA (whales, dolphins, and porpoises), Sirenia (sea-cows), and Pinnipedia (seals, sea-lions, and walruses) represent the main groups of marine mammals. Of these the Pinnipedia are not found in the Indian seas.

The phylogenetic relationships of present-day marine mammals have given rise to much speculation but it is now accepted that their ancestors are to be sought among the first land mammals. Whereas the fishes have evolved from primitive aquatic ancestors and are perfectly adapted for life in water, the lung-breathing arrangements which the marine mammals have inherited from their progenitors may be a considerable handicap, for instance the necessity of surfacing for breath makes whales an easy target for whale-hunters.

The marine mammals represent several independent lines of evolution, but have come to resemble each other in various ways on account of their similar mode of life. The amphibious Pinnipedia are an offshoot from the primitive Carnivora, while the Sirenia exhibit marked affinities to the Ungulata. The Cetacea, regarded by some as the closest relatives of the earliest mammals, have become highly specialised for life in an aquatic medium. Various gradations of secondary adaptations to the aquatic environment can be traced. Marine mammals thus offer an excellent instance of convergent adaptations in different groups resulting from a similar mode of life.

ADAPTATIONS OF MARINE MAMMALS

Shape of the body. In keeping with their aquatic mode of life this group of animals has developed a torpedo-shaped body, tending towards a fish-like form. This is exemplified in the whale by the total elimination of the neck, the insensible merging of the tapering body in the tail, the disappearance of the external ears, the modification of the forelimbs into flippers, the absence of the hindlimbs which have either disappeared altogether or remain only as concealed vestigials, and the development in many forms of a fold of skin along the back resembling the adipose dorsal fin found in some species of fish. Among the Cetacea movement through the water is made easier by a skin which is naked except for a few sensory bristle-like hairs about the lips.

Locomotion. Swimming in the Cetacea and Sirenia may be termed
tail propulsion ', being effected by up-and-down strokes of the
tail combined with complicated movements of the horizontally-
placed tail-flukes, the whole producing an effect like the rotatory
drive of a ship's screw. In consequence the hindlimbs are unneces-
sary, an apparent reason for their becoming vestigial or disappearing altogether. Many of the Cetaceans have a speed of 15
knots. The Blue Whale has been known to attain 20 knots and to
keep up this speed for several minutes. Dolphins are much faster
and easily keep pace with ships travelling at 30 knots and
over.

Skeletal system. Variety in the construction of the vertebral column
is possible because in the water it has little weight to carry. In the
Cetacea the bones are spongy, an adaptation which helps towards
buoyancy. In the Sirenia, on the contrary, the skeleton is massive,
its great weight helping to keep the animal at the bottom of the
shallow waters in which it browses. In the whales a ' telescoping '
of the head and the cervical vertebrae is evident, for there is a shortening of the anterior part of the skull and the cervical vertebrae are
almost or completely fused. This has resulted in the central part of
the braincase being proportionately higher and wider, and the
brain shorter and broader. For some reason not yet understood the
skull in the toothed whales is slightly asymmetrical—a peculiarity
that may be carried over to other features, e.g. the position of the
blowholes, and the external colouring. With these changes in the
skull, the external nostrils have moved upwards to become the
' blowholes ' on top of the head, two in the whalebone whales and
one in the toothed whales. They are provided with special valves
for shutting the opening when the animal is under water, and communicate directly with the windpipe instead of opening into the
throat as in land mammals.

Integument. The marine mammals have a layer of dermal fat or
blubber which is greatly developed in the whales and may be several
inches thick. This acts as a storage reservoir for food and probably, when metabolised, of water. The whale is a warm-blooded
animal, and this layer of non-conducting blubber acts so well as a
heat insulator that, at times, in dead whales the heat produced in
decomposition cooks and even chars the deeper layers of the flesh.
It adds to the buoyancy of the animal and possibly its elasticity faci-
litates necessary changes in volume when deep diving. The sweat
and oil glands have little value for aquatic mammals ; as a result
these glands are absent.

Mouth armature. The Sirenia graze with their well-developed lips ;
in consequence their teeth are little used and are greatly reduced
in size. The Dugong (*Dugong dugon*) males carry a pair of tusks in

the upper jaw, and in both sexes there is a horny pad in the lower jaw concealing rudimentary teeth.

Striking modifications in the mouth armature of the whales form the basis of their division into two groups, those with baleen being commonly known as the whalebone whales (Mysticeti) and those with teeth as the toothed whales (Odontoceti). In the former group the teeth are completely absent in the adults, although traces may be seen in the foetus thereby suggesting their evolution from toothed forms. The baleen or whalebone, consisting of rows of transverse plates of keratin with hair-like bristles on the inner edge hanging down from either side of the upper jaw, helps to strain the minute planktonic food on which these whales live. The Odontoceti subsist mainly on fish ; their jaws are slightly elongated and carry numerous teeth being thus well adapted to hold their prey. In the Killer Whale the jaws and teeth are strong and capable of biting into their prey, which usually consists of other whales and seals. Some toothed whales live on the giant cephalopods found in the greater depths of the ocean. In such forms the teeth are feebly developed and are present, as in the Sperm Whale, only in the lower jaw.

Adaptations for deep diving. Some whales dive to great depths—the greatest depth known to have been attained is about 800 fathoms (1500 m.). When a whale comes up to breathe it may surface several times in quick succession, and then go under for a period varying from twenty minutes to half-an-hour. Harpooned whales have been known to remain submerged for as much as one to two hours. Certain physiological adjustments explain the ability of the whale to remain submerged for long periods and to dive deep and come up again in a comparatively short time without suffering from caisson disease or the ' bends '.

Unlike land mammals, when a whale breathes there is an almost complete change of air in its lungs. So the whale begins its dive with a good supply of oxygen. As the whale goes down its metabolic rate falls and its heart beats very slowly. Also, the respiratory centres of the whale are very insensitive to carbon-dioxide. All this acts as a device for economising the oxygen available.

When a diver ascends rapidly from the depths nitrogen dissolved in his blood at the high pressures associated with great depths is released into his circulation. This acts as an obstruction and causes the ' bends ', which in a severe case may lead to death. This is avoided to a large extent in the whale by the fact that, as the pressure increases with the depth, the alveoli of its lungs collapse and the air from the lungs is driven to the bronchial tubes, the trachea, and the nasal passages, where very little nitrogen passes into the blood. Another adjustment that helps is the presence in various parts of the body of the *retia mirabilia*, complicated networks of blood vessels, which divert the bloodstream from the muscles. Also, a quick elimination of the dissolved nitrogen is effected by an increase in the rate of the heart beats as the whale rises. Experiment has shown that seals are not completely immune from gaseous embolism ; it is therefore probable that the rise of the whales to the surface of the water is not as rapid as is generally imagined.

GESTATION AND PARTURITION

The Sirenia and the Cetacea give birth to their young in the water. Practically nothing is known about the breeding habits of the dugong except that, like the manatees, it nurses its young at teats placed at the axils of the flippers. The manatees carry for about 150 days and give birth to one young. Among whales, one calf per litter seems to be the rule and the period of gestation may vary from about six months to a year or more. In the Bottlenosed Dolphin (*Tursiops truncatus*) the new-born baby has been observed to rise to the surface to breathe within ten seconds of its birth, and to begin sucking in about an hour and a quarter. Among the larger whales, the period of nursing varies and may extend from six to about twelve months.

GROWTH, SIZE, AND LONGEVITY

New-born whales are of comparatively large size, being in some cases one-third the length of the adult. The rate of growth is very rapid, and the giant Blue Whale and the Humpback (*Megaptera novaeangliae*) become sexually adult when four to five years old.

With the support of the water to counterbalance the force of gravity, aquatic animals are free to attain large sizes. A female Blue Whale attained a length of 113 ft. (about 34 m.), being thus much longer and several tons heavier than the giant dinosaurs *Diplodocus* and *Brontosaurus*. The smallest cetacean measures about 4½ ft. (1½ m.) in length. Steller's Sea-cow (*Rhytina stelleri*) of the Behring and Copper Islands in the north Pacific, now extinct, attained lengths of 26 to 33 ft. (8 to 10 m.), being thus much larger than its existing relatives the dugong and the manatees. The dugong does not exceed 12 ft. (3.5 m.), and one 10 ft. (3 m.) in length was found to weigh 325 lb. (147.5 kg.). The female dugong appears to be slightly smaller than the male.

Nothing definite is known about the longevity of whales. They are probably long lived ; a Killer Whale recognizable by physical peculiarities is known to have lived for at least eighty years. Equally little is known about the longevity of the Sirenians.

MIGRATION

Most species of whales migrate periodically between the sub-
polar and the tropical latitudes. For instance, in summer the
Humpbacks of the southern hemisphere frequent Antarctic waters
and in winter are seen off the coasts of Australia and Madagascar.
Recoveries of marked individuals have shown that several more or
less segregated populations occur, corresponding to their separate
Antarctic and winter sub-tropical resorts. Similar migrations are
also believed to occur in other oceanic species such as the rorquals
which, in summer, come together in restricted zones in high latitudes and, in winter, are dispersed over a very wide area extending
to the sub-tropical regions.

MAN AND MARINE MAMMALS

Among animals, marine mammals as a natural resource to man
are second only to the terrestrial ungulates. Whaling and the seal
fur industry affect the economy of many nations. Although
commercially important species of whales, such as the Blue Whale,
the Finner Whale or Common Rorqual, and the Sperm Whale,
are known to occur in the Indian seas, whaling is mainly restricted
to the north Atlantic and the Antarctic Seas. The harpoon gun and
steam-operated whalers and factory ships have completely revolu-
tionized the whaling industry. As a result of the increased killing,
whaling in north Atlantic waters declined and the whalers extended
their activities to the Antarctic. Fortunately, since 1937 the whaling
industry is governed by an international convention imposing a
number of rules and regulations and restricting the whaling season
to a period of three months. No part of the whale is wasted; even
the bones, after the extraction of the oil, are made into fertilizer.
The magnitude of the industry may be gauged from the fact that
some of the ships used are well over 20,000 tons gross tonnage and
capable of processing 1500 whales in a single season. Between
1929 and 1939, the annual world catch of whales varied from 24,000
to 44,000, yielding about half a million tons of oil. Post-war whaling
has brought into use reconnaissance aircraft, radar, and asdic
devices to locate the quarry.

Indiscriminate killing was responsible for the extermination of
Steller's Sea-cow within a few years of its discovery. The living
Sirenians are not hunted but stray specimens of the dugong caught
in fishing nets are killed for their meat and fat.

Fur seals and sea-lions are valued among other things for their
fur, skin, and fat.

THE BLUE WHALE

Balaenoptera musculus (Linnaeus)

Plate facing p. 289

Local Names. Hindi *magar māchch, hūt, raghwa* ; Mar. *devmasa* ; Tamil, Tel., and Mal. *thimingilam* ; Kan. *thimingila* ; San. *thimi.*

Size. Average length measured from tip of snout to notch of tail flukes : 74 ft. (22.5 m.) in males and 77 ft. (23.5 m.) in females, with a corresponding weight of 80 (81 tonnes) and 85 (86 tonnes) tons respectively. Maximum length recorded 113 ft. (34 m.) and weight 150 tons (152 tonnes).

Distinctive Characters. Body streamlined and hairless except for a few hairs on the lips ; colour slate-blue mottled blue-grey with the tip and undersurface of the flippers whitish. Some animals have a yellowish colour on the underside, attributable to a thin film of diatoms ; hence the common name Sulphurbottomed Whale. The head is longer than in other rorquals ; the dorsal fin low, small, and placed well back. The flippers are long and tapering, in length approximately one-seventh of the body length. The ventral grooves number 80 to 100. The baleen plates including the fringes of the frayed inner border are jet black. This colour is characteristic of the species.

Distribution. The higher latitudes of both hemispheres in summer. In winter more widely distributed in arctic, temperate, and less commonly in tropical waters.

Habits. The largest of the rorquals, in fact the largest animal in existence, the Blue Whale like most other whales is an inhabitant of the open ocean, and strandings and off-shore sightings are rare. They usually move in schools of two or more. Distinct migratory movements occur, in summer towards the Arctic and Antarctic latitudes where planktonic crustacea grow in profusion, and in the winter towards the temperate waters to mate and breed.

The Blue Whale lives more or less exclusively on the oceanic prawn *Euphausia superba* in the Antarctic and a similar crustacean *Meganyctiphanes norvegica* in the Arctic. Extensive shoals of these crustaceans known as ' krill ', sometimes covering several square miles of ocean, occur at or near the surface where the temperature is less than 2° Centigrade. The capacity of the open mouth is considerably increased by the flexibility of its pleated undersurface allowing the mouth to hang down as a huge bag. When full of plankton the mouth closes and the contraction of the pleats squeezes out the water between the fringed baleen plates. The stomach of specimens captured in winter is usually empty and it is generally assumed that the oil stored in the blubber, bones, and muscles supplemented by small quantities of pelagic crustaceans supplies nourishment in winter.

Blue Whales become sexually mature at the age of 4 to 5 years. Pregnancy lasts for 10 to 11 months. The calves, which are about 23 ft. (7 m.) in length at birth, weigh 2½ to 3 tons (2.5 to 3 tonnes). Calves are weaned after 7 months and at weaning weigh 23 tons (23.5 tonnes) and have a length of about 50 ft. (15 m.). Normally one young is born at a time. Pregnancy occurs every two or three years.

The Blue Whale has been so extensively hunted since the invention of the steam catcher and the harpoon gun that its numbers have been severely depleted. A certain amount of protection is now afforded by restricting the number that may be captured.

Three other species of *Balaenoptera* occur in Indian seas and are likely to be stranded on Indian shores. The **Finner Whale** or **Common Rorqual** [*Balaenoptera physalus* (Linn.)] is second in size to the Blue Whale, the maximum length being about 85 ft. (26 m.) and the average 65 ft. (20 m.). The flippers are shorter, approximately one-ninth the total length. In colour it is bluish grey above and white below, including the undersurface of flippers and tail flukes. The colour of the head and shoulder is asymmetrical, the pigment usually extending further down on the left side than on the right. This asymmetry affects also the inside of the mouth and the baleen plates, the plates on the right for about one-third their length from the snout being white and the rest of the plates dull blue-grey streaked with pale ashy-grey and yellowish grey. The fringes are yellowish white throughout. There are usually 60 to 90 ventral grooves. The **Sei Whale** (*Balaenoptera borealis* Lesson) is smaller, maximum 60 ft. (18 m.), average : males 44 ft. (13.5 m.), females 48 ft. (14.5 m.) ; bluish black above with the flanks, flippers, and flukes dark grey. White on the underside from the chin backward ending well above the tail. The flippers are small measuring approximately one-tenth to one-twelfth the total length, ventral grooves 30 to 60, baleen plates black with frayed inner edges white. The **Piked** or **Lesser Rorqual** (*Balaenoptera acutorostrata* Lacépède) is the smallest among the rorquals, reaching a length of 37 ft. (11.5 m.). It is blue-grey above and white below with a characteristic white patch or band on the upper side of the flippers. The baleen plates are yellowish white and the flippers in length one-eighth of the total length.

Another baleen whale likely to occur in Indian waters, though no stranding has so far been recorded, is the **Humpbacked Whale** [*Megaptera novaeangliae* (Borowski)]. This species has a short and stout body, large head, pleated underside, large tail flukes, and a small recurved dorsal fin set far back. The flippers are extraordinarily long and narrow, one-third of the total length of the body, which does not exceed about 50 ft. (15 m.).

THE SPERM WHALE

Physeter catodon Linnaeus

Plate facing p. 289

Size. Large males may reach a length of 60 ft. (18.5 m.). The females are about half the length of the male.

Distinctive Characters. It is readily identified by the square-cut head, which is almost one-third of the size of the entire body and contains spermaceti in liquid form within a fleshy tank above the skull and also impregnated in a layer of spongy tissue immediately below. The head is asymmetrical and the single blowhole opens to one side. The narrow and underslung lower jaw has up to 30 large teeth, which fit into sockets in the palate when the mouth is closed. There is no dorsal fin. The flippers are small but wide. The tail is wide and deeply notched. The smooth skin of the body may bear scars caused by the suckers of cuttlefish, the main food of the animal. The normal colour is of varying shades of black, the ventral side being lighter. There is one record of a white specimen.

Distribution. Tropical, temperate, and arctic waters of the oceans of the world.

Habits. The Sperm Whale or Cachalot is the largest of the toothed whales or Odontoceti. It is usually seen in small parties which occasionally join up to form large schools. In the summer old bulls are seen in Arctic and Antarctic waters but the younger bulls and females normally occur in tropical and subtropical waters. It is believed to be a powerful diver and to remain under water for periods exceeding an hour. On the surface it attains a speed of over 10 knots when chased. Sperm Whales feed on squids and cuttlefish and can swallow squids 16 ft. (490 cm.) and more in body length. They occasionally take fish of quite large size. Their breeding habits are not fully known. The animal is believed to be polygamous. Breeding occurs about March to May in the Northern Hemisphere and about September to December in southern waters. Gestation period is about 15 to 16 months. One young at a birth is normal, two rare. The calf at birth is about 14 ft. (430 cm.) long and is weaned at approximately a year.

The Sperm Whale is commercially important. The oil from its blubber is of finer quality and greater in quantity than that of other whales. The spermaceti forms the base for some of the finest lubricating oils. Sperm Whales also yield ambergris, a light inflammable substance formed in its large intestine by bacterial action. This is used as a fixative for highly priced perfumes. There is only a single record of the stranding of this species in Indian waters.

The **Pygmy Sperm Whale** [*Kogia breviceps* (Blainville)] is occasionally stranded on Indian shores. This little animal hardly exceeds 12 ft. (3.50 m.) in length and like its larger cousin feeds on cephalopods. There are 9 to 13 teeth on each side of the lower jaw. A rudimentary pair embedded in the gum of the upper jaw may occur. In colour it is black above and light grey below.

THE COMMON DOLPHIN

Delphinus delphis Linnaeus

Plate facing p. 289

Local Names. Tamil *pomigra*.

Size. 8 ft. (240 cm.) in total length.

Distinctive Characters. The snout is prolonged into a long narrow beak separated by a groove from the forehead. Both jaws contain numerous small teeth exceeding 35 in number. As in all toothed whales there is a single blowhole. Pectoral fins and dorsal fin falcate. Body slender. Skin hairless and smooth. In colour black or dark grey above, underparts whitish, and sides with bands of fulvous or ochre. A ring of black circles the eye.

Distribution. Tropical and temperate seas of the world.

Habits. The Dolphin is known from very ancient times and has figured in the myths and legends of the earlier civilizations of the Mediterranean. It is usually seen in schools, which are occasionally of considerable size. The Dolphin is one of the fastest among the oceanic animals and is capable of attaining over 30 knots. A curious habit recorded of this species is the practice of riding the bow waves of ships in the manner of a human surf-rider and based on the same principle. Dolphins produce numerous underwater sounds as means of communication between members of a school and also echolocate their prey. Co-operation between members of a school giving assistance to injured and otherwise-disabled individuals has been noticed. The food consists of fish, mainly of shoaling species. The young are believed to be born in summer.

Several other species of the smaller toothed whales have been reported from Indian waters. Among the Dolphins the **Plumbeous Dolphin** (*Sotalia plumbea* Cuvier) is similar in dimensions to the Common Dolphin but is distinguished by its long snout, from tip to eye one-sixth the total body length. The dorsal fin is long but low. Teeth number 34 to 37 in each row. The **Red Sea Bottlenosed**

Dolphin [*Tursiops aduncus* (Ehrenberg)], known as *gadamu* to fishermen of the Vizagapatam area, grows to a length of 7 ft. (2 m.). It is distinguished by its well-defined snout about 6 in. (15 cm.) in length and teeth 23 to 28 in each row. The pectoral and dorsal fins are falcate. Pectorals about one-fifth of total body length. In colour dark grey above with darker fins and pinkish ash-grey below having irregular darker blotches. The **Indian Broadbeaked Dolphin** (*Lagenorhynchus electra* Gray) has a shorter beak, not as distinct as in the dolphins described above. In colour it is similar to *Tursiops aduncus* except for the absence of blotches on the underside.

A single record exists of the stranding at Armada, Baroda, of a **Killer Whale** [*Orcinus orca* (Linnaeus)] the largest member of the family Delphinidae and the most formidable of aquatic mammalian predators. The mouth has 10 to 12 large teeth on each side of the jaw. The colour pattern is distinctive, black above except for oval white patches above the eye and white below, which extends to the flanks behind the dorsal fin. The dorsal fin, which attains a length of 6 ft. (180 cm.), and the pectorals are disproportionately large in old males.

The **Little Indian Porpoise** [*Neomeris phocaenoides* (Cuvier)], Family Phocaenidae, is distinguished by the absence of a dorsal fin. The snout is rounded and a band of tubercles occurs from above the pectorals to above the vent. In colour it is uniformly black ; purplish patches may occur above the upper lip and throat. This species frequents tidal creeks. Length about 4 ft. (120 cm.).

THE GANGETIC DOLPHIN

Platanista gangetica (Lebeck)

Plate facing p. 289

Local Names. Hindi *sus, susu* ; Bengali *susuk, sishuk* ; Sanskrit *sisumar* ; Assamese *hiho, seho, huh* ; Sindhi *bhulan, sunsar.*

Size. Generally 7½ to 8½ ft. (2.3 to 2.6 metres) in total length, although there is one record of a specimen measuring 13 ft. 2 in. (4 metres). As a rule, the females are larger than the males.

Distinctive Characters. The body is fusiform, the head being prolonged into a compressed beak or rostrum which is slightly enlarged distally. The number of teeth may vary from 27 to 32 on each side of each jaw, there being a slightly higher count in the lower than in the upper jaw. The teeth which are pointed and conical in the young become blunt bony projections with age. Unlike the true dolphins, a very short neck is evident in *Platanista*. Dorsally, a fleshy ridge forming a rudimentary fin is seen about mid-length of the body excluding the beak. The pectoral flippers are more or less triangular in shape and measure about one-sixth the length of the body. The eyes are about the size of a pea and are devoid of the crystalline lens. The blowhole is a longitudinal slit and the tail flukes are horizontally placed. The colour ranges from dark lead to sooty black, the older individuals having a few lighter patches on the sides.

Distribution. Found in the Ganges, the Brahmaputra, the Indus, and their larger tributaries to the bases of the hills. They are also seen in the tidal limits, but do not enter the sea.

Habits. Although the Gangetic Dolphin is found in small groups in certain parts of the rivers, it appears to be essentially non-gregarious. Its regular absence from some parts of the rivers during the hot months is an indication of migratory tendencies, the governing factors of which may be food, temperature, increased salinity in the tidal limits during the hotter months, or some other factor still not understood. They usually rise to the surface to breathe for a few seconds after remaining immersed for about a minute. The jaws of the animal are well adapted for browsing on bottom-living crustaceans and cat-fishes. Life in turbid waters has resulted in the extreme reduction of the eyes which are probably not of much assistance to the animal in such an environment. During the monsoon months the Gangetic Dolphin descends to the tidal waters and is often taken in the fishing nets. At this time an individual dolphin may occasionally be seen proceeding in a series of leaps.

The breeding habits of the animal are not yet fully known, but it has been noticed that one or rarely two young are born between April and July after a period of gestation of about eight to nine months.

Nets and harpoons are used in some places to capture these animals for their meat. The oil taken from the fat is used for burning lamps and for various other purposes.

The Indus Dolphin which was described as a separate species (*Platanista indi*) is now considered conspecific with *P. gangetica*. *Platanista* itself is an offshoot of the marine Cetacea, and ranks along with the other freshwater dolphins, namely the Amazonian Dolphin (*Inia geoffroyensis*), the La Plata Dolphin (*Pontoporia blainvillei*), and the Chinese Lake Dolphin (*Lipotes vexillifer*) as a zoological curiosity.

THE DUGONG, or SEA-COW

Dugong dugon (Müller)

Plate facing p. 289

Local Names. Tamil *kadalpudru, avilliah, kadalpanni* ; Malayalam *kaddapanni* ; Singhalese *muda ura, talla mala.*

Size. Attains about 10½ ft. (3.2 metres) in total length, but generally between 6½ and 8½ ft. (2 and 2.6 metres). A specimen about 11 ft. (3 metres) in length may measure about 6½ ft. (2 metres) in circumference. The females are generally smaller than the males.

Distinctive Characters. In general body form the Dugong resembles more the Eared Seals than the Cetaceans. The belly is more or less flat while the back and sides are rounded. The neck is absent and the head which is massive is somewhat truncate anteriorly. The tail flukes are horizontally placed and a thickened fold of the skin is seen extending dorsally from about the commencement of the tail to its tip. The forelimbs are flattened flipperlike and the mammae are situated just behind them almost in a line with their posterior edges. The mouth of the animal is small and the upper lip projects considerably beyond the lower lip and is in the form of an extensive horseshoe-shaped fleshy pad overhanging the mouth. Three types of hairs can be made out on the body, two on the aforesaid facial disc and the lower jaw and the third over the whole of the body including the limbs and the tail flukes. The disc-like upper ' jaw pad ' bears long fine bristles which are probably sensory in function and on the two ridges on the sides bristles which are shorter and blunter than the spines of the porcupine. Four and eight incisors on the upper and the lower jaw respectively and five molars on each side of each jaw make up the full complement of teeth in the young animal. In the adults only two upper incisors and two or three molars on each side of the upper and the lower jaws are present. The incisors or ' tusks ' which are very pronounced in the male project through the skin of the upper lip, while in the female they may or may not pierce the gum. The nostrils are crescentic in shape and placed on top of the head. The eyes are small, beady, and deeply sunk, and the eye glands well developed. The external ear is in the form of a small circular aperture about 0.4 in. (10 mm.) in diameter. The colour is variable and in a freshly killed specimen may vary from dull brownish grey dorsally to grey on the sides and flesh colour ventrally.

Distribution. The Red Sea, and the shores of the Indian Ocean between 22° 50 N. and 18° S. latitude from East Africa to Australia, and Formosa in the Pacific. Dugongs have been observed in the Gulf of Kutch, on the coast of Malabar, the north-west coast of Ceylon, around the Andaman Islands, and in the Mergui Archipelago. The typical name *D. dugon* has been ascribed to those from the Indian Ocean. The ones from the Red Sea and the coast of Australia were described as distinct species, *Halicore hemprichii* (=*H. tabernaculi*) and *H. australis* respectively, but are now considered conspecific with *D. dugon*.

Habits. The animal is clumsy and sluggish in its habits and not particularly adapted for rapid motion. At one time it was very abundant in the Gulf of Manaar. In fact, there existed a Dugong 'fishery' of some importance in the Gulf of Manaar, as the flesh of the animal is highly esteemed by the local people and special nets were used to capture the animals while they were in their feeding grounds. The animals are so scarce now that only occasionally a specimen is caught in fishing nets when they visit the shallow waters to browse on the sea grasses which form their main diet. Females with young have been seen throughout the year, but those in the Gulf of Manaar have not been observed to clasp their young and stand up with part of the body showing above water as the Red Sea Dugong has been noted to do. The latter habit has probably given rise to the numerous stories about mermaids! The Malays regard the tears of the Dugong as a powerful love-charm.

Bibliography

A few references are given beiow to supplement those mentioned in Mr. Prater's preface, at page xix :—

Bourliere, François. The Natural History of Mammals. George G. Harrap, London 1955.

Bourlière, François. Mammals of the World. George G. Harrap, London 1955.

Champion, H. G. A Preliminary Survey of the Forest Types of India and Burma. *Indian Forest Records* vol. 1, No. 1 : 1-286 ; 1936.

Ellerman, J. R. The Fauna of India, Mammalia, vol. 3, Rodentia (in two parts). Manager of Publications, New Delhi 1961.

Ellerman, J. R. & Morrison-Scott, T. C. S. Checklist of Palaearctic and Indian Mammals 1758-1946. British Museum, London 1951.

Gee, E. P. The Wild Life of India. Collins, London 1964.

Norman, J. R. & Fraser, F. C. Giant Fishes, Whales and Dolphins Putnam, London 1937.

Sanderson, Ivan T. Living Mammals of the World. Hamish Hamilton, London 1955.

Talbot, Lee Merriam. A Look at Threatened Species. *Oryx* vol. 5, Nos. 4 & 5. Fauna Preservation Society, London 1960.

Wroughton, R. C., *et al.* Bombay Natural History Society's Mammal Survey of India. Reports 1-46. *J. Bombay nat. Hist. Soc.* vol. 21, No. 2 to vol. 33, No. 3 ; 1912-1929.

Wroughton, R. C., *et al.* Scientific Results from the Mammal Survey. Nos. 1-49. *J. Bombay nat. Hist. Soc.* vol. 21, No. 2 to vol. 33, No. 3 ; 1912-1929.

Index

(Bold-face references relate to illustrations)